e/90

D0875658

WITHDRAWN

The
Barren
Zone

The
Barren Zone

a novel by
Toyoko Yamasaki

TRANSLATED BY JAMES T. ARAKI

UNIVERSITY OF HAWAII PRESS
HONOLULU

CONTENTS

FOREWORD

In this, the first of four linked novels depicting Japan's recovery from postwar desolation and its headlong rush into frenzied economic expansion, the story I wish to tell is that of the spiritual agony of the tens of thousands of unfortunate Japanese whose lives in Siberian prison camps were as barren as was the physical setting of their captivity. I am grateful for the assistance given to me by those survivors, named on the final page, whose testimonies enabled me to use the vehicle of fiction to present truths that historians have been unwilling to verify and relate. This first volume is concerned with the period from 1945 to 1959.

Osaka, Japan

1

THE ENCOUNTER

Daimon Ichizo, president of Kinki Trading Company, began each working day in his office by looking out at Osaka castle, below which the Dojima River flowed sash-like and eternal through the sprawling city. On this special morning the towering citadel stood out in sharp relief against a clear sky, its dark tiled roof and white walls gleaming in the winter sunlight. Once the fortress of the mightiest of combative feudal lords, the citadel called up visions of war in Daimon and fired the aggressiveness that sustained him in the world of business.

Content with the rewards from this morning's ritual, he turned his attention to a wall-sized map of the world, etched into a wide copper panel and lighted with red and blue bulbs—red for branch offices, blue for local agencies. A clock showed the exact hour of the world's important time zones. Through gold-rimmed glasses Daimon glanced with satisfaction at the Audemars Piquet watch on his thick wrist. At that hour night covered the whole western hemisphere. But the other half of the world was astir, and his thoughts quickened as he imagined his three hundred agents carrying on Kinki's business in all those foreign cities.

Barrel-chested, five feet six inches tall and weighing one hundred and sixty-five pounds, Daimon showed the vigor of a man much younger than his fifty-six years. His smooth face still glowed from contact with the brisk December wind outside.

On his desk lay documents neatly stacked—some requiring his approval, others to be read and evaluated during the day. He reached for the international market quotations. However busy he might be, he always checked the daily quotations of principal international commodities. New York cotton, Chicago wheat, Sydney wool, Singapore rubber, and London sugar were quoted in both American dollars and British pounds.

Suddenly Daimon's face expressed annoyance, and his big hand reached for an interoffice phone. "Get me Irokawa, Wool Department. Urgent!"

His phone rang almost immediately. "Sir! This is Irokawa."

"The price of Australian wool's shot up. What's the reason?" The president spoke sharply. Australian wool, stabilized at one pound and sixty pence a fortnight ago, had crept up slowly and moved past one pound seventy. Now, all of a sudden, this morning it went up to a pound eighty-four.

"People in the wool trade have suggested a variety of reasons," Irokawa replied confidently. "Some say there's been a sudden surge in demand from Europe and the United States, following a change in fashion styling. Others think it's caused by a drought that's wiped out the sheep in Queensland. We're unable to pinpoint the cause. But some of us in the Wool Department noticed a strange shifting of prices nearly three weeks ago. We've been in close touch with the Sydney branch office ever since, and we've been buying daily. We've already bought futures to fill our quota through March of next year."

"What's the outlook?"

"I doubt if the market will ever reach one pound ninety. So I'm thinking of selling now at a thirty percent profit and pulling out." Irokawa was reacting with the quickness expected of a department chief in the front lines of trading. His attention was on the sure profit.

"No!" Daimon shouted. "The market will definitely hit two hundred. Keep buying all you can get until it does."

"Two hundred? But we have no basis on which to . . ."

"No 'buts'! If the pastures of Queensland die, chances are those in New South Wales will dry up too. When that happens, there won't be any more Australian wool. So keep buying until the price hits two hundred!" He hung up.

Kinki Trading Company, with three thousand employees and an estimated capital of almost four billion yen, was one of the ten biggest general trading houses in Japan. Originally it had been a wholesaler of textiles in the Semba district of Osaka, and even now, in 1958, textiles made up sixty percent of the merchandise it handled.

Daimon Ichizo had come to Kinki Trading after graduating from Osaka Higher Commercial School in 1922. Not long after, he was chosen to be the branch manager in Peking; there his principal duty was to hunt through the vast interior of China for enough cotton to satisfy the Japanese need. Later, in Japan, he was trained in the thick of skirmishes with spinning mills and textile plants, and had successfully survived countless economic battles. He and the former president, who had died two years before, carefully laid the foundations of a major trading company. In less than two years as president, Daimon established a remarkable authority within the company because of his extraordinary ability to read the market and to use his keen intuition boldly.

But he was troubled by a recent trend. Trading companies that had previously made up the *zaibatsu*—those powerful industrial and financial conglomerates that were broken up following the war—had begun to regroup and were gradually regaining their former strength. If that trend continued, Kinki Trading would be no match for them even if it drove all of its production departments at top gear, setting higher and still higher goals. It was limited in what it could produce. What Kinki needed was systematic organization that would enable it to meet the former *zaibatsu* firms head on. Above all, it required men whose ready grasp of broad issues would lead to quick, accurate decisions and immediate action.

His secretary brought in more documents and his commitments for the rest of the morning. "You have the Cotton Industry Club meeting to attend at eleven. I hope you can approve these before you leave."

Daimon normally maintained a busy schedule. Now, with the year's end close at hand, he was even busier and often took paper work home with him. "I'll get it done. Right away."

The document requiring his approval dealt with jet fighters to be purchased by the Defense Agency. They reminded him of something else. "Wasn't I supposed to interview Iki Tadashi today?"

"Yes, sir. Mr. Iki is scheduled to be here at ten-thirty."

Daimon removed his glasses, examined the papers, and quickly made decisions: seven proposals approved, three rejected, and two to be returned for further study. He handed the sheaf of papers to the secretary, then reached into his desk drawer for Iki's resumé:

Current Address: Unit 490, Yamato-gawa Municipal Housing, 45 Kitajima-chō, Sumiyoshi-ku, Osaka.

Registered Domicile: Yuza-cho, Akumi County, Yamagata Prefecture. Registered on date of birth, November 21, 1912.
Training and Experience:
  Entered Tokyo Junior Military Academy, April 1926.
  Graduated from Army Academy, July 1933.
  Assigned as staff officer, Fifth Army (Eastern Manchuria), June 1940.
  Assigned as staff officer, Army Operations, Imperial General Headquarters, December 1940.
  Assigned as staff officer, Kwantung Army, February 1944.
  Promoted to lieutenant colonel, March 1945.
  Reassigned to staff, Army Operations, Imperial General Headquarters, April 1945.
  Despatched to Kwantung Army as special emissary from Imperial General Headquarters, August 1945, and interned in U.S.S.R. at termination of hostilities.
  Released from internment and repatriated, December 1956.
Occupation: unemployed.

His résumé was nothing less than a military man's listing of the stages in his career. Daimon studied the photograph. It showed a forty-six-year-old man wearing an ill-fitting civilian's suit. The sunken cheeks and the hollows under his eyes were undoubted testimony to the harshness of the man's long internment in Siberia. His forehead was prominent, and the eyes were direct and clear, although with more than a suggestion of melancholy in the lids and brows. But eleven years of brutal confinement had not dimmed the brightness in those eyes.

Daimon opened the letter that accompanied the résumé. It was addressed to him personally. Its message, in characters written with a brush rather than a pen on traditional and inexpensive stationery, was as forthright and precise as the man's military history:

Request

Item: I wish to be spared the indignity of being interviewed, subjected to a personal inspection, and then rejected.

Item: Because I was deprived of freedom of speech and of activity for eleven years during my detention in Siberia, I do not wish to be similarly restricted now.

Item: I wish you to understand that I have no knowledge whatever of commerce and have not acquired skills in calculating or bookkeeping, for which I am ill-fitted.

4

A faint smile played about Daimon's lips. This was the story of the man he had been trying to recruit for more than half a year. Each of Kinki's earlier offers had been met with a firm but courteous refusal. Executives of Kinki Trading Company wondered openly why Daimon was so interested in hiring a former staff officer of Imperial General Headquarters. For a short while after the war many firms had sought out the more prominent former staff officers and upper-echelon commanders, and had exploited their status and personal connections for business gains. But the war had ended thirteen years ago. What benefits could a former army officer, especially a repatriate from Siberia, bring to Kinki, a trading company that had its roots in Osaka, long considered the commercial capital of Japan?

In fact, Daimon cared little about the prestige or connections of former military men. He was attracted by their operational and organizational skills. True, no one could possibly gauge how effectively that special ability could be applied to private industry. But to him logic suggested that he should seek out men of surpassing ability from among former staff officers: they were the men on whom the country had relied, on whose training great amounts of the nation's resources had been spent. Calculated at the present rate, tens of millions of yen had been spent on preparing each of them for duty. The probability that such a man would be a successful leader was excellent, Daimon convinced himself. At the very least he should look this special man over and then decide whether or not he could use him.

Daimon's interest in Iki Tadashi had become almost an obsession. After a third urging, Iki had submitted his qualifications; and, when negotiations had proceeded to the point of a personal interview, he had presented Daimon with those three conditions. His first requirement, to be spared the indignity of being rejected after an interview, could be interpreted as being either an expression of arrogance or simply as a request that he be allowed to keep some of the dignity he prized. Whichever way he read those conditions, Daimon had allowed himself to yield to the will of the man whose visit he awaited with extraordinary excitement.

Iki Tadashi carefully locked the front door of his modest home. It was one of the more than three hundred such dwellings in a municipal housing project on the north bank of the Yamato River,

5

each unit consisting of three rather small rooms furnished with mats and a tiny kitchen. All the houses were plain, but their well-tended little gardens gave a softness to the setting. He dropped his key in the wooden mail box he himself had made and stepped into the street.

From the wives in the neighborhood, busy hanging up their laundry, he drew only momentary attention; they were accustomed to seeing him around at that time of the day. He nodded a solemn greeting toward them as he turned toward the Suminoe Station. Two years had passed since he'd joined his family in that small house upon his return to Japan aboard the very last repatriation ship from the Soviet Union. He was still without a job. The only work experience he'd ever had was that of a staff officer in the Imperial Army. For those two years he had lived off the earnings of his wife, who was employed in the Public Welfare Department of the Osaka Prefectural Government. On this fateful day, having said goodbye to his wife, their daughter, who attended high school, and their son, still in middle school, he had cleaned the house and would buy the vegetables for supper, as he did every day. Usually he went into the city to find employment for the men who had been his subordinates in the army. Today was different, however: this morning he was going to Kinki Trading Company on his own behalf.

He found the train relatively empty, the hour being already past nine o'clock. His thoughts were heavy as he rode into the city. He had not yet made up his mind about joining Kinki Trading. He had declined those two earlier invitations to join the company, but the most recent overture had come at the insistence of the president himself, and could not be dismissed abruptly. He had responded by sending in his résumé, to which he attached a personal note for the president. He was uncertain about his ability to work in the rapidly changing world of private industry, especially in a trading company. He might not be in touch with the times; eleven years of his life, spent in Siberia, had done nothing to prepare him for working in this new Japan. Most people still looked down on former military men, and he was suspicious of the motives of this Daimon Ichizo, whom he had not met. He was determined to have nothing to do with any scheme that called for exploiting his former position. A year earlier he had been approached by the Defense Agency in Tokyo but had been firm in refusing to commit himself once more to the military. He hoped that Daimon would not want to talk about his former career. Other people could not possibly understand why his participation in the planning of the war in Asia still weighed heavily on his mind.

At Namba Station, Iki transferred to a bus that took him through streets crowded with year-end shoppers. The fourteenth New Year since the end of the war was only a few days away. Abundant stocks of merchandise and brisk trading helped almost everyone to forget that not too long ago the country had been ravaged by war. Only Iki and a very few people like him still lived in the state of shock which most of their countrymen had felt in the first years after the war. He reached into his overcoat pocket and touched an envelope he had put there only yesterday. It held a registered letter sent to him by a former subordinate for whom he had found a job; with the letter came a note wrapped around some cash: "Dear Colonel, this isn't much, but I hope you can use it to treat your family to dinner." Iki recalled the man's face. "That rascal," he muttered, smiling for the moment.

At Korai Bridge, where he got off the bus, he could see the new Kinki Trading Building rising at the next intersection. Soon he pushed open the glass door at the building's main entrance. Just inside he stopped, surprised by the well-dressed workers busy at their desks. He gave his name to the receptionist, who assigned someone to escort him to the seventh floor, where a secretary took him into the president's office.

The large desk near the window faced the door; sitting behind it Daimon Ichizo looked steadily at Iki as he walked in. Iki's own clear eyes were fixed on Daimon, who immediately broke the silence. "That was an interesting letter you wrote me, Mr. Iki," he said, motioning his guest toward a chair.

"I may have sounded brash. I'm not good with words."

"Quite the contrary. Your letter showed me that eleven years in Siberian camps haven't softened you a bit. You've been back for two years now. Why haven't you taken a job yet?"

"Those years were needed to find employment for my subordinates who came back with me on the last repatriation ship. And, too, I needed to regain my health."

"Still, two years is a long time. Have you been waiting for any particular opportunity you have in mind?" That possibility was very important to Daimon.

7

"Not really. Let me say only that I've been extremely cautious about deciding on a second career. I mustn't—I definitely mustn't make a mistake this time."

"Have you decided to join us? There'll be no problem in agreeing to your three conditions."

"I'm grateful for your consideration. But the truth is I'm still uncertain."

"I can understand that." Daimon leaned forward. "Naturally you'd be wary about joining a trading company when—as you say—you don't know much about business. And you'd be afraid that we might take advantage of your former position for business purposes. Let me make myself clear. What I'm interested in is your experience with tactics and organization. I want to put that to use in my company." The intensity in Daimon's gaze appeared in his voice as well.

"But I should think there would be fundamental differences between army tactics and civilian enterprise. . . ."

"Differences? I'd say that an army command and a trading company are fundamentally the same. Let me put this in my own way. Back in Meiji times, the army was started with close to zero capital investment. All the government needed was penny postcards to call up men to train as soldiers. Nowadays, a trading firm is an operation of people and telephones—hardly any capital investment to start with either. What matters is how the people and their brains are put to use to keep the enterprise afloat—or to sink it. Don't you see how much alike they are?" He burst into hearty laughter.

Despite his prejudices, Iki was impressed with this bold decisive man. Having been trained as a staff officer, he was well aware of his disinclination to work closely with anyone except men endowed with the ability to command, and he sensed a fatefulness in this encounter with Daimon.

"What do you say? Will you join us?"

Iki answered after only the briefest of pauses. "Yes, if you will allow me to." He bowed respectfully, a courtesy Daimon found natural in a former military officer—and becoming in a new employee.

"Well! Looks like I've finally got my wish." Daimon smiled broadly. "By the way, where in Siberia were you interned?"

"They kept me in several places—Khabarovsk. Taishet. Also in

8

Lazo, which is about two hundred and fifty miles north of Magadan on the Okhotsk coast."

Daimon quickly found those places on his wall map.

"Eleven years certainly was a long time. What was the worst part of it? Hunger?"

"Far worse than hunger was the loneliness of solitary confinement."

"Solitary? I thought you men lived in internment camps. You were actually in prison?"

"I was sentenced to twenty-five years at hard labor for war crimes."

"Because you were on the staff of our Imperial General Headquarters, I suppose?"

"They called it the crime of abetting capitalism."

"So they took a man from a country that operates on a capitalistic system and charged him with abetting capitalism . . ." Daimon's interest was aroused. But Iki felt as if a partly healed wound had been slashed open with a scalpel. His eleven years in Siberia had been like eleven eons in the Hell of Frozen Lotuses. He desperately wanted to erase all memory of those years from his mind. But Daimon's probing had reopened the wound, from which dark blood and foul pus gushed forth anew. And in his mind those terrible memories rose up—

At that moment a huge airliner flew above the city. The roar, growing louder like that of an enemy bomber approaching overhead, drew Iki's thoughts up out of the past, more than thirteen years before . . .

2

DISINTEGRATION

At Imperial General Headquarters on Ichigaya Heights in Tokyo, Lieutenant Colonel Iki Tadashi of the Imperial Army stood motionless, as if frozen, having just heard about the suicide of Minister of War Anami. This shock came on the evening of August 15, 1945. Earlier in the day the Emperor had spoken to the nation over the radio.

Officers and men who heard the imperial command to end hostilities were dazed. After that, the news report—"This morning at dawn, Minister of War Anami died by his own sword"—came as a shattering blow. At the final conference in the presence of the Emperor, held the previous day in the palace air-raid shelter, Minister Anami had been determined in his opposition to unconditional surrender: he insisted on negotiating for peace only after a "decisive battle" had been fought on Japanese soil. But once the Emperor announced his decision to end the war, Anami had deferred to the imperial wish. At dawn this morning he had written his last testament—"With my death I seek forgiveness for my great crime"—and committed *seppuku*. Iki, a staff officer in Operations at Imperial General Headquarters, was deeply moved by Anami's death; it had been planned and carried out in accord with the strict tradition of Anami's profession as a soldier.

"Colonel, the Chief-of-Staff wishes to see you." The voice of a noncommissioned officer brought Iki's thoughts back to the present. He hurried toward the office of the Chief-of-Staff, located on the second floor at the opposite end of the building from the Operations room.

He opened the door and saw General Umezu seated as usual at his desk. The general's handsome, dignified face showed the effects of deep anguish and fatigue. Until the very end Umezu and Anami had insisted on fighting a decisive last battle. Anami's death had affected Umezu profoundly, far beyond the comprehension of Iki and others.

When Iki drew himself to attention before the Chief-of-Staff's desk, the general looked up at him for a long moment. "I'm sending you on a crucial mission," he said slowly. "You are to fly to Shinkyo tomorrow and convey His Majesty's decision to the Kwantung Army Headquarters."

Even after the Emperor's broadcast—a historic event, for the sacred voice had never before been heard on the radio—Imperial General Headquarters had been besieged with telephone and telegraph messages from the many army headquarters in Southeast Asia, China, and Manchuria, all seeking clarification of the process that had brought about the order to terminate hostilities. Even more troubling, all messages questioned the authenticity of the order. The Kwantung Army in Manchuria had sent this message: "Although His Majesty's wish has been expressed in person over the radio, we are unable to comply. We had anticipated the Soviet Union's entry into the war and we shall send all 700,000 men into battle. We shall seek a possible miracle by risking total annihilation."

"We can't do anything with them by telephone or telegraph," General Umezu continued. "You go and talk to them directly. Explain His Majesty's wish, and tell them that Imperial General Headquarters is *ordering* Kwantung Army Headquarters to comply. You were a staff officer of the Kwantung Army. They were your colleagues, and you should be able to convince them."

Four months earlier Iki had been recalled to Tokyo from the Kwantung Army to help plan the decisive battle on homeground. He thought of the 700,000 officers and men who had devoted hearts and minds to preparing for eventual war with the Russians. Even when a large part of their troops and ammunition had been diverted to Southeast Asia, they had not wavered. Now at last they were engaged in combat against the Soviet Army, which had declared war only seven days before it invaded Manchuria.

"Of course I shall do my best," Iki replied to General Umezu. "But probably many officers in the Kwantung Army have interpreted the Emperor's broadcast as being only an address to the general public, not to the troops. They might not recognize the

11

need to surrender—until they are given orders from Imperial General Headquarters. So I wish to take them an official order from you to lay down their arms. I don't think I can persuade them without that."

General Umezu considered Iki's request. A communiqué received from the Philippines earlier in the evening had stated that the command there would not cease combat unless it was ordered to do so by Imperial General Headquarters. Ordinarily a cease-fire order would be drafted by a staff officer in Operations and then issued by the Chief-of-Staff. But today no one in Operations had been willing to prepare that fateful communication.

"You draft the order," Umezu said.

The irony underlying this command sent a shock through Iki. In 1941 he had drafted the order to initiate hostilities with the United States. Now, in the moment of Japan's defeat, he was being ordered to draft the cease-fire command. The wheel of fate had turned a full round, he was thinking.

Just then a staff officer burst into the room. "Sir! We've received a phone call from Kwantung Army Headquarters, objecting to our order. They said: 'We shall initiate an attack on the Soviet Army; we cannot, at this juncture, agree to an unconditional surrender.' "

"We've no time to lose." Umezu turned to Iki. "Write the order immediately, and leave for Shinkyo in the morning. We'll communicate with the Soviet, American, and British forces and request safe passage for you. Remember, you are to return here the moment your mission is accomplished."

Iki came to attention, crisply repeated the order he had received, saluted, and left the room. In the hallway he stopped to look out a window. The air reeked of gasoline. Several fires lighted the darkness in the front garden. Men darted in and out of the shadows, shouting, carrying boxes full of papers. They were burning heaps of secret documents and encoded instructions.

"How can the Imperial Army surrender?" a voice bellowed. Sobs of grief mingled with the shouting, the urgings to hurry. "No one at the Academy taught us anything about defeat!"

The firelight revealed the figures of anguished officers and men, their uniforms stained with sweat, their faces twisted by despair. Iki wanted to run out into the yard, to join them in giving vent to their grief. But he had to write the order.

Although the lights were on, the Operations room was deserted. Every drawer and cabinet door had been pulled open, and papers lay scattered over most of the floor. The disarray made mockery of the fact that, until the day before, this very office had been part of the headquarters that commanded the 4,500,000 men of the Imperial Japanese Army.

Iki pushed aside the clutter on his desk and sat down to write. He took sheets of lined paper from a drawer, removed the lid from the box holding his inkstone. He always used the traditional brush and Chinese ink to draft commands of Imperial General Headquarters, even those to be sent by telegraph. No rule required the use of brush and ink, but he could not bring himself to use a modern pen, a thing so alien to Japan, when he thought that his every word would affect the fates of Japan's men on the battlefields of Asia.

The noise outside the building grew louder. Iki moved the inkstick back and forth against the wet stone, concentrating on the sentences he must compose. From the time he entered the Junior Military Academy at the age of fourteen, and throughout the twenty-four years since, spent in the Army Academy and the War College, he had been trained only for victorious campaigns. He searched his memory, but the terms for writing a cease-fire command to end a lost war simply would not come to him.

Time wove its silken cocoon about him, and gradually he regained the composure necessary to an Operations officer. At last he began to write the order to halt all combat by Japan's warriors across the conquered seas.

At five o'clock the next morning, accompanied by a first sergeant, Iki boarded a headquarters reconnaissance plane and left the mist-shrouded field at Tachikawa Air Base. An army briefcase across his lap held the cease-fire order from Chief-of-Staff Umezu addressed to the Kwantung Army commander: "The purpose of Imperial General Headquarters is to carry out the import of His Imperial Majesty's order. You must, therefore, terminate all combat action. I entrust the Kwantung Army Headquarters with authority to negotiate a cease-fire with the army of the Soviet Union."

General Umezu's parting words, "You are to return," lingered in Iki's mind. In his capacity as a special emissary, Iki was obligated to return; but, even more important, General Umezu had implied that he was not to risk his life needlessly. Already Iki had given much thought to his fate. He realized that he must find a suitable place for the soldier's death that now awaited him. But the inexorable sacrifice to honor must await the completion of his mission.

The plane landed for refueling at the army air base near Keijo, or Seoul, and almost immediately took off again in the direction of the Manchurian city of Ch'ang-ch'un, which Japan had renamed Shinkyo, "New Capital."

Shinkyo shone white in the glare of the August sun. The hardy plane trees lining the city's streets glistened, still green beneath the powdering of dust. As Iki was driven into the city he saw that the doors of all the shops and houses were shut tight. His driver moved cautiously through the congested streets. Thousands of Manchurians were fleeing to the countryside; most were pulling carts filled with small children and wrinkled elders. Occasionally Iki's car passed Japanese residents who were loading their belongings into trucks.

The car began to climb the long slope of Daido Boulevard, which appeared to rise into the clouds. The broad avenue was jammed with frightened people and loaded vehicles of every possible kind. Iki noticed a woman carrying only a few personal belongings and leading her small child. She made him think of his wife and children in Tokyo. Ever since the ninth of August, when the Supreme War Council met, he had slept in the officers' quarters at Ichigaya without once returning to his home in Koenji, in Suginami Ward. He had spent his last night in Tokyo composing the cease-fire command and putting his office in order. He'd had no time to telephone his wife. Perhaps that was just as well, he thought, for a call would have caused her unnecessary worry. He did not doubt that, although he might find his own escape from disgrace in suicide, his wife would raise their two children and would herself endure the life ahead.

Open cars filled with soldiers sped northward on the railroad tracks. The Kwangtung Army, which had not accepted the cease-fire, was massing its forces at the border to defend it against the invading Soviet Army. Iki knew that Japan's units in Manchuria lacked sufficient ammunition. Because both troops and supplies had been diverted to the southern front, the Kwantung Army no longer had the strength for which it was once feared.

They passed West Park and approached a four-story building with high gables and wide eaves, patterned after Japanese castles of the sixteenth century—the Kwantung Army's headquarters. Here Iki had worked until four months before. He saluted as the guard at the main gate presented arms.

The final staff meeting of Japan's army in Manchuria was held in the Operations room. Twenty-six staff officers, including Commander-in-Chief General Yamada and Chief-of-Staff Lieutenant General Hata, were convened to decide the fate of the Kwantung Army. The Soviet Army had already crossed the border and was pouring into Manchuria. Each moment's delay could mean the loss of thousands of lives. Lines of strain marked every face in the room.

A young staff officer spoke out the instant Iki finished reading the cease-fire order. "We must refuse in no uncertain terms," he said forcefully. "On August 10th Imperial General Headquarters ordered an all-out operation to crush the Soviets. That was only six days ago. Now it orders unconditional surrender. Well and good. But what does Headquarters have to say about preserving Japan's status as a nation? In the imperial proclamation His Majesty is specific regarding his wish to maintain Japan's status as a nation. How do we know the Allied Powers will honor any pledge following a surrender that's unconditional?"

Iki had no answer to this challenge. The point had been debated on August 14th in the imperial presence, and, despite uncertainty on this point, ultimately the Emperor's will had prevailed.

"At this rate the Japanese will cease to exist as a people," another staff officer said somberly. "We've got to take a stand! We've no choice except to fight for the concessions that will preserve Japan's status as a nation."

"Whether we win or lose the battle is of little consequence," another argued. "Our duty is to fight to the last man. If Japan survives, the memory of our annihilation will be an inspiration to our people as they rebuild the country."

The younger officers, openly belligerent, declared their intention to reject the order. Iki looked at General Yamada. The Commander-in-Chief had been sitting stiffly, his expression unchanged despite the turbulence of his thoughts as he weighed the decision he must make. Hata, the Kwantung Army's foremost expert on the Soviets, had not said a word.

15

"I have a question for Colonel Iki," General Yamada finally broke his silence. "I've heard that the Army insisted until the very end on fighting a decisive battle on Japanese soil. What undermined the Army's position? Please tell us. You were recalled to Tokyo to assist in the planning of that battle. You should be able to take an objective view of the situation."

The general's question had been calculated to calm the young officers. Iki answered promptly: "About the end of July, those of us entrusted with planning the final battle were prepared to deploy our forces on the assumption that the American invasion of southern Kyushu would take place along three fronts—the Miyazaki coast, Ariake Bay, and the west and south shores of Satsuma Peninsula. And we assumed that the most crucial battle would be fought in the outlying regions of Tokyo against landing forces at three fronts—Sagami Bay, the Kujukuri-ga-hama coast, and the Kashima coast. But now the realities are different. Increased bombings of our cities have heavily damaged facilities for production of military material. Our fuel reserves are exhausted. The only alternative left was for each man and each tank to fight an individual suicidal battle. At the conference on August 14th His Majesty said that he did not wish to see his people subjected to more misery, and he rejected the Army's request for a decisive last stand on the home islands."

The situation in Japan, as Iki described it, was far worse than any of them had imagined. The staff officers fell silent.

"What's happening in the homeland is not our business!" a younger man shouted. "You were once one of us, with your life on the line along with the rest of us in the Kwantung Army. And that was only four months ago. Now you dare to come to us with a cease-fire order! Coward!"

"That's right!" another cried. "We've held the border against the Soviets for more than ten years. We've honored Tokyo Headquarters' injunction 'to maintain peace.' We held back despite Soviet provocation because we were concerned about the future of the Manchurian nation. Now you're telling us to abandon all of Manchuria without so much as a skirmish, to abandon the million and a half citizens of Manchukuo to a fate no one dares to guess. You're telling us to submit to the shame of being taken captive! I ought to run you through with my sword!"

Those who wanted to argue became enraged. Some leaped up in fury. Violence hung in the air.

"Settle down!" Chief-of-Staff Hata's command rang through the room. "What sense do you find in disobeying His Majesty's command, and then talking about preserving the nation? We're subjects of His Majesty and, if we're to remain so, we must immediately suspend operations in compliance with his sacred wish. If you insist on continuing this war, do so. But strike off my head first. Then do what you wish."

General Yamada had been listening, with eyes closed. "I'm in complete agreement with the Chief-of-Staff," he said quietly. "His Majesty's wish has been made known to us. Anyone who disobeys becomes an outlaw or a guerilla. And I've no intention of commanding a band of guerillas. We've no choice except to honor the imperial wish. Whether in victory or in defeat, we have one duty only—to obey the imperial wish."

Having spoken his mind, Yamada closed his eyes once more. A glistening tear coursed down each cheek. The deep silence that settled over the room soon became unendurable. Tears and muffled sobs at last brought release—and resolution.

"My friends, we're disbanding the Kwantung Army," General Hata said. "This Army has had an admirable history of twenty-six years. This is the last time we shall be together. So I would like to have a farewell drink with you. I want to thank you for the many years of loyal service you have given to this unit."

Saké and cups were brought to the table. The twenty-six officers stood and, in silence, drank the saké in a ritual of parting. Then they left the room, one by one. Only Iki and General Hata remained.

"Well done, Iki," Hata said. "Fly back immediately and report that the Kwantung Army, in compliance with the imperial wish, accepts the cease-fire order issued by Imperial General Headquarters."

"Sir, I respect your wish, but I would like to report to Tokyo by telephone and stay here, in the Kwantung Army Headquarters command."

"You can't do that. You're assigned to the staff of Imperial General Headquarters."

"That's true. I've been with them for four months. But before that I worked under you for more than a year, planning operations against the Soviets. I want to stay with the Kwantung Army."

"You have your orders. It's your duty to return. Try to understand why General Umezu gave you those orders. As Chief-of-

Staff of the Kwantung Army, I won't allow you in this command. Get back to Tokyo!"

Iki looked at his watch. Five o'clock. He had been at headquarters for two hours. The flight from Shinkyo to Tokyo would take at least nine hours. He must hurry to the airfield.

Still agitated, he left the Operations room and was rushed to a waiting car by the sergeant who had accompanied him to headquarters. They threaded their way through streets more congested than before. As they neared the airfield, he noticed the strange maneuverings of a light plane coming down out of the clouds in the northeast. Its angle of descent indicated that the pilot intended to make a landing. But then the craft leveled off instead and started to circle the field unsteadily. It was a Type-93 Army trainer, nicknamed the "Red Dragonfly," used by cadets in flight academies in Japan. Iki was puzzled, for that plane should not have been flying anywhere in Manchuria. He urged the sergeant to drive faster.

A fire truck and an ambulance waited beside the runway. Everyone watched the trainer as it made a wavering descent.

Iki pushed his way among the maintenance crew to a lieutenant who was tracking the plane through binoculars. "Where's that trainer from?" he asked. "Orders for flight academy cadets to evacuate have already been issued."

The lieutenant recognized the cordon that identified Iki as a staff officer and saluted him. "Sir, it's a trainer used by the fifty-ninth class of the Toyooka Flight Academy. The cadets arrived here last month for flight training, and were ordered to return as soon as we learned that the Soviets have entered the war. The cadets hadn't been fully trained, and several got off course and went down on the way home. According to a report that's come in over the radio, this pilot was going home by way of Seoul but was attacked by Soviet planes over Kirin. He's barely managed to fly back here for an emergency landing."

"Where was his plane hit?"

"From what I can see, the tip of the left wing . . ." Before the lieutenant could finish, the trainer, swaying crazily, touched down at the far end of the landing strip. The fire truck and ambulance sped off toward the aircraft, followed closely by Iki in his car. The trainer's left wingtip was shorn off, and bullet holes riddled the fuselage. Although blood flowed down one side of the pilot's face,

Iki could tell that he was no more than twenty years old. The cadet managed to climb out of the cockpit, then fell unconscious to the ground. Medical corpsmen gathered around him to administer emergency aid.

"Will he live?" Iki asked the medical officer in charge, after he'd examined the youth.

"He has a scalp wound and a bullet through his left thigh, but it's a clean wound. He'll be all right if we can stop the bleeding. We'll take him to the hospital right away."

"Wait," Iki said. "Let's send him back to Tokyo in my plane. Get him ready."

"But, sir," the sergeant protested, "our reconnaisance plane can carry only two passengers besides the pilot."

"I plan to stay in Shinkyo. I'll report to Imperial General Headquarters by phone. But, to be sure they get it, I want you to make a verbal report for me as soon as you get back."

"But, sir, military regulations forbid—"

"That cadet has already received his orders to return home. He's been wounded on the way, and no regulation will be broken if he proceeds on another aircraft. The Soviet Army is already in Hailar, so you'd better leave quickly."

The cadet was still unconscious as they lifted him into the cabin. By giving up his place on that plane returning to Japan, Iki gave up his chance for a safe retreat. "This is for the best," he told himself as he watched the plane leave the runway and fly eastward into the darkening sky, toward Japan. He had decided, soon after entering Kwantung Army Headquarters, that he was one of Japan's soldiers who must not survive a lost war.

On August 18 the sky above Harbin Airport was dark gray, the color of lead. In the distance thunder rumbled, as if foretelling doom.

Iki Tadashi stood with the Japanese delegation, awaiting the arrival of an aircraft that would bring in the Soviet officers with whom they would negotiate the cease-fire agreement. The delegation consisted of Lieutenant General Hata, Major General Nohara of Intelligence, Colonel Omae of Political Affairs, Lieutenant Colonel Kawashima of Operations, Consul-General Miyakawa from Harbin, and several supporting officers.

Kwantung Army Headquarters, on August 16, had decided to

abide by the orders from Tokyo delivered by Iki. On August 17 it had issued orders to all its units to cease hostilities and surrender their arms to the Soviet Army. Negotiations for a cease-fire had been initiated through the Soviet Consulate in Harbin.

The Soviet Military Mission in Harbin had notified the Japanese that Marshal Vasilevsky, chief of the Far East Command, would represent the Soviet Union at the negotiations. The delegation representing the Japanese Army was instructed to be at Harbin Airport that afternoon.

At 4:10 p.m. several Soviet planes appeared from the east and circled above the airport, apparently reconnoitering the area for indications of threats by Japanese troops. Soon a formation of more than a dozen planes roared through the clouds overhead. The squadron was unexpectedly large for the purpose of flying the Japanese delegation to a site for negotiating the cease-fire. Iki, suddenly alarmed, looked at General Hata, speaking nervously to General Nohara beside him.

As soon as the planes landed, Soviet soldiers carrying automatic rifles swarmed out from the aircraft and swept the runway clear of Japanese troops. The Russians moved quickly, occupying the hangars, maintenance sheds, and all other structures in the area. All Japanese soldiers in the airport, as well as employees of Manchurian-Mongolian Airways, were herded at bayonet point into a far corner of the airport compound. The Japanese Army delegation was not allowed to move from the space beside the wall outside the waiting room.

Within fifteen minutes Harbin Airport was fully secured by the Russians. Then, assured of safety, a group of officers emerged from an airplane and walked directly across the field to the Japanese delegation.

"I am Major General Shelekhov," one of the officers said in a shrill voice, speaking in Russian, of course. While Consul-General Miyakawa translated the unfamiliar language for them, the Japanese officers stared at rows of brightly colored ribbons decorating Shelekhov's olive-green tunic as he glared arrogantly down at them. "Where is Chief-of-Staff Hata?"

Hata stepped forward. "Is Lieutenant Colonel Iki of the Imperial General Headquarters here?" Shelekhov asked, emphasizing each word.

"I am here," Iki replied.

The Russian looked him up and down with icy contempt. In the communiqué sent through their Military Mission, the Soviets had specified that "Iki of Imperial General Headquarters" be included in the Japanese delegation. To avoid implicating Imperial Headquarters, however, Kwantung Army Headquarters had taken the precaution to state that Iki had already left for Japan. The alert Soviets detected this ruse: "Our radio interceptors have monitored information pertaining to Iki. We know that he reported to the Imperial General Headquarters by telephone, then entered the command of the Kwantung Army."

With Consul-General Miyakawa interpreting for him, General Hata said he wished to conclude a cease-fire agreement with the Soviet Far East Command at the earliest possible moment.

"The meeting with Supreme Commander Marshal Vasilevsky has been postponed until tomorrow," Shelekhov said haughtily. "In the meantime, you will provide us with a register of all Kwantung Army officers in this area, as well as with registers of all guard units in Harbin."

The Russian delegation boarded automobiles seized from the Kwantung Army and drove off to the Soviet Consulate, taking the Japanese officers with them.

Next morning the Soviet plane carrying General's Hata's delegation left Harbin Airport at seven o'clock. As they flew over the Mu-tan River, Iki was stunned by the scene that unfolded below— the steel bridge demolished, houses reduced to ashes, hills pocked with brown craters. Black smoke billowed into the sky above the Sui-fen River in the distance. Apparently the cease-fire order had not yet reached the front lines.

The plane crossed the border into Siberia and landed on an unpaved runway in a narrow field. Judging from its location amid mountains near the border, the landing strip probably was the secret airfield of Zharkova. No time was given the Japanese to study their surroundings; they were rushed into jeeps and driven to a wooden building not far away. The building had been put up in a hurry. The floor of rough unfinished lumber was covered with blankets in place of a rug—as a courtesy, perhaps, to the delegation representing the Japanese Army.

A loud knocking at the door caused the apprehensive Japanese to turn and watch it open. A plump officer entered, followed by enlisted men who brought in quantities of caviar, smoked salmon, and white bread. The Japanese were astonished to see such delicacies in a battle zone. "I don't think you gentlemen have had breakfast yet," the cheerful officer said as he uncorked a bottle of champagne. Members of the delegation looked at each other somewhat foolishly, as they considered the novel idea that military personnel would drink alcohol in the morning.

"Please help yourselves," the courteous Russian said, "and let me know if you have any favorite dishes I can serve at lunchtime."

"We appreciate your kindness, but we wish to meet with Marshal Vasilevsky as soon as possible," General Nohara said. "At what time will the meeting take place?"

"I'm only your host," he tittered. "I wouldn't know anything about that. Are you gentlemen fond of Russian food?"

"We're asking you about the hour of the meeting," Iki said, annoyed with this officer who could think of nothing but food. "If you don't know, will you go to your command headquarters and find out right away?"

A bit reluctantly their host consented to do so and waddled off. Several hours passed without word from him or any other Russian. Twice more the Japanese asked Consul-General Miyakawa to repeat their request. Finally another officer came to inform them of the scheduled hour; he added that the Japanese were to be represented only by Chief-of-Staff Hata and Imperial General Headquarters staff officer Colonel Iki.

General Hata shook his head. "If I'm to discuss any specifics in my capacity as chief-of-staff, I must have my staff officers with me. And I must have Mr. Miyakawa, our Consul-General in Harbin, as interpreter." Thirty minutes later the officer returned to say that Hata's requests had been approved.

The Japanese were taken by jeep to command headquarters, a number of wooden buildings much like the one they had left, set amid sparse groves of white birches that covered the surrounding hills. Other structures stood along either side of the road leading to the headquarters buildings. At several checkpoints guards lifted bars to let them pass. The entire installation was concealed from aerial observation with an admirable thoroughness. Huge camouflage nets covered the road and all buildings. That explained why the reconnaissance flights of the Kwangtung Army's intelligence staff had failed to locate the Soviets' general headquarters.

The Soviet headquarters, a building made of logs, was painted light green on the outside. But the main conference room was crude and bare of furnishings except for a Soviet flag on a staff, a cheap table, and a number of unpainted chairs. The whole place showed the obvious haste with which the Soviet Far East Command had been established there. It was one more proof of the Russians' guile: they had planned to abrogate their neutrality pact with Japan and enter the war just as Japan was about to surrender to the Allies, thus allowing them an easy conquest of Manchuria. Iki burned with anger at this revelation of Russian deceit.

At 3:30 p.m. Soviet Supreme Commander Marshal Vasilevsky entered the room, accompanied by Marshal Malinovsky, Zabaykal area commander, Marshal Meretskov, Commander of the Maritime Territory, and the chiefs of the Far East Air Command and the Pacific Fleet. The Japanese delegates stood and saluted.

An electric tension filled the room as the Japanese and the Russians faced each other from opposite sides of the conference table. They had been adversaries for more than ten years, observing each other across the Manchurian-Soviet border, preparing themselves for an eventual clash. Now, without having fought a full-scale war, they were meeting at a table—and taking their places as victors and vanquished.

In the silence the Japanese heard the music of an accordion accompanying a Russian folksong. Russian soldiers were singing, jubilant in easy victory. Sadness, then bitterness, crossed General Hata's bold features as he thought about the 700,000 despairing men of the Kwantung Army. But visible emotion vanished in the instant, as he started the discussion.

"In accordance with the order of His Imperial Majesty of Japan, the Kwantung Army has decided to cease hostilities with the Soviet Army. We wish to implement this decision as quickly as possible."

Marshal Vasilevsky spread out a map on the table and began talking about a suitable place for the Kwantung Army to be assembled for the surrender. Occasionally one of the other marshals would add a comment, a suggestion or a reminder.

While the Japanese reply was being interpreted, Iki had time to study the powerful men seated across the table. He knew much about Marshal Vasilevsky, Stalin's chief-of-staff in command of the

Red Army, ten million strong, a man renowned for both intelligence and bravery. Marshal Malinovsky, seated next to Vasilevsky, had fought magnificently against the Germans at Stalingrad. Marshal Meretskov had served as commander of the Soviet Army against Finland. But of them all, only Vasilevsky bore himself with the dignity of a true general. Malinovsky had a self-righteous look, and a suggestion of cruelty lay behind the condescension with which he regarded these emissaries of the vanquished Japanese. The diminutive Meretskov fidgeted continually, and berated the Japanese whenever they paused to think about questions directed at them. With the exception of Vasilevsky, who was born in 1895, all the other Russians were men in their forties who had been made generals in a hurry, in response to the urgencies of war. Iki fought back the feeling of helpless, suffocating fury at the thought of being forced to sue for peace from such sinister men.

Slowly, the conditions for surrender were worked out in great detail.

"I expect the Japanese Army to maintain strictest order in the process of surrendering," Marshal Vasilevsky declared, "and to provide its own troops with food during the first several days. Each unit must bring its own provisions to the point of assembly. Until the Soviet Army arrives, maintenance of order in the Shinkyo area shall be the responsibility of Japanese Army Headquarters."

Having accepted Vasilevsky's orders, General Hata spoke earnestly on behalf of the Japanese Army. "I wish to make three requests. We have submitted to defeat, but I ask that we be accorded customary military courtesies. As you may know, we in the Japanese Army have always abided by the code of the samurai, and I ask that our officers be permitted to wear their swords. Second, I seek the assurance that you will do your utmost to protect Japanese civilians and expedite their return to Japan. And, last, I ask that Japanese army personnel be interned in Manchuria, where we are assured of adequate housing, food, and clothing. I should like to add that we expect you to abide by international law governing prisoners of war, as stipulated by the Geneva Convention."

Marshal Vasilevsky conferred at length with his colleagues, then rose to speak. "We shall permit the Japanese military to wear their insignia and swords, and we shall permit officers of general rank to retain their aides. I assure you that the Soviet Army will accord Japanese officers and men proper military courtesy.

"The protection of your civilians and their early repatriation are matters of humanitarian concern for which our country will do its utmost," Vasilevsky continued. "However, we cannot agree to the internment of Japanese troops in Manchuria. The officers and men of the Japanese Army will first be disarmed, then interned in Siberia until the Soviet Army completes its occupation of Manchuria."

Vasilevsky refused to comment on the request to observe the rules of the Geneva Convention, despite Hata's repeated mention of the subject. Perhaps Soviet policy, determined in Moscow, dictated Vasilevsky's refusal to answer a question pertaining to international law.

General Hata, visibly alarmed by Vasilevsky's attitude, spoke again: "I would like to make a request regarding food supplies for internees. Rice is the staple of the Japanese, and without it we shall not be able to sustain ourselves physically. I ask that you take this into consideration."

Shaking with anger, Marshal Meretskov shouted that this was an impossibility. Vasilevsky, however, said he would see that the ration of staples for each man per day would consists of three hundred grams each of black bread and of rice. The Japanese could not insist on more.

"I trust you will consider that amount of staples to be absolutely minimal for our sustenance," Hata said, by way of confirming this commitment from Marshal Vasilevsky.

"Moreover," he added "I ask that you allow us to maintain adequate means of transportation and communication. We shall need to transmit orders issued by the Soviet Far East Command to all our units."

Marshal Vasilevsky agreed to this request, and the meeting was concluded.

"Are you gentlemen in any way dissatisfied with the quarters we've provided?" one of the lesser Russian officers asked as the Japanese were leaving. Hata stopped to say that the delegation was grateful for its accommodations.

"The plane that brought you here has gone off on a flight to Sakhalin Island," said the Russian. "You'll be staying in those quarters for the time being."

The Japanese showed signs of surprise. Hata spoke immediately. "Then we ask that you provide us with another aircraft."

"Unfortunately, all of our planes have left for Manchuria and China," Vasilevsky replied.

"In that case," countered Hata, "send one of our planes from Harbin to take us back."

"No. I've made this decision to keep you here in my capacity as Supreme Commander."

Hata was astonished by the implications in this abrupt reply: Marshal Vasilevsky did not believe that the Kwantung Army was actually surrendering, and was holding the delegation as hostages until all units did surrender!

"We must be taken back immediately, in order to put our agreement into effect in a peaceful and expeditious manner," Hata emphasized.

"In that case you must send men to replace you." This was an undisguised demand for hostages.

"We agree. We'll dispatch them as soon as we get back."

Vasilevsky's severe expression softened noticeably, and he ordered a plane readied for them.

The Japanese delegates were driven back over the same road toward the airfield. The ghostly whiteness of the slender birch trees seemed to float up out of the grayness of dusk, like suggestions of the white robes associated with death.

They found a reconnaissance plane provided for them at the airfield, but were forced to wait until maintenance work on it was completed. Already impatient to depart before sunset, they were irritated by the slowness of the Soviet crew and wondered if their departure was being delayed purposely.

At last the Japanese settled into their seats with sighs of relief, and the plane lifted off about eight o'clock, for the last phase of their mission, the flight back to Shinkyo. But they were restless and worried, thinking of the task that awaited them—the need to establish communication with each of the imperial army groups in Manchuria.

As they flew into the space above Kirin, a flash of lightning flared, followed by a roar of thunder. In moments they were enveloped by black storm clouds. Pelted by rain, rising and sinking unsteadily, the plane continued to fly on for what seemed to be much too long a time. Iki wondered if the pilot was following the correct course. He became uneasy when he realized they had exceeded the normal flight time.

The Soviet officer with them also appeared to be nervous, and went frequently into the pilot's cabin. After his last visit there he spoke excitedly to Consul-General Miyakawa, who translated the information. "Visibility is poor because of the weather, and the plane is almost out of fuel."

A flurry of concern swept among the Japanese. The thought of crashing to his death entered Iki's mind. But he remembered the group's responsibility for the fate of the 700,000 men of the Kwantung Army, and he moved toward the pilot's compartment. He brushed aside the Soviet officer who tried to stop him, stepped inside, and sat down next to a startled pilot.

During his year and a half as operations officer for the Kwantung Army, Iki had studied dozens of maps and memorized the topography of all of Manchuria. Not one river or mountain was unknown to him. He looked out at the terrain below, and saw that they had flown past the tracks of the Dairen-Shinkyo Railway. He could speak some Russian—perhaps enough for this emergency.

"Turn left and look for a river," he said from the co-pilot's seat. If he could find the Sungari River, he would be able to sight familiar landmarks. The pilot made a wide turn, to the left.

"Look! A river—the Sungari!" the pilot shouted. The rain had been left behind, and they saw the reflection from a large body of water. Iki recognized the man-made lake in the hills southwest of Shinkyo.

"That's a lake," he said. "Now fly north and look for a railroad."

He directed the pilot to fly at a lower altitude, to search for the Manchurian Railway tracks which passed through the city of Shinkyo. Soon they saw below them the smooth surface of the Sungari River, and beside it a row of small, evenly-spaced blurs of light.

"Follow the tracks to the south, and you'll find the Shinkyo Airport."

Ten minutes later they saw the Shinkyo Airport's beacon light. But the airfield was completely dark, the runway invisible. They were almost out of fuel. Iki told the pilot to keep circling the field, in order to attract attention below. Gradually the darkened field was dotted with small fires. In minutes the dry grass around the field was blazing, and they saw the runway.

"Go in for a landing!" Iki shouted. The pilot pulled hard on the controls, to level off over the landing strip; the plane hit the ground hard, bounced, and settled on the runway. Iki slumped in his seat, looking at the burning grass beyond the window. Saved from an unsoldierly death, he thought. But saved for what?

An automobile drew up at the main entrance to the Kwantung Army's Headquarters. A Russian officer had come for the man who would replace Chief-of-Staff Hata as hostage. The man specified by the Soviet Far East Command was Major General Takemura, the Deputy Chief-of-Staff. Takemura, who suffered from gastric ulcers, had coughed up blood the day before. The strain of excessive work had taken its toll, and his colleagues expressed genuine concern over his being sent alone to Zharkova. They had tried to replace Takemura with someone else, but the Russian officer considered the effort a ruse and rejected their request.

"Take care!" The officers of the Headquarters staff called out to him as, standing in a line at the entrance, they said farewell to General Takemura. Iki could not find words to express his feelings.

"Don't worry," Takemura told them. "Fortunately I can get by with my Russian. Be sure to look after the Commander-in-Chief and the Chief-of-Staff." Takemura spoke in his usual brisk, cheerful manner, but his body told them of his resignation to the uncertain fate that lay ahead.

Iki watched sadly as the automobile carried Takemura away. Then he went down to the underground Communications room and dispatched a report to headquarters in Tokyo, detailing the movements of the Soviet Army subsequent to the cease-fire agreement and describing how General Takemura had been taken as a hostage. About him more than a dozen Signal Corps operators were trying to communicate the cease-fire order to the divisions, brigades, and battalions strung out along the front lines. Those battle lines stretched over more than 1,800 miles, and, as with the Japanese, the Soviet High Command too had not yet been able to notify all its units. The Japanese and the Russians were still engaged in combat at a number of points, and grim news continued to trickle in.

The guard detachment at Hun-ch'un sent a summary telegram: "The Regimental Commander has killed himself. He did so after committing all subordinates to a pledge to cease hostilities and disarm." No more communications came from that unit.

Undoubtedly the commander had committed suicide after convincing his reluctant subordinates of the need to obey the imperial wish. He had fulfilled his duty as commander and then killed himself. He had died a warrior's death. Iki was profoundly affected by the purity and intensity of his loyalty.

Another message came through. The operator grew pale as he received the last part of it. "Sir, it's from the heavy artillery battalion at I-ho!" he cried out. He handed the slip to Iki, who read it quickly: "We cannot surrender without having fired a shot. Therefore we have decided, all of us, to be blown up by our own artillery shells."

"Get in touch with them," Iki ordered. "Use the telephone, the telegraph. Try everything! I've got to get through to them!"

He prayed silently as several operators tried desperately to get through. The commanding officer of the I-ho Heavy Artillery Battalion had been his classmate at the Army Academy.

"Good!" an operator exclaimed. "We've made contact by telephone. I think it's the battalion commander."

Iki grabbed the phone. "Watase? This is Iki. Obey the order! It's from His Imperial Majesty. Don't be rash."

"Iki! I didn't know you were in Shinkyo." Watase's strong voice carried through the crackling static.

"I brought the cease-fire order from Imperial General Headquarters, and stayed on. We negotiated a cease-fire with the Soviet Army yesterday. We're doing everything we can to stabilize the situation. I know how you feel, but you've got to bear it. Tell your unit to surrender. You've got to!"

Watase did not answer.

"Don't do it now, Watase," Iki pleaded. "First see that your men surrender to the Soviet Army. Then you can do what you feel you must."

"I can't do that. In no way can I get my men to change their minds. They're determined. We've got twelve tanks grouped in a circle and wired together for detonation. My men are all aboard. We've no more time, Iki. Goodbye!"

"Don't, Watase!" Iki shouted into the phone. "Don't do it!"

"I'll be going on ahead of you. You stay a while and see that everything is taken care of properly." Watase spoke quietly, as brave men will do when they have accepted death. Iki's shouts went unanswered. He heard only static, until an ear-shattering explosion came through the line before it went dead. The phone fell from Iki's hand. He had failed in his attempt to save those lives. A whole battalion of heavy artillery, 113 determined men, linked together by a common fuse and a shared destiny, had vanished in a thunderous blast and in a gigantic column of flames shooting heavenward. Iki sat in a daze, surrounded by the appalled operators. After a few moments he stood up, quietly left the Communications room, and walked back to his place in the Operations section.

Tactical operations having ceased, the room was unused. Its doors and windows were closed tight and the air within was stifling. Iki stood before the large map laid out on a table in the center of the room. This map of Manchuria, six feet wide and twelve feet long, was decked with miniature forests of blue and red markers, pinpointing the locations of all friendly and enemy units. Red markers showed where the Soviet forces were penetrating the regions along the border; blue markers, shifting away from the Soviet-Manchurian border, represented the defending Japanese units—the Kwantung Army's divisions, mixed brigades, and tank units. All for nothing! Iki groaned, remembering how he and his staff had gone sleepless for many a night, studying the shifting markers along the border, desperately devising strategies and tactics for eventual combat. At one time the Kwantung Army had accounted for a third of the Imperial Japanese Army, and had the strength to challenge the entire army of many a first-rate power. No longer. Soon it would not exist. Responsibility for its disintegration lay with the top echelon of command—with Imperial General Headquarters of which he had been a part. He had actually heard the violent blast that took the life of his friend. How could he endure to go on living?

He drew himself straight, his eyes still fixed on the map. "In times of national emergency, the self is no weightier than swan's down." Iki remembered this epigram from his first days as a cadet at the Junior Military Academy. Perhaps since then he had always been prepared to accept death. He thought fleetingly of his wife and two small children, but most urgent in his mind was the need to shape his own end. He drew his revolver from its holster, making sure the chambers were filled. Watase had said "We cannot surrender without having fired a shot," and he had died with his men, still believing in the invincibility of the Japanese Army, which never had known defeat. He is more fortunate than I am, thought Iki, who had borne the bitter humiliation of defeat.

He wiped the perspiration from his brow, raised the revolver to his temple. The door burst open and a noncommissioned officer rushed into the room. In his excitement he did not notice Iki's intention.

"Sir! I've been looking all over for you. We've just received orders from the Soviets to vacate our headquarters."

This was an incredible demand. The Soviet Occupation Army in Shinkyo had been given the big Army Club building, just across the street, for its headquarters.

"That's preposterous! What did the Commander-in-Chief say? And the Chief-of-Staff?"

"I don't know, sir. The Russians have come here in trucks. They're armed, and they've forced their way into the building."

Iki jammed his revolver back into its holster and ran to the office of the commander-in-chief. Russian soldiers already occupied the room, forming a semicircle around the Japanese officers who had assembled there.

"Your orders are to vacate this building immediately and move into the Navy enlisted men's building," the Russian officer in charge said harshly. Ignoring General Yamada's protests, he insisted, "If you refuse, we must take it by force."

In the expectant silence Yamada rose slowly from his chair. The others followed his example.

An hour later General Yamada and his staff officers climbed into the one remaining Headquarters truck, taking with them only a few personal belongings. The enlisted men moved out on foot.

Once beyond the gate the officers looked back at the beautiful lines of the Kwantung Army Headquarters building, which for fourteen years had been an imposing symbol of Japanese expansion on the continent. The tiled roof soared high against the cloud-banked summer sky. At once they noticed that the golden imperial chrysanthemum crest had been torn away from the white plaster wall below the uppermost central gable. The lighter emptiness left on the wall where for so long the crest had gleamed was a heart-breaking symbol of their capitulation, of their lost cause.

The truck, under Russian escort, moved away at slow speed. Everyone, from the commander-in-chief down to the enlisted men, wept openly as each looked back, time and again, at the captured citadel. Iki cursed himself for failing to take the right moment to die.

The moving of the Kwantung Army Headquarters to the Navy building, situated a little more than a mile north of the former headquarters, was soon completed. Japanese staff officers still constituted the headquarters, but only in name; they had been stripped of all command prerogatives, and in effect were being held in enforced detention. The only arms the Russians allowed them to keep were the revolvers carried by the duty officers and a dozen or so rifles issued to guards who manned the main gate. One radio set was all they were permitted for communicating with the world beyond Shinkyo.

A week went by. General Hata, depressed and worried, stood beside the window to his office. "Look, Iki, more Russian troops coming in for the occupation . . ." Iki saw the column of Russian soldiers marching toward them from Shinkyo's central railway station. The men wore dirty, rumpled uniforms, but their rifles were new and shiny. Weary from long travel, many were stopping at wayside puddles, cupping water into their hands to drink. Others used knives to split open cans of rations and scooped up the food with their fingers. In the opinion of the disciplined Japanese, they appeared to be no different from a horde of animal-like primitive tribesmen from a distant plain.

Iki turned away from the window. He knew that more and more Soviet ground troops were coming into Shinkyo. Drunk with victory and vodka, they were on a rampage of looting, rape, and violence. Drink made them savage, and they turned the lives of resident Japanese into a nightmare. Innumerable complaints were registered with the Kwantung Army Headquarters by refugees as well as by officials of the Manchurian government, but the staff were helpless. All they could do was to ask the Soviet authorities to discipline their troops, and to hasten the repatriation of resident Japanese. Their pleas were ignored. When some members of the Manchurian-Mongolian Development Group reached Shinkyo and huddled down in the city's western plaza, Russian soldiers stripped them of all their possessions, even their underwear. They presented a strange and pitiable sight, with head and limbs projecting from the burlap bags someone had given them to cover their nakedness. For three days they had nothing to eat, only foul water to drink.

"If they're left as they are," Iki reported to General Hata, "they'll die of starvation or freeze to death when winter begins. We've got to let Imperial Army Headquarters know what is happening and ask them to take action."

With Hata's consent, Iki went to the Communications room and tapped the keys of the telegraph: "Refugees in Shinkyo are being stripped of their few belongings by Soviet troops; some have had no food for several days. We have manpower available to ship coal into the city for heating, but cannot obtain permission to effect shipment. Clothing, bedding, and housing have vanished by way of requisition and pillaging. We anticipate countless deaths by starvation and freezing during coming winter. Our requests for clarification of intent of Soviet authorities have gone unanswered. Japan, as a nation, must make a concerted effort now to expedite repatriation of our citizens."

Iki repeated this plea daily by wireless. The Imperial General Headquarters in Tokyo conveyed the request repeatedly to the Soviet High Command, only to have it rejected.

On September 5 a Soviet officer wearing a major general's insignia entered the Navy enlisted men's building. "I've come as emissary from General Khabarov, Commander of the Shinkyo Occupation Army," he announced. "I wish to see Commander-in-Chief Yamada and Chief-of-Staff Hata."

Sensing the unusual, Iki and other staff members accompanied Yamada and Hata to the meeting. The Soviet emissary wasted no time. "Commanding General Khabarov has ordered all members of the Kwantung Army in Shinkyo to be assembled at the former General Headquarters. I've come to escort Commander-in-Chief Yamada and Chief-of-Staff Hata. The two of you will come with me now."

The Russian major general spoke politely, but the note of authority in his voice was unmistakable. The Japanese knew that the time had come for them to be disarmed. They were prepared for this event. Carrying only a few personal articles, they left the Navy building.

When they reached the former headquarters and entered the

compound, they found about a thousand Japanese soldiers who had been stationed in Shinkyo assembled in close formation. About fifty civilians were there as well. The soldiers stepped to either side, opening a pathway for their officers. Iki felt their questioning glances as the officers walked, lips drawn tight, into the space where General Khabarov awaited them.

Khabarov thrust out his chest as he addressed the Japanese: "Pursuant to the order of Marshal Vasilevsky, Chief of the Soviet Far East Command, the Kwantung Army Headquarters unit is to be disarmed. All personnel presently in Shinkyo are to be transferred to other designated areas."

"As Commander-in-Chief of the Kwantung Army," Yamada replied, "I shall give the order for my unit to disarm." He mounted the steps to the reviewing stand and stood there in silence, looking at the many faces ranged below him.

"Men!" he said at last. "You have served our country well over a long period of time. The fortunes of war did not favor us. We were compelled to cease hostilities, and now we face the inevitable demand to disarm ourselves. But remember that the order to disarm has come from His Imperial Majesty, and you will not bear the shame of being taken captive in war. As Commander-in-Chief I shall bear the responsibility for that. You men must return to your homes and serve your parents. Serve them as sons with the same dedication with which you have served your country as soldiers."

Many men wept as they heard their commander's parting message. For a few moments Yamada could not continue, as he fought back the emotion rising within him.

"In giving up your arms," he continued, "act in a disciplined and orderly manner, as would befit the Japanese Army."

Not one of the men moved. Until that day each had regarded his rifle as a weapon bestowed upon him by the Emperor. Because the rifle was sacred, it was given constant care and valued above everything else, even one's life. Moreover, for them the battle order, "You shall not endure the shame of being taken prisoner alive," was still inviolable.

"Lay down your rifles!" Khabarov shouted, suspecting a dangerous mood in the crowded compound. The Russian soldiers raised their automatic rifles.

Yamada spoke sternly to his soldiers: "Any untoward incident here will be in violation of the imperial wish. Stack rifles immediately!" He looked out at the rows of faces, twisted by grief and pain and humiliation. At last, a few soldiers broke ranks, to stack their rifles in the prescribed manner.

The summer sun beat down on men and weapons alike. The Japanese, stripped of arms, desolate, stared blankly at the dark shadows cast by the rifles they had been forced to give up. Disintegration of the Kwantung Army was complete.

General Yamada and his staff of twenty-five officers were led into the headquarters building.

"Now we shall proceed with the disarming of you gentlemen," Khabarov declared. "According to Marshal Vasilevsky's directive, you may keep your swords. Please lay down your pistols."

Khabarov's broad puffy face revealed the cruel delight of a victor. General Yamada removed his pistol and placed it on the table Hata and the others followed him. No one spoke, and the only sounds were made as each officer laid his pistol on the table.

Iki felt almost unbearable anguish as he gave up his sidearm. A soldier can suffer no greater shame, he realized. A country should not go to war, he thought. If it should find that war is necessary, then it must be sure to win.

Later the twenty-six officers were taken to Shinkyo Airport and put aboard a plane bound for an unknown destination. Following an overnight stop at Harbin, their flight continued northward. Only then did they understand that they were being flown to Siberia.

Two hours after leaving Harbin, they saw the Amur River, a wide, black slash in the wilderness that separated Manchuria from Siberia. Knowing what it meant, Iki looked down in sorrow on the great river far below.

The plane flew across the river, across the border, into Soviet territory.

3

THE INTERVIEW

"**I**'m sorry I've kept you waiting so long," Daimon said, rousing Iki from his thoughts. "I didn't think the executive meeting would last that long."

Iki had been sitting on the big couch in the president's office, indifferent to the passing of time. Daimon sat down opposite him, on the other side of a coffee table on which a silver cigarette case, a lighter, and an ashtray were neatly arranged.

"I've imposed on you because I didn't want to cut our conversation so short," he said, lighting a cigarette, taking up the talk easily just where they'd stopped. "I doubt if any of us can imagine the dread you must have felt when you heard yourself being sentenced to twenty-five years at hard labor in Siberia."

Daimon's casual reference to that dread brought more unwanted memories into Iki's consciousness.

"I make a point of not telling anyone about Siberia, of not ever referring to it in conversation." Two years at home had not been long enough to help him forget those eleven years of imprisonment.

"I'm sorry. I'm in the habit of wanting to know everything . . . of asking questions until my curiosity is thoroughly satisfied."

A buzz on the intercom broke the tension. "I have a phone call from our office in Indonesia for Mr. Ichimaru," Daimon's secretary said. "I've told them that he's away in Africa. Would you like to take the call?"

Daimon picked up one of three telephones on his desk, immediately involved. "What's that? The Indonesian cabinet's decided on the amount of textile imports? You're sure it includes a hundred thousand bales of cotton yarn? Who gave you that information?"

His grip on the receiver tightened. "Okay! It's reliable if it came straight from Unton."

Unton, Indonesia's Minister of Economics, had covert ties with Kinki Trading and was a trusted source of information. "But how recent is this information? Decided at yesterday's cabinet meeting? And? . . . You heard about it last night at a reception at Unton's house?"

Daimon looked at his watch. Usually a minimum of nine hours would be required for a telephone call to come through from Djakarta to Osaka; furthermore, a two-hour time difference must be taken into account. The manager of the Djakarta branch had placed the call about midnight, immediately after he had heard the tip. Judging by the absence of fluctuation in price so far along in the day, Kinki was the only trading company in Japan to have heard this report.

"Good work! I'll get an order out for a bulk purchase right away." Daimon picked up another receiver with his left hand even before he had laid down the one in his right, and asked for the head of the Cotton Yarn Department.

"No one else should know about this," he warned, having quickly summarized the message from Djakarta. "The price this morning was 199 yen. It's sure to go up to 250. It's another Indonesian deal, so we'll capitalize on the secrecy and go for the short-term gain."

Daimon directed his business with the speed and precision of a machine. The domestic market price for cotton yarn had hit rock bottom in 1958 as a result of overproduction. Producers were utterly dependent on export as the only avenue to revival; Indonesia's bid for one hundred thousand bales would be considered a godsend. As Daimon turned again to Iki, they heard a light rap on the door and a short, wizened man in a black suit stepped into the office.

"They told me you had someone with you," he said, giving Iki a sidelong glance. "I was at Otomo Bank, so I thought I'd drop in." He spoke softly, in a familiar manner.

"You know you can walk in here anytime, Mr. Kitoh. Have a seat." Daimon got up from his place opposite Iki and moved to his swivel chair behind the desk.

"Stay," Daimon said as Iki stood up to leave. "It's quite all right. Mr. Kitoh of Chukyo Textiles is an old friend."

Kitoh was owner and president of a firm that handled half of all the cotton yarn produced in Japan. He was known to be an uncanny and successful speculator.

"How is it today?" he asked, perching on the edge of a chair.

"Not all that good," Daimon shrugged.

"All I'm doing these days is stocking up on a commodity with a negative margin. Quite a bit of it. So my sword stays out of its scabbard. How about you?"

"I'm ready to start buying," Daimon replied.

Although mystified by their conversation, Iki could not miss the glint of interest in Kitoh's eyes in response to Daimon's remark.

"You've got information! What is it?"

"Indonesia is good for a hundred thousand bales."

"You're letting me in on good news. I've got fifty thousand. Do you want any of it today?"

"How about ten thousand?"

"Fine." He stood up. "I'll be running along."

It had been a brisk exchange. As Daimon did, Kitoh too concentrated exclusively on the business at hand. He turned and left as quietly as he had entered.

"That was a timely interruption," Daimon said. "I've just made a transaction worth eight billion." His manner was light and casual, as if he'd just concluded one of many routine transactions for the day.

Iki had understood none of the conversation—it was expressed in coded language. The two, after exchanging a few cryptic remarks, had concluded a transaction valued at eight billion yen, a sum equivalent to one-fifth of the total capitalization of Kinki Trading Company. Although Iki found the process baffling, he marveled at the shrewdness and daring of the men who managed it.

"You seem puzzled, Mr. Iki," Daimon chuckled. "I don't suppose you understood much of what we said, so I'll explain it. It's all useful information to someone who knows. Do you remember hearing Kitoh say 'How is it today?' when he came in? He wasn't inquiring about my health. He was asking about this morning's market. Then he talked about stocking up on a commodity with a negative margin—meaning he's been buying steadily at low prices even though he'll resell at a net loss. His sword stays out of its scabbard because he needs it to fight off the wolves. In other words, he's complaining about the squeeze he's caught in. Frankly, I wasn't sure that I should let him in on what I know about Indonesia. But I decided I'd better do so because what I need right now is a sure source of supply. Kitoh was grateful, of course. For the moment. He now has fifty thousand bales of cotton yarn in his warehouse, and has agreed to sell me ten thousand at a low price. I'd never give away a business secret the way I just did, except to Kitoh. We have few secrets between us. Can't afford 'em."

The deal he'd just witnessed and Daimon's explanation made Iki realize even more the wholly alien nature of the world of business and his utter inability to cope with it. He had been unable even to follow the logic behind Daimon's explanation of a simple transaction that would be easily understood by someone familiar with the language of business.

"I said earlier that I would accept employment. But now I'd like to decline after all. I've only known the military world. And just now you've made me realize that I'm not at all suited for a job in business."

Daimon laughed loudly. "We've alarmed you, Mr. Iki. But that's only natural. When Kitoh and I talk business, we're enough to frighten people already established in the trade. Look at the castle, Mr. Iki." He pointed to Osaka citadel, its majestic white walls and intricately tiled roof shining in the winter's sun. Daimon's eyes glistened as he looked out on this monument to might. But Iki saw only its resemblance to the fallen citadel of the Kwantung Army at Shinkyo.

"When I come into my office in the morning, the first thing I do is take a good look at that castle. If you want to take a castle, you have to win the battle first, you know. I look at that castle every day, to remind myself of the importance of winning. That's all that matters to me. When you were an army staff officer, I'm sure winning the war was on your mind every day of the year. My business is commercial tactics, yours was military tactics. What's the difference?"

"In commerce," Iki answered, "tactics are employed for the sake of profit. The purpose of commerce is remote from that of military tactics. I repeat, I've known only the military. I'm afraid I'm very remote from the world of business."

Daimon leaned forward. "Don't think of commerce as something having to do wholly with profit-making. Economic strategy and the tactics of trading companies go hand-in-hand with the effort to revive Japan's economy. Instead of soldiers you have commodities, but the tactics are exactly the same. You either advance or retreat in a military operation. You have no other alternative. You either buy or sell in a commercial operation, and again you have no alternatives. Quick and accurate judgment, immediate implementation, concentration on winning, absolute dedication to victory—that's what commerce is all about. Is that so different from the military? If you can't understand that, Mr. Iki—and I know that once you had a brilliant mind—then this must mean you've been undone by those eleven years in Siberian camps."

Daimon sounded as if he were scolding Iki. His voice had the authority of a general commanding a thousand divisions. Iki felt a rising of interest, almost of excitement, as if the emptiness within him were filling with energy under the steady flow of an incoming charge. He had not felt such energy in many years. Nevertheless, his memory of the short meeting between Daimon and Kitoh remained too vivid, too jarring, inducing considerable uneasiness. He wavered between the two extremes—of yielding to Daimon's persuasiveness, and of resisting it.

"Time you made up your mind, Mr. Iki. If you're thinking you should help to make amends for the lost war, then put your training and experience in tactical warfare to good use. Apply it to the planning of commercial strategy that's so badly needed to develop our country's economy. In any event, I'll be expecting you at work. Here. Tomorrow."

Daimon did not pretend to wait for Iki's reply. With a calculated show of busyness he hurried out of the office, on the way to his next appointment.

Iki left the train at Suminoe Station and went straight to nearby shops to buy things for supper. At a vegetable store in the middle of the block he bought the items his wife had listed: two slices of fried beancurd, a slab of *konnyaku*, one large white radish, a bunch of green onions—frugal fare, to be paid for from his wife's earnings. Carrying those purchases wrapped in a sheet of newspaper, he walked home along the embankment of the Yamato River. Flowing placidly, it sparkled in the rays of the afternoon sun.

Although Iki had accepted a job at Kinki Trading Company, he wished that he might linger in his present state of relative free-

40

dom, passing the time much as the Yamato River flowed, unhurried and without concern about its destination. His daily routine included cleaning the house after the other members of the family left in the morning, and spending his afternoons in the city helping former subordinates find employment. Whenever no special reason required that he go into the city, he had time to read magazines and books before the afternoon stroll to the markets near the station to shop for supper. It was not an entirely unenviable life.

He took the house key from the mailbox and pushed open the stubborn sliding door. His home, no different from hundreds of others, consisted of a four-mat room, a six-mat room, and a tiny kitchen. From the entrance, which opened on the small four-mat room, he could see the two apple crates converted into study-desks for his children and, on the wall between the two desks, a large formal photograph of himself in the uniform of a lieutenant colonel, hands resting on the hilt of his sword, the staff officer's cordon hanging from his shoulder. Undoubtedly that photograph had sustained the children's hope for his eventual return during the eleven years of his absence. But the father who came back to them bore little resemblance to the man preserved in their cherished photograph. The father returning wore the shabby clothes of a repatriate. With sunken cheeks and unsightly gaps left by lost teeth, he had aged far beyond his years. "That's not my father," Makoto said, backing away when Iki tried to embrace him. The boy could not accept him even after Iki settled in with the family. Now a middle-school student, he occasionally allowed his father to be affectionate, with a pat on the shoulder or an indulgent smile. But Naoko accepted her father with unquestioning love, openly rejoicing in his return from the very first day.

Iki changed into a pair of old trousers and a woolen sweater, then took the small charcoal stove outside the kitchen door to start the fire. He touched a match to a crumpled newspaper, placed a few pieces of charcoal upon it, and began fanning the flames. The charcoal smoldered and gave off smoke, but refused to start burning. He persisted, for it must be glowing by the time Yoshiko came home.

Just as the first blue flames began to spread over the charcoal, he heard Naoko and Makoto slide the door open. "We're home, Dad!"

"You came home together for a change." Iki's greeting was low,

41

tender. "You must be freezing. Come here. I've just started the fire."

He brought the stove inside, and the two children huddled around it, warming their hands. Soon Naoko went to the kitchen to wash the vegetables; she must have everything in order for her mother to begin cooking. Affectionately, Iki watched her, quiet and intent, moving from shelf to table to sink and back again.

At six o'clock Yoshiko joined her family. As she paused just within the doorway, her soft smile and bright patch of knitted scarf, almost hidden by a drab woolen jacket, gave each of them a feeling of warmth and cheer.

"Hello, Mother." The children, too, smiled happily as they took her purse and shopping bag. While Yoshiko tied an apron about her waist, she spoke to Iki. "Dear, how did things turn out today?"

"The president of the company decided to hire me on the spot."

She did not recognize the light-hearted jest. "I'm so relieved. . . . Everyone says that Kinki Trading is the oldest trading company in Central Japan. Certainly the best known."

"That's probably true. Mr. Daimon seems to be a man of fine character and certainly a farsighted businessman."

"You won't change your mind then, will you?"

"Well . . . I just can't help feeling that a trading company hardly needs my special talents. It's a world of business, you know, where everyone's concerned with money and profit . . . But we can talk about this later," he suggested, when he saw the flicker of apprehension in the faces of both wife and daughter. "Let's eat."

After dinner Iki and Naoko went to the public bath, leaving Makoto at home, waiting for a friend to pick him up for the same purpose. The bath was a ten-minute walk away. During the better stages of his detention in Siberia, Iki had been able to bathe only once in every ten days, when he would be given a ration of two buckets of hot water. Now he reveled in an abundance of hot water and delighted in the pleasure of relaxing in the neighborhood bath for almost as long as he liked. As usual, he and Naoko agreed to meet in thirty minutes at the entrance, which separated the men's side from the women's. Iki went into the men's side and undressed. Although he was five feet nine inches tall, he weighed only 110 pounds. Gaunt he might be, but he still stood straight as a warrior. He stretched out his emaciated body in the tub and lay

42

still, resting his head against the tiled rim. As soon as he closed his eyes he was overcome with drowsiness. He realized how he'd been drained of energy by a mere two hours spent that morning in the office of Daimon Ichizo. And at once the drowsiness ended, chased away by vague fears about undertaking a career in the unfamiliar world of commerce.

At the proper time, he dressed and hurried toward the entrance, lest he keep Naoko waiting. She was not there, of course. He shook his head as he thought of how women, even girls, seemed to require twice the time a man felt was necessary, and crossed the street to buy a bag of hot rolls at a peddler's stall. As he was tucking the parcel under his sweater, to keep the rolls warm for Yoshiko and Makoto, Naoko ran toward him, with water still dripping from her short hair.

"I'm sorry, Dad. I took a little longer because I was washing my hair."

Iki brought out his damp towel. "You mustn't catch cold," he said, trying to dry her head with light touches of the towel. Her hair was like her mother's, coal black and silky.

"We'd better hurry home so that mother can come for her bath before the place closes."

As they walked along the darkened road, Naoko stopped abruptly, facing him. "Dad, I want to ask a favor of you."

"What is it? Can't it wait until we get home?"

"When you were talking about Kinki Trading, you sounded as if you were still trying to make up your mind. Please take the job! I don't want you to go to work for a place like the Defense Agency."

Iki had been asked many times to join the Defense Agency. The year before, a major had come to Osaka from headquarters in Tokyo with the express purpose of persuading him to join the Agency.

"Why not?"

"Mother was miserable all those years while you were away. Because you were a soldier. Oh, I'll be happy, too, when you start working. But, please! Don't ever become a soldier again." Naoko, a high-school student, was not repeating the idea of pacifists. Iki knew that her concern for her mother—and for him—was genuine.

"I understand how you feel. I'll take a regular job, one that will keep me here, at home. So don't worry."

Never, since he first aspired to be a soldier, had Iki made a decision that was not dictated by military concerns. But since he returned from Siberia, other considerations—a father's, a husband's—were determining his actions and his choices.

Lying in bed beside Yoshiko that night, he found words to express the gratitude he felt, acknowledging the hardships and miseries she had endured for eleven years. "At last you can stop working," he finished, gently.

"Have you really decided to accept the position at Kinki Trading? I have the feeling you're forcing yourself to take this job."

"The truth is, I wasn't sure about it at first. But I've thought it over a great deal. And now I've decided to accept the job."

"I'm so glad! I knew that the Defense Agency could offer you a better salary. And I was more or less resigned to moving to Tokyo. But now I can stop worrying about such a big change."

"We'd be able to live much better if I went to work for the Defense Agency."

"That doesn't matter to me. I'd much rather see the four of us living together with no worries. Those eleven years were horrible —always hoping you were alive, and always wondering if you were dead . . ."

In the two years since Iki's return, Yoshiko had never before spoken about her trials while he was gone. Now, in only a few words, she had dared to release her secret thoughts. She was soon asleep. But sleep did not come easily to Iki. During those two years his worst memories of Siberia had gradually faded, the wounds to his spirit had begun to heal over. But today the wounds had been torn open by Daimon's inquisitiveness. While he lay awake, listening to Yoshiko's even breathing, inevitably his thoughts drifted back to those years in the icy hells of Siberia.

4

SIBERIA

The Siberian autumn lasted but a short while. Already in the first week of October the air was chilly.

The twenty-six officers of the command staff of Kwantung Army Headquarters were held prisoner at a place not far from the Amur River, on the outskirts of Khabarovsk. The leaves on the white birch trees had been a vibrant green when the Japanese arrived. As fall came on, a yellow tint appeared in the upper branches of the trees, and reached quickly downward, until the countryside became a shimmering expanse of golden foliage. Then, almost overnight, the leaves fell, stripping the trees and exposing the naked land to the ravagings of winter.

The prison camp had been a training center for the Soviet River Fleet. Facilities were spare, but at least they provided a number of smaller rooms in which groups of officers could find some degree of privacy. A rectangular area slightly larger than two hundred yards wide by a thousand long formed the enclosure that contained the Japanese prisoners of war. Soviet guards patrolled the perimeter. Within the compound the officers were permitted to govern themselves.

They were kept busy for a while, as they settled into their quarters, sorting out belongings and cleaning the rooms. After that they lived in idleness. A month went by with no word from the Soviet authorities.

One day the prison camp commandant requested the officers' help in harvesting potatoes. The harvest in a nearby *kolkhoz*, or collective farm, had fallen behind schedule because of a shortage of workers. Although international law forbade the use of prisoners of war for labor, the Japanese decided to cooperate for a few hours daily, considering the work a form of exercise.

The commandant led them on a forty-minute walk to a large *kolkhoz*. One tract, enclosed by a wire fence, was neatly cultivated; obviously it was a private field owned by the family occupying the house at the center of the tract. But the other farms, all parts of the collective, were full of weeds. Iki, critical as ever, thought that the mere sight of those fields explained why the *kolkhoz* had difficulty raising its level of production. The *kolkhoz* officials happily welcomed the Japanese, promising them four percent of the harvest as compensation; and, with much laughter, they demonstrated to the inexperienced military officers how real farmers bring in a crop of potatoes.

The Japanese generals having been exempted, two dozen officers, in teams of three, worked the field. Following instructions, one man in a team dug up the plants, the second man separated the potatoes from the roots, and the third carried them in a basket to the collecting point, where in exchange he received a ticket from an official. Only a few tools were provided—some old shovels and dull sickles. The younger officers used sticks to loosen the hard reddish-black soil. They covered their faces and necks with towels to protect themselves from the many wasps hovering above the field, and soon were perspiring even though the day was chilly. Despite the monotony of working furrows half a mile long, they talked very little. As Iki labored with his companions, he had time to think about his native village so far away.

Mt. Chokai rose near the village of Sugizawa in Yamagata Prefecture. By now its summit would be covered with a mantle of fresh snow. Iki had been sickly as a child. His father, principal of the local primary school, had looked favorably on Tadashi's fondness for books, hoping that the boy would follow in his own footsteps and become a teacher. But Tadashi's grandfather, gruff and stubborn, had insisted on the importance of physical conditioning and forced his grandson to massage his body week in and week out with a towel soaked in cold water. Perhaps thanks to that regimen, by the time he was a fourth-grader he was as hardy as any child in the farming village. He no longer came straight home from school to read books, but roamed the nearby fields and hills until dusk. In winter, when five to six feet of snow lay on the ground, he went into the hills to chase wild rabbits. That was enough to worry even his doughty grandfather.

When Iki was in the sixth grade, the prefectural regiment held

46

maneuvers in the foothills of Mt. Chokai. He was fascinated by the spectacle of the infantry, cavalry, and artillery simulating warfare in the autumn fields, and by the stirring sight of the standard-bearer holding high the regimental flag—a crimson disc in a rectangular field of white, with sixteen crimson stripes radiating outward to the tasseled border. Subsequently he applied for admission to the Junior Military Academy in Tokyo, and was accepted in the spring of his fourteenth year.

The three-year curriculum at the Junior Academy emphasized foreign languages and correct ideological thought more than military drill. From among French, German, Russian, and Chinese, Iki chose to study German. In addition, he was placed with an instructor from the Ueno Music School and given lessons on the piano, an instrument unknown to the people in his provincial village.

Only after he matriculated at the Army Academy was he fully involved in military training. After his second year, he was assigned to six months' training in an active regiment, serving three months as a senior private and three as a sergeant. There he learned the soldier's daily routine, which included the care of his rifle, cooking simple meals, and laundering his uniform. The upper division curriculum at the Academy was heavily weighted toward pure military science. After graduation he became an apprentice officer; although his insignia were those of a master sergeant, he wore an officer's sword, identifying him as a member of the elite corps of the Japanese Army.

Iki's first assignment as a newly commissioned second lieutenant sent him to the regiment of his native Yamagata Prefecture. In 1937, when he was twenty-five years old and a first lieutenant, his regimental commander nominated him as a candidate for the Army War College. He took the entrance examination and, among a thousand applicants, was one of the fifty to qualify for admission. Courses at the War College dealt exclusively with staff-level operations. Students applied themselves to the history of warfare, but the curriculum emphasized tactics and strategy for divisions and larger units. They used no textbooks. A class of fifty students was divided into four platoons of varying composition, each competing against the others in devising solutions to tactical problems assigned to them daily. They analyzed and discussed their assignments together, thinking up solutions to problems, until midnight, often later. Thus they accustomed themselves to the exhausting rigors of staff-level planning, during which every young officer maintained absolute calm and self-control as he solved complex tactical problems, none of which could be regarded as unsolvable.

When he graduated from the Army War College at the head of his class, Iki was awarded a sword by the Emperor himself, and delivered the valedictory speech in the imperial presence. Those were precious memories . . .

"What's wrong, Iki? You're just standing there in a daze. If you keep on daydreaming we won't finish our furrow."

Colonel Tanikawa, chief of Information, a man from his own prefecture, called him back to reality. Tanikawa, who had served for many years in the Department of Military Training, was an officer who always looked after his men. Iki could speak freely with him.

"Colonel Tanikawa, should we be harvesting potatoes like this? —When I think of the plight of our civilians in Manchuria, and of our 700,000 enlisted men, who are probably living in far worse conditions than ours, I can't help wondering if this is right—for a few of us to be getting by with such light work."

"We can do nothing about this, you know. We can try complaining to Stalin, but that won't make any difference." Tanikawa paused, as if to assure Iki that he understood his distress. "Think about other things—your responsibility, for instance. Your orders were to return to Imperial General Headquarters after delivering His Majesty's pronouncement. You still have the responsibility of reporting to Japan. Imperial Headquarters no longer exists, so you'll be reporting to the people of Japan. Your duty is to make a full statement about the condition of our men of the Kwantung Army. Those men are without weapons, and they're at the mercy of the Russians. What will happen to them? You'll have to find out in order to tell their story."

Only a month earlier, this group of officers had been flown from Shinkyo to the Khabarovsk Airport, where they were put in jeeps and exhibited along the main thoroughfare of the city. Iki had been almost maddened by that experience of complete degradation.

"I'm at fault for letting myself get emotional," he said, "but the disgrace of having to endure this . . ."

"You're young, and a bit too sensitive in some ways. You're

48

dejected and humiliated, I can see. But think of Japan's humiliation. Survival is no longer a matter of individual wish. You have to think of yourself as a citizen of Japan and realize that your first duty is to survive these troubles. Remember, you were a staff officer of both the Kwantung Army and Imperial General Headquarters. If you feel any responsibility at all for having led our army, and our country, into these degrading circumstances, then fulfill the obligation that's still yours. Observe—and remember the fate of the Kwantung Army. Live—and become a witness to history."

"And now," Tanikawa ended his lecture lightly, "please get some water for us. All this work has made me thirsty."

Because the well water was not safe to drink, the *kolkhoz* officials gave the Japanese officers a basket of tomatoes instead. Not having eaten fresh fruits or vegetables since they arrived in Siberia, they relished the tomatoes, even though those were not fully ripened. By the time they finished their work, the bright red sun was close to the horizon of the broad plain. Dusk would come quickly.

The party began the long walk back toward camp, carrying their bundles of potatoes. Iki kept his eyes on Colonel Tanikawa, ahead of him, looking every inch the wizened village elder sauntering along contentedly, his day's work done. He thought of what Tanikawa had told him: however great the humiliation, he must continue to live. He drew a deep breath. Tanikawa had freed him from the dark emotions—frustration and loss of self-respect over his failure to meet death—which had oppressed him since the day of Japan's defeat.

Mornings and evenings became much colder. To keep the cold air from creeping into their rooms, the Japanese sealed the edges of window frames with strips of old newspapers, using a paste they made by boiling scraps of bread and grains of rice. All the windows had double panes. As Iki was sealing a window in the north wall, he noticed a dead fly that had been trapped when the outer pane was installed in late summer. He looked down at the black husk, as if it were an ill omen. Where would he be in the spring when the time came to remove these strips of paper? Would he even be alive? Or would he, too, be a shrivelled thing, as dead and as black as this ill-fated fly? As he lifted his eyes, he saw a jeep being driven into camp. He watched as it slowed to a stop. The man who stepped down from the jeep was their Deputy Chief-of-Staff, whom they had not seen since the Russians took him away as a hostage.

Iki ran out to greet Major General Takemura. "Sir, I'm happy to see you well!"

The other officers rushed toward him. "Takemura!" Chief-of-Staff Hata's eyes were misty as he welcomed him. "How are you? You must have had a difficult time . . ."

Takemura appeared haggard, but wore his usual gentle smile as he described life as a hostage in Zharkova. He had been kept at Far East Command Headquarters, but was not subjected to interrogation. Two weeks later he was transferred to a prison camp at Voroshilov, where he met General Kita, Commander of the First Area Army, Lieutenant General Shimizu, Fifth Army Commander, and other Japanese officers from the eastern sector.

"I'm glad for your news," General Yamada said. "I hadn't heard anything at all about them since coming to Siberia. I was worried. They were all well, were they?"

"They were quite well, but I feel sorry for them now that the weather's become so cold. General Ushirogu of the Feng-t'ien group and others were told they would be taken to Shinkyo for a conference to negotiate a cease-fire. So they boarded the train without taking any of their belongings with them. As it turned out, they were tricked into boarding a train for Siberia."

Takemura himself was still wearing his summer uniform. "Our fellow officers at Voroshilov asked me to convey this message to you," he continued. "They want you, General Hata, to ask the Soviet Army to expedite the repatriation of the men of the Kwantung Army and to have them repatriated to Japan by way of Manchuria."

"Asking will be useless," Hata replied. "Immediately following the end of hostilities, the Soviet Army declared all members of the Kwantung Army prisoners of war. That was in violation of accepted international practice. I don't think they have any intention of releasing us. Besides, they don't have the transportation to carry out an early and simultaneous repatriation."

Hata had made this assessment on the basis of his knowledge of the Soviets—he knew them better than did anyone else in the Kwantung Army. But the younger staff officers objected.

"Don't you think your assessment is too pessimistic?" one of them asked, turning red with anger. "Shouldn't you give some serious thought to the wishes of the officers at Voroshilov and present the Russians with a strongly worded demand?"

Iki stopped him. "I believe the Chief-of-Staff is right. The other day we were asked to fill out a questionnaire which is supposed to provide them with personal information. One of the items in that questionnaire concerned Japan's tactical and strategic planning in the war with the United States. We should know by now that the Soviet Union fought Germany first, then Japan much later, and that now their potential enemy is the United States. They've already indicated that they want to keep the 700,000 of us hostages, to be used as pawns in the Soviet-U.S. negotiations over policies for the occupation of Japan. I strongly doubt that we can have any hope of early repatriation."

Some of the officers agreed with Iki and argued with those others who insisted on pressing the Russians for repatriation. The situation was discussed daily, and with increasing vehemence. But the hopes of those who believed in the value of making demands faded as the days grew shorter, and the cold more intense.

At last deep snow covered the ground. Since the buildings they occupied had been built to serve as a summer training site for the Soviet River Fleet, no means of heating their quarters were available. Caulking the windows had added little to their comfort; in freezing temperatures they bundled themselves in their overcoats twenty-four hours a day. General Hata repeatedly asked for heating equipment, but always the reply was the same: "Soon." At night temperatures fell to twenty degrees below zero Centigrade or more. Death by freezing would come in a matter of weeks.

One night, as Iki was drifting off to sleep after lying awake for hours in the cold, the glare of a flashlight in the pitch-dark room awakened him. Behind it he made out a Russian officer, accompanied by three soldiers.

"Where's Iki?" the officer demanded. When Iki sat up, the officer barked, "Come with me! The rest of you, don't move!"

"What do you want, at this hour of the night?" Iki asked.

"I only have orders to take you along," the Russian officer said. "Get your belongings and come with me."

Colonel Tanikawa quietly slipped some winter underwear and a pair of heavy socks into Iki's bag of clothing. When he spoke a few

51

words to Iki the Russian officer growled, "No talking." Tanikawa extended his hand, and Iki gripped it tightly in silent farewell.

Surrounded by four hulking Russians, Iki went out into the bitter Siberian night. A flash of fear shot through him when he saw the dark outline of a sedan parked within the camp gate.

"Get in!" The officer opened the rear door and pushed him toward it. Iki had never seen such a car before—jet black, and windowless, a thing to be dreaded at sight.

"Where are you taking me at this hour?" he asked.

"How should I know?" the officer said. "Just get in!" Two guards thrust the muzzles of their automatic rifles into Iki's back, forcing him into the sedan. A tiny bulb shed a dim light over the interior. The seats were wooden benches. The guards got in with him and slammed the door shut.

At first Iki could guess the direction in which he was being taken, but after a few minutes the car took a turn that confused him. He wondered what fate awaited him. Exile in the interior? A firing squad? Why had they come for him in the middle of the night? The chilling thought of General Nohara, Chief of Intelligence, entered his mind; Nohara had vanished two weeks before, and had not been heard of since.

The car stopped, and guards ordered Iki to get out. As he stepped down, he guessed that he must be in Khabarovsk, judging by the old buildings from the Czarist era. But no signs identified the building they entered.

They took him into a room beside the main entrance. Large portrait photographs of Stalin and Beria hung on a wall. Stalin was presented in a marshal's uniform, complete with a row of medals, looking down commandingly and contemptuously at the viewer below. Beria wore a high-collared jacket; his round face, thin lips, and beady eyes conveyed more than a hint of cruelty. Iki knew that he must be in the Khabarovsk headquarters of the Ministry of Home Affairs, better known at the N.K.V.D.—the Soviet secret police.

"This way," a guard beckoned, and Iki followed him into the hallway, where he saw many men busy at work despite the late hour. The guard led him to one of the many interrogation rooms that lined the hallway.

The rectangular room had a window with an iron grill; the

walls were covered with layers of a thick fabric, to deaden sound. As Iki stood, studying the strange room, the door behind him swung open and two men entered. One, a husky army officer about forty years old, promptly sat down at a desk. The other, wearing a civilian suit, practically dissected Iki with sharp, cold eyes before sitting next to the officer.

"I'm the Japanese-language interpreter," the civilian said. "You may sit there." He pointed to a wooden chair before the desk. Iki sat down, holding his sword close to his side. The Russian officer drew himself erect, as if to look down on Iki, keeping a watchful eye on his every move.

"I'm Major Yazef," he said, "investigator of the Khabarovsk area headquarters, Department of Internal Affairs. I'm sorry to call you out so late at night, but I must interrogate you as soon as possible concerning crimes committed by the Japanese Army during the war. Japan has surrendered unconditionally, so she should have no secrets to keep. I expect you to be frank in confessing crimes that have been committed against the Soviet Army. If you conceal the truth, you will be punished in accordance with the law. You understand this, of course."

The interpreter's Japanese was faulty, but the threatening tone was clearly conveyed. Now Iki understood why he had been brought there.

"First, I want your personal history," Yazef said.

Iki repeated what he had written down on the questionnaire filled out several days earlier for the team of investigators from Moscow: the date and place of his birth; his education and training at the Junior Military Academy, the Army Academy, and the Army War College; his assignment as a staff officer at Imperial General Headquarters, Kwantung Army Headquarters, and again at Imperial General Headquarters.

"Your dossier shows that you became a lieutenant colonel at the age of thirty-three. That's quite a high rank for so young a Japanese officer. You must come from a family high in the aristocracy. Or are you related to the emperor?"

"My father was just a country school teacher. And we're not members of the aristocracy," Iki replied.

"That cannot be," the Russian retorted. "I have here the personal histories of all staff officers of the Kwantung Army Headquarters. Not one of them reached your rank at such a young age. You're lying about your family background."

"But I have nothing to lie about. I happen to be the son of a country school teacher."

"Let's move on to the next question. Give me a detailed description of the organization of the Imperial General Headquarters."

"Imperial General Headquarters is a large war-time organization. It's divided into Army and Navy components, each having departments labeled General Affairs, First, Second, and Third. The First Department is concerned primarily with tactics and strategy, the Second with intelligence, and the Third with transportation. In addition, signal and communication sections were formed."

"You were in the First Department, engaged in the planning of war operations. What is the chain of command in operations planning?"

"In all instances, Army plans are directed by the Army chief-of-staff, and those of the Navy by the Navy chief-of-staff."

Yazef pounded his fist on the table. "You know that the emperor is the supreme commander of the Imperial General Headquarters!"

"The Imperial General Headquarters is placed under His Majesty, as the Grand Marshal," Iki explained, trying to stay calm. "In the case of the Army, plans formulated by the First Department are presented by the chief-of-staff to His Majesty to obtain his approval as a matter of formality, but all operations planning is completely under the direction of the chief-of-staff. It would be a mistake to think of the Emperor as the supreme commander. His role is nothing at all like that of Marshal Stalin in your country."

Iki's explanation, stated in Russian by the interpreter, apparently was not understood by Yazef, who pounded the table again, reddening with anger.

The interpreter, alarmed, leaned forward and spoke soothingly. "The Major isn't questioning you about your responsibility. Why not just agree with whatever he says? If you keep on contradicting him, that won't be good for you."

Iki, nevertheless, began again to explain.

"Enough!" Yazef raged. "Obviously you're evading my questions. If truths aren't forthcoming, I can take certain measures. Keep that in mind. Now tell me how the war between Japan and the United States started, and describe the war plans at the outset of hostilities. Write it down. I want the details."

Iki filled out two sheets of coarse paper, taking care to avoid mentioning specific dates, names, or numbers. The civilian translated what Iki had written and handed the translation to Yazef, who took the sheets eagerly. Iki contemplated a ceiling corner while Yazef read.

"This is an insult!" Yazef shouted when he had finished. "You've written what any child would know, and the rest is lies. This is an affront to the Ministry of Internal Affairs!"

"I had no such intention," Iki replied. "I wrote what I knew." And he fell silent, ignoring Yazef's noisy threats.

Yazef suddenly changed direction. "What about the planning of anti-Soviet operations? You participated in the planning, didn't you?"

"I did not. Before I was transferred to the Kwantung Army, I was on the planning staff for our operations in the south."

"You knew about the anti-Soviet planning at Imperial General Headquarters, of course."

"Yes, I did. But they were operational plans to be put into effect in the event of an outbreak of war between Japan and the Soviet Union. They were never activated."

"That's a lie! What kind of orders did Imperial General Headquarters issue to the Kwantung Army during the Russo-German war? Tell me!"

Until then Iki had not worried about being interrogated by Major Yazef, a mere local investigator. But with this shift Yazef's questions were becoming incisive. And his suspicions were well-founded. He insisted that as soon as Germany began to invade Russia, the Kwantung Army was supposed to concentrate its strength on the Soviet-Manchurian border, in order to tie up part of the Soviet Army.

But Iki would not admit that such an order had been issued by Imperial General Headquarters. "You have no evidence whatever for such an operational plan by Imperial General Headquarters."

"You're saying, then, that the Kwantung Army alone decided to concentrate its troops on the border to threaten our eastern front."

Trapped by Yazef's reasoning, Iki could not reply immediately. He felt the sweat of fear trickling down his sides.

"That's not so. As you've said, during a certain period our troop strength in Manchuria did increase. That happened when Japanese units were passing through Manchuria on their way to fight the British."

"Everything you say is lies! Japan and Germany were partners in a plan to conquer the world. That's a known fact. You were on the Kwantung Army staff for more than a year, and you come up with this nonsense! In your heart you're still an enemy—you haven't surrendered at all. Think that over thoroughly tonight. You'll have a good chance to do so."

As Yazef stalked out of the room, two guards entered, grabbed Iki by his arms, hauled him to his feet, and savagely pushed him toward the door.

The black windowless sedan stopped beside a high brick wall. In the dimness Iki saw that the wall joined with a barbed-wire fence, which formed an enclosure. As he passed through the gate of the prison, he felt as if he were entering a deep forbidding cavern.

They led him to a room at the far end of an immense building, where a first lieutenant seemed to be expecting him.

"I'm the warden," he said, matter of factly. "I have orders to confine you here in Khabarovsk Prison."

"Prisoners of war can't be confined in prison," Iki said heatedly. "That's illegal. It violates conditions of the cease-fire agreement exchanged with the Soviet Far East Command."

"What the Red Army does is no business of mine. We're under direct orders from the local headquarters of the Ministry of Internal Affairs. If you have complaints, tell them to the investigator in the morning."

In the same indifferent manner the warden ordered a guard to examine Iki physically. He showed none of the soldierly attitudes that Iki had observed in many of the front-line officers of the Red Army. This Internal Affairs officer was a policeman, and a rather bored one at that.

The guard led Iki to a quarantine room and ordered him to remove his wristwatch, sword, and jacket. He checked the jacket closely, turning the pockets inside out, even ripping open the seams of the lining. When he was finished, a medical officer entered the room.

"Remove all your clothing," he said.

"Wouldn't the upper body be sufficient?" Iki protested.

"Strip," he said coldly.

The guard seized hold of Iki's belt, but Iki pushed him away and undressed. The physician touched a stethoscope against his chest in a few places. Suddenly he grasped Iki's lower jaw, forcing him to open his mouth wide, and made a close check of all parts of the oral cavity. He inspected his ears, then made him bend over on all fours, in order to probe the rectum with his finger, feeling for cyanide capsules that Iki might use to commit suicide. The examination finished, he ordered Iki to take a shower.

Iki was taken to a small room with several shower heads. The guard handed him a towel and a piece of soap half the size of a matchbox; then shaved the hair from Iki's head, armpits, and pubic region. Although the guard explained that the purpose of the shaving was to rid him of lice, Iki trembled with indignation. He realized that such emotion was entirely meaningless, isolated as he was in a regional prison in a foreign land. No one could help him. Having showered, he went to a a dressing room and found a set of disinfected clothing laid out for him. His sword and wristwatch were missing.

"Where is my sword and my watch?" he demanded.

"We're holding them for you until you leave," the guard said with a sneer. "That's a prison rule. Besides, a sword is a deadly weapon. Have you ever heard of a prison where convicts are allowed to carry weapons?"

Iki dressed hurriedly. He was taken from the basement to the ground floor, across the courtyard, then along a darkened corridor. They stopped before a small iron door. Within was a cell, less than six feet square, dimly lit. Iki could make out a steel cot, a blanket, and two wooden buckets, one for urine, the guard told him, the other for water to wash in—and to drink.

"I have to go to the latrine. Now." Iki said. The guard hesitated, then motioned him to follow. The latrine was a large barrel topped by two straddling boards. When he had finished and asked for paper, the guard look at him curiously.

"Give me paper," he said again, in basic Russian.

The guard looked puzzled, shook his head, and said, "None." Iki tore off a trousers cuff with which to clean himself. Then he was taken back to his cell. The guard shut the iron door with a clang. To Iki, the echo sounded like his soul being ripped from his body.

Faint with dread, he tried to comprehend the limits to his tiny cell, to this world in which he would be the solitary inhabitant. The thick iron door had a peephole fitted with an insert of thick glass. From his position, the round piece of glass glowed like an unblinking, watching artificial eye. Holding his breath, he listened for sounds. But the silence was absolute. He could be driven insane, he understood, if he were to stay here for long. Don't break, he told himself. He became conscious of his own breathing, something he'd rarely found time to notice before. He might survive this vicious treatment if he called upon the strength, the inner calm, that had enabled him, even under great stress, to help plan military operations for the four and a half million men of the Japanese Army.

Having so reasoned with himself, Iki gained some peace of mind. He lay down on the narrow cot next to the wall, to give rest to his body. As he was dozing off he saw a line of bedbugs crawling toward him across the wall. The sight made him instantly awake. Sleep did not come easily, as he lay tormented by the cold and the itching bites of the bedbugs. At six o'clock the next morning he was awakened and taken to the latrine to empty his urine bucket. Then he washed his face with water from the second bucket. At seven o'clock breakfast—a piece of black bread weighing about six hundred grams, nine grams of coarse raw sugar, and a bowl of hot water—was thrust in through a small opening beside the door. At noon he received two ladlesful of barley gruel and some cabbage soup. The cabbage must have been spoiled; he could not swallow the bitter stuff.

Early in the afternoon the guard swung open the iron door. "Come out!" he called. Iki, told to put on his uniform, was escorted to the warden's office.

"We're sending you off," the warden said, shoving Iki's wristwatch and personal belongings toward him across the table.

"Where's my sword? I want it back."

"I can't return your sword because you're under arrest, charged with war crimes."

"Japanese officers are allowed to wear their swords. That's specified in the agreement made with Marshal Vasilevsky. You must give it back to me!"

Iki strung together all the Russian words he could remember in making this protest. His sword was sacred; it symbolized his highest aspirations as a military man. He had received it from the Emperor himself, on the day he graduated from the Army Academy at the head of his class.

"You don't have the authority to deprive me of my sword! It's illegal!"

The warden simply ignored Iki's anger. The guards hauled him outside, where the same dark sedan awaited him. Although Iki expected to be taken back to the local headquarters of the Ministry of Internal Affairs for further interrogation, the car sped on toward a destination he could not have imagined even in the worst of dreams.

Surely the dull rumbling he heard was the sound of a train. They seemed to be on a road running parallel with some railway tracks.

As the black sedan rolled to a stop, someone opened the door. Iki looked out on the converging tracks of a railroad yard. They had indeed arrived at Khabarovsk Station. Pedestrians were crossing the litter-strewn tracks in all directions, ignoring the shouts of station guards that they must follow the walkways.

Iki was marched across the tracks toward a train parked on a far siding. He saw a long row of haggard men dressed in all sorts of clothes, from filthy uniforms to filthier rags, with shabby bundles slung over their shoulders. They were closely guarded by soldiers carrying automatic rifles. He knew then that the cars waiting on this siding were used for transporting prisoners. He felt a new surge of loathing at the way the Russians continued to disregard the cease-fire agreement, throwing war captives into prison and exiling to the Siberian interior those who would not cooperate with their interrogators. He felt concerned for General Yamada, General Hata, and the others from whom he had been separated the day before.

When he entered a steel car, he was appalled. A yard-wide corridor ran its length, between a steel side furnished with windows and a continous grating made of heavy iron bars. Behind the grating was a row of dim compartments, partitioned off by iron grills; each compartment had three tiers of bunks built into two sides. Actually these bunks were simply wooden shelves. Each compartment was occupied by six or seven men—apparently Russians, Ukrainians, Mongolians, and Koreans. A bedlam of shouts, moans, and wails rose from the prisoners, as from caged animals. Iki was taken down the corridor to a smaller compartment at the end, which he would occupy by himself. Obviously the Russians considered him a very special prisoner. A guard stood outside his compartment.

Through the iron grating he asked the guard, "Where is this train going?"

"*Ya nye znayu,*" the soldier answered, moving away to talk with other guards. Iki overheard a few words, such as "*Yaponskii soldat*" and "*vopros,*" all suggesting that he was being taken somewhere for intensive interrogation by the N.K.V.D.

Eventually the train moved slowly out of Khabarovsk Station, and soon he heard the wheels crossing a bridge. He stood up to look out the windows opposite the grating of his cage and saw the Amur River, its surface a sheet of ice.

The train crawled westward across the snow-covered plain, an unending expanse of white. For several hours Iki sat up after he could no longer stand, looking out at the grim unchanging land. Finally, overcome by the strain of the night's interrogation and by horror at the treatment he was receiving, he fell back on the bunk, his overcoat still wrapped around him, and slept.

As long as the train continued its slow westward journey, Iki spent his daylight hours staring at the wide icy plains of Siberia, forever stretching away into the distance. At night he drifted off into disturbed sleep. He wrote the date of each passing day on the inside cover of a small notebook he carried among the personal belongings he'd been allowed to keep. This exercise required but a few seconds each morning.

The number of captives in the car, as well as the din they made, increased day by day. In each compartment the number of occupants grew from six or seven to twelve or thirteen as more prisoners were loaded aboard from towns along the way. A bunk was wide enough for only one man to lie down in. When the upper and middle bunks were occupied, eight or nine men had to share the two lower bunks and the floor space between them. Prisoners started a rotation system, exchanging places at two-hour intervals, but this soon ended in chaos. The inmates, of several different races and languages, included murderers and thieves as well as political offenders. They bickered and fought continually for choice places, which all too often were seized by the biggest brutes. And the wrangling over food was loud and incessant.

Before boarding the train, each man had been given several days' supply of black bread and salted fish. Some of the prisoners had eaten up all their allowance, and so preyed mercilessly on men newly shoved aboard, a further cause for quarreling. The overburdened toilet was still another reason for raucous complaint.

Eventually the prisoners had to be taken to the toilet by turns. Alert to the possibility of escape, the latrine guard kept the toilet door open and his automatic rifle trained on the prisoner within. During the first few days, each man was given three or four turns at the latrine. But as the car became more and more crowded, the fortunate ones were escorted to the toilet once in the morning and once in the afternoon, but not at all during the night.

Sometimes the train moved on continuously during the whole day and night; at other times it stood idle for hours on sidings somewhere along the way. Seven days after it left Khabarovsk, the train and its cargo arrived at a large station. A sign told Iki that this place was called Chita. Rows of houses stood nearby, and warmly-clad people trudged through the streets. Not far from the station, factories belched smoke into the gray sky.

Iki looked out upon the strange sight of a major railroad station crowded with carloads of prisoners, each train guarded by a detachment of security troops. He had heard of "escort armies" serving within the Soviet Ministry of Internal Affairs, but the function of those military units had been a mystery. Now he knew that they had been created for the purpose of convoying prisoners. Escort armies most certainly would be needed to supervise the systematic transportation of the countless millions of prisoners who made up a large part of the nation's total labor force.

Impatient guards shouting *"Davai! Davai!"* herded more prisoners into a train on the next track. While watching the gray line of disheartened victims, Iki was surprised to see the bright colors of an expensive bridal *haori,* draped over the shoulders of a woman walking beside a Russian officer on a distant platform. The officer probably had been on occupation duty in Manchuria and brought the beautiful coat home as a souvenir. It resembled the *haori* Yoshiko had worn on their wedding day.

When he returned to the Yamagata Regiment after graduating from the War College, Iki, already a captain at the age of twenty-seven, was much sought as a bridegroom. Kept busy by his regimental duties, he tended to ignore the many photographs of eligible young women brought to him by go-betweens trying to arrange a marriage. He finally agreed to a request for a *miai*, an introduction to a prospective bride, because his regimental commander urged him to do so. Thus he met the daughter of General Hamada, commander of Japan's expeditionary force in China. Although Miss Hamada was a beautiful young woman with a cheerful disposition, Iki disliked the way she mentioned her father's rank a bit too often. To Iki, this implied that she expected him to rise to the same highest level.

Iki ultimately withdrew from discussions of an arranged marriage with General Hamada's daughter. Instead, he wrote Colonel Sakano, one of his instructors at the War College, asking for his daughter in marriage. He had visited the colonel's home frequently, together with some of his classmates. Although he had exchanged greetings with Sakano Yoshiko, he had never actually talked with her. Colonel Sakano, most surprised to receive this proposal from a former student, did not conceal his delight. His brief reply to Iki concluded, "It is her wish as well as mine."

During his next leave, Iki traveled to Tokyo to call on the Sakanos at their home in Ogikubo. The sitting room was very simply furnished, its only decoration being a flower arrangement of simple elegance—one spray of white plum blossoms, signifying the coming of spring. As Sakano Yoshiko served him tea, Iki found in her slim loveliness a quality that suggested inner strength—the serene purity of a fragile plum blossom combined with the hardiness that brought the tree to flower in the frigid air of late winter. When official permission for them to marry was issued in the name of the Minister of War, a simple ceremony was held, attended only by members of the immediate families and Iki's regimental commander, who served as the formal go-between.

Iki's father promptly declared that he wanted to build a house for his son and daughter-in-law, but Iki objected to the extravagance. Then his father wished to put an equivalent amount of money in a savings account in his daughter-in-law's name, but Yoshiko insisted that she preferred to live on her husband's salary. In truth, Iki's father was pleased by Yoshiko's declining the offer, because it showed her determination to serve her husband well, under all circumstances that fate might bring.

Iki's pay of seventy yen a month allowed them no luxuries.

Yoshiko had been brought up in an officer's home, where frugality and perseverence were regarded as traits of paramount importance in a wife. She never spoke of their limited income, just as she never protested when, all too often, their budget was strained by the need for Iki to spend evenings with his colleagues and subordinates. When she was carrying their daughter Naoko, and later their son Makoto, she never once complained about the discomforts of pregnancy. Each time she returned to her parents' home to give birth to the child, thereby relieving her husband of any cause for worry or bother.

After his assignment to Imperial General Headquarters, Iki's preoccupation with duties there left him little time to devote to his family. Yoshiko kept the children healthy, and taught them the importance of moral integrity. One day, when Naoko persisted in begging her mother to buy an expensive blue-eyed doll, Yoshiko said to her: "If you get into the habit of always having your way, you won't grow up to be the kind of lady who can marry a fine officer like your father." In Siberia Iki recalled with fondness those words and her tone of voice. He acknowledged his good fortune: his wife and children were safe at home in Japan. General Hata, General Takemura, and many other officers lived in silent torment. Their families had been sent off on the homeward journey from Shinkyo aboard a crowded refugee train after Russia had invaded Manchuria. The generals did not talk about their families, because they did not know what had happened to them.

With a lurch the train began to move steadily away from Chita, resuming the course of its westward journey.

On the morning of the ninth day, Iki noticed that the view outside his car looked somewhat brighter. The train was crawling along the edge of a huge lake, its surface frozen over, reflecting the sunlight. But the brightness did not last; by noon the sky was gloomy again. Mountains pressed against the lake shore, and from time to time the train passed through long tunnels. Judging by the topography, Iki identified the body of water as Lake Baikal.

The train traveled along the shore of the lake for an entire day and night. The next morning it veered away from the shore and soon rolled into Irkutsk Station. Irkutsk was an old city, with row upon row of aged buildings. The dome of a church rose above the snow-laden trees.

63

The moment the train stopped more prisoners were pushed into the cars. Each compartment, which held six or seven prisoners at the start of the journey in Khabarovsk, and twelve or thirteen when the train reached Chita, was crammed now with at least twenty occupants. Thus far Iki had traveled by himself, but at Irkutsk his cage was opened and three men were thrust inside.

Two of the newcomers were swarthy middle-aged Russians. The third, dressed in grimy summer clothes, was an Oriental. He had no overcoat despite the biting November cold, and he dragged his worn laceless shoes as if they were weighted with cement. His haggard face gave Iki no means of guessing his age. He noticed Iki's interest in him.

"Are you an officer of Kwantung Army?" he asked softly, in Japanese.

"Yes. And you?"

"I was with a branch of the Manchurian Electric Corporation."

"But how does someone from Manchurian Electric, a civilian . . ." Iki asked in disbelief.

"They said I'd been intercepting Soviet radio broadcasts, and accused me of being an anti-Soviet intelligence agent. They grabbed me at Feng-t'ien Station as I was boarding the refugee train with my family. They put me on a freight train for ten days, and shoved me in a prison in Chita for interrogation. None of the charges is true, of course. I denied everything. But that did not help. Then they accused me of falsifying information and threw me into a prison in Irkutsk. I'm being sent off somewhere else. I wonder where?"

He bent over, coughing violently. Iki's heart went out to the pathetic fellow, obviously sick with tuberculosis.

"But your clothes?" he began.

"All your doing," the gaunt man said sharply, as if blaming Iki personally for everything wrong in this world. "The fault of you people at Kwantung Army Headquarters. You weren't concerned at all about us resident nationals. You sent your military dependents out first—and left us civilians to shift for ourselves." He began in anger, but soon subsided into a hoarse whisper as his mind turned to other worries.

"I keep wondering if my wife and daughter got safely across the thirty-eighth parallel. If they didn't—and when I think of what might have happened to them—I don't know if I have the strength to go on living . . ." His voice trailed off, as tears gathered in those sunken eyes.

"I don't mean to offer excuses," Iki said, "but please let me explain. When the Soviet Army started to invade Manchuria, our very first concern was the evacuation of our resident civilians. Around August 13th, as I recall, we issued an emergency order for all civilians to board a train provided by the Manchurian Railway. But the civilians objected to the order, saying they couldn't possibly pack their household goods on such short notice. We couldn't let that train leave empty. That's the only reason we ordered all military dependents and Army civilian personnel and their families to assemble immediately at the railroad station, carrying only their personal effects, and sent them off."

Iki had not actually seen the evacuation, because he was still in Tokyo at the time. But he had read the report sent from Shinkyo to Imperial General Headquarters in Tokyo. Convinced by his sincerity, the sick man kept quiet for a while.

But later he challenged Iki upon another point.

"I hope you won't mind my asking a frank question," he said, although more calmly this time. "Anti-Soviet operational planning should have been uppermost among the concerns of the Kwantung Army. Why couldn't you people have predicted that the U.S.S.R. would revoke the neutrality pact and enter the war?"

The staff at Imperial General Headquarters had been well aware of that possibility, of course. But they had trusted the fact that the agreement was supposed to remain in effect for one year following its abrogation by either party. Also, they had miscalculated the speed with which the Soviet Army, having just finished its war with Germany, could shift its divisions to the Manchurian border. According to their estimates, the Russians would not be able to transport sufficient troops, ammunition, and supplies to the Soviet-Manchurian border before November. But Iki, still the staff officer, mentioned none of these facts. They were secret— and they were damning.

"And another thing—why were you people so naive as to think that Russia would abide by the cease-fire agreement?"

"You must understand that we received very little information about the situation in Europe after the German surrender. And we had no idea the Soviet Army would treat Japanese soldiers and civilians the way they have. After all, we hardly fought them—

certainly not in the way we fought against the British, Chinese, Americans, and Dutch. Admittedly, we were at war with the Soviets—but only for a week."

Iki long ago had resigned himself to the possibility of being imprisoned, even executed, at some desolate place in Siberia, just because he was a military man. But to think that a Japanese civilian would be dragged from one Siberian prison to another, merely because he had listened occasionally to Soviet radio broadcasts! Raging inwardly at the thought that a nation would capture noncombatants and throw them into prisons with criminals, Iki was unable to continue so reasoned a conversation with this wreck of a man.

Three miserable days later, an escort guard told the Japanese civilian to prepare to get off at the next stop, Taishet. He carried nothing with him, so he had no preparing to do; he just sat there, hunched over, trembling with cold and weakness. As the train entered Taishet, Iki quietly slipped his overcoat over the man's shoulders.

"You can't live without an overcoat in this cold," the man said, trying to give it back. "You'll be going farther into the interior, where the country's colder."

"I've been in the Army a long time, and I'll be all right," Iki insisted. "Whatever happens, just make sure you survive. You're a civilian, a noncombatant, and if you hold on you'll get back to Japan."

When the train stopped at Taishet, Iki said farewell to the man, with a pat on the back and an encouraging smile.

At Taishet, the prison train was switched to a branch line and resumed its journey into the interior.

A guard told Iki to leave the train at a small station about forty miles north of Taishet. More than a dozen political prisoners also were taken off the train there, turned over to soldiers of the escort army, and herded away through knee-deep snow.

The few sleighs and carriages gathered in front of the station disappeared, and with them went the people. Only Iki and his guard were left standing on the platform.

"We wait here for transportation," the soldier explained. Holding the collar of his greatcoat tight around his neck he squatted down under an eave of the station building. Iki, wearing only his winter uniform, felt the piercing cold in his very bones.

An hour went by. Worn out by two weeks of travel, he sank into a stupor. Remembering the fallen birches along the shore of Lake Baikal, a tangle of bleached and broken limbs among the rocks, he imagined himself dead, a heap of bleached bones disintegrating in the icy wastes of Siberia.

As Iki, numb and dazed, looked out over the waste land of barren snow, a horse-drawn sleigh approached the station. He was fully alert when the sleigh stopped. An officer stepped out of it and came toward him. Apparently surprised by Iki's youthful appearance, the officer asked his name to confirm his identity.

"I am Lieutenant Nikolai," he added, waving Iki toward the sleigh.

"Where are we going?" Iki asked, as gratefully he sank into the conveyance. Receiving no answer, he tried again: "Are we going far?"

"No, not very far," the lieutenant replied as he took up the reins. The sleigh moved on to a solitary road that cut straight across the land. Blizzards had shaped the plain before them into a sea of undulant white, its sparkling surface broken by occasional wedges of green, where trees thrust themselves above the snow.

Just as the sleigh reached the top of a rise, snow fell about them in thick swirls, brought by the full fury of the wind roaring down the slopes of mountains beyond. The stinging pain in Iki's ear lobes gave way to numbness; the icy wind knifed through his thin uniform. Unable to bear the agony spreading through his limbs as well, he burrowed into the loose straw that covered the bottom of the sleigh.

Fighting its way through the blizzard, the sleigh passed several villages in the foothills. At long last Iki saw the vague outline of a tall building upon a prominence ahead of them and realized that the isolated road led directly to that hill top. As they drew nearer, he saw a stretch of wooden wall and a barricade of barbed-wire fences. What had appeared to be a tall building was merely one of four guard towers rising at the corners of a compound. The towers were manned by armed guards. He recognized that this was a lager, a prison camp.

The sleigh pulled up in front of a sturdy gate made of logs, with a carved wooden hammer and sickle prominent on its crossbeam. A sentry, wearing a heavily padded overcoat that reached to the tops of his boots, opened the gate slowly, pushing hard against the force of the wind.

When the sleigh came to a stop within the gate, Iki stood up, brushed the straw from his shoulders, straightened his uniform, and stepped down as if to a parade ground. Except for Lieutenant Nikolai no one was present to see him. The compound was more than five hundred yards square. The enclosure contained twelve rows of flimsy wooden barracks. Their rooftops were covered deep with snow, and beneath the eaves the small windows were iced over completely.

"This is a lager, isn't it?" he asked Lieutenant Nikolai.

"You are right. This is Taishet Camp Eleven. You'll be taken in as soon as we examine you."

Guards led Iki into a nearby building and ordered him to undress. After a thorough search of his body, for metal objects or drugs that might be used for escape or suicide, Nikolai went through his personal belongings—underwear, toilet articles, and a two-volume paperbound Japanese edition of Tolstoi's *Resurrection*, taken hastily from the bookshelf as he was leaving the Kwantung Army Headquarters building. Nikolai passed over the books without comment, but looked up when he caught sight of the fountain pen in the inside pocket of Iki's jacket.

"I was told you were an important man in the Japanese Army. You should not keep a pen. Not good. I'll hold it for you."

After the examination, Lieutenant Nikolai continued in the usual bored manner of prison wardens who must say the same warning over and over again. "Now I shall inform you of our regulations. They are to be strictly observed. You are assigned to Barrack Number Three. You are not to go within two meters of the fence unless you have permission to go there. If you do go that close, you will be shot without warning. To go to the latrine at night you must receive the sentry's permission. You will be allowed to bathe once in every ten days. As a rule, officers are not assigned to labor, but they are expected to do such work as is required for their maintenance. You will wake up at six o'clock, and go to bed at ten. Bugle calls will tell you when. That is all."

He ordered a guard to escort Iki to Barrack Number Three. Night had fallen, and light from the barracks windows glowed feebly. As Iki neared his assigned shelter, he heard the voices of men within. He caught his breath sharply, for they were speaking Japanese.

The guard opened the double doors. Iki winced as he took his first breath of the stale air, heavy with the smell of hundreds of unwashed men. In the dim light he saw a room full of Japanese officers still wearing army uniforms. Some leaned against tiers of double bunks, others sprawled across them. He stood there, just within the door, while the nearer officers stared at him in a shock of surprise, curiosity, and uncertainty. Then an officer near the door stood up, and immediately others sprang to their feet, crowding around him.

"Did you come alone?" "What outfit are you from?" These and other questions came in quick succession from the gaunt, tired men. A bearded major quieted the others before speaking: "I'm Terada, tank batallion commander, Fifth Army, I-ho sector, now serving as leader as this barrack. What unit are you from?"

Because at Khabarovsk Prison Iki's uniform had been stripped of its cordon and insignia, he stood before them without any identification at all. So he revealed his identity in words and in bearing. "I'm Lieutenant Colonel Iki Tadashi, staff officer, Imperial General Headquarters."

They looked at him bewildered, even stunned. "From Imperial General Headquarters. . . . And you are interned in Siberia?" Terada asked in alarm. But then, remembering his good manners, he said, "Come, come in! Sit down, and tell us the news."

Iki related the circumstances that had sent him there. Then he told them about Commander-in-Chief Yamada and the other ranking generals who were interned in the prison camp at Voroshilov.

"Our commanding officer, General Shimizu, is safe!" Terada exclaimed. "The chain of command in the Fifth Army fell apart when we were disarmed at Mu-leng, and I've been worried because I heard nothing more about him. I never expected news of his safety to reach me here in Siberia!"

"Where are you gentlemen from?" Iki asked. "Now your turn has come to talk."

"Most of us are from the infantry and heavy artillery units of Mu-leng and I-ho, where the heaviest fighting took place. We didn't find out about the end of hostilities until August 19th, four

69

days after the war ended officially. Combat ceased that afternoon, and we were disarmed at once. The Russians put a thousand of us on a freight train at Tun-hua." Major Terada clenched his teeth. "We were on that train for twenty-seven hellish days—until we got here."

"Twenty-seven days!" Iki exclaimed. The others raised their voices, angry and resentful about the inhuman way in which Russians transported prisoners of any kind in Siberia.

"Our units were assembled at Tun-hua following disarmament. Then on August 23rd, we were forced to march the hundred and twenty-five miles to Kirin, in scorching heat and without a long rest. They yelled *'Davai! davai!'* all the way. They prodded us with bayonets, to keep us marching day and night through insufferable temperatures and dust. We never thought we'd survive that march. Most of the men threw their backpacks away, keeping only their food and blankets. Some of the men cut their blankets in half to lighten the load, then eventually threw away the half they had kept because even that became a burden. Most of us managed to get to Kirin. There we camped out of doors for a month, before they pushed us onto a freight train. A Soviet officer gave us a farewell speech, telling us that we were being sent home in accordance with the cease-fire agreement and that we must obey their commands and depart in orderly fashion. That was just a big lie to get us on board without incident—they were afraid of the Kwantung Army's reputation as an army of samurai. We were happy enough to board the train, believing we'd be sent through Harbin to Vladivostok and repatriated from there on Japanese ships.

"But the train crossed the Sungari River and kept heading westward, right past Chita, the last junction for Vladivostok. Until then we'd endured all the hardships because we thought we were on our way home—to Japan. When we learned the truth, we couldn't believe what was actually happening to us. With our hopes destroyed, the rest of the trip was a nightmare.

"Forty of us were packed into a fourteen-ton freight car. Naturally, there wasn't space for all of us to lie down in. So we made double bunks out of scrap wood. By then the cold was intense. We used a metal drum as a stove, and for fuel burned dead branches we picked up whenever the train stopped. We stuffed the slits and cracks in the cars with strips of cloth from our clothes, but the rain seeped through them, turning to ice. We were freezing, and we were starving. All the food we'd transferred to the train from our warehouse disappeared—probably appropriated by Soviet officers. They fed us kaoliang gruel that had been polluted. Most of us got diarrhea, and many of us lay helpless and weak, passing bloody excrement. After we left Irkutsk, we picked up an infestation of lice, which led to an outbreak of typhus. The sick were quarantined in the last train, but we saw very few of them again. We don't know how many of them died or what happened to their bodies . . ."

The officers related their experiences, and—like them, as long as they lived—Iki would never forget their tribulations. But finally Terada saw the effect that Iki's troubles had had on him. "You must be exhausted," he said. "When the bugle sounds at six in the morning, you'll have to get up with the rest of us, no matter what. You'd better go to sleep now." He cleared half the space on one side of his bunk. "Here," he pointed.

The instant Iki lay down, he fell asleep. The next thing he was aware of was the insistent bugle call.

Outside, the morning was still dark. The only light in the barrack came from wicks of cotton string inserted into old tin cans, each holding a bit of coal oil. Two hundred and fifty men stirred in the semi-darkness, rising from four rows of double bunks. Two rows extended down the center of the barrack, one row along each of its longer walls. Iki and Terada shared a lower bunk against a cold wall. Iki was dressing when the barrack door opened and a Russian officer and a pair of cooks came in with a large vat.

Major Terada, as barrack leader, called out: "Assemble with your mess tins!" The officers rushed to crowd around the steaming vat, each holding out his tin can.

"Kaoliang gruel again!" Several observant prisoners shouted out the bad news, arousing groans of disappointment from many others.

"Hey! Why so little?" cried one. "It's watery on this side! Stir it some more!" protested another.

As the gruel was being ladled out, each man studied his tin can with eyes sharpened by the greed born of hunger. The mess officer would scoop the watery stuff from this side of the vat or that, would add a little more to one tin cup or reduce the amount in another. As he tried to satisfy the complainers, the gruel rapidly lost its warmth. Iki was reluctant to hold out the empty tin that Major Terada had given him to use; but he had been hungry the night before and, after some hesitation, he offered his can to be filled. But by then the vat was almost empty, and he received only a little of the liquid that was left at the bottom. Having no spoon, he lifted the can to his lips, when Major Terada stopped him.

"Here, take mine. I'll try to find a spoon for you today."

"Actually," Terada explained later, "the officers' barracks are not too bad. Russian soldiers on kitchen duty are afraid to go into our enlisted men's barracks. Sometimes they're waylaid outside by men who threaten them to get extra portions before the serving starts. Some of our enlisted men have made crude balancing scales to weigh the portions because, they say, there's a difference in weight between the old-style mess tin and the newer ones made of Alumite. Some fellows have even made rulers, with which they measure the exact width of the slices of bread they're given."

The bearded Terada grinned as he talked about the primitive behavior of his countrymen, but Iki was shaken at hearing this new proof that men deteriorate when they are faced with starvation. Men who had faced death joyfully together as comrades in arms were adversaries now, contending over an ounce of watery gruel or a few millimeters in a slice of bread.

After breakfast, about half of the two hundred and fifty officers dressed for working outdoors, where they would gather firewood. A Russian soldier ordered the other officers to report to the medical room for routine physical inspection.

Obeying this order, Iki and Terada left the barrack. Although two hours had passed since reveille, the sun had not yet risen above the horizon. Under those forbidding skies, the lager presented a dreary sight, relieved only by a few thin stands of Siberian pine and birch trees, remnants of the extensive natural forests growing outside the compound.

Iki was surprised to see a prisoner in a tattered German army uniform. Judging by his pale, wrinkled face and emaciated body, he had been brought to this lager long before the Japanese came. He asked Terada if indeed German prisoners were there.

In this matter, too, Terada provided Iki with answers to questions. "The prisoners in this camp are mostly Japanese, but a few hundred Germans and Hungarians are here, too. We don't see much of them because our quarters are segregated. Once we were allies, so they're friendly. When we first got here, they called us 'comrades.' In fact, they taught us quite a bit about living in a lager."

"You see those small buildings beyond the pine grove?" Terada pointed. "The nearest one is the medical room. Then comes the mess hall for prisoners, and then the laundry room. I don't like the idea of your being assigned to mess-hall duty or firewood-gathering, but we have a number of over-age officers with us—the ones who were called up from the reserves just before the end of the war. They can't work. So I'd be grateful if you would join the work details. You could help fulfill our quotas."

"I'd intended to," Iki said.

When they entered the medical building, they saw dozens of naked Japanese, both officers and enlisted men, standing in line. The Russian medical officer did not bother to apply his stethoscope to a chest or even take a pulse rate. He ordered each man to turn around, pinched the buttocks thus presented, and, on that evidence, assigned him to the first, second, or third grade. Men placed in the first two grades were considered fit for hard labor, those in the third for light labor. The rare few who were classified as fourth grade suffered from advanced nutritional deficiencies. Iki found no difference between this procedure and that used in the grading of beasts of burden. Some men with protruding ribs and painful swollen bellies were assigned to grade three, fit for light labor.

"Remember the way we used to grade the horses we requisitioned, by pinching their haunches?" Terada said, trying to be cheerful. "The Russians have a policy of classifying everyone they can as grade one or grade two, and then assigning them to hard labor. I doubt if any of us here belongs in grade two. We're grade three material at best. —Well, I'd better be going to work. See you later."

Iki got in line behind an elderly Japanese officer and undressed. Eventually, the lager's medical officer, having worked his way along the line, stopped in front of him.

"Are you a newcomer?" he asked through his interpreter. "And where did you come from?" he added, stroking his full beard.

"From the general-grade officers' lager in Khabarovsk."

"Hmm . . . the generals' lager? The food must have been pretty good there," he said with a snicker. The meals at the lager at Khabarovsk, Iki recalled, usually consisted of soup, bread, and one or another kind of salted fish, but they had never been appetizing or filling. Even so, they were known to be far better than those provided at other lagers.

"That explains why you're fleshy." With a wave of his hairy hand the medical officer motioned Iki to turn around. He pinched Iki's lean buttocks, flicked them with a forefinger, testing their bounce.

"Grade one. Hard labor, starting tomorrow," he decreed.

Iki had been inspected and graded. Like an animal. Like something lower than a horse. He eased his humiliation by telling himself that this was the reality of imprisonment. A fact to be accepted . . .

At eight o'clock the next morning Iki joined his comrades at the lager gate, waiting to be sent out on a work detail. The sun had not yet risen. The men standing in the snow in column formation, five abreast, shivered as the cold penetrated layers of clothing to reach the thin flesh beneath.

"One, two, three . . ." The sentry counted off each five-man row as the column marched out the gate. Having counted to ten, he held up the rest of the column to allow the first fifty men to be assigned to the custody of security guards outside the gate. He started to count off the next ten rows, but became confused because the men were not well aligned.

"Halt!" he roared, and started counting again. In the meantime, those ahead were kept waiting in the cold, their cheeks already reddening under their caps.

Major Terada issued an order in Japanese: "Everyone move forward with linked arms. This sentry can't count." The men complied, the satisfied sentry shouted "Khorosho!" and allowed them to pass. Again they waited while the security guard made a recount of the men under his care, and at last they were ready to move off.

The daily passage of work details along the road had packed the snow down hard. Iki had trouble keeping his balance and frequently leaned on Terada to keep from slipping and falling. The two-mile walk to the logging site was a formidable distance for men weakened by internment. Enlisted men, being younger and hardier, fared better than did the officers. One elderly officer, a reactivated reservist, often lagged behind. The security guard, shouting obscenities, prodded him with the point of his rifle. When the officer staggered, the guard whistled for his dog.

"Wait!" several Japanese shouted. "Can't you see this man is weak?"

"You damned prisoners! Keep your mouths shut!" The young Russian soldier bared his teeth.

They struggled up an incline, where the road narrowed into a path that led into a virgin forest of red pine, silver birch, and Siberian cedar. The forest stretched out on all sides, silent and haunted. Occasionally a branch would bend under the weight of accumulated snow, dropping it with a soft thud upon the deep drifts already covering the ground. When the faint whispers died away, the unearthly silence returned.

Finally they arrived at the logging site. After a thirty-minute rest, they were put to work in two-man teams. Iki was paired with Major Terada. They were told to use a long cross-cut saw to fell trees that soared more than seventy feet above the ground.

"This is dangerous work," Terada warned, patting the trunk of a huge pine with a diameter of more than three feet. "You could be crippled, even killed, by a falling tree, so be careful. I'll make a notch in the trunk right here, and that'll be the direction of its fall. You just sit for a while, and watch."

"You're not used to this work," Iki said. "I was raised in the foothills of Mt. Chokai in Yamagata, and I've seen how it's done." He persuaded Terada to give him the ax. But he could not keep his feet steady as he swung, and the ax merely glanced off the trunk. Terada laughed, and Iki did so, too.

"The best lumberjacks—even those from Sakhalin—stay away from logging in Siberia," Terada said, taking back the ax. "For me, the work was killing at first, but I've been doing this for a month now and I'm getting used to it. Watch now. The notching has to be done exactly right. If it isn't, the tree can come down where you least expect it. We've had some nasty accidents."

He brushed the snow away from a point near the base of the tree, took careful aim, and swung the ax mightily. The blade bit into the bark. In slow, forceful rhythm he swung again and again, until the notch was perfectly cut. Then he lay down the ax and stopped to catch his breath.

"Let's start sawing," he said, after a few moments. They began on the side directly opposite the cut. After half an hour of steady sawing, Iki was panting. His hands were numb, his arms weak. Terada continued to push and pull, while his beard grew stiff with slivers of ice. After two hours of effort, the saw blade reached the center of the trunk. As it did so, the giant pine tree gave off a loud creak.

"Just a little more to go. Move away when the blade nears the point of the notch." They advanced the saw slowly.

"Now!" Terada shouted. They ran headlong, almost before their hands left the saw. The great tree swayed, lost its balance, gathered speed as it fell, shearing off branches of other trees, even breaking massive trunks, before it hit the ground with a roar that split open the silence in the forest.

As a boy, Iki had watched tree-cutters in the countryside around his home village, but the logging he had seen then was child's play compared to what they were required to do in Siberia. Flying branches, some more than a foot in diameter, could easily kill a man caught in their path.

"Now we trim the branches." Terada, standing astride the trunk, sawed off the great heavy boughs, then trimmed away the smaller branches with his ax. Iki followed Terada's example. The morning's weak sun hid behind clouds, and the temperature fell even lower. What earlier had been a dull throbbing in Iki's hands and feet now became intense pain. This unrelieved pain and the unrelenting cold caused his eyes to fill with tears, and the tears would try to freeze.

Cold and hunger had weakened Lieutenant Colonel Iki before Terada decided they must start on their second tree, and he was very unsteady on his feet. During lunch he hugged the fire and ate his piece of black bread greedily, forgetting all pretense at an officer's dignity. The other men, wise in the ways of survivors, melted snow in a metal drum set over a fire. When the water boiled, each worker took some in a tin can, dissolved a spoonful of sugar in it, and drank it as he ate his bread.

"This is the only way to get warm," Terada told Iki. "And, besides, after this you'll feel as though you've eaten a full meal." Heeding the advice, Iki drank some hot sugar water and soon felt its good effect.

"Colonel!" someone cried out. "Colonel Iki!" Iki turned toward the source of the shout. "Sir, is it really you? It *is* you! Sir, it's me— your orderly!"

"Marucho!" Iki exclaimed, overjoyed. Marucho had been his personal orderly during his tour of duty with the Kwantung Army. But the joy of reunion was tinged by sadness as he noted the changes in Marucho's appearance. His square face, once jolly and agreeable, had lost its fullness, and the eyes were dull and sunken, sparkling no longer. He was still generous at heart, however, just as he had been before.

"I'd heard that a staff officer from Imperial General Headquarters arrived here. The rumor reached our barrack last night. I didn't think it could possibly be you, but even so I couldn't help wondering. I bribed a guard so that I could come here today and find out for myself. —What happened, sir? You were supposed to be in Tokyo."

"I was sent back to Shinkyo on an errand, and decided to stay on with the Kwantung Army." He did not say any more about that errand and its consequences.

"Sir, are Mrs. Iki and your children well?"

"Probably." Iki said as much as he honestly could, being reasonably certain that they had escaped from Tokyo and found refuge at his parents' house in Yamagata. "How about your family? Are they all right?"

"That's what bothers me, sir. Frankly, I was happy about the war ending, because then I thought I'd be going back home to the wife and kids. But look where I am now—in Siberia, up to my belly in snow, chopping up trees. My wife is probably having a terrible time running the barber shop by herself. Maybe she thinks I was killed. . . . Maybe she's married to someone else . . ."

Iki knew Marucho's barber shop in Osaka and his attractive, sensible wife. "That's nonsense," he said. "She's a fine woman. She'll take care of your shop and your children while you're gone. And she'll be waiting for you when you get back. My wife has always praised her."

"Do you think so? She can't match Mrs. Iki, I know, but she has a good heart. Still, I worry about her. Sir, could you talk to the camp commandant about letting me send a letter to her? Sir, it would mean a lot—"

"War prisoners are allowed by international law to communicate with their families. But the Soviet Union hasn't even drawn up a decent register of those who are being held prisoner. Eventually, I believe, they'll be persuaded by world opinion. Then we'll be able to send letters out."

"Eventually? That's a long time! That's cruel! Sir, you're the brilliant Colonel Iki, who received a sword from His Imperial Majesty. Back in the old days you could solve anything. Now, right here, can't you figure out a way for me to get a letter out to my wife? Please help me, Colonel. I'll work for you the way I used to when I was your orderly—I don't care if they laugh at me for doing your laundry. I'll start work tomorrow."

He brought his palms together and bowed. Iki could not help laughing at this comical performance, but Marucho looked as if he was about to cry. "Sir, you think it's funny. I'm willing to do anything for you! Sir, how can you be so hard-hearted?"

"All right," Iki yielded. "I'll ask them to give us permission as soon as possible. But be patient." He gave Marucho a reassuring clap on the shoulder. Marucho blinked and smiled happily. Iki found himself returning the smile. For the first time since becoming a prisoner of war, he had been touched by an expression of genuine human affection.

The first of January was a holiday in Russia, and no work was required of prisoners that day. The Japanese had been preparing for their own New Year, stretching their ingenuity to devise decorations and special treats.

They hung boughs of fir at either side of the barracks doors because they resembled the traditional pine-branch decorations that grace entrances to Japanese homes at New Year festival. In Iki's barrack two hundred and fifty men arose promptly at six o'clock, put on their uniforms, and assembled in the compound, in formation, facing east, the direction of their homeland. The stars above looked like glittering crystals of ice in the black sky.

Overcome by a confusion of emotions as they sent their thoughts eastward, they stood in silence. Their nation shattered, themselves captive in an enemy's land, they prayed for the resurrection of their country and for their early return to it. A voice, singing softly, broke the sacred silence. Soon the lone singer was joined by others. The strains of Japan's national anthem swelled up, as every man lifted his voice with his hopes, raising the music of *Kimigayo* against the dark and sunless sky.

In the barracks once again, they ate (through the courtesy of their Russian hosts) a special New Year's fare—gruel much thicker than usual and salty caviar—and then settled around their favorite game boards to play or look on.

"Happy New Year, dear Japanese officers!" Two German officers walked in, calling out greetings in German. These prisoners from Germany very seldom came into the barracks of the Japanese, but this day gave excuse for an exception. Their usually pale faces were reddened with drink.

"Happy New Year, my cheerful friends!" Iki responded in German, and shook hands with the two, a major and a lieutenant. The major was eager to talk to Iki, a man his own age.

"I know that the New Year for you is the equivalent of Christmas for us. I came to offer you felicitations on behalf of Deutschland. Here's our gift—from the officers of the German Army to the officers of the Japanese Army."

The major held out a bottle of vodka, which brought a gleam to the eyes of the Japanese nearby. They had lived without the taste of alcohol since the day they set foot in Soviet territory.

"We can't imagine a finer gift." Iki felt happy because he could express his comrades' appreciation in the major's native tongue. "But how did you ever manage to obtain such a gift?"

"Quite simple." The young lieutenant boasted. "When we transported lumber to the docking point last week, we sold a load of it to the transportation officer."

Their daring amazed the Japanese, who, at most, would occasionally sneak a few narrow planks on to their cargo sledge for repairing things in the barracks.

"Even though the transportation officer is receptive to trading, I'm amazed that you were able to get past the supervisors," Iki said admiringly.

"No one in this lager can't be bought," the lieutenant said. "The lager commandant is a reservist who used to be a school teacher. Oh, he looks like a decent sort, but he thinks nothing of black-marketing food, clothing, and other supplies intended for prisoners. Some 'teacher'! The only one who doesn't follow his example is Lieutenant Nikolai. Nikolai's a member of the Communist Party. But I don't think he's ever reported the misconduct of the commandant and his staff. He pretends to see and hear nothing. Why he's so generous, I cannot think."

Iki remembered Nikolai, the lieutenant who had met him at the railway station. He had not seen him since that day. Why, he wondered again, had Lieutenant Nikolai, political officer and Party member, taken the trouble to meet him at the station?

The German officers talked on easily. "Do you know why their discipline breaks down so completely where material things are concerned?" the lieutenant asked. "Because they—the whole country, in fact—are exhausted from the war with our Deutschland. It was too much for them. If we had made a thorough climatological study of Russia, and outfitted our troops with decent cold-weather gear before going to war, Deutschland would never have lost to Russia. Hitler made no strategic errors, but he can be blamed for repeating Napoleon's mistake about Russia's weather."

"We're prisoners now," the major declared, "but the world situation is changing constantly. One day we'll return to Deutschland. And when that day comes, I'll be back in the army. Next time we'll pulverize Russia. A war can be won as long as a country's people retain their fortitude. Remember my name and my face, gentlemen, for when the time comes, I'll be the marshal of the German Army. I'll be even greater than Hitler was."

The Germans were a bit drunk, but they demonstrated impressive pride in their country, blazing no less fiercely after three years in a Russian prison camp. They were not at all like the Japanese, who appeared to drag their tails between their legs, completely resigned to their demeaning fate after only a few months' imprisonment. As passive as slaves, Iki thought, including his resigned self among the lot.

Not long afterward, he had the chance to see a convincing display of German pride. It happened on a day when a group of hardy prisoners, thirty-five years of age and under, was sent out for road work three to four miles beyond the usual logging site. Seeing a cleared strip fifty yards wide running through the length of the forest, Iki guessed that a railroad was being built along that route. When assigned to the Kwantung Army staff, he had known about plans for the Baikal-Amur railroad—a line that would eventually link Taishet, on the western shore of Lake Baikal, with towns far to the east, on the banks of the Amur River.

A German crew joined the Japanese. They were given the work of leveling tree stumps that projected above the partly finished road bed.

After completing their scheduled hours of work for that day, all the men were ready to board the trucks at four o'clock, for the ride back to camp. The officer in charge of the security guards, however, tried to persuade them to continue working "just a little while longer," to clear the few remaining stumps.

80

When Major Terada objected, the Russian officer retorted: "In that case you'll stay here till morning. Do you think you won't care whether you have food to eat? And shelter to keep you from freezing to death during the night?"

Recognizing the threat, and realizing that the extra work would not take much more than half an hour, the Japanese went back to work. But they heard the uproar in the area where the Germans were working. "*Davai!* Move! You damned German fascists!" "Shut up, you stupid Ruskii!"

By the time the commander of the guards rushed in to investigate the reason for this commotion, the Germans were marching in formation toward the trucks.

"Halt! Halt or we'll shoot!" the six guards shouted, waving their automatic rifles. But the Germans ignored them and swarmed into the trucks.

"Why aren't you finishing the job?" the officer screeched. "The Japanese have agreed to finish. Why can't you?" He pointed to the Japanese watching the confrontation with saws and axes in their hands.

The German major who had visited Iki's barrack on New Year's day spoke up: "The Japanese may do as they please, but we refuse to acknowledge the need to work beyond our scheduled hours."

The Germans were specifying their rights and responsibilities, and refusing to be abused—on the very teutonic ground of logic.

"In the Soviet Union we shoot saboteurs!" the enraged officer screamed. "Come forward, all of you! Five at a time!"

More than sixty Germans leaped out of the trucks, regrouped themselves in a column, five abreast. The five men in the first row took a resolute step forward. No words were spoken, but the contempt in the Germans' faces was unmistakable: shoot if you dare, they were saying in a brave charade. Then see what happens to you.

No one broke the ominous silence. The Germans stood their ground. The Japanese watched with bated breath, wondering what would happen next. Rescue came in the crunch of boots upon snow. Everyone turned to see Lieutenant Nikolai approaching the Germans.

"The temperature is falling rapidly," he said calmly. "We'd better wait until tomorrow to finish up. That's all for today."

The triumphant Germans—they expected no more, no less,

even from enemy Russians—threw condescending glances at the meek Japanese as they quickly climbed back onto the trucks.

"You seem to be fascinated by the defiance of our German guests, Mr. Iki," a voice beside him said in slow, clearly enunciated Russian. The cool gaze of that pair of brown eyes, set in the austere face of Lieutenant Nikolai, disconcerted Iki.

"I'm not so much fascinated with their defiance as I am impressed by the German spirit—their pride as a people, undiminished despite the death of so many of their comrades—more than a hundred thousand, I believe—on their way from Leningrad to Siberia, and during their three years here in your lagers."

"So . . . An interesting thought. By the way, isn't the work here at the lager too strenuous for you, a staff officer of the Imperial General Headquarters?"

It was a strange question, but Iki answered it immediately. "I'm no exception. The work is taking its toll of every prisoner. Daily."

"I'm sorry to hear that," Nikolai said. "You really must be very careful while you're working here." He turned and strode away. Thinking about the implications of this parting remark, Iki sensed in the imperturbable Lieutenant Nikolai something sinister, something to be feared.

5

THE VANQUISHED

The grim Siberian winter gave way to spring. Beneath the warmth of April's sun the great cover of snow melted and trees brought forth new buds. As the days grew warmer hope for their repatriation revived the spirits of the interned Japanese. But the stir of excitement did not last. With the thaw, construction of the Baikal-Amur railroad began in earnest, and soon the prisoners were being driven at a ruthless pace.

"You war prisoners have been maintained at great cost to the Soviet government," the lager's commandant told them. "Your work level went down during the winter. Now that the weather's getting warmer, I expect you to increase your workload, to compensate the Soviet Union for the extraordinary sacrifices it has made on your behalf." When he finished this speech he assigned standards of performance far harsher than those he'd imposed for logging, and threatened to keep all the prisoners on the work site until every man fulfilled his quota for the day.

They were taken in trucks to the wide swath that other laborers before them had cleared through the virgin forest. Iki's task was to loosen hard earth and haul it to the roadbed. Only with much effort could he drive the pickax into the solid ground. And he lacked the skill to guide the wheelbarrow steadily across the movable plank that served as a ramp to the unfinished bed. In the afternoon of the first day, already near exhaustion, he staggered and his wheelbarrow missed the ramp, toppling over. He was ashamed of his weakness, and knew that he was falling behind in his work and would be keeping the others waiting at the end of the day. Wearily he bent down to straighten the wheelbarrow.

"I'll do it, Colonel!" Marucho quickly set the barrow upright and shoveled the spilled dirt back into it.

"Thanks," Iki murmured, still breathing hard.

"Sir, you're still too soft to do this kind of farmers' work. I'll come back and help you as soon as I've finished with my job." As he hurried away he looked back, giving his colonel an encouraging grin.

Once again, Iki guided the wheelbarrow carefully along the narrow ramp, dumped the dirt upon the insatiable roadbed, and hurried back for another load. As he raised the pick a jeep pulled up near him. Lieutenant Nikokai sat beside the driver.

"Put down your tools, Mr. Iki, and get in," Nikolai said, almost gently. He ignored Iki's questions about where they were going. A bundle on the back seat contained Iki's personal effects. He understood at once that he was being taken away, unnoticed by a thousand other Japanese working on the site, without even time to say goodbye to Terada.

A bewildering series of events awaited Iki. He fully expected to be taken even farther into remotest Siberia, to die on the frozen tundra. But much to his surprise, he was sent all the way back to Khabarovsk.

The city was unlike the Khabarovsk he had known six months before. White birches were thick with new green foliage, and old brick buildings and domed churches stood out against the bright blue sky of spring. As they drove along Iki recognized the district headquarters of the Ministry of Internal Affairs. Their jeep continued past other landmarks he remembered, into the suburbs; then, for another hour, they followed the Ussuri River until they stopped in front of a small dacha set amid a grove of white birches. It was one of a cluster of dachas built on a low hill overlooking the river.

The villa was old and worn, but its interior showed traces of an earlier opulence, from the time of the czars. A wide hallway led to a sitting room fitted with a splendid crystal chandelier. The house was strangely quiet.

They locked Iki in a bedroom on the upper floor. With delight he contemplated the luxury of a soft clean bed, but the pleasure vanished as soon as he noticed the heavy curtains and tight shutters that separated him from the world outside. He sat on the bed, wondering about his abrupt removal from the Taishet lager to a dacha in suburban Khabarovsk. Only a few minutes passed before he heard footsteps, then the turning of a key in his door. A Russian captain and an interpreter entered.

"You may relax in this room for the time being," the captain said. "We also have two Japanese generals staying in this dacha. You'll meet them after dinner." He made a perfunctory search of Iki's person and left.

Iki ate both lunch and dinner in his room. The generous meals included white bread and butter and thick vegetable soup—undreamed of fare in the lager at Taishet. To Iki everything increased the mystery. And who were the Japanese generals hidden away in this dacha?

After dinner, as he lay dozing on the bed, the captain returned. "Come and meet your fellow officers," he said, slightly more affably than before.

Iki heard conversation from the floor below as he approached the staircase. When he recognized the voice of Deputy Chief-of-Staff Takemura he rushed down the stairs.

"So it was you!" General Takemura exclaimed, with both surprise and satisfaction. "Lieutenant General Akitsu of the Continental Railway Command is here with me."

General Akitsu lifted himself with obvious effort from the sofa. "You look tired, Iki," he said. The tall, lean general had changed remarkably—his once black hair was completely white, the cheekbones more prominent than ever, the deep-set eyes soft with misery. Seeing these superior officers made Iki all the more puzzled: why had he, a field-grade officer, been brought here, together with two such important generals of the Kwantung Army?

The weather was unusually cold for the month of May. Accustomed to hoping for warmth while lying fully clothed in a hard bunk in a crowded barrack, Iki could scarcely believe that he stood in the warmth of this large sitting room, with its comfortable sofas, soft chairs, and glowing fireplace.

"Where were you taken?" General Takemura asked. "And what's happened to your uniform? It's so worn and shapeless."

Iki described the life of Japanese prisoners at the Taishet prison camp. The generals had heard that captive Japanese military personnel were being used as laborers for railroad construction work, but had no idea of the conditions in which they lived. When they learned the truth from Iki, they could only shake their heads in sorrow.

"Has General Hata been well?" Iki asked, seeing the need to speak of something else.

"The Chief-of-Staff was taken to the Ministry of Internal Affairs district headquarters in Khabarovsk a few days after you were. He was taken back and forth five times altogether, and imprisoned each time. In the end he was so weak that he had trouble climbing stairs. They took him away two weeks ago—to be hospitalized, they said. We've had no news about him since then. Rumors say that they took him to Moscow."

"To Moscow? By himself?"

"That seems likely. The rest of us, too, have been tossed back and forth between Internal Affairs and prison a number of times. The interrogations became so intensive that we felt something was going to happen soon."

"What do you think will happen?" Iki had been isolated in Taishet for so long that he did not know what to expect anymore. "And why did they bring the three of us together here?"

"Neither General Akitsu nor I can understand this. We were brought here from the generals' lager in Khabarovsk. In the week we've been here, we've been left alone—no questions, no demands. It's a typical Russian technique. They treat you like a guest when they expect to get something out of you." General Takemura knew the Russians well: he had been taken as a hostage to Zharkova just as the war was ending, and since then he had also spent time at the prison camp in Voroshilov.

"Nothing they do should surprise us," the taciturn Akitsu said, looking not at them but into the flames seeking escape up the chimney.

Beginning the next day, Iki, Takemura, and Akitsu were taken to Khabarovsk daily for interrogation at the headquarters of the Ministry of Internal Affairs. They were questioned separately, with the purpose of eliciting specific answers to two questions. First, which of the three—the Emperor, or the civil government, or Imperial General Headquarters—had exercised supreme authority in determining highest level Japanese policies during the war? And second, was Japan's strategy with respect to the U.S.S.R. equivalent to a war of aggression?

Iki's interrogator was the same Major Yazef who had questioned him half a year earlier. When Yazef was dissatisfied with a reply from Iki, he would rephrase his question. But, although the words might change, in fact he asked the same questions over and over, continuing late into the night, sometimes until daybreak. He allowed Iki (and presumably himself) to sleep for three or four hours, then resumed the interrogation, repeating the same questions throughout the morning and the afternoon. Yazef gave the impression that he considered this procedure entirely legal; he relied only upon words, and always stopped short of physical violence. Iki thought that he himself would lose his sanity if he were subjected to such insistent interrogation for as long as a month. He found strength in observing the way the elderly Akitsu and Takemura endured this ordeal with unfailing dignity.

One afternoon when Iki arrived at the interrogation room he was greeted by Yazef, positively beaming. "This is an affidavit of the information you gave me in the course of the interrogation. After the interpreter reads it to you, in Japanese, please sign it." He handed a document, written in Russian, to the civilian interpreter.

"If I am to sign it, it must be in Japanese," Iki objected.

"If you've told the truth, what is the difference whether it's in Russian or Japanese?" Yazef ended this brief exchange by telling the interpreter to proceed.

All the statements regarding anti-Soviet operations emphasized Soviet innocence, and contrasted that with the aggressive intent of the Japanese Army. The distortions angered Iki.

"I told you that an offensive strategy was dictated by the plans for 1941 and 1942. But I also told you that planned strategy after 1943 was unquestionably defensive."

"The purpose of your affidavit is to set forth facts known to you when you were on the Operations staff of Imperial General Headquarters," Yazef argued. "We have supplemented your statements concerning war plans since 1943 with information obtained from your generals. I believe everything is correct." Again he urged Iki to sign the affidavit.

Five days later, Iki, Akitsu, and Takemura were summoned to the Ministry office, where Major Yazef told them that they would appear as witnesses for the Soviet Union at the International Military Tribunal for the Far East, then being held in Tokyo. The three, aghast at this turn of events, protested vehemently. Yazef's order came as a greater shock to them than had the imperial decision to end the war. This would be the ultimate humiliation—to appear as witnesses in a military court where their former superiors and their nation were on trial. Yazef ignored their protests. The order, he said, had come from the Soviet Ministry of Internal Affairs in Moscow, and therefore must be obeyed.

Iki could not sleep that night. He lay awake thinking over the choices that lay before him. Refusal was not one of them, for he was a captive and could be thrust forcibly into the trial. He would be spared this degradation only if he succeeded in taking his own life.—Or, on the other hand, should he seize the opportunity to testify at the Tribunal in behalf of his own country?

When the first light of dawn appeared, he was recalling the day he had returned to the Kwantung Army Headquarters, mission fulfilled, and had stood in the deserted Operations room, his finger touching the trigger of the pistol that could have ended forever all humiliation, all worry. He no longer carried a revolver or a sword. Nor—and this he saw clearly, at last—did he have the freedom to take his own life. If he were to die, another staff officer would be forced to take his place.

He could hear one of his companions in distress stirring on the other side of the wall. Like himself, General Takemura had spent a sleepless night.

The three Japanese officers persisted in refusing to appear as witnesses at the International Military Tribunal. Although interrogations had ended, they were kept in confinement for another month. One night Major Yazef appeared at the dacha.

"We have received a directive from Moscow," he told them. "If you gentlemen persist in your refusal to testify at the Tokyo trial to what you have already acknowledged in the signed affidavits, we must conclude that the contents of the affidavits are false. If that's so, we'll have to start interrogations over again. What's your answer?" It was an undisguised threat.

"Then you're forcing us to appear at the Tribunal," General Akitsu said.

"That's right. And if you refuse, we'll have to take Chief-of-Staff Hata out of the hospital and send him in your place." Yazef had set up an effective trap.

"We have no choice," Akitsu said. "Under these circumstances, we'll offer testimony—but only on the contents of the affidavits. If your government tries to make us testify on any other subjects, we'll refuse. Our refusal will be absolute. Is that understood?"

"I can promise that no other demands will be made," Yazef said, with many nods of satisfaction. He left promptly, as if running away before they could change their minds.

Iki doubted the value of Yazef's assurances, and urged Akitsu to insist on written confirmation of his promises.

"This will be a matter of sticking to our resolution, each of us, and of doing no more than we've agreed to do," Akitsu said. "If you're coerced into saying more than you wish to, the solution to that problem is simple—you must die." He paused for only a moment. "Now that our course of action is settled, let's relax until the time comes to leave. We ought to have them take us down to the Ussuri River for a bit of fishing."

Two mornings later a loud rap on his door awakened Iki. The room was lighted only faintly by a pale dawn beyond the shutters. As he sat up in bed, a guard came in.

"Get into these. You're leaving." The guard handed him a new lieutenant colonel's uniform, undoubtedly taken from the stocks left in the Kwantung Army warehouse. In the hallway he met General Akitsu and General Takemura, also dressed in crisp uniforms with appropriate insignia.

Guards drove them to Khabarovsk Airport. Major Yazef met them there, accompanied by a medical officer, an interpreter, and three soldiers. On the runway a PBY Catalina amphibian, acquired through Lend-Lease from the United States, warmed its engines.

"Is that the plane we're taking to Tokyo?" Akitsu asked.

"That's right," Yazef replied airily. "We'll fly nonstop to Tokyo."

Looking down from the PBY's window, Iki saw the indented coastline of the Soviet Maritime Provinces. He noticed the direction from which the rays of the morning sun entered the cabin, and knew they were on a southeasterly course away from Khabarovsk. They were flying along an air route that soon would take them due south. If the craft maintained its air speed of about 180 miles an hour, they would be over Honshu in five hours. He closed his eyes. In a few short hours he would set foot in Japan, to be a Soviet witness at the International Military Tribunal. He shrank from the indignity of the task he must perform before that court of inquiry. He glanced at Akitsu and Takemura. Both sat silent, arms folded, their inner distress betrayed by troubled expressions.

The Japan Sea spread out below them like a carpet dyed a deep indigo. In the distance lay a large green island, ringed about with white caps breaking upon its shores. "There's Sado," Takemura said softly.

Southeast of Sado Island stretched the Niigata coast of Honshu. Iki put his face against the window, looking with love at the beautiful green land below. He yearned to hear the lapping waves on Japan's shores, and bit his lips to suppress the flood of emotion rising within him.

The aircraft circled over Sado Island several times, then turned east into the skies above Niigata, flying over low ranges of mountains, a network of rivers, and, nestled here and there in the valleys, small villages and rice fields. Iki remembered Tu Fu's celebrated poem—"The nation torn asunder, Only hills and rivers remain"—and he understood as never before how simply the Chinese scholar, more than a thousand years ago, had lamented the devastation of his country.

The PBY landed at Haneda Airport near the southern end of Tokyo Bay. The Russians led the way out of the aircraft. An American flag, flying atop the airport tower, caught the attention of the Japanese. The Stars and Stripes forced the reality of an "occupied Japan" upon them with stunning impact. American Army jeeps screeched to a stop alongside the PBY, and armed MPs leaped out to surround them.

"What's the idea?" an American officer shouted angrily. "You were supposed to rendezvous with an American plane over Sado, and be escorted from there to Haneda. You do know Japan is now under U.S. occupation?"

Major Yazef, speaking through an interpreter, chose to be equally blunt: "We arrived over Sado earlier than scheduled because of strong westerly winds, and we circled over Sado long enough before flying in to Haneda. Your plane didn't appear. There's your reason!" To the Japanese this verbal fighting was evidence of the U.S.-Soviet confrontation already far advanced in Japan.

Russian jeeps carried the three Japanese officers toward central Tokyo. The Yokohama-Tokyo highway ran through a low, desolate plain, level but for an occasional rusting skeleton rising out of the scorched rubble. The unobstructed view of tiny fishing boats sailing in the deep waters off Omori beach was oddly picturesque. They drove on past Shinagawa, toward the heart of the city, through burned-out city blocks stretching as far as the eye could see. The war had ended a year before, but as yet few signs of recovery could be seen. In some places, flimsy shacks hastily thrown together on empty lots gave shelter to the shabby, dispirited Japanese walking along littered streets.

"This is dreadful! I never thought it would be this bad . . ." General Akitsu murmured. Having spent the last months of the war in Manchuria, he was not prepared for so much ruin. The center of Tokyo was a graveyard of gutted buildings. The Great Earthquake of 1923 had not been as destructive.

The jeeps drove them past Hibiya Park, along the wide boulevard beside the moat around the Imperial Palace, and turned right into an area of office buildings that had escaped the bombing, pulling up in front of a red brick structure that Iki recognized as the Mitsubishi Building. A Russian soldier stood guard beside the Soviet flag at the entrance. The Japanese officers were led to the third floor and past closed doors to the end of the hallway, where they were assigned quarters. The room Iki would share with General Takemura had been an office; slightly less than twenty feet square, it had been converted into a sleeping room by the addition of two beds and two armchairs.

Major Yazef was almost friendly at the prospect of giving his charges into the care of someone else. "This is the Soviet Mission in Japan," he explained carefully. "The third floor is occupied by persons connected with the Far East Military Tribunal. We still don't know when you gentlemen will appear before the Tribunal, but you'll be notified soon by a responsible officer of the Mission. I'll be leaving you now. Try to get some rest."

Iki and Takemura were instructed to take their meals with Akitsu, in his room across the hall. Their first meal was typically Russian, but with the added treat of fresh vegetables grown in Japan. Takemura ate heartily, but Akitsu, unusually wan and preoccupied, scarcely touched his food.

"Aren't you feeling well?" Iki asked, thinking the long flight might have tired him.

"I'm all right. Perhaps I'm unusually depressed by the ruin I've seen—far worse than I had imagined. It's made me think . . . The politicians were the ones who made the decision to start the war, but the military were responsible for losing it. Now that I've seen what's happened to Japan, I keep thinking about my share of the blame . . ." He lapsed into a brooding silence. In a few moments, however, he spoke with more animation: "Come, let's get to sleep early tonight. You two must be as tired as I am.—But, before you go, I want to say how I've appreciated the concern you've shown me all along."

They returned to their room. Takemura soon fell asleep, but sleep did not come easily to Iki. He raised the shade and looked out at the few dim lights to be seen in the city. A number of people hurried along the streets below. Thinking of his wife and children, alive, he hoped, somewhere under the same Japanese sky, he felt an intense yearning for them. Unable to contain himself any longer, he was about to speak out his feelings to Takemura. Just in time, he remembered that Takemura's situation was far worse than his. He did not even know if his wife and children were alive, much less safely back in Japan; when he parted from them in Shinkyo, the Soviet Army was overrunning Manchuria. Yet he had not once spoken of his concern. Takemura's fortitude helped Iki to quiet the turmoil within—and to regret his own immaturity as an officer.

That night Iki dreamt of his family.

Irises were in full bloom in their small garden in Koenji. They were celebrating Makoto's first Boys' Day, and Iki's father had traveled the great distance from Yamagata to spend the day with them. Holding his year-old grandson on his lap, he said, "I hope you grow up to be a fine soldier like your father, so that the Emperor will give you a sword too." His fondness for the child was boundless.

Four-year-old Naoko looked unhappy. "I wish I were a boy, Grandpa," she said. Snatching the warrior's helmet off the shelf, she put it over her head and struck a pose, like that of one of the heroic samurai dolls being displayed for the holiday. "Shame on you, acting like a boy," her mother said. Intent on greater mischief, especially upon defying Iki, Naoko ran out of the room to the veranda. As she bounded from the veranda to the garden, the crimson chin straps came untied and the helmet fell off.

"Oh, the chin straps!" Yoshiko gasped, growing pale. "We can tie them back together," Iki said, laughing. "But helmet straps have always been linked to victory," his wife said. "Remember the samurai proverb, about tying the chin straps tighter after winning a battle?" She picked up the helmet and tried to tie a knot in the braided cords. But the ends of the knot kept falling apart. After each failure, Yoshiko became even more distressed.

When Iki, too, tried to tie the braids, they snapped suddenly in many places, and the crimson knots became spurts of blood sprayed about by a gust of wind. "I wonder if something terrible will happen to you," Yoshiko cried, her tear-filled eyes looking fearfully into his. He pulled her close, and she pressed her face against his breast.

The next morning, after Iki had shaved and dressed and was about to leave with Takemura to join General Akitsu, a guard entered carrying two breakfasts on a tray. "You are to eat here today," he said, more quietly than guards usually spoke to him.

"Why is this? Yesterday we were told to take all our meals in General Akitsu's room." Something was wrong, they realized, and both moved toward the hallway.

"Stop! Stay in this room!" the guard shouted, barring the door with his body. Iki and Takemura looked at each other in surprise. Soon after the guard withdrew, locking their door, they heard a commotion in the hallway and in Akitsu's room—doors slamming, people rushing in and out, men talking excitedly in Russian and in English. But they did not hear Akitsu's voice. When, after a long time, all became quiet again, Takemura knocked on his own door to attract the attention of the guard, and told him they wished to see Major Yazef. He came promptly.

"Why can't we go to General Akitsu's room?" Takemura asked.

"Because General Akitsu died this morning of a heart attack."

"General Akitsu . . . died?"

Yazef's stiff expression, obviously a deception, strengthened their disbelief.

"We would like to see the general's body," Takemura said.

"You cannot. Against regulations."

"The general was in good health in Khabarovsk. And last night too! I can't believe his heart suddenly failed. How did he die?" Iki pressed Yazef for an answer, but Yazef said only that the general had suffered a heart attack. Evidently he knew nothing more.

Had Akitsu taken his own life? Iki recalled what the General said at Khabarovsk, when he suggested that the three of them declare in writing their refusal to testify to facts not contained in their affidavits: "If you're coerced into saying more than you wish to, the solution is simple—you must die." He must have known then that he could not bear to take the witness stand in a court where his colleagues and superiors were on trial, and at that very moment must have determined to commit suicide. Last night, after seeing the utter desolation of Tokyo, his strong sense of responsibility had caused him to do then what he had been intending all along to do in time.

"Please let us pay our last respects—just a glance," Iki pleaded.

"I'm sorry. His body was taken away by the Americans, for an autopsy."

Iki knew that he must control his rage against the loss of a respected leader with whom he had shared military defeat and, even more galling, against the senseless denial of his right to pay his last respects to that leader. Trembling violently, he fought to hold back the fury mounting in his throat, raging to be heard.

That afternoon they were visited by an American officer, accompanied by MPs and an interpreter. The officer questioned them about General Akitsu's behavior during the last days. He made a thorough search of their bodies, clothing, and personal effects, obviously looking for poison capsules or sharp instruments. Overhearing the MP who had searched him say that he had found no cyanide, Iki knew that General Akitsu had taken his life with poison.

Later that day, Iki and Takemura were moved from the Mitsubishi Building to a large Japanese-style house, hurriedly taken over by the Russians.

Their new quarters were in Kioi-cho, on the opposite side of the Imperial Palace, not far from Sophia University. The death of General Akitsu had cast a shadow over them; even the Russians, apparently chastened by his death, were surprisingly solicitous and accommodating. Iki and Takemura were given separate rooms on the upper floor, overlooking a large garden. And they were permitted to take walks in the garden, under the watchful eyes of guards in civilian clothes.

Because their appearance at the Tribunal had been postponed, they waited in almost unbearable idleness. Only a wall separated them from the world of freedom; beyond that wall they heard the footsteps, voices, and laughter of their fellow Japanese and the noise of their activities. To be deprived of all freedom in the hopelessly remote isolation of Siberia was not as intolerable as being held captive in Tokyo, so close to the liberties they yearned to enjoy.

A month went by before Yazef came to see them. He reported that he was ordering civilian suits for them because uniforms of the defunct Japanese Army were inappropriate for witnesses appearing at the International Tribunal. A Japanese tailor showed them the fabrics: dark blue serge for the suits and, for shirts, pink Fuji silk. Iki objected to the color of the silk, but Yazef insisted that pink was in fashion these days.

Soon after they received their new clothes, they were informed of impending visits by Soviet Chief Prosecutor Golunsky and American Chief Prosecutor Keenan. Their interview with Golunsky was a simple matter. But excitement swept through the Russians as they awaited Keenan's visit. Yazef became even more concerned about their comfort, and several times said, "Be very careful when you talk to Keenan." It was a needless worry, for neither Iki nor Takemura had any thought of complaining to the American or of trying to gain favor with him.

They met in the big living room on the ground floor. Keenan came with an interpreter and two stenographers. An officer from the Soviet Mission and Major Yazef were also present. Keenan appeared rather ordinary, hardly the sharp, abrasive type reporters for the Japanese press had made him. He asked questions in a business-like manner.

"How are you being treated in the Soviet Union?"

"We're receiving normal treatment."

"What do you mean by 'normal'?"

"We're treated as all war prisoners are."

"Can you think of anything that might shed light on General Akitsu's suicide?"

Takemura drew himself straight in his chair and answered, "His Excellency General Akitsu and I shared the same quarters for four months before we were brought back to Tokyo. Not once did he give so much as a hint of planning his death. His decision to die had to be a very personal decision."

Keenan waited for a moment, then asked: "Are the statements in your affidavits, and in General Akitsu's, based on truths?"

"Yes, they are. But, of course, allowances must be made for nuances of language that may have been altered in the course of translation."

"For my own information, I'd like your opinion of the assumption that the Emperor of Japan did not possess the power of veto."

The officer from the Soviet Mission interrupted him, insisting on the inappropriateness of the question.

Considered in light of the U.S. occupation policy, Keenan's

question evidently was directed toward affirming the American position—disassociation of Japan's Emperor from responsibility for instigating the war. The American attitude contradicted that of the Russians, who were determined to put the responsibility on the Emperor, who could then be brought to trial.

In the days following their interview with Keenan, Takemura and Iki were treated with renewed concern and courtesy—as if they could be expected, in return, to testify favorably on behalf of the Soviet Union.

Major Yazef called on them a second time. His two prisoners thought that he assumed a disagreeable familiarity when he said: "You've been in Japan more than a month now, and I'm sure a day doesn't go by without your thinking about your families. I plan to arrange matters so you'll be allowed to see them."

"I appreciate your kindness," Takemura said immediately, "but that's quite unnecessary, if not impossible. My wife and children were in Manchuria when the war ended. The oldest of my four children was only fifteen. I doubt that they got out alive."

Iki hesitated, overwhelmed by longing for his family. Yet he showed not a hint of struggle. "My family has been missing since I left Tokyo. But I thank you just the same."

"It's no trouble to me," Yazef said with a shrug. "Our intelligence network is very efficient. We'll make every effort to locate your families." So intent was he on making use of family affection to get them to do his bidding that the sensibilities of his prisoners did not ever enter his mind.

When the time drew near for Iki and Takemura to appear before the Military Tribunal, Soviet Prosecutor Golunsky himself came to the house in Kioi-cho to inform them of the date—September 18, four days later.

As soon as Golunsky left the living room, reeking of Russian tobacco, Iki stepped out on the terrace and looked up at the cloudless autumn sky. A small glittering object crossed his field of vision, coming to rest on a branch of the nanden bush near the door. Once again he perceived, as he had in youth, that the dragonfly, with its thin, opalescent, silvery wings and slim body of bright scarlet, was a creature of delicate yet magical beauty. He held his breath, studying his discovery, envying its freedom, while it rested only a few feet away.

Hearing someone approaching, he turned—and beheld Major

Yazef. With some difficulty he suppressed a grin. Such a thing to see, after the dragonfly! Yazef wore a baggy blue serge suit, with a double-breasted jacket, of course, and a shirt too small made of the same pink Fuji silk as Iki's. He cut a crude, provincial figure, made all the more ridiculous by his newfound idea of his importance.

"I have wonderful news for you, Mr. Iki," he sank into a stage whisper. "Thanks to our intelligence network, we were able to locate your family."

Iki's reaction was instinctive. "My family! Really? Where are they?" Yazef had told him only two days before that his family could not be found, either at the address he'd used in Tokyo or at his registered domicile in Yamagata. The Russian saw that, with his good news, he had succeeded in breaking through Iki's reserve.

"Of course you'll want to find out about your wife and children, and to see them again. We've taken great pains to bring you this opportunity, and you mustn't reject our kindness."

"No. I do not wish to see them." Iki drew a long, slow breath. "But I would like to know where they are living."

"In Osaka. Mrs. Iki and your two children are living in a neighborhood called Suminoe, in Osaka."

Suminoe was not a familiar name. Iki had really been expecting that Yoshiko and the children would be living with his parents in Yamagata. If they had moved to Osaka, they should have gone to the house of her father, Colonel Sakano, in Tezukayama. Worries sprang forth faster than he could find words for them. Perhaps Sakano had died? Perhaps his house had been destroyed in the bombings? Families of former military officers were the hardest pressed to earn a living in postwar society. How could his wife, husbandless and fatherless, possibly work and take care of two small children?

"You *will* see your wife and children, won't you?"

Iki hesitated. His thoughts raced as his eyes sought the dragonfly—in vain. It had gone away, on its erratic course, unplanned but free. His own presence in Japan was no less a miracle than resurrection from death, and his family's survival an incredibly kind gift of fate. After testifying at the Military Tribunal, he would be taken back to Siberia and might not live to see them again. He must see them! And yet, if he were to submit to temptation and agree to see his wife and children, he would most certainly become known as a witness who testified for the U.S.S.R. out of gratitude for Soviet kindness. Thousands of the Kwantung Army's soldiers and officers were still denied the right to communicate with their families; they did not even know if their wives, children, parents, were alive. How, then, could he accept a privilege they were refused?

"No, I do not wish to see them." he said again, firmly. "But I would like to know why my family is living in Suminoe."

"That's something you might ask when you see them."

"You don't have to tell me if you don't wish to. But I ask you not to mention bringing my family to me any more."

"Mr. Iki, if you persist in this stubborn refusal to see them, you may live to regret it. Think it over, and let me know if you change your mind. I can bring them up from Osaka right away."

At dinner that evening, Iki related the incident to Takemura and asked the general if he'd heard anything about his family.

"The Russians continue to worry me with questions about them. From what I've been able to learn, they've not come back from Manchuria. I wouldn't have expected my family—a woman and four young children—to return safely to Japan." He spoke in a matter-of-fact way, as if he were resigned to their fate, whatever it might be. He chose not to comment on Iki's dilemma. This, of course, made Iki all the more determined that he could not possibly allow himself to be reunited with his family.

Three more days passed. Because their appearance before the Tribunal was scheduled for the following day, Iki was in the bedroom reviewing material for his testimony. He heard several urgent raps on his door, and Yazef calling. "Some people to see you, Mr. Iki." Yazef, all cheer and color, brought himself into the room.

"Golunsky again?"

"No. Someone else. Mrs. Iki and your children. We brought them here from Osaka. They're downstairs waiting for you! Come!" And he called down to Iki's wife. "In a moment."

Iki got up and started walking toward the door. Then he caught himself, recognizing the trap that was about to be sprung. His face twisted with fury, he wheeled upon Yazef. "I will not see them." Send them back to Osaka. And don't interfere again with my family!"

"I don't understand you at all. They were on a train all night, coming here from Osaka. They want to see you. Listen! You can hear their voices."

"Damn you!" Iki growled as he pushed Yazef out the door and slammed it shut. Behind the door, he stood still, listening for sounds from below. Naoko was six years old, Makoto was three; neither would understand the reasons for their trip to Tokyo. But Naoko would be old enough to pull away from her mother and run about shouting, "Where's daddy?" He had an overwhelming desire to rush downstairs and gather Naoko, Makoto, and Yoshiko into his arms. He fought back the impulse, listening to what was happening below. He heard Yazef's voice, and doors being opened and closed. He did not hear Yoshiko, who, realizing that her husband would want to be spared the humiliation of being seen as a prisoner of war, doubtless spoke softly to the children to quiet them. But then perhaps the children were silent because they were frightened by the strange surroundings and the alien Russians.

"Here, Iki. A present from your children," the guard said, coming into the room and handing him a doll made of colored folding paper. Iki took the doll and lifted it to his face.

Hearing the hum of a motor, he looked out the window and saw Yoshiko walking away from the house, leading Naoko and Makoto by the hand toward the car parked before the gate. More slender than he remembered her, she wore a conservative kimono of appealing simplicity. The children had grown taller; his heart skipped a beat when he saw their thin wrists and ankles, sticking out from clothing they had outgrown.

Car doors were slammed shut, and the automobile disappeared from view. In the dark silence, Iki felt the tears begin to come. He looked down at the paper doll in his hand, and gave way at last to weeping.

The Russians provided an official automobile for Iki and Takemura's solemn ride to Ichigaya Heights, where sessions of the International Tribunal were held.

The white-helmeted MP guard stopped the car as it rolled up to the gate. He examined the passengers' identification papers, then motioned to the driver to proceed. The car moved along the slowly curving road cut into a bank overlooking a bed of silver-tasseled miscanthus grass. Until the end of the war the buildings at the top of the slope had housed the Japanese Army Academy and Imperial General Headquarters as well. Now those very buildings were being used to stage the trials that were to determine the guilt or innocence of members of the Japanese Army. The choice of place emphasized the fact that the Allied nations were determined to teach the Japanese people a lesson they would not soon forget.

Iki and Takemura left the car at the main entrance, where an officer of the Soviet Mission met them. He escorted them to the second floor lounge that was reserved for trial witnesses. Formerly the lounge had been the conference room, located between the Operations room and the office of the chief-of-staff. Iki had used that room daily during the last weeks of the war, and he was familiar with every piece of furniture in it, every nick on every table and chair.

While the Russians scurried about, checking details of their scheduled routine, Iki stood quietly by the window overlooking the inner courtyard, now thronged with newcomers—members of the Tribunal staff and the ubiquitous MPs. He closed his eyes and remembered that courtyard the last time he had seen it. On that evening, Japanese officers and enlisted men, still dismayed after hearing the Imperial Voice declare that the war was ended, rushed about setting fire to great piles of secret documents. The gasoline-fed flames leaped high into the air. Gradually, the haggard face of Chief-of-Staff Umezu floated up into Iki's vision of flames. Today General Umezu sat in the dock among the accused, along with others classified as Class A war criminals. As the time for his testimony drew near, Iki felt a growing nervousness and a disgust with himself.

"General Takemura," he said. "Do you really think the Allied nations are capable of making an impartial assessment of our testimony?"

"I really wonder," Takemura said in his casual way. "The inquiry into Soviet-Japanese relations has been going on for ten days. Golunsky began his presentation with references to the Russo-Japanese War, going all the way back to 1904–1905. I think we can assume that the trial will be conducted under the pretext of legal proceedings, but that it will allow the victors to avenge themselves fully against the vanquished."

As if confirming Takemura's assumption, Yazef came in, bursting with energy, announcing, "The court is in session. Colonel Iki, you're the first scheduled witness."

Iki exchanged glances with Takemura and stepped out into the hallway, where an armed MP waited to conduct him to the courthouse.

The courtroom of the International Military Tribunal for the Far East occupied about thirty-six hundred square feet of floor space. Before the surrender, this room had been the auditorium of Imperial General Headquarters.

The room was crowded—more than seventy people took some part in the Tribunal that day.

Flags of the eleven prosecuting nations were displayed behind President Webb and the other justices. The courtroom, brighter than day in the glare of floodlights, had been divided into three levels: the justices, occupying an elevated bench along the south wall; the prosecutors and interpreters dispersed throughout the middle section; and the defendants, seated in a dock along the north wall, just above the row of tables for the Defense Counsel. The witness stand occupied the center of the room, facing the justices. In the defendants' dock sat Tojo Hideki, Itagaki Seishiro, Togo Shigenori, Kido Koichi, and twenty-two other men—in all, twenty-six of the twenty-eight Japanese officers and civilians who had been designated Class A war crime suspects. Missing were Matsuoka Yosuke, who had died of tuberculosis since the war's end, and Okawa Shumei, who had been declared insane.

Chief of the Soviet Prosecution Golunsky was conferring with his assistant as Iki entered the courtroom. As soon as he caught sight of Iki, Golunsky requested permission to examine him.

A hush settled on the courtroom as an MP led Iki to the witness stand. All eyes—those of the Prosecution, the Defense, the Bench, the gallery of newsmen—were turned on Iki, the youngest and, in some respects, the most unusual witness to take the stand since the trials had begun. Dazzled by the intense lights and the impressive setting, Iki could not locate the dock in which his former superior officers would be seated. With considerable effort, he adjusted the headphones in order to listen to the interpreter.

"The witness will, according to the regulations of the court, swear that . . ." President Webb spoke in the measured phrases of Churchillian English, and his instructions were translated into Japanese through the headphones. Iki raised his right hand, as he had been taught to do, and took the customary oath such as Westerners require, to tell the truth to the best of his ability, and not to suppress or conceal any part of that sacred and inviolable truth.

Prosecutor Rosenblit conducted the examinations in behalf of the Soviet Union. "State your name please."

"Iki Tadashi."

"Your age?"

"Thirty-four."

"Your position and rank before the surrender?"

"Staff officer, First Department of the Army, Imperial General Headquarters, with rank of lieutenant colonel."

"Were you on duty in the First Department of the Army between December 1940 and February 1944?"

"Yes, I was."

"Are you now a prisoner of the Red Army?"

"Yes."

"I have the Prosecution's Japanese-language transcript of your affidavit. Is this your signature?" Rosenblit showed him the document.

"Yes, it is."

"Are all statements in this affidavit true?"

"Yes."

The Prosecutor's arrogance was distasteful, and Iki answered him as briefly as possible.

"Mr. President," Rosenblit said, "I hereby introduce as evidence the complete text of the witness's affidavit." He presented the five-page document that Iki had signed weeks before.

Webb declared that the document would be accepted as evidence, and Rosenblit pressed on: "If you have no objections, Mr. President, I should like to read the entire text."

"That would take too much time," Webb said. "Could you read only the necessary excerpts?"

"All of the affidavit is important, Your Honor. I request permission to read it in its entirety."

With Webb's grudging permission, the Prosecutor began. "I am Iki Tadashi, former lieutenant colonel of the Japanese Army. In December 1940 I was assigned to General Staff Headquarters; then, in October 1941, I was appointed to the First Department of the General Staff. I served in this department until my transfer in February 1944 to the staff of the Kwantung Army. I was recalled to the above department in April 1945. The following is the synopsis of facts known to me by virtue of my assignments during the period stated above.

"First. During the period of my service in General Staff Headquarters, my duties were in the area of general administration and included both maintaining custody of secret documents and destroying outdated documents. War plans were kept in the active file for two years, after which I destroyed them. I customarily committed the gist of the plans to memory before destroying them. Among the war plans for 1939, which I destroyed in the spring of 1941, was one designed to be activated in the event of a Soviet-Japanese war; it can be summarized as the amassing of forces in Eastern Manchuria to take the offensive against the Soviet Far East.

"Second. In October 1941, I was appointed to the Second Section, or Operations Section, of the First Department of General Staff Headquarters. During this period of assignment, my duties initially concerned troop transportation. Subsequently I participated in operational planning for the First Department, and in this capacity was acquainted with anti-Soviet war plans for the years 1941 and 1942. According to the 1941 plan, in the event of a Soviet-Japanese war the Kwantung Army was to send its main force into the Soviet Maritime Provinces, deploy units in the areas of Blagoveshchensk, Kuibyshevka, and Hailar, and commit the reserve troops to Harbin. In the first stage of the war, the Kwantung Army was scheduled to occupy the areas of Voroshilov, Vladivostok, and Iman; in the second stage, Northern Sakhalin, as well as Nikolayevsk and Komsomol'sk in the Amur River region . . ."

Rosenblit's deep voice droned on.

Throughout Iki's interrogation in Siberia, he had told the truth about his duties, as long as his statement were not damaging to Japan or the officers of the Japanese Army. He knew that clumsy lies could lead eventually to discrepancies, a more harrowing interrogation, and possibly damaging consequences for other Japanese prisoners.

". . . The war plan for 1942 called for an accelerated offensive. Approximately thirty divisions were to be assembled in Manchuria; their main strength was to be deployed in eastern Manchuria, with smaller units in the area of Sun-wu and Hailar. The plan for 1943 was identical. I do not know if the plan for war with the Soviet Union was meant to be implemented. I was a member of the First Department of General Staff Headquarters, and I was familiar with the military aspects of operational planning. I was not familiar with policies regarding the implementation of war plans."

"Defense may now cross-examine the witness." President Webb spoke as soon as Rosenblit finished the reading. During the short lull that followed, Iki looked across the courtroom, seeking the defendants and found them—two rows of Japanese prisoners seated in the raised dock. In the center of the front row sat General Tojo, in an attentive attitude, arms folded, chin drawn in. Next to Tojo was Vice Admiral Oka, former Chief of the Military Affairs Bureau of the Navy Ministry. And next to Oka was Chief-of-Staff Umezu, his gaze fixed on a point directly in front of him.

"Defense Counsel Kiyose may cross-examine the witness," said President Webb.

More floodlights were turned on, and people in the courtroom shifted their attention to Kiyose Ichiro, second-in-command for the defense, as well as personal counsel for General Tojo. Iki was struck by Kiyose's shabbiness. The small man's gray hair was lusterless, in need of trimming. He wore a pair of clumsy Japanese army boots that emphasized the threadbare condition of his ancient dark blue suit. Without question, Japan's preeminent defense attorney cut a pathetic figure; he was practically a symbol of his people, who had dared so much in war, only to be defeated so disastrously.

"Please begin, Counsel Kiyose," Webb said, and Kiyose, calm and unassuming, turned toward Iki.

"On page five of the affidavit that has just been read, you state: 'I did not know if the plan for war against the Soviet Union was meant to be implemented. I was a member of the First Department of General Staff Headquarters, and I was familiar with the military aspects of operational planning. I was not familiar with policies regarding the implementation of war plans.' Does your statement mean that the government customarily included war plans among its annual plans, even though it may not have had any intention of going to war against a particular nation?"

Iki's mind raced in an effort to understand the purpose behind Kiyose's question. "I have no knowledge of decisions made by either the cabinet or the Supreme Military Command," he replied, "However, I can say that war plans were formulated annually."

"Let me put it this way," Kiyose said. "You state that you participated in operational planning. Was the planning executed by order of the cabinet—that is, the government?"

"Operational planning was always executed by order of my superior officer. It was not directly related to the cabinet."

"Would you say, then, that the formulation of a war plan against a specific country does not constitute evidence that there was intent on the part of the government to engage that country in war?"

Kiyose apparently was trying to establish a distinction between the formulation of war plans and the intent of initiating a war of aggression.

Webb interrupted the proceedings. "Mr. Kiyose, your question is concerned with a matter outside the contents of the witness's affidavit. Furthermore, the witness's rank does not qualify him to testify on the point you have raised."

Kiyose withdrew his question and asked for information that Iki had furnished to the Soviet interrogator, only to have it deleted from his affidavit.

"You have testified regarding the plans for 1941 and 1942. Was the Kwantung Army provided with new operational plans in 1944 and 1945?"

"Yes."

"Essentially what kind of plans were they?"

"The plans for both 1944 and 1945 called for strategically defensive operations."

"Defensive operations? Now let me ask you about offensive operations. My understanding is that the term 'offensive operations' does not necessarily imply territorial aggression. It that correct?"

Kiyose based his legal maneuvers upon a wish to protect Japan from the unilateral judgment that the Allied government were attempting to inflict upon her. His fervor was transmitted to Iki, and perhaps to the Soviet Prosecution as well. Golunsky stood up, his bear-like body dwarfing Kiyose's.

"I object on the grounds that the witness is not qualified to answer the question."

"Counsel Kiyose," Webb said, "do you have a legitimate reason for asking that question?"

"Yes, I do," Kiyose replied unhesitatingly. "The witness has testified concerning war plans. I believe that we should know the precise differences between 'defensive' and 'offensive' operations in order to understand his testimony fully."

Webb gave permission to proceed.

Iki felt Golunsky's withering glare as he answered Kiyose. "In military parlance, 'offensive' and 'defensive' refer to the mode of operation. Whether or not an offensive operation is to result in territorial aggression is determined by the objectives of a war, not by the course of operational planning."

"You spoke of an increase in troop strength in Manchuria in the period after 1940. Were the added troops ever transferred elsewhere or otherwise reduced in number?"

Kiyose was referring to the Kwantung Army's "special maneuvers" that called for the immediate addition of 300,000 troops to be available for an attack on the Soviet rear following the German invasion of Russia. The Soviet Prosecution had made an issue of the special maneuvers, persisting in its attempt to prove that they had been meant to prepare for a war of aggression against the Soviet Union. Iki understood the point that Kiyose intended to emphasize: whatever the purposes of the special maneuvers might have been, they had become irrelevant when Germany collapsed. Thus, Kiyose wanted to demonstrate that in 1945 Japan had no intention of invading the Soviet Union.

"Of the troops sent to augment the Kwantung Army in the summer of 1941, a considerable part was diverted to the Pacific area after 1942," Iki replied.

"No more questions," Kiyose said, satisfied. Iki allowed his body to relax, along with his mind. He had kept both under extreme tension, knowing that his answers would affect the fate of General Umezu, who had been in command of the Kwantung Army.

Iki was told to remain on the witness stand. As he awaited further questioning, he looked at General Umezu. He had last seen the former Chief-of-Staff on the night of August 15, 1945. Umezu had ordered him to return without fail to Tokyo from his mission to Shinkyo; he had, in effect, ordered him not to take his own life. Iki had indeed returned—not as an honorable officer, but as a prisoner and as a witness for the Soviet Prosecution. He looked intently at Umezu, trying to find some meaning in his expression.

"As Counsel for Defendant Umezu, I wish to cross-examine the witness," said a young American lawyer who had been exchanging whispers with Kiyose.

"Counsel Blakeney may proceed," Webb said.

Iki had been told that the counsel for the defense included several American lawyers selected by the Allied Powers. The tall American began immediately. "Will you describe the conditions under which you are being held prisoner?"

Members of the Soviet Prosecution appeared to be startled by the question.

"In the early part of September last year, I was interned in the general-grade officers' lager in Khabarovsk, along with the Commanding General and the Chief-of-Staff of the Kwantung Army. I was later transferred to Taishet Labor Camp Eleven, and then to a villa on the outskirts of Khabarovsk."

"Where were you interrogated for the information contained in your affidavit?"

"I was interrogated at the Khabarovsk headquarters of the Soviet Ministry of Internal Affairs."

"Were you put in prison?"

"Yes, I was."

"In what prison, and for what reason?"

"I'm not certain of the reason. I was told to reconsider my false testimony, and then I was put into Khabarovsk Prison."

"Did you actually present false testimony?"

"No, I did not. My intention all along was to tell the truth."

"Was your testimony influenced by the fact of your imprisonment?"

"Mr. President!" Golunsky objected loudly. "The question is wholly irrelevant, and I ask that it be stricken from the record."

"Does Counsel have reasons for questioning the witness further regarding his interrogation in Siberia?" President Webb asked.

"No, Mr. President. If I may have the witness answer this one question, there will be no need for further questioning. Will the witness proceed, please."

"My testimony and my imprisonment are separate matters," Iki said soberly. "My concern throughout was to tell the truth."

The American picked up an English translation of Iki's affidavit, flipping open the pages. "Did you participate in operational planning in the First Department of General Staff Headquarters?"

"Yes, I did."

"Was operational planning conducted entirely by General Staff Headquarters, or did outside agencies provide assistance or suggestions?"

"I do not think agencies outside General Staff Headquarters were involved in the planning itself."

"You are saying, then, that the commanding general of the Kwantung Army was not involved in the planning of military operations against the Soviet Union. Is that correct?"

107

Iki understood at once that Blakeney's question was aimed at exonerating General Umezu.

"Precisely. Operations conducted by the commanding general of the Kwantung Army were mounted in compliance with orders received from the chief of General Staff Headquarters in Tokyo."

Iki realized, as well, that he must continue to exercise extreme caution in answering Blakeney's questions, for a misstatement would direct responsibility for the war beyond and above General Umezu to the late Marshal Sugiyama, Army Chief-of-Staff, and ultimately to His Imperial Majesty, as Grand Field Marshal of the Empire.

"In your affidavit you state that the anti-Soviet war plan for 1942 was a plan for offensive operations. May we assume that the plan was based on the military maxim, 'The best defense is a good offense'?"

"Offense is the best means of defense. That is a cardinal principle in tactical warfare," Iki replied.

"Did war plans—for example, the one designed against the Soviet Union—specify when they would be put into practice?"

"No specific dates were given for commencing operations."

"Was it anywhere stipulated in those plans that they were not to be put into effect until so ordered by Imperial General Headquarters?"

"I do not recall such a stipulation. In any event, the plans were not of a nature that they could be translated into action at the whim of commanders in the field."

"Let me return to the anti-Soviet war plan for the year 1939. Was that plan put into effect?"

A negative reply would destroy the credibility of the Soviet charge that Japan was responsible in 1939 for the clash at Nomonhan on the Manchurian-Mongolian border.

"No, it was not put into effect," Iki answered.

"Was that the case also with the 1940 plan—that it was not put into effect?"

"Anti-Soviet operational plans were purposely drawn up by General Staff Headquarters for the eventuality of an all-out war between Japan and the Soviet Union. The war between Japan and the U.S.S.R. did not begin until 1945. Therefore, no anti-Soviet war plans were put into effect until August 8, 1945, when the Soviet Union abrogated the Neutrality Pact."

Blakeney was pleased with the success of his cross-examination.

"I have one more question to ask. In preparing the annual war plans, what data did you use for estimating the resources and military strength of the Soviet Union?"

"The study of Soviet economic resources, military strength, and capabilities was the responsibility of the Second Department, which was the intelligence wing of General Staff Headquarters. I do not have detailed knowledge of their operations."

"When the First Department formulated its plans, did it not utilize data compiled by the Intelligence Section?"

"Yes, it did."

"When you were with the First Department, what was your assessment of the relative strengths of the Soviet Far East Army and the Kwantung Army of Japan?"

"The Prosecution objects," Golunsky said, rising to his feet. "That question is irrelevant and immaterial."

Webb conferred with the justices next to him and said: "I ask Counsel to restrict his questions to planning in which the witness was a direct participant. But you may ask about Japanese estimates of Soviet military strength and whether or not war plans were founded on those estimates."

Blakeney asked Iki to answer as indicated.

"I recall that General Staff Headquarters' estimate of Soviet ground forces in the Far East in 1942 was in the neighborhood of twenty-five divisions."

"What was the strength of the Kwantung Army that year?"

"As I recall, we had fifteen divisions in Manchuria in the Kwantung Army command."

"Would it be correct to say that the ratio of twenty-five to fifteen remained constant after 1942?"

"In making a study of comparative strengths," Iki answered, "we were required to evaluate and compare air strength and ground strength, as well as geographical conditions, the effectiveness of the lines of communication, and a considerable number of other factors. Since I do not recall all that information, I cannot comment precisely on the ratio of over-all military strength."

"But is it not true that the strength of the Japanese Army was less than your own intelligence section's estimate of Soviet Army strength at the time you were with General Staff Headquarters?"

Blakeney's question put Iki in a quandary. Locked away in his mind was secret information which he had learned in his capacity as a staff officer of Imperial General Headquarters, but which he

109

could not reveal without being charged with treason. "Are you referring to troop count?" he asked, stalling for time.

"Troop count would be a significant item. Give me any comparative figures you can remember."

Iki squirmed. "I just can't remember . . . I cannot answer the question," he replied at last.

"No more questions," Blakeney said, and sat down.

"Well, then, Witness Iki . . ." Webb started to excuse him from the stand.

"Mr. President!" Chief Counsel Keenan called out.

"Please proceed, Mr. Keenan," Webb said.

This Keenan was not the nondescript middle-aged lawyer who had come to the house in Kioi-cho to meet Iki and Takemura. Today he was magisterial.

"I have a request to make on behalf of the Prosecution. The witness is a prisoner of war in the Soviet Union. He is under the jurisdiction of the government of the Soviet Union. However, I ask that he be kept available for the time being, so that he may be called upon again to serve as a witness for the Prosecution. I am entering this request because I have been told that he is sought for an appearance at a separate trial now in progress in the Soviet Union, and that the Soviet authorities plan to send him back immediately upon the conclusion of today's proceedings."

Iki could not believe what he'd heard. What could this mean—his presence sought at another trial taking place in the Soviet Union?

"Mr. President," Kiyose said, rising to his feet. "The Defense also requests that witness Iki be kept available for further testimony."

"The Defense will be permitted to summon this witness whenever it wishes. The witness may be excused."

The MP escorted Iki back to the waiting room. Iki, upset by Keenan's revelation, did not hear what General Takemura said to him as he went past, on his way to the witness stand.

Lights in the Kioi-cho house burned into the late hours that night; the usually quiet neighborhood rang with shouts and laughter as Yazef and his Russian colleagues celebrated their release from the worrisome responsibility of preparing their Japanese charges for appearing in the courtroom. After dinner they continued drinking, and their noisy merriment sounded once more in the streets.

But on the upper floor, where Iki and Takemura faced each other across their small dining table, the mood was one of deep dejection. Iki sat, wordless, toying with his food, sickened by humiliation and bitterness at being forced to testify. Although in the morning Takemura had masked his feelings with an air of indifference, by evening he'd become as morose as Iki. Since leaving the court at Ichigaya Heights, he had not said a word. He had secluded himself in his room, and now he sat slumped over half a bowl of cold soup, unable to touch the rest of the meal.

From below came the stamping of feet and the strains of a spirited Russian folksong sung by Yazef, a baritone who prided himself on his repertory.

Iki decided to end the brooding. "Sir, if you're not feeling well, I can have the table cleared."

"Let's leave it until they come to clear things away." Takemura straightened up. "Iki, did you have to testify on matters not mentioned in your affidavit?"

"I was afraid they would make me do so, but fortunately that didn't happen. And you?"

"The same, fortunately. I was half expecting the Russians to go back on their word and demand testimony that would be damaging to Japan. But, after all, the trial is being conducted jointly by eleven nations. And there's so much friction between the U.S. and the Soviet Union that the Russians seem to be inhibited, and very cautious."

Because Takemura had been chief of the Russian section of Japanese Army Intelligence before being assigned to the Kwantung Army, Iki was curious about how he fared under cross-examination.

"You probably had a difficult time because of your previous involvement with anti-Soviet intelligence," he began. "I was questioned primarily about operational planning at General Staff Headquarters—whether it was an annual affair and whether or not the Japanese government had any intention of engaging Russia in war."

"With me the Soviet Prosecution dwelt on two issues," Takemura said. "One concerned the time I was chief of the Russian section. I used to pass on information about Russia to the military attaché of the German Embassy in Tokyo. The other concerned our having used our military attaché in Moscow to gather intelligence on the Soviet Union. They tried to say that my actions constituted spying, and were in violation of conditions stipulated in the Japan-Soviet Neutrality Agreement. They know as well as we do that nothing's wrong about exchanging intelligence. Everyone knows that gathering intelligence is a primary function of all military attachés stationed in all foreign countries. Japan wasn't the only one. It's being done right now among the eleven Allied nations of the Prosecution. The Defense cross-examined me to show that the Soviet Prosecution was taking exception to accepted international practice. All I did was sit there and agree with the examiner. That silly Golunsky kept glaring at me!" Takemura managed a chuckle.

He was back in character again, holding up to mockery even an adversary as formidable as Golunsky. Iki recalled how he himself had all but frozen under Golunsky's cold stare.

"Did Dr. Kiyose cross-examine you?" Iki asked.

"Yes, he did. Mostly about Japan's relationship with the Soviet Union. I read an article about Kiyose in some newspaper the other day. He lost his downtown office in a big air raid, so he moved into a burned-out school dormitory farther out. He walks from there to Ichigaya. —Quite a distance. That explains the army boots, I guess.— You've got to admire him—at his age, standing up to all those justices of the Allied Powers. I felt myself cleansed by seeing a Japanese like him, with such a strong sense of mission and wholly devoted to his defeated country."

"He impressed me, too. But I was a little worried during the cross-examination. I was afraid he might call attention to the obvious slant of my testimony, and then ask me questions that would force me to talk about Soviet injustices. You know what the consequences of that would be, to our men in Siberia. He was taking me in that direction, but stopped just in time. I'm not so sure about the American counsel Blakeney, though, the way he applied pressure . . ."

"Dr. Kiyose is sensitive to our position," Takemura said. "I realized that quite soon, when he was questioning me about events after the Kwantung Army Special Maneuvers. He was careful not to lead us into making statements that would be pointedly damaging to the Soviet Union. He knows what the Russians would do to us when we get back to Siberia. I'm sure that's why he didn't push us for more."

"I wasn't aware of that," Iki said, grateful again for the kind of consideration that could come only from a countryman.

"I must admit, Iki, how miserable I felt, being put on the witness stand. I thought I'd become used to their humiliations after the surrender, and after living in one of those lagers. But this experience today was the worst—seeing my superior officers lined up as defendants in a criminal trial. Some of them were very close to me." He shook his head, sighing. "There was a time when the victors simply killed the defeated generals, made slaves of the conquered troops, and took the women and the loot for themselves. That was crude, but it was honest—compared with the way men torture captives today, under the pretext of giving them a legal trial."

"What kind of sentence do you think our generals will receive?"

"Hanging for most of them, I suppose, or life imprisonment, at best," Takemura said dully.

The pounding of big feet on the stairs interrupted them. The door was thrown open and Major Yazef staggered in, his face flushed, his breath smelling of vodka. "It's all over, gentlemen, so why are you so glum?" Drink made Yazef even more difficult to understand. "I just got word from the Soviet Mission that your departure might be delayed. But you're to be prepared to leave at any moment."

Seeing Iki and Takemura exchange glances, Yazef resorted to a bully's teasing. "You two seem worried that your friends in Siberia will accuse you of selling out to your country. If you do what we tell you to do, we'll take care of you. We'll see that you're protected when you get back."

Offended by Yazef's insinuations, the two said nothing.

"You won't be spending many more nights in Japan," Yazef said, thoughtlessly. "I've brought you some saké. Drink up! Forget your worries, and have a good night's sleep." He deposited a large bottle on the dining table and lurched out the door.

"General, I'll be going back to my room," Iki said. When the corridor was clear he bowed and left. Back in his own room, he dropped wearily into a chair, and picked up the folded-paper doll his children had brought to him. Soon he would be leaving Japan. His wife and children had come to this very house. And yet he

113

would leave for Siberia without having spoken to them, embraced them. He was shaken by a desperate wish for just one more glimpse of them. And instantly he felt shame for his weakness.

Another week went by, and still they sat in the house in Kioi-cho.

One gloomy morning a fine rain spattered against the window panes, and the first chill of autumn penetrated their rooms. Iki put on his new uniform. Having only a few toilet articles and some underwear to take with him, he was ready to go at a moment's notice. Although Yazef had told him to keep the blue serge suit that was tailored for him, he had refused to accept the thing. He detested the suit; it was nothing more than another kind of uniform, issued by the Soviet government, to be worn during his appearance as a witness for the Soviet Prosecution. He had asked if he might, instead, keep some of the Japanese newspapers he had been allowed to read while in Tokyo, but Yazef rejected his request, giving the excuse that doing so was against the Ministry of Internal Affairs regulations. On this stormy day Iki carefully read once again the morning paper, because it might well be the last printed Japanese he would see for a long while.

"Purging of Public Officials" declared the front-page banner-line. Of 7,945 men investigated, 899 were to be removed from office. This figure did not include former professional military men, who were automatically debarred from employment in any government office. In Japan's postwar society, military officers made up a caste of helpless rejects, excluded even from the lowest level of civil service.

When the knock sounded on his door he put down the paper, reached for his personal effects, and prepared to leave. But the guard informed him that a Japanese visitor was asking to meet him and Takemura. The guard escorted them to the living room, where Major Yazef and his interpreter waited. A Japanese woman, somewhat past middle age, and dressed in a formal black kimono, sat on a sofa beside a coffee table.

"This is Mrs. Akitsu," Yazef said, genuinely polite for once. "We arranged this meeting because she wished to talk to you about General Akitsu. We can allow you thirty minutes." He would not leave the room, of course, but he did withdraw to a chair near the window.

Both Iki and Takemura were deeply touched. Each had hidden

114

his sorrow over General Akitsu's suicide, and had not even talked about it. They bowed solemnly to the widow, whom they had not met before. They had heard that General Akitsu sent her and their daughter back to Japan from Manchuria in 1944.

Mrs. Akitsu stood, and bowed formally to each in turn. "I'm sure my husband troubled you from time to time when he was alive," she said softly. "I wish to thank you. Now that I have conducted the forty-ninth-day memorial service, the time has come, I think, to see you both. I'm sure my husband would have wanted to bring us together . . ."

She had walked to the house in the rain, and droplets of water still glistened in her black hair. Her eyes, set in a pale, drawn face, were dry and sad, as if all tears had been shed. She spoke clearly, with the self-control to be expected of an officer's wife.

"How did you find out where we were?" General Takemura asked. Their appearance at the Tribunal during the week before had not been reported in the papers.

"I was notified of my husband's death last month and told to go to the Soviet Mission for his ashes. I thought he had died in a prison camp in Siberia. But when I received his ashes, I was told that he had committed suicide the day after he was brought back to Japan and that his body was cremated after an autopsy. I overheard two men talking about other Japanese who had come back with him. I asked for their names, but they seemed to think they shouldn't tell me. I went back a number of times, because I wanted to learn whatever I could about the circumstances of my husband's death."

Although she spoke calmly, her thin, white hands, placed properly on her lap, were trembling.

"I'm glad you came," Takemura said. "The truth is, we're about to be flown back to Siberia—this afternoon, I believe. I'm sure it was the will of His Excellency, General Akitsu, that brought us together."

"Can you tell me how he died? . . . Was it a soldier's death?"

"We dined with the General the night before he died. His manner was no different from usual. In fact, he was the one who expressed concern for us, and sent us off to bed early, saying how tired we must be. I should have been more sensitive. I blame myself."

"You're not at all to blame. The people at the Soviet Mission said he took cyanide. Is that true?"

"Yes, according to the people who performed the autopsy."

"Where did my husband get the poison?"

"He must have obtained it from the chief medical officer in Shinkyo when the war ended. The Russians checked us quite thoroughly a number of times—our bodies, our clothing, all our possessions. How the General could have kept it concealed is a mystery. But he did, and I can only believe that he intended all along to take his life."

As she listened, her shoulders shook, and tears fell down her pale cheeks. Iki's own eyes filled with tears as he thought of the late general, who had arranged his lonely end like a true samurai. Akitsu had suffered, caught in a web of complications which, after long and painful reflection, had locked him into the precise place and moment of his death. He chose to wait until he returned to Japan. For only then, at that time and in this place, the suicide of the ranking officer among the three Japanese witnesses for the Soviet Prosecution must be regarded as a protest against the falseness by which the victors of a war prosecuted the vanquished, not on an execution ground but in a court of law. General Akitsu's suicide could well have been the reason that the Prosecution's lawyers did not attempt to extract additional testimony from Iki and Takemura. Iki felt that for him to have survived and to be alive in the presence of Mrs. Akitsu was wrong, another injustice dealt by fate.

Yazef came forward from his observation post. "Your thirty minutes are up." he whispered.

"Please," Mrs. Akitsu turned in desperation to Iki. "Didn't my husband leave a token of remembrance?"

"I'm sorry," Iki said. "He seemed no different from usual, and it never occurred to us that we might not see him again. General Takemura and I were in separate rooms, and were not even allowed to pay our last respects . . ."

"Just a minute," Takemura said, searching through his pockets. "Before saying good night, the General gave me a pack of cigarettes. I put it in a pocket of my uniform and—because I seldom wore my jacket since—forgot about them. The General liked to smoke, and at the time I wondered why he should take just one cigarette and give me the rest of the pack. Now that I think back, he must have meant for it to be a remembrance."

Mrs. Akitsu looked sorrowfully at the pack that Takemura laid on the table before her. She held it for a moment, as if to feel the

116

warmth of her husband's body. Then she wrapped it carefully in a white handkerchief, and placed the precious packet in the sleeve of her kimono.

She rose reluctantly when Yazef, this time in full baritone, reminded everyone that they'd already spent five minutes more than the rules permitted.

"And is your family well, General Takemura?" she asked, while moving toward the door.

"The truth is, their whereabouts are still unknown."

"I'm sure Mrs. Takemura will bring your children back safely. Please take good care of yourselves . . . for the sake of your families."

Takemura and Iki accompanied her to the front door. Erect, grieving but unbroken, Mrs. Akitsu walked out into the slanting rain. She turned around once, bowed in their direction, and vanished beyond the gate.

The wind and the rain continued into the afternoon. Their departure, they were told, would be postponed. Later, however, the winds subsided and, although five o'clock had already passed, Yazef rushed them out to Haneda Airport. Iki and Takemura half suspected that the Russians feared that a postponement of their flight might result in their being summoned to testify in behalf of the Defense. Promises and assurances, even when given to the Tribunal, meant nothing to the Ministry of Internal Affairs.

Soon they were airborne. The bright sea, the moss-colored mountains, and the curling rivers they had seen as they flew in from Khabarovsk were hidden in darkness. They saw only the few scattered twinkling lights of places in their homeland where life went on, despite the destruction of war. Iki was very conscious of the empty seat beside him, a reminder of General Akitsu's death. It was also a reminder of the utter uselessness of his appearance at the Tribunal.

Once, in the dark void below, he saw a single spark of light, perhaps from a fishing boat far off the Noto coast. The light disappeared almost as soon as his eyes had found it, but he kept his forehead pressed against the window, searching for some further sign of home. This might be his last farewell.

As they flew beyond the edge of the Japan Sea, the PBY's pilot increased its altitude and set course for Khabarovsk.

6

TURBID CURRENTS

Once more spring came to Khabarovsk, the third since the Pacific War ended. A year and a half had passed since Iki Tadashi's return from Japan after his appearance before the Tribunal in Tokyo. He and General Takemura were sent to the same suburban dacha in which they had been housed before going to Tokyo. This time, too, they lived under constant surveillance—being kept "available," they were told, for a possible second summons to the Tribunal in Tokyo. For Iki the enforced idleness was unusually punishing.

One day guards took General Takemura away. With that change in attitude on the part of the Russians, Iki knew his turn would soon come. And it did, without any preliminary indications in the dacha. One afternoon a guard came into Iki's room, saying, "Get your things and follow me! Quickly!"

The speeding jeep bearing Iki and a pair of guards crossed the long bridge over the Amur River, its usual placid flow transformed into a roaring, muddy torrent by the spring thaw. Soon they entered the city of Khabarovsk.

Many new brick buildings lined the streets. People on the sidewalks were dressed far better than he remembered seeing them during the last time he had been driven through Khabarovsk. The Soviet Union appeared to be recovering with astonishing speed from the economic devastation of the war with Germany. Iki thought about the 700,000 men of the Kwantung Army. What changes, he wondered, had they undergone in the past year and a half?

Six miles beyond the city the jeep arrived at the Khabarovsk prison camp, a typical rectangular compound enclosed by double lines of barbed-wire fences. Guard towers rose at each corner. The guards took Iki inside the main building and turned him over to the lager's officials. A Russian officer made a rapid check of his few possessions.

"Everything's in order," he said. "That man will take you to your barracks and tell you what you're to do." He pointed to a short, plump Japanese about forty years old, still wearing the uniform that identified him as an enlisted man.

"Comrade Yasuda, this is Iki. Get him processed."

Yasuda smiled obsequiously at the Russian officer while bending in a way that was part bow and part cringe. "I'll take him to headquarters immediately," he said; then, to Iki's astonishment, he declared, "I'm grateful for the protection of the Soviet Union!"

The moment they were outside the building, Yasuda moved aside and looked Iki up and down contemptuously.

"What's the idea of—" Iki said, annoyed by such impertinence. But Yasuda cut him short.

"You'd better watch your language when you talk to me. I'm Yasuda Tokichiro of the Democratic Committee. Remember that. Now come along!"

Iki was baffled by Yasuda's needless arrogance, and even more so by his cant. Why would a Japanese prisoner say anything so ridiculous as "I'm grateful for the protection of the Soviet Union?" And in a place like this! Why would an enlisted man address a superior officer with such impudence? And in such a shared captivity as this? What was the significance of the Democratic Committee in this camp for prisoners of war?

Judging from the appearance of the Khabarovsk camp—six barracks, a dispensary, a mess hall, and supporting facilities, all concentrated on about two and a half acres—it held between seven and eight hundred prisoners. Most of the inmates must have been out on work detail, for the compound looked deserted.

Above the door of the barrack they entered hung a conspicuous sign: "Democratic Headquarters." Yasuda led Iki into a crudely partitioned office. The wall facing the entrance was dominated by badly painted portraits of Lenin and Stalin. Numerous posters, inscribed amateurishly with red ink in Japanese characters, were pasted on the other walls in random fashion, proclaiming the usual messages:

"Long live the Soviet Union, Bastion of World Peace!"

"Win the Production War before May Day!"

"Destroy the Emperor System! Build a Democratic Japan!"

"The Emperor is a Doorman for Western Imperialism!"

Iki was especially offended by a cartoon depicting the Emperor attended by a tail-wagging dog wearing the insignia and sword of a Japanese Army general.

"Hey! Don't just stand there with your head in a bucket," Yasuda bawled. "Sit down in that chair." Iki obeyed, seething inwardly. Yasuda settled behind a desk, and glanced occasionally at him over the rims of his glasses as he pretended to read through a set of papers.

"We ordinarily ask a newcomer his name, rank, outfit, what he's been doing since the war ended, and so forth and so on. In your case, we already have all that information. You're Iki Tadashi, former lieutenant colonel. This says here that you were a staff officer in Imperial General Headquarters at the start of the war, chief Operations officer of the Kwantung Army, then recalled to Imperial General Headquarters to assist in planning the last homeground battle on Japanese soil. Well! How impressive. A key man of the Japanese military, I'd say."

Iki did not bother to reply.

"Don't act so big!" Yasuda shouted. Infuriated by his insolence, Iki looked at Yasuda, as only an officer can blast an enlisted man with a glance. Yasuda flinched, then giggled foolishly to cover his uneasiness.

"The political officer has told me about you," Yasuda blustered. "You don't seem to know anything about our democratic activities in these new times. That explains why you think you're still such a big man. You'd better learn, right now, that this camp is no longer run by officers of the Japanese Army. We of the Democratic Committee run it. That's the first thing to get into your hard head. The same thing is true in all prison camps. Your old military system has been abolished, and we live and work democratically, on the basis of equality. Each according to his deserts. We now bask in the joy of labor—all thanks to the great Soviet Union and our comrade Stalin!"

Yasuda was caught up in the excitement of his delusions. Every word he spoke confounded Iki, reminding him of the incredible articles he had read in a Japanese tabloid while he was living in the dacha outside Khabarovsk. He could not believe that the *Nip-*

pon Daily was the work of Japanese minds or hands. He had dismissed it as Soviet propaganda, shrill and unsubtle, but now he was hearing from Yasuda exactly what he had read in that newspaper. Yasuda was pushing him into a world that, once upon a time, he had refused to believe existed.

Yasuda observed Iki's reaction with the kind of superior air that an inept teacher accords a stupid child. "I can see you're surprised," he said, with a sly smile. "Being the reactionary you are, I'm surprised you were able to denounce the Emperor and Tojo."

"What do you mean?"

"Forget it. We all know about you. No sense in trying to cover it up."

Hiding the alarm he felt, Iki hated the sight of this pompous Yasuda enjoying himself. "What is it you're trying to tell me? Stop talking in riddles and come straight to the point."

"Still trying to cover it up? Then let me remind you, Mr. Staff Officer of Imperial General Headquarters. Year before last, you and the deputy chief-of-staff appeared at the Tokyo trials as witnesses for the Soviet Union, and you exposed every crime ever committed by Tojo, the top Army command, and the staff of the Kwantung Army. That's known all over Khabarovsk."

"What kind of nonsense is that?" Iki retorted, stunned. "Of course I appeared at the Far East Tribunal. But whatever else you've just said is a complete contradiction of the facts."

Yasuda tossed a hand, curled his lips in an elaborate sneer, dismissing anything Iki might say. "Everything about it was reported in our Nippon Daily. I can understand that you might not have meant everything you said, and I don't blame you for saying things on the spur of the moment to protect yourself. But we see no sense in making excuses now that it's all over. As far as we of the Democratic Committee are concerned, the past is past. So long as you're willing to join us, we'll be willing to welcome you as a true comrade who's overcome the old militaristic ideology. Think about that."

Iki, unable to bear any more of Yasuda's distortion of truth, leaped up from his chair and headed for the fresh air outside.

"Wait, you!" Yasuda shouted, menacing, now, where earlier he had been merely insinuating. "I didn't say you have to make up your mind right now." He opened the window to let in the sound of men singing in the distance. "Hear that? One of our work units is coming home. Take a good look. And listen to 'em, too. You'll see how we've changed."

The chorus of voices came nearer. Beyond the barbed-wire fences Iki saw Japanese prisoners, five abreast, marching toward the enclosure with a red banner held high in the lead.

The gates were opened, and the "International" rose to its climax as the column came to a halt. While a head count was taken and the roll was called, the red flag, still held high, fluttered against the darkening sky. Finally, the two hundred men broke formation and moved into an open space facing the Democratic Headquarters, in which Iki stood, observing them. They sat down on the cold ground, in a circle, hunched over, resembling an army of snails. A young soldier sprang into the center of the ring.

"Now we'll review our operation for today!" he shouted in a rough voice that reached everyone in the compound. "Those guilty of sabotage, step forward!"

No one moved, no one made a sound.

"You're being given the opportunity for self-criticism. If you don't come forth on your own, we'll find you and put you on trial. Who sabotaged our efforts today? Those who know, raise your hands!"

A number of hands shot up, as in a classroom, and several names were called out.

"Come forward!" the young fellow in the center of the ring ordered the prisoner whose name had caught his attention. An emaciated man, well into his fifties, was shoved into the circle.

"Give your name, former rank, and former title!" the leader barked at the helpless man, who was old enough to be his father.

"Kagawa Tsunehisa, colonel, formerly commander of Unit 7994 of the Kwantung Army."

"So you were a unit commander! Comrades! This Kagawa is a well-known reactionary. When we first came to Russia, he took advantage of his position as barracks chief to keep his men from following the orders of the Soviet Union. He claimed the men in his barracks were tired and weak, and then he had the nerve to stand by while men from other barracks took up the slack. Let's give him a lesson!"

"No objection!" the mob roared. Several young men, wearing

arm bands denoting their membership in the Youth Brigade, surrounded the colonel.

"Kagawa laughed on the job," one of them said. "He's not serious about working for the fatherland of us laborers and farmers. Whatever he claims as his work credit for the day should be reduced twenty percent!"

"No objection!" the crowd yelled.

"This shirker went to the latrine three times during the work period. He's deliberately slowing down the construction project. That's an act of sabotage against the Soviet Union. Reduce his credit another twenty percent!"

"Even more," another said. "Kagawa has been an enemy of us in the Youth Brigade. We've been giving all our energies toward increasing our quota, but he's deliberately refused to cooperate with us. His work credit should be reduced another ten percent— fifty percent in all!"

When the accusers stopped, the leader added his opinion to the attack. "With May Day coming, we should be striving for even higher quotas to speed our building of the fatherland. But this reactionary has sabotaged our efforts.—Now, you! Stand up and criticize yourself!"

Colonel Kagawa, his lips closed in a tight line, remained silent.

"Why don't you answer? You have a mouth, don't you? Are you making fun of us? Do you think what we've been saying is funny?" Working himself into a frenzy, the leader struck Kagawa on the shoulder. The colonel reeled.

"I had diarrhea," he mumbled. "I had to go to the latrine three times during the work period."

"Murderer!" the leader shrieked. "How many of our comrades did you help to murder when you were a commander? Can you even remember? You saved your own skin, and now you have the nerve to use that flimsy excuse for sabotage. An ultra-reactionary like you ought to be worked to death." He swung his fist at Kagawa.

"That's right!" another soldier yelled. "He's the pawn of imperialism! Don't let him get back to Japan alive!"

"Make fertilizer out of him!"

Amid a frenzy of shouts, screeches, and jeers, every man in the group rose to his feet. Like savages, the mob formed a tight circle about Kagawa, taunting him with gestures and threats. Gradually the circle contracted, like a closing sphincter, and Kagawa, at the center of the whorl, was spun round and round by the crush of bodies.

Iki was horrified by the brutality of those young activists. In two years the Russians had succeeded completely in transforming the character of their captives.

Yasuda wasted no time. "Well, Iki, what's your impression of our corrective demonstration?"

"Corrective demonstration? That wasn't a demonstration. It was more like a mass murder."

"What you saw was mild. When they deal with a real rotten reactionary, they squeeze in around him until he's lifted up in the air, and then they drop him. Hard. When the reactionary hits the ground, he wakes up enlightened. That's what they did the other day to a fascist named Tanikawa, a colonel who used to be information officer for the Kwantung Army. I heard that his enlightenment left him with a few broken ribs . . . Too bad."

Yasuda cackled, showing purple gums above yellow teeth. Iki shuddered. Tanikawa was the companion who had told him long ago, in a field where they harvested potatoes: "Whatever happens, live on. Your mission is to live on and become a witness to history." That advice had given him the strength to endure the shame he felt over having survived a lost war. He had not seen Colonel Tanikawa since leaving the lager on the bank of the Ussuri River two and a half years before. And he was deeply troubled at learning that Tanikawa, more than fifty years old now, should have been removed from the lager for high-ranking officers and thrown among this collection of madmen.

"Is Colonel Tanikawa still here?"

"I sent him off to the forestry camp in Komsomol'sk. And that's just a starter for such a devil. He kept us all fooled with his lies, right up to the end of the war. We'll have him dragged through every lager in Siberia. That's only what he deserves. As for you, you'd better report now to your barrack. You start work tomorrow."

Yasuda told one of the young soldiers who had just come in to escort Iki to barrack number three, next to headquarters building. Once again Iki was sickened by the foul air of the barrack. The stench of unwashed bodies and sweaty clothes was even stronger when he sat down on a lower bunk that someone assigned to him.

"Hello—My name is Iki," he said to the young soldier lying in the bunk to his left.

"My . . . my name is Hosono . . ." the slight, timid-looking soldier answered uncomfortably, his eyes avoiding Iki's.

The soldier lying in the bunk to his right, pretending not to hear when Iki addressed him, opened a book entitled *A Short History of the Soviet Communist Party.* The others around him also ignored Iki, refusing to acknowledge his salutations. But Iki noticed their curious glances when he took his few possessions out of the cloth sack in which he carried them. At last he lay down on his bunk wrapped in the single threadbare blanket that had been issued to him.

Coal oil lanterns were turned off at the prescribed time. Except for the dim rays of lights outside that entered through the filthy window panes, the barrack was dark. Iki lay awake, still tense, unable to think about anything except the experiences of the day. He was among his own countrymen, but they treated him as if he were an alien, an enemy. He thought of Tanikawa's refusal to compromise his principles as an army officer, even though refusing had cost him painful injury. His heart ached for Tanikawa, aged and abused, and without a friend to comfort him.

"Iki—" someone said softly. Startled, he looked up and saw the dark bulk of a man beckoning to him.

"Who are you?"

The dark figure waited, making certain that the men nearby slept before he came close.

"Mizushima—of Headquarters," he whispered into Iki's ear.

"Major Mizushima?"

Iki trained his eyes on the man. In the dimness Iki saw a lean face. He recognized Mizushima, youngest of the staff officers. He was only twenty-eight years old when, at the last meeting of the Kwantung Army staff on August 16, 1945, he spoke up vehemently for a fight to the finish. He had been a strikingly handsome young man, but here, in Khabarovsk camp, Iki would not have recognized him.

"Don't make any noise," Mizushima said. "The Democratic group is always listening and watching. Go out to the latrine. Lieutenant Colonel Kamimori will be there, too."

Mizushima moved away quietly. Iki waited a few minutes, then slipped out of the barrack. The temperature outside was below freezing, and his breath turned white as he walked toward the latrine, about a hundred yards toward the back of the lager. As he approached the latrine, two men came out of it and motioned him toward a narrow path. He followed them at a discreet distance, until they disappeared inside a warehouse.

He followed them into the warehouse. Mizushima quickly shut the door. Beside him stood Lieutenant Colonel Kamimori Kenji, who had been Iki's classmate at both the Army Academy and the War College. Kamimori, a year older than Iki, had been Operations officer of the Third Army when the war ended. He was as gaunt as Mizushima, but his eyes gleamed fiercely under thick brows.

"Kamimori! You're well," Iki said, grasping his hand.

"Where in hell have you been all this time," Kamimori growled. He had noticed Iki's uniform, rumpled but clean; his own was worn and shiny with accumulated grime. And he was irritated by Iki's healthy complexion, which gave no sign that he had known hard labor. Quick tempered as ever, Kamimori had leaped to the conclusion that Iki must have been excepted from prison labor for some very special reason. Iki explained, with more than a hint of apology, why he and General Takemura had been confined for a year and a half in a dacha in a resort area near Khabarovsk.

"In some ways, you had a rougher time than those of us here," Mizushima said sympathetically. But Kamimori, known for his stern insistence upon integrity, continued to look at Iki as if he had done something wrong in order to gain special favors.

Iki could not resent Kamimori's suspicions. "Please tell me," he changed the subject. "Was Colonel Tanikawa here until a month ago? I heard this from a man named Yasuda, who said he's with the Democratic Committee."

"That's true," Kamimori said. "They picked on him continually for having been Information officer of the Kwantung Army. Even during meals they'd taunt him with remarks like 'How dare you eat food provided by Stalin!' But Colonel Tanikawa neither made concessions nor allowed himself to be baited. He never played into their hands. I suppose you could call it passive resistance."

"I wonder how he is? Yasuda told me that several of his ribs were broken."

"That would never have happened if we'd been here," Kamimori said angrily. "Mizushima and I were serving out a hard labor sentence, in a quarry miles from here, and we learned about his injury only when we got back. Colonel Tanikawa is a stoic. But when we went to see him at the dispensary, he was bathed in sweat, fighting the pain. Three days later he was gone. They told us he'd been transferred to another lager. But how can we be sure?"

Boots treading upon the pavement outside interrupted them. The two pulled Iki down behind bales of hay near the door. The footsteps stopped in front of the warehouse. A guard opened the door, swung the beam of his flashlight once around the inside, shut the door, and was on his way. Sighing with relief, the three sat down to talk. After this Kamimori relaxed.

"How could the Russians have brainwashed our men so completely in so short a time?" Iki wanted to know.

"They've used a very clever strategy," Kamimori said. "For a year they told us to maintain our usual military organization. They gave preferential treatment to officers. Only officers were assigned as barracks chiefs and appointed to the negotiating team that represented prisoners. That, they knew, would be the way to get the most work out of our enlisted men. The soldiers were kept in a state of extreme fatigue and near starvation. That's when the Russian political officers went to work on them, blaming us, their officers, for having led them into an unjust war—and an unsuccessful war, at that, which landed them in prison camps. Once they got anti-military sentiment kindled among the troops, they launched their 'Siberian democratic movement.' "

"They did that in easy stages." Mizushima supplied some of the details. "First, a 'friendship association' was formed, with the backing of the political officer. The men spent their leisure time together, composing haiku and making wall posters. In time, the posters included articles criticizing our Imperial Japanese Army. The political officer located former Communist Party members among the prisoners and helped them to publish the *Nippon Daily*. No one took the paper seriously at first, because it carried so many articles supporting communism and advocating the abolition of the Emperor system. But the men were starved for news—for that matter, for anything printed in Japanese. They kept reading the same slanted articles over and over again, and eventually they started to believe what they read. Finally, Party members cooperated with the political officer to organize the Democratic Committee. That committee now runs the camp. We haven't reached the end, yet—"

"Who is this Yasuda Tokichiro I met today?"

"He's a lackey of the Soviets. When we first got here, he sidled up to Colonel Kagawa, his barracks chief. Yasuda served him as a personal orderly and often was given leftovers from the officers' mess. When the enlisted men began to criticize the officers in secret, Yasuda was the first turncoat. He went to the Russians' political officer and denounced Colonel Kagawa for 'harboring anti-Soviet tendencies.' As a result, Kagawa was relieved as barracks chief, and Yasuda was sent to a training school for activists in Khabarovsk. When he got back, he made quite a record for himself, urging the men to denounce one officer after another. That's how he got appointed to the Democratic Committee."

Iki thought how well suited to the role of betrayer was the contemptible Yasuda, a man who could not even speak anymore without revealing how rotten he'd become.

"We'd better get back to the barracks." Mizushima warned. "We've been here for nearly half an hour."

Kaminori stood up, looking hard at Iki. "I want to tell you something. How you go about taking care of yourself in this camp is your business. But you'd better not betray us."

Iki flared up. "That's an insult! What exactly do you mean by that?"

"Don't play the innocent with us. You appeared at the Tokyo Tribunal as a witness for the Russians, and testified for them. I was disgusted by your performance—even if you were hired to do it."

"You believe that, Kamimori?" He lunged at Kamimori, ready to hit him.

"Wait, Iki, wait," Mizushima said, holding him back. "That's what we read in the *Nippon Daily*. The same article that also said that the Russians made arrangements for you to see your family."

"Yes, my family did come to see me. But I didn't see them."

They met Iki's denial with disbelief. Only he and Takemura could fully understand the shame of being taken back to Japan, humbled under foreign rulers, and of being forced to testify at a trial of their former superiors, all accused as war criminals. He had resolutely cut himself off from his own flesh and blood, fearing that if he saw them, he might fail to live up to his obligations as a loyal Japanese and as a loyal officer of the Japanese Army. Suicide would have been easier than appearing before the tribunal. Only now did he realize the irony in his present situation —where he was looked upon with damning suspicion by his former colleagues, and treated with contemptuous familiarity by members of the Democratic Committee.

At six o'clock the next morning the prisoners slid from their bunks as the compound reverberated to the jarring clamor of an iron rod striking a steel rail.

Iki had slept very little but, of course, got up with the others, saying "Good morning" to Hosono. Although he avoided looking at Iki, Hosono managed to mumble "Good morning." Iki's other neighbor had already gone outside.

"Hey, you!" The ugly challenge rang throughout the barrack. "Still dreaming about the days when you were still a colonel? Quit stalling! Get up and get to work!"

The victim was Colonel Kagawa, who had been painfully beaten the evening before. He was having much trouble lifting himself out of his bunk. A middle-aged soldier from the next bunk reached out to help him, but was immediately rebuked for his kindness.

"If you have time to help a reactionary, you should spend it on memorizing the *Short History of the Soviet Communist Party*. Or have you already memorized the book?"

"Well, no . . . What I mean to say is . . . I made a mistake in trying to help a reactionary." He scurried away as though guilty of being caught in a shameful deed.

After the roll call the men spent the interval before the morning meal in study groups of twenty, learning songs of the revolution. The call to assemble for work sounded at eight o'clock, immediately after a breakfast of thin gruel and weak tea. They fell into marching formation, five abreast, and moved out at the command of Soviet guards.

The young activists carried their red banners high, shouting support of the fatherland. "Work hard for the Soviet Union!" they bawled. "Let's finish the five-year plan in four years!"

All the other prisoners parroted the slogans. As he moved along with his barrack mates, Iki reflected on the spiritual weakness of people who are cut off from their homeland and therefore from national ties. Japanese people are not endowed with a strong sense of individuality or of self-reliance, he told himself, and so they tend to fall in easily with the crowd. Here, too, the strong impose themselves upon the weak, and the weak are too timid to protest their transgressions. Even so, as matters are going now, both the strong and the weak are yielding too easily to the pull that is drawing them into the vortex of "Siberian democracy." What, he wondered, has happened to our renowned Japanese fortitude? To our patience and honesty?

The prisoners marched three miles to a construction site near the outskirts of Khabarovsk. Four brick apartment buildings to house Soviet workers were being erected on a slightly elevated plot about three acres in extent. Work on each unit had progressed as far as the third floor. Amid the drone of huge trucks and massive cement mixers driven by Russians—probably obtained from America or brought back as reparations from Germany—about eight hundred Japanese prisoners worked as busily as an army of ants.

Iki was assigned the task of hauling bricks to the third floor. The carriers worked in pairs, bearing a wooden litter loaded with twenty bricks, each weighing between four and five pounds. The ramp leading to the third floor had to be climbed carefully. After hauling a half dozen loads, Iki's hands throbbed, despite the cloth gloves he wore. He had been paired with Hosono, the small, timid man in the bunk next to him. Although Hosono shunned Iki in the barrack, because he feared being accused of fraternizing with a reactionary officer, on the work site, where he could lose himself in the crowd, he expressed his natural gentleness. The activists gave themselves the easier jobs of throwing bricks into the litters. As soon as a load of twenty bricks was counted off, Hosono would stack them so that Iki's end, the front of the litter, weighed less than his end. Iki soon noticed Hosono's consideration and asked him to distribute the weight evenly, but, saying nothing, Hosono continued to bear the greater share of the burden.

Later in the morning, the crew leader paired Iki with Kagawa. The colonel had not borne up well under the brutal beating. His eyes were glazed and yellowed, and he breathed with difficulty. Iki pitied the man more than ever, especially because Kagawa bore a close resemblance to Colonel Tanikawa. "I'm younger than you, so I'll take the rear," Iki said. As Hosono had done for him, he distributed the load to favor Kagawa.

After another hour of hauling, Iki's gloves were torn and bloody. "This work is too hard for you, Iki," Kagawa said, breathing heavily. "I'll carry the rear."

"No, no!" insisted Iki. "I'm not used to this work, but I haven't been beaten by those savages."

"Stop wasting time, you old fool!" the crew leader shouted. "That goes for you, too, tenderfoot!"

"If you try any kind of sabotage," yelled a man nearby, "we'll send you flying from the top floor."

Similar threats came throughout the day from the activists and members of the Democratic Committee, as they made the rounds, checking on the amount of work done and recording the results on their charts. Brick carriers, bricklayers, cement mixers—everyone had a quota to fulfill.

After a while Iki noticed that the litter he and Kagawa were carrying was larger than those being used by activists wearing the Youth Brigade arm band. He asked Kagawa about it.

"Oh, the larger ones are for us reactionaries," Kagawa said, as if this treatment was to be expected. Neither one noticed that Yasuda stood behind them.

"And what's wrong with that?" Yasuda demanded, shoving Kagawa. "Why do you say things to cut down Comrade Iki's joy in his first day of work?" He ordered one of the activists to relieve Iki as Kagawa's partner.

"Listen, Yasuda," Iki said, holding his anger in check. "I find no joy in this work. I'm trying to understand why we submit to this hard labor for the Soviet Union."

"You talk like that because you've been well treated all your rich man's life. You've never been really hungry. Some day, when you're so hungry that bricks start looking like rice cakes to you, you won't be talking that way to me." Abruptly Yasuda turned away and strutted off, to persecute some other reactionary officers.

Having had nothing but watery gruel for breakfast, Iki's shrunken stomach knew the meaning of hunger well enough. After the crews had worked continuously for three hours, the bell rang for a fifteen-minute break. Iki looked about for Mizushima and Kamimori but did not see them. He sat down near Hosono, who was mending his gloves with deft fingers.

"Thanks for helping me out this morning," Iki said. Hosono scratched his head, in the typical Japanese gesture of embarrassment.

"I have some thread left over," he said, nodding at Iki's bloodstained gloves. "Let me mend those."

"Thanks, but I can do them myself if you'll lend me your needle and thread." The needle was a piece of wire with a sharpened point and a small loop at the other end, and the heavy thread had been made by twisting together ravelings from discarded cement sacks.

"I wonder where Colonel Kagawa is?" he asked innocently, as he set about mending his gloves. He remembered how tattered Kagawa's gloves had been. Hosono pointed toward one of the buildings. Kagawa was hauling bricks, holding up the heavier rear end of the litter and being dragged along by the activist at the front end. Even from a distance Iki could see how unsteadily Kagawa's feet moved on the treacherous ramp. Not far behind them another pair of haulers climbed the ramp with firm steps. Iki gasped when he recognized the two men.

"Why are Kagawa and Mizushima and Kamimori being made to work during the rest period?" he asked.

"Because . . . because they're reactionaries," Hosono murmured.

After the day's work Iki returned to camp weak from fatigue and hunger. The roll call was soon ended, but the leader of the squad did not dismiss his twenty men. Instead, he ordered them to sit down on the cold ground.

"Comrades!" he said. "We've time for self-examination, for reflection on whether or not we're satisfied with the work we did today on behalf of our fatherland, the Soviet Union."

They had engaged in a "marching discussion," on the subject of compulsory education in Japan, even while they trudged the three miles back to the camp. They had concluded that the Soviet system of education under Stalin's direction was the more beneficial, whereas education in Japan under the Emperor only exploited the people. Now, back in camp, the squad leader demanded further "ideological reflection." The absurdity of submitting to more useless talk at the end of an exhausting day disgusted Iki. But most of the men, afraid of being labeled "reactionary," spoke out in favor of more intensive labor and achieving higher production levels for the Soviet Union, for the fatherland.

"Tomorrow let's be even more firmly united!" the squad leader cried. "We want to be well prepared for the production contest! We want our barrack to win!"

He dismissed them in time to join a line at the mess hall entrance, where activists handed out meal tags. Each meal tag bore a number. Those who had completed less than eighty percent of their work quota were issued a tag marked "one," and would be given 250 grams of bread. Those who had achieved from eighty to one hundred percent of their quota were given a "two" tag, entitling them to 300 grams of bread. The "three" tag, for 350 grams of bread, was given to those whose work for the day had exceeded the norm. If the chart showed that a prisoner had achieved 126 percent or more, he was issued a "four" tag for 450 grams of bread. The soup each man received varied in amount and content according to the number on the tag. Only then did Iki understand why everyone in his work squad had been very much concerned with the percentage figures on the chart. He understood, too, that because the daily food supply per person for the prison camp was fixed, the meal-tag system resulted in the strong taking food from the weak. "And they talk about exploitation in Japan!" Iki thought—to himself, alone.

Iki stood in line, expecting to receive the very least. He had hauled bricks in the morning, but had been shifted in the afternoon to the relatively easy task of stirring the mixture of cement and sand. To his surprise, Yasuda sought him out and handed him a "four" tag. Although he knew that he should refuse it, lest he play into Yasuda's plan to lure him into the Democratic Committee, Iki took the tag because he was weak from hunger. Even Yasuda's conspiratorial smile did not make Iki give back that most precious tag.

When Colonel Kagawa reached the head of the serving line, the cook's helper greeted him noisily. "Well, well! Even a reactionary is given a 'number one' tag. Here you are—catch!" He pushed an aluminum plate with some soup and a small piece of bread toward Kagawa. The abrupt movement caused some of the soup to spill.

"What are you doing?" Kagawa protested. "Fill the cup to the level I'm supposed to have."

"It's your own stupid fault.—Go 'way!—Next!"

Kagawa persisted. "I've always fulfilled my quota one hundred percent, but I'm always given a 'number one' tag. At least give me what I'm entitled to."

Young soldiers in line behind Kagawa began to jeer. All were members of the Youth Brigade. "Since you hate Stalin, you should be happy at getting as little soup as possible from Stalin."

"You've had your turn, old man! Get out of the way!"

"Wait a minute," Kagawa said, turning upon them. "I've got to get the full meal. Without it, I won't have the strength to climb into my bunk, much less to lift a shovel. Please! Give me a little more!" He dropped every last shred of dignity to plead with the cook's helper.

"Just like a beggar," sneered one of the activists. "If you're so hungry, get down on the ground and beg for it. Let's see you kowtow!"

"I have a better idea," said another. "If you'll spin around three times and say 'Banzai for Stalin!', then I'll let you have a sip of my soup."

The teasing grew louder, more impatient. Scared away, Kagawa left the serving counter. When his turn came, Iki exchanged his meal tag for a large piece of bread and a ladleful of soup with a few pieces of codfish in it, and went searching for Colonel Kagawa. But he could not find him in the crowd.

"Iki! Over here!" Mizushima called him from a table nearby. The other officers at the table shifted about to make space for him. As soon as he sat down and laid his tin platter on the table, everyone could see his generous serving. Mizushima had worked the whole day, straight through the rest periods, hauling bricks up the ramp, but his ration of bread was much smaller than Iki's, and his watery soup contained no pieces of fish. Iki felt miserable over having accepted Yasuda's purchase price. The other officers knew precisely how much work he had done that day, and they eyed his meal with suspicion and envy—and greed.

"Has Kamimori finished eating?" asked Iki, breaking the intolerable silence.

"No, he hasn't eaten. He's in the guardhouse."

"The guardhouse? What for?"

"He went to the Democratic Committee chairman to insist on canceling the production contest among the barracks that's scheduled to start tomorrow. He told him that the contest would

134

exhaust the men to the point of endangering their lives. The chairman reported him immediately to the political officer, and the political officer threw him in the guardhouse on a charge of plotting systematic sabotage of work."

Iki expressed admiration for Kamimori's courage.

"Iki," Mizushima said, "you must realize that we have only three ways of getting by in this camp. One is to be like Kamimori, living according to the codes of our Japanese Army, making no compromises. The second is to go the opposite way, as Yasuda and others of the Democratic Committee have done, selling their souls to the Russians. The third is to *pretend* to be a believer in Communism and to do everything you're told—for the sake of *damoi*, the chance 'to return home.' The vast majority of us haven't the guts either to stay wholly Japanese or go the other way and sell out to the Russians. That's sad, but that's the way we Japanese are. Since childhood we've been warned constantly never to defy the majority. Well, the Russians have exploited our weakness to the hilt."

A sudden commotion across the mess hall cut short Mizushima's instruction. A crowd had formed around Kagawa, on hands and knees, with a sign reading "ultra-reactionary" dangling from his neck. Two young activists held him down, and a third stuck a postcard in front of his face.

"Say 'woof!' if you want it!" he ordered. "Go ahead, bark! You can't have it until you do."

He waved the postcard before Kagawa's eyes. It was a message from Kagawa's family, a reply to the first letter he had been allowed to send home. Twisting himself from side to side, Kagawa used all his strength trying to shake the men off.

"Kagawa! You dog! Say 'woof!' and open your mouth." The soldier brushed the postcard against Kagawa's lips. "Then you can have it."

"I've waited three years to hear from my family. Please let me read it! Please . . ."

"Sure, I'll let you read it. Just say 'woof!' and I'll lay it down on the floor so you can pick it up with your teeth."

When the activist snickered, Iki exploded in anger. "You're the one who's a dog!" he shouted, pushing into the middle of the circle. "Enough is enough!"

When the soldier drew back in surprise, Iki snatched the postcard from him.

"What in hell do you think you're doing!" the activist yelled, trying to grab Iki by the throat.

"What any decent human being would do. If you have any complaints, take them to the Democratic Committee." He pointed to Yasuda Tokichiro, standing on a table top to get a better view.

"You can't insult the Democratic Committee and get away with it!" the activist screeched. "We'll put you on trial!"

"Let's get him!" a number of others cried, closing in on Iki.

"Go ahead!" Iki shouted back, despite the fear that gripped him. "When you're finished, I'll write up a report of what happened today and send it up to the camp commandant and the office of the Ministry of Internal Affairs in Khabarovsk."

Iki had learned, from his experiences with Major Yazef, how Russians dread appeals or complaints addressed directly to the upper echelons of the Soviet political hierarchy. He raised the threat in sheer desperation, but it had an immediate effect. The activists, suddenly quieted, looked to Yasuda for direction. He was as confused as they were. Taking advantage of the moment, Iki knelt on the floor to help Kagawa. He removed the sign from around his neck, lifted him to his feet, and put the postcard into his bloodied hand.

During the next month, Iki changed almost beyond recognition. His uniform, frayed at the elbows and knees, hung upon him, stinking with sweat and dirt. His body, beneath the rags, was reduced to skin and bones. But his will remained unbroken.

The activists seldom took their eyes off him. One of them would position himself in front of Iki during the morning flag ceremony, to make certain that he sang while the red flag was being raised. If Iki failed to sing loud enough, the departure for work would be delayed until he sang a whole verse. If he neglected to participate in the marching discussions, the column would be brought to a halt until he conformed. In these and other ways the activists took advantage of every opportunity to demonstrate to everyone his "ultra-reactionary" tendencies.

At the construction site Iki was taken off the easy job of mixing the cement mortar and assigned exclusively to hauling bricks. The prisoners were setting bricks for the building's fourth floor. Because the ramp was too steep to permit the use of litters, each carrier took his load up in a shoulder bag.

"Assemble, Yaponskii!" the red-bearded Russian supervisor called out whenever the big trucks from the brick factory arrived.

"Today we will work even harder for our Fatherland, the U.S.S.R.!" members of the Youth Brigade shouted in unison as they climbed into the trucks to unload the bricks. Iki and others waited their turn behind the third truck. His barracks neighbor Hosono was unloading that day, and Iki noticed that several of the fifteen bricks Hosono piled in his shoulder bag were chipped, thereby lightening his load slightly. When he stood up, straining under the weight, Hosono helped lift the bag. He gave Hosono a nod of thanks, and moved away. He dared not say a word, lest Hosono be accused of sympathizing with a reactionary. He joined the file of men trudging slowly up the steep ramp, like an endless line of ants, crawling from ground level to the fourth floor. He saw Colonel Kagawa, not far ahead, forcing his weary body upward, every step labored and unsteady.

When he reached the top, the squad leader wrote a note on his chart. Standing beside the leader was Yasuda, as watchful as ever. Ignoring Yasuda, Iki unloaded his shoulder bag and went back to the truck for another round. When he got there he found that Hosono had been replaced by a member of the Youth Brigade.

"Here comes Mr. Staff Officer of Imperial General Headquarters," said the bully. "He should be rewarded for his great fighting spirit."

The activist tossed more than the usual number of bricks into Iki's bag. When he stood up, the added weight made him stagger.

"Put in the right number of bricks," Iki said sharply. "You know what the norm is."

"Quit complaining, reactionary!"

"It's not a complaint. It's a demand."

"Comrades!" the activist called out. "This former staff officer of Imperial General Headquarters dares to question us! He's insulting the Youth Brigade!"

Half a dozen activists rushed over to the truck, crying, "Put him on trial!" They hoisted Iki to the bed of the truck. "Fellow comrades! This man worked at the Imperial General Headquarters and took his orders from that fascist Tojo! He used us as cannon fodder!"

When the excitement reached a noisy pitch, Yasuda stood up, raising both arms to quiet the crowd.

"Comrades!" he cried. "Our duty calls for us to denounce this stinking reactionary. Right now!"

Hundreds of fists shot up into the air as the men roared back, "Now! Now!" The lust for violence made them ugly.

"Hey, you! Reactionary! Give your name, rank, and title!"

Iki stood silent and motionless.

"Hey, you! You have ears, don't you?"

"Say something! Have you lost your guts?"

"This bastard still thinks he's running us from headquarters!"

"Make him criticize himself!"

"Repeat what you said at the war crimes trial!"

"Drag him down here! Let's spin him!"

The jeers became a terrifying uproar. Iki fully expected that the devils meant to tear him to pieces.

Yasuda's command cut through the noise. "Hosono! You do it!"

They pushed Hosono to the front, amid cheers for him and curses for Iki. Pale and trembling, he stood there, not looking at Iki.

"What's the matter? Are you a friend of this reactionary?"

Alarmed by that dangerous thought, Hosono shut his eyes and blurted, "Hey, you!" He heard shouts of approval. "Y-you . . . d-damned re-reactionary!" he stammered. "S-still think y-you're at headquarters?"

"At-a-boy! Keep going!"

"D-don't you know the m-meaning of di-diametrical materialism?"

They roared with delight. Someone had taught the near-illiterate Hosono the Marxist catchword and he, characteristically, mangled it.

"You're doing fine," Yasuda said, encouraging him. "Teach Mr. Staff Officer here the meaning of 'dialectical materialism.' "

"I- Iki! Diametrical materialism means . . . wh-when you're in a strange country, you follow its ways. This here's the Soviet Union, you know. Not Ja-Ja-Japan. N-now, y-you criticize yourself!"

Hosono's conclusion was accompanied by more shouts of approval. Iki looked down at his twisted face, where drops of saliva gathered at the corners of his mouth. The crotch of his trousers was wet, but no one else seemed to have noticed that. Although Iki had been determined not to give in to Yasuda and his bullies, the sight of timid, powerless Hosono filled him with compassion.

"You are right, Hosono. I understand you. I accept what you've said."

The crowd shut up in amazement—until a few jeers ended the silence of surprise.

"The staff officer has criticized himself!"

"The reactionary Colonel Iki has surrendered to Private Hosono!"

"Hosono did it! He did it!"

"Imperial General Headquarters today announces that Private Second Class Hosono has destroyed Staff Officer Iki Tadashi!" Raucous laughter, followed by contemptuous, bitter remarks restored the onlookers' hostility.

"We lost the war because boneheads like him were running headquarters! Get him!"

Several husky activists swarmed over Iki, dragged him from the truck, and threw him to the ground. They began to kick him.

"Yaponskii!" The red-bearded supervisor came running. He was furious. "Sabotage!" he yelled. "Now is work period!"

" 'Twenty-four-hour campaign' for Iki!" the activists shouted triumphantly, scattering in all directions. The milder onlookers went back to their work, leaving Iki alone, lying on the cold earth.

Muddied and bruised, Iki tried to stop the flow of blood from his nose. When he got back on his feet, he saw Yasuda standing nearby. Iki would never forget the expression upon that fat face: it mixed glee, derision, satisfaction, and hatred, all at once, in a way that marked him as being the worst enemy Iki had ever known.

At five o'clock the prisoners marched back to camp. There the activists immediately surrounded Iki, bawling, "Time to get started on your 'twenty-four-hour campaign.' "

"I've completed my quota for the day," Iki retorted.

"The quota for a reactionary is never completed. We'll keep you working till you drop dead."

The activists caught sight of Colonel Kagawa, trying to reach the safety of his barrack.

"Hey, old fool! Teach this man how to clean the latrine."

The outdoor latrines were nothing more than straddling boards laid over a deep trench. The accumulated excrement would freeze when the temperature dropped to fifteen degrees below zero. At any time, summer or winter, deposits from so many men would soon fill the trenches. Iki chipped away at a frozen heap with a pick, and tossed the icy chunks into a tub used for transporting the wastes to a dump outside the lager. Exhausted from the day's labor, and hungry, he felt dizzy as he swung the pick. He had almost chipped away a heap when another swing of the pick broke through the icy crust and sent a spray of stinking liquid into the air, causing him to gag. Colonel Kagawa quickly exchanged his pick for a long-handled dipper, with which he scooped the foul mixture out of the pit and into the tub.

"Colonel Kagawa," Iki said, resting on his pick for a moment, "I'm sorry you got dragged into this because of me."

"Don't think about it," Kagawa replied. "I'm always being made the goat by these mad dogs. But you, Iki—I don't like the way Yasuda's been looking at you. You must be careful of him. Once you're branded a reactionary in this camp, you're flirting with death. And this 'twenty-four hour campaign' is a dangerous thing—men have gone crazy, even committed suicide, because of it."

The following day was Sunday, but Iki, Kagawa, Mizushima, Kamimori, and others who had been labeled "reactionaries"— more than a dozen in all—were forced to work in the compound while the others rested. Their assignment that day was to tidy up the "forbidden zone"—the two-yard strip along the inner barbed-wire fence. The strip was covered with river gravel, carefully raked and swept, so that anyone stepping on it would leave distinct footprints. The guards in the towers had orders to shoot any prisoner who walked on that strip.

Iki worked with a broom, leveling the gravel of no-man's-land, where no one might pass, where nothing could grow. He paused for a moment when he saw the dried stalk of a weed long dead, emerging from the barren earth at the foot of a fence post. Even weeds cannot survive here, he was thinking.

"Iki—" Kamimori called from a place close enough for him to speak softly. "Is it true that you subjected yourself to self-criticism when you were denounced yesterday?"

Iki nodded.

"Why didn't you stand up to them, as I do? I've been thrown in the guardhouse lots of times, but I've never compromised yet. I've met them head on every time."

"These men aren't sane," Iki said. He was thinking about good-hearted and frightened Hosono, with his "diametrical materialism." "I see no sense in meeting them head on. They'll grow out of this foolishness in time. I believe we should use better sense—try to ignore them until the madness leaves them."

"Use better sense? Are you trying to tell me that what you're doing is rational? To put the matter kindly, you're being 'flexible.' To put it bluntly, you're a calculating coward, using your wits to protect yourself. That's what I don't like about you."

"Listen, Kamimori. You can't get by in a place like this by continually saying what you think is right. You've got to consider situations where your own stubborness will bring harm to others."

"I'm aware of that. I invoked international law when we first came here, and refused to let any of our officers work. But now the Russians have set up a system in which everyone has to work for his meals. If I'm to be fed, someone has to do my share of the work. When I found that out, I started to work—but only to get myself fed. That's as flexible as any of us needs to be. We have no excuse for other compromises—like indulging in self-criticism."

"I haven't compromised myself," Iki said. "Whatever I do, I do with the welfare of all 700,000 men of the Kwantung Army in mind, not for my own benefit."

"That's all the more reason why you should act in strict adherence to the code of the Army."

"Listen to me, Kamimori. We're in a situation where everyone's in danger of going crazy—with some Japanese informing on one another, others even ready to murder their brothers in arms. What's important now is for us to do whatever we can to reduce the toll taken of our men."

Iki spoke emphatically in an attempt to persuade Kamimori, but succeeded only in irritating him. "You're spineless! I don't want to talk to you!"

As Kamimori turned away, they saw Colonel Kagawa lying on the ground, gasping for breath. They rushed to his side and lifted him up. "We've got to get you to the dispensary right away," Iki said.

Kagawa shook his head. "No use. The medical officer does only what the Democratic Committee tells him to do. He won't treat reactionaries."

"In that case, I'll go to the dispensary and drag him here," Kamimori said.

"Please don't!" Kagawa begged. "If they find out I can't work any longer, they'll give me an injection—to kill me."

Kamimori, scarcely hearing him, ran off to the dispensary. Iki helped Kagawa toward the shelter offered by a lone pine tree.

"Water . . ." Kagawa gasped.

"I'll get some right away. Sit here."

Iki ran the fifty yards or so to the nearest faucet, filled the communal drinking can with water, and hurried back. But Kagawa was not where he had left him. He looked about frantically—and found him moving like a sleepwalker toward the barbed-wire fence.

"Stop!" he shouted. "Colonel Kagawa! Stop! Wait!" He ran as fast as he could toward the broken old man.

"They're calling . . . they're calling . . . my family—" Kagawa cried out, in joy, seeing only the open space beyond the fence.

Iki, mindful of the guards, turned toward them. "Wait! Don't shoot!"

The sharp reports of rifle shots echoed throughout the compound. Under the impact of several bullets Kagawa's body bounded into the air before it fell upon the gravel. Iki moaned in horror. A guard came down from the tower and hurried toward Iki and his companions, kneeling in the dirt at the outer edge of the gravel strip where Kagawa lay.

"Why did you shoot when I asked you not to?" Iki demanded.

"He was trying to escape."

"That's not so! He was sick in his mind and didn't know what he was doing. He wasn't trying to escape. How could he escape from this place?"

"But there's the proof. Look where he is." The guard pointed at Kagawa's body, shedding bright blood on the thirsty gravel they had leveled so recently. He turned to the officer of the guards, arriving on the scene, to explain what had happened.

"No problem here," the officer said. "A clear case of attempted escape. Take care of the body. You know what to do." He ordered a horse-drawn refuse cart to be brought to carry the body away.

"Wait!" Iki said angrily. "Your guards disregarded my signal to hold fire! Shooting a prisoner of war is a violation of international law!"

"That's very strange," Yasuda sneered. "This camp is administered by we Japanese, and all decisions and actions are the reponsibility of our Democratic Committee. This reactionary Kagawa's recent behavior showed quite clearly that he was planning to escape. Therefore, his body should be turned over to the Soviet authorities."

"You and your devils on the Democratic Committee drove Colonel Kagawa out of his mind! The least you can do is give him a decent burial."

"According to regulations, the Soviet authorities are empowered to dispose of a criminal's body. We're just following regulations," Yasuda said flatly. Then, to the amazement of everyone, he helped the Russian guard lift Kagawa's limp body onto the cart. Several hundred Japanese watched him do so, but no one said a word—except for Iki.

"Damn you, Yasuda! You're a beast! You're not human!—We'll bury Colonel Kagawa ourselves."

Iki shoved Yasuda aside and reached toward the cart. A second guard stepped forward and trained his automatic rifle directly on Iki alone, while his companion and Yasuda stuffed Kagawa's body into a long burlap sack. They tossed the shapeless bundle upon the cart. A husk . . . As dead as last year's weed, unable to grow in no-man's-land . . .

The garbage-collector flicked the reins over his mule, and drove away.

As summer neared its end, the prisoners talked more than ever about *damoi*—going home.

Freight cars from the Siberian interior, filled with Japanese prisoners of war, had been arriving at Khabarovsk Station almost daily since late spring. And everyone had heard about a general shifting of Japanese prisoners in camps in the vicinity of Khabarovsk. Recent rumors said that the Japanese in subunit ten of the Khabarovsk-area system would be leaving Khabarovsk Station aboard *damoi* trains. Subunit ten was less than two miles away from subunit eleven, where Iki was interned. To the inmates of Camp Eleven *damoi* seemed very close.

Having lived for almost three years in a Siberian prison camp, the men were weakened and dispirited almost beyond saving. They felt that repatriation must come within a few months if ever they were to return home alive. If, for any reason, they were excluded from the *damoi* group, they would spend yet another winter in Siberia. The prospect of being condemned to such treatment was terrifying.

The day's work done, Iki sat on a clump of grass near the barracks; he welcomed these few moments alone, while waiting for his group's turn to enter the mess hall. Although the time was past seven o'clock, the sky was still lighted by a waning glow in the west. Beyond the barbed-wire fences, two rounded hills rose above the grassy plain, iike a pair of humps on a camel's back.

Memories of his native village, long absent from his thoughts, captured them now as he gazed at those Siberian hills. Mt. Chokai, whose flawless cone distinguished it as the "Fuji of the Northeast," rose majestically before him. Apples would be turning red in the village of Yusa, where his aged parents awaited his return. His thoughts lingered only for the moment on his chances of being sent home. His fellow prisoners might be freed for repatriation to Japan, but most certainly he would not go yet. He did not doubt that he would spend many more years of imprisonment in Siberia, but, after having survived so many difficulties, he was sure of his determination to endure them in the future. He felt his resolution weakening, however, whenever he dared to think about an early return. He knew he must banish all such hope from his mind.

The Democratic Committee exploited the prisoners' excitement over *damoi* to intensify its programs. Prisoners were led to believe that only those who pledged their loyalty to the Committee would be listed in the registry of the fortunate ones to be repatriated to Japan. On the job site they were incited to compete with one another to exceed their assigned work norms—because of course they would want to demonstrate to the Soviet Union their gratitude for the protection and care they had received for the last three years. During their evenings in the barracks, they were urged to study Marx and Lenin—to prepare themselves the better to serve as "fighters for the revolution" upon returning to Japan. They were driven to make senseless and continuous efforts to prove themselves worthy of repatriation.

Iki remained an exception in his barrack. No one talked to him. Hosono, once the only man who would talk with him, slept in the next bunk. Unable to face Iki after he had denounced him, even though he had been forced into doing so, Hosono had asked to be assigned to another barrack.

"Hey, reactionary! Time to eat," a former lieutenant called out to Iki. The younger officers who shared Iki's barrack had picked up the habit of addressing him as the activists did. He walked slowly toward the mess hall, disturbed by a sight he could not quite understand. Instead of the usual line, moving along, a throng of activists hung around the door. Nearer the entrance, he saw what was happening.

On the threshold lay a board in which a crude carving of a chrysanthemum flower had been cut—with sixteen petals. It was unmistakably a representaion of the imperial crest. Activists were forcing each prisoner to step on the symbol as he entered the mess hall to receive his meal tag.

"Ah, the Emp's crest—so what?" said a soldier, grinding his boot into the carving.

"Alright. Next!"

A young officer followed, putting both his muddy shoes on the crest.

"Next!"

A middle-aged enlisted man walked up to the board, then stopped.

"What's the matter? Still afraid of the Emperor? Why so? Remember how we were herded into the army? By his orders. With a notice that cost a lousy *sen* to mail? Come on. The Emperor's human, and so are we. Step on it!"

Frightened by their very presence, the soldier closed his eyes and took a stiff, resolute step forward. He swayed as his foot came down on the crest.

"That's not good enough. You can't pass unless you spit on it too."

The soldier blanched, his lips twitched.

"What's the matter? Go on, spit on it, or we'll keep you off the *damoi* train. Then you'll end up as bone meal in Siberia."

Trembling all over, the soldier spat.

Iki refused to look any longer at this stupidity. Japanese soldiers of the twentieth century were doing to one another precisely what the shogun's government had done in the seventeenth century, forcing suspect Christians to trample upon engraved crucifixes and images of Jesus. Those who trampled upon the chrysanthemum crest would be rewarded immediately with food and approval, and eventually with passage home; those who refused would be labeled "ultra-reactionaries," worked brutally, starved, and perhaps prevented from ever returning home. "Siberian democracy" had sunk these Japanese into a state even worse than mad. These men had become monsters, still sane, but all the more perverse for that reason.

Iki's turn came.

"Here comes Honorable Mr. Staff Officer of Imperial General Headquarters!" Several activists welcomed him with exaggerated bows and insulting salutes.

"Iki," Yasuda said, "go ahead. No need to hesitate." He spoke with an even stronger sense of importance, as newly-elected vice chairman of the Democratic Committee. "Just step on it. If you do, even an ultra-reactionary like yourself might have a chance for *damoi.*" His smirk turned to derisive laughter.

"Take this board away immediately." Iki snarled at Yasuda. "You're shaming the whole Japanese race."

"Shaming the Japanese race? That's ridiculous. We have only one fatherland, and that's the Soviet Union. Our return to Japan will be a beachhead landing on the shores of an enemy island ruled by the Emperor. Men who haven't the guts to step on this crest will be useless to us when we get back to Japan. Step on it, Iki! Or you won't even get a 'number one' meal tag tonight."

Iki knelt before the board and, with a sleeve of his tattered uniform, started to wipe the crest clean of mud and spittle. As he lifted the board, he was thrown down violently and pinned to the floor. The more he struggled the more crushing the weight of the bodies became, and the tighter the grip around his neck. As he gasped for breath, his mind reeling, he heard Yasuda's scornful shout: "You put your foot on it, Iki! That's the end of that! You pass."

"We made him step on it!" another man yelled.

"Our splendid Staff Officer stepped on the Emperor!"

"This ultra-reactionary even laid his ass on the crest!"

Their disrespect, more than their taunts, aroused a furious resentment in Iki. The instant they relaxed their hold, he shook them off and sprang to his feet.

"You filthy coward!" he shouted, grabbing Yasuda by the shoulders and throwing him to the floor. Iki lifted him up, pounded the fat and flabby face, and again knocked him to the floor. Blood streamed from Yasuda's nose and mouth, and his eyes were wide with terror. Iki, worn almost to a skeleton, unsteady on his feet, yet relentlessly beating Yasuda, struck fear into the activists. Cowards all, they backed away. Not one of them tried to help Yasuda, even when Iki struck again and again, and started to choke him.

"Stop it, Iki! You'll kill him!" Mizushima and Kamimori pulled Iki's hands away from Yasuda, sprawling unconscious. Iki stared down at that bloody hated face. Kamimori lifted an eyelid, already swelling. "He's all right. Still alive. Just unconscious. Iki, go back to your barrack. Hurry! We'll take care of the rest."

Mizushima pushed Iki out the door—too late. The political officer and several armed guards were rushing into the mess hall. The commissar needed only an instant to find the culprit. Pointing at Iki, he yelled, "Fascist! Throw him in the guardhouse! In solitary!"

At the north end of the camp, the guardhouse stood in bleak isolation—a clammy cubicle built of stone, dark and cold as ice.

During all his years in the army, Iki had never seen the inside of a guardhouse. He had been empowered to punish enlisted men when he was a company-grade officer. But never had he sentenced any of them to confinement, nor had he been curious enough to see what a guardhouse was like.

So, in this new abode in Khabarovsk, he examined his cell with mounting dread. It had only one small barred window in the door, through which food was passed. He shuddered convulsively in the freezing box. The stink of excrement from previous occupants rose from the slimy floor. When his legs trembled with exhaustion, he sat down on that same floor; when he could no longer bear the cold and the stench, he stood up, rubbing his arms and legs to give them some warmth. After several hours, intense hunger increased the misery of that numbing cold.

With night, cold and hunger grew unbearabie. At the best of times in that lager, rations were so meager that a man was always hungry. Without anything to eat, Iki knew, he would soon freeze to death. He shouted several times for the guard, but received no answer. In the silence that followed his call, he thought he heard the faint sounds of a man moving about in an adjoining cell.

"Anyone there?" Iki called, his mouth close to the wooden wall between them.

"Who are you?" the reply came, muffled, yet youthful.

"Iki Tadashi of barrack three. Who are you?"

The man did not answer. Iki tried again, louder this time. "I'm from barrack three. Which barrack are you from?"

Receiving no answer, Iki almost shouted. "Listen! The Democratic Committee took a dislike to me. That's why I'm in here. Is that what happened to you?"

"Not at all," the man answered. "But don't talk so loud. The guard might hear you, and I don't want any more trouble."

This neighbor wanted silence. He had been condemned to a Soviet lager, which in itself was a huge prison; he had been confined to a guardhouse within that prison, then locked in a solitary cell within that guardhouse. Yet he was afraid to be caught talking to a fellow Japanese prisoner who had been labeled "ultra-reactionary." Broken by the Siberian democratic movement, he had withdrawn into silence. All he wanted now was merciful solitude.

As the hours passed, Iki tossed and turned on the freezing putrid floor, unable to sleep. About midnight a surly guard brought him a slice of black bread and a cup of water. He had had neither food nor drink for more than ten hours.

The next morning he was awakened by the racket of Japanese prisoners in the compound, shouting Soviet slogans and singing revolutionary songs. Their excitement over *damoi* had been mounting steadily. Most of them had accepted instruction by activists of the democratic movement in the hope of being allowed to return to Japan. In their eagerness to assure that return, many had acted with unwarranted viciousness, even to the point of denouncing and slandering their own countrymen, thereby sending some to their death. Those eager and unprincipled men were guilty of deeds that would forever blacken the reputation of Japanese war prisoners in Siberia.

After three days and nights in solitary confinement, Iki no longer remembered a time when his body did not tremble with cold. On the fourth evening the loud clanging of the alarm summoned the prisoners into the compound. Other than reveille, the only occassions for that jarring noise were emergencies—as when an attempt to escape was discovered, or when lager officials came from Khabarovsk for a surprise inspection. Iki pressed his ear against a crack in the outer wall of his cell and heard the bustle of men gathering in the open area. A guard bellowed for quiet, and a brief announcement was made in Russian. And then a tumult of shouts and cheers broke out.

148

"*Banzai! Damoi! Damoi!*"

"We're going home!"

The shouting swept into singing. The Japanese prisoners sang the "International." The song came to their lips automatically—as a spontaneous, ingenuous expression of gratitude for being released and in the hope that the louder a man sang the greater would be his chances of going home in one of the first *damoi* groups.

Iki moved back from the wall. Like everyone else he had prayed for the day when every prisoner in this camp would be sent back to Japan. But his joy for those who were going home mingled with aching pity for those who had died—from starvation, from disease, from the breakdown of spirits that led to madness and to death.

He heard a light rapping on his cell door, a whisper. "Iki, this is Mizushima." While the entire camp rejoiced over *damoi*, Major Mizushima had slipped into the guardhouse.

"You're taking a chance coming here," Iki said.

"I've come to say goodbye. My name isn't on the *damoi* list. I expect to be sent off into the interior. Even farther away from home . . ."

"Is Kamimori going with you?"

"No. He's already been taken away. I don't know when he went."

"I'm not too worried about him," Iki said. "He'll be stubborn and tough wherever he goes, and he'll survive. Make sure you survive and return to Japan, Mizushima. I intend to do the same."

"Take good care of yourself, Iki—" Mizushima passed a piece of bread and a lump of raw sugar through the barred window. They were part of his dinner rations for that day.

"I don't need it," Iki pushed back Mizushima's hand. "I just sit here all day long. You're the one who needs food. Please keep it."

"We won't be seeing each other any more, Iki. You keep it— please."

This was Mizushima's deed of farewell. Although they had talked often of surviving and of returning to Japan, both knew that they had little chance of staying alive, and even less of seeing each other again. Humbly, Iki accepted the gift of bread and sugar —and of friendship. He tried to say something, but the words would not come. Mizushima, too, could not speak. Each looked

149

quietly at the other for a moment. Then Mizushima slipped away, as quietly as he had entered.

The prison camp hummed with excitement the next day. The men behaved as if they were drunk with saké. They sang revolutionary songs at the tops of their voices. While standing in line for the pre-*damoi* physical check-up at the dispensary, they engaged one another in heated debates about the principles of Marxism. As they wrapped up their few battered belongings, they continued singing rousing versions of the "International." In his cell Iki heard the uproar from morning till night. His fifth day in solitary confinement was the long-awaited day of *damoi* for most of the prisoners in that lager.

The Japanese activists planned to the last detail the ceremonies of their final morning—the raising of the red flag, the salute, and cheers for Marshal Stalin, the thrice-repeated "Banzai!" for the generous Soviet Union. At a command, they fell into column formation and, five abreast, marched through the great gate, singing the "International." Iki was allowed to watch them go from the guardhouse window. The men being freed wore ill-fitting trousers and thick quilted coats with stand-up collars, issued to them by the fraternal Russians. The backs of those coats, wet by a light rain, shone in the morning sunlight as the squads moved out in unison, firm footsteps ringing out smartly to the cadence of their song. They would take a train from Khabarovsk to Nakhodka, where a ship flying the flag of the Land of the Rising Sun would be waiting to take them home.

Watching them go, with his hopes to be among them, Iki gripped the window sill, assailed by loneliness and yearning. In a corner of his mind he knew that he was on the edge of collapse. Yet, as the last men in the column disappeared in the distance, he reminded himself that his time for *damoi* had not yet come. He could not go home until he had seen the last of the 700,000 men of Kwantung Army returned safely to Japan.

7

WAR CRIMINAL

The chilling rain had stopped. The autumn sun, hidden beyond rain clouds, shed its weak rays on Iki as he emerged from solitary confinement in the guardhouse. The camp was deserted. A confusion of footprints in the muddy road, made by hundreds of other Japanese now homeward-bound, told him that he had been left behind. —The only Japanese in this lager not to be going home.

"Here, take this. Let's go!"

An officer of the guards thrust into his hands the kerchief holding Iki's personal belongings, and led him out the compound's main gate. A windowless van awaited the lone prisoner.

An hour later, as Iki left the darkness of the van, he recognized the "White Prison" in Khabarovsk, where he had been confined three years before. This White Prison had been built to hold political offenders during the pre-trial stages. Convicted political offenders, as well as common criminals, were confined in the "Red Prison."

Following the routine body check, Iki was led along a corridor to the far end, where an iron door opened into a large room containing a row of cells. He was locked in cell nineteen, which he would share with four Europeans.

"What are you doing here?" a young Russian asked. "I thought all Japanese were being sent back to Japan."

"I don't know," Iki answered cautiously. After his years in Soviet prison camps, prisons, and dachas, Iki heard and spoke Russian about as well as the natives did. But those same years of experience had taught him to be very careful about what he said—and how he said that.

"Then you must have been connected in some way with intelligence during the war. Most of the Yaponskiis sent to this prison are former MPs, secret service men, police, or diplomats."

The talkative Russian had mentioned all the categories of Japanese whom the Soviet Union had rounded up for "retaliation." The Soviets labeled them "men with a past." After being so identified, they had been denounced, even beaten, certainly avoided, by fellow Japanese of less importance, sometimes on the slightest provocation. How the Russians treated them remained a mystery.

"I was in operations, not intelligence. The security officials probably have the two confused."

"So you were an operations officer," a German officer spoke up. "So, also, was I—a lieutenant colonel with General Staff Headquarters of the German Army. I knew your ambassador, Mr. Oshima, in Berlin."

The German seemed to be full of contempt for his other cell mates, but evidently felt an immediate liking for Iki. Moreover, Iki could speak fluent German with him, having learned the language during his years at the War Academy in Tokyo. In the course of their talking, Iki remarked that Ambassador Oshima had been designated a Class A war criminal at the Far East Military Tribunal. The German interrupted him, angrily denouncing the Nuremburg tribunal as an arbitrary trial imposed on the leaders of a defeated nation by punitive victors.

"But, you see," the Russian interjected, "the situation with you is very different from mine. You two foreigners are being held prisoner in a country that was your enemy. But I was tried and convicted by my own countrymen—for having spent time in a German prison camp. I was a first lieutenant in the Red Army and a loyal Party member, too, and I fought well in the war until the Germans captured me near Leningrad. After the war ended, my government asked me to come home to the Soviet Union, to rejoin my family, to be welcomed as a hero who'd fought courageously in defense of the fatherland. And I was one of the men who happily returned to Russia—only to be accused of being a German spy. Without a sign of understanding for our plight as prisoners of the Germans, they condemned me, and thousands of others, to spend the rest of our lives in Russian prison camps.—Let me tell you about my friend, who was operating a state farm. He was turned in just because he'd left a sack of potatoes overnight in his backyard. He was arrested for embezzling state property—that's a political offence in my country—and sent off to a labor camp in Chita. Because of logic like that, thirty-five million of my people are convicts."

"That means convicts make up one-fifth of the Soviet population!" one of their cell mates exclaimed. "A country can't get labor any cheaper."

"Where are you from?" Iki asked.

"Warsaw," he answered, brushing back his graying hair. "I'm Polish, and at home I was a civil servant, not a soldier. The N.K.V.D. picked me up off the street one afternoon. I should have expected that, because I'd spoken critically of the Soviet Union that morning at a city council meeting. Even in our own country we were afraid to answer the door bell, never knowing when the N.K.V.D. might be there . . ."

"You people are lucky because you have a country," a middle-aged Russian broke in. "You can serve out your term, then—if you live—return to your country. We White Russians cannot do that. I was separated from my family in Harbin. If we had a country we could call our own, we might have a chance of meeting our families again some day. Because our country has been taken away from us, once we become separated we're separated forever."

Iki was pained to hear his tale, perhaps the saddest of all those recounted by his cell mates. The White Russians had had a home of sorts in Harbin until the Soviets drove the Japanese out of Manchuria. Now the White Russians had no place at all to go. Here was another instance of tragedy following upon defeat in war.

The very next day the White Russian was called out by a prison guard, and never returned. About a month later, the Pole was taken away. Iki's turn came soon after, in the middle of the night. That happened in March of 1949.

Guards put Iki into the same windowless van that had brought him to the White Prison and drove him to the Khabarovsk headquarters of the Soviet Ministry of Internal Affairs. The setting was too well known to Iki. Although he arrived late in the night, the huge building hummed with activity. Stalin and Beria still looked down arrogantly from their places on a wall near the entrance.

Iki was led upstairs, questioned briefly to establish his identity, then taken into a small room farther down the hall. Seated at the table were an interrogation officer and a civilian interpreter.

Would he be repeating his experience of three years before, he wondered. No one had told him yet why he was to be questioned once again. Resolutely he sat down opposite the sharp-eyed Russian legal officer.

"I'm Captain Sarnov, the examining judge," the officer said. "You're being held as a war crime suspect, and I've been assigned to investigate the charges against you."

Iki stiffened. He had heard, during his visit to Tokyo, that Class B and Class C war crime suspects were being tried in the countries where the alleged crimes had occurred. But he had not expected that the Soviet Union, after unilaterally abrogating the neutrality agreement with Japan, would try officers of the Japanese military who had already suffered several years of imprisonment. Border skirmishes between minor units of the Soviet and Japanese armies could hardly be considered a war. Besides, to him the very idea of "war crimes" was, at the very least, farfetched, a strain upon the intelligence of honest men.

"I advise you to answer truthfully. If you do, the Soviet Union will be generous. If you give false information, you most certainly will never see Japan again."

Sarnov's threat, right at the beginning, and his staging of the interrogation late at night were calculated to unnerve Iki.

"I see you were attached to Imperial General Headquarters from 1940 to 1944. Tell me about the Russian section of your Intelligence Department during those years. First, who was chief of the Russian section?"

"I was assigned to Operations. I know nothing about the Intelligence Department."

"Ohh . . . Why, then, were you sent to the Soviet Union on a spying mission in 1943?"

The question took Iki by surprise. He had indeed been sent on a secret assignment to the Soviet Union in 1943, while Russia was reeling from the German invasion in the West. The top Soviet command had remained in Moscow, but foreign missions and embassies had been moved to the relative safety of Kuibyshev on the banks of the Volga River. Iki had been assigned briefly to the Japanese Embassy in Kuibyshev. How had the Soviets learned this bit of secret information, not only about himself, but also about Japan's very methods of operating its intelligence system?"

"I visited your country between May and August of 1943," he replied. "My orders were to deliver information concerning personnel matters to the military attaché at our embassy in Kuibyshev. But my trip had nothing to do with intelligence activities, as you allege."

"If that was the case," said Sarnov, frowning, "your passport should have identified you as Major Iki Tadashi of the Japanese Army General Staff Headquarters. I'd like to hear your explanation for this."

Watching Iki carefully, Sarnov, laid an immigration form document on the table and, with a long white finger, pointed to the photograph affixed to it.

"Do you know this person?" he asked. The photograph showed a thirty-one year old Japanese man, dressed in civilian clothes with hair relatively long and well groomed. The name on the document read: "Takahara Hiroshi, Embassy Clerk, Foreign Ministry."

"It's my picture," Iki admitted.

"Of course it is. Your military hair cut would have taken weeks to grow out to the length shown in the photograph. Obviously your entry into the U.S.S.R. was secret—and carefully planned. What was your mission? I want the details."

"I've told you: to relay information directly to our military attaché—nothing more. I went as a diplomatic courier simply to avoid the needless inconveniences that all military officers met in those days when traveling in countries at war. The Russian war with Germany was then at its height. Military officers were used as couriers by all countries, including your own. It was an accepted international custom."

In 1943 Iki had been instructed to study the effect of Germany's invasion, to gather information on Soviet armed strength along the Siberian-Manchurian border, and to assess the likelihood of the Soviet Union's joining the Allied Nations in their war against Japan. But, naturally, he would not admit this to Sarnov—or to any Soviet official.

"I'm not concerned with international customs," Sarnov snapped. "Did you enter the Soviet Union by yourself?"

"I traveled with my superior officer at staff headquarters," Iki replied truthfully, certain that Sarnov must know all about his accomplice. He glanced at the clock on the wall. Two o'clock in the morning.

"Your route of travel?"

"From Vladivostok to Khabarovsk, then by the Trans-Siberian Railway to Kuibyshev."

"Was a White Russian riding in your compartment?"

"One may have been, but I'm not sure. —How could I know?"

"Then I'll tell you. A White Russian spy working for the Kwantung Army boarded the train at Irkutsk and passed on to you information concerning Soviet troop movements along the Trans-Siberian Railway. Isn't that so?"

The Japanese Army had employed several White Russians as spies in Russia and Germany, and Iki had indeed made contact with a White Russian agent on the train.

"I remember only talking about the scenery with other travelers in the compartment."

"You're lying! A passenger in your compartment became suspicious of you two Japanese and reported your actions to the Ministry of Internal Affairs. We know that, during the whole journey, you and your partner took turns sleeping. You two were able to observe every eastbound train, and make a note of its destination and an estimate of the number of troops and kinds of weapons it carried."

Diplomatic couriers generally traveled in pairs, partly for protection, partly in order to be observant around the clock. As long as Sarnov refused to recognize the fact that couriers of all countries systematically collected intelligence wherever they went, Iki had no choice but to deny his charges.

"If a foreign traveler in Russia talks with other passengers, or even looks out the window at the Russian landscape, is he automatically considered a spy?" he retorted.

"I want the names of the people you saw at Kuibyshev," said Sarnov, quickly shifting to another line of attack. "And I want to know what documents you delivered."

"I saw Ambassador Azuma, Counselor Ushiba, Military Attaché Hayashi, and his deputy Gomi. I delivered a letter from Japan's foreign minister addressed to the ambassador, as well as several encoded documents from our foreign and war ministries."

"What did the foreign minister's letter say?"

"I didn't read it," Iki replied, although he had been briefed on the contents of the letter in order to convey the message orally in the event the document was lost.

"You're lying again! We have the evidence. And we have witnesses."

"Where are they?" Iki was firm, for by then he knew only too well the technique of seizing upon any vacillation or show of doubt in a prisoner as a wedge to expand the scope of interrogation. Sarnov scribbled irritably on his note pad.

"Here's your report," he said finally, putting down his pen. "Sign it!"

Iki listened with disbelief as Sarnov's account was interpreted into Japanese. He had been accused of spying while traveling across Russia in the guise of a civilian courier.

"No. This report is nonsense. I won't sign it."

"You'll be sorry if you don't!"

Iki retreated into silence. Sarnov called a guard. "We both have plenty of time" he reminded Iki. "I'll let you think it over for a while."

At dawn, Iki was driven back to the White Prison through a howling blizzard. On arrival, guards took him directly to a solitary confinement cell.

They kept him in that cramped solitude for a month.

The cell had one small window in the wall, near the ceiling. It was too high to allow him to look outside, but during the day it did admit some light. One morning he noticed that a moving object interfered with the rays entering the cell. Looking up, he saw a sparrow perching on the window sill.

The bird was grooming itself, ruffling its soft feathers, twisting its head in quick, jerky movements, scratching itself vigorously with a tiny claw. Seeing it, Iki thought of his children. When he stood up, the visitor flew away.

Suddenly crushed by loneliness, Iki stared at the wall; its very grayness obliterated images that could have brought him greater sorrow. His eyes searched the grimy surfaces as they often had, studying scratchings that told of the bitter anguish and utter despair of men who had dwelt there before him. Although inmates were searched for sharp objects, some had managed to bring in nails or splinters of glass with which to cut messages upon the plastered walls.

Among the few inscriptions he could read was one written in Japanese characters: "Starved and afraid—a convict. Mother, I'm still alive! May, 1949, Morikawa Takeshi."

Another, in Russian, read, "There is no God!"

When he closed his eyes, Iki imagined that he could hear the moaning of the terrified and abandoned man who denied the existence of God. How could any man, deprived of all hope, go on living in these hideous cells? Did the Russian who denied the existence of God write that bleak message precisely because he believed in God? Unable to endure the torment, had he cried out to God to confirm His existence, had he invoked Him and pleaded for His saving grace? Was his own faith in Japan simply another form of faith in a supreme being?

When the light had faded from the small window, the guards outside switched on a naked electric lamp attached to the ceiling. It stayed on all through night, shining on the prisoner below for the benefit of inspecting guards, and was turned off only when daylight again brightened the cell.

The loud click of a key unlocking the door called Iki back to reality.

"Out!" a brawny guard commanded.

"Am I to be questioned again tonight?"

"Right."

"But I haven't had my supper yet." He expected to be interrogated through most of the night.

"Sorry," the guard said with unusual sympathy, "but the van's already here."

This time they took Iki through a maze of corridors to the hallway that led directly to the prison entrance. From the other end of the hallway came two guards, dragging a half-conscious prisoner between them. The guard accompanying Iki stopped in confusion. He called out loudly to the oncoming guards, who turned their limp prisoner toward the wall. Such curious behavior led Iki to believe that the other prisoner was a Japanese.

"Look straight ahead and keep walking!" his guard commanded, twisting Iki's arm behind his back to make sure he obeyed.

Even so, Iki had time for a quick glance at the other man, and saw that he wore a Japanese officer's uniform. At that instant the other prisoner raised his head. Although bruised and haggard, he was young, still almost a youth. Iki guessed that he was one of the newly commissioned second lieutenants assigned to the Kwantung Army in the last days of the war. For an instant Iki sent the signals of eyes and face that encouraged him to take heart, but his guard pushed him onward.

The young officer shouted in desperation: "Second Lieutenant Hori Toshio of Strategic Brigade! Sentenced to death!"

Iki spun around. A guard tried to clap a hand over the youth's mouth, while shoving him forward. But he broke loose, and cried, "Death by firing squad! Tell my father and mother in Fukuoka!"

"They can't shoot you, Hori!" Iki shouted back. "Keep your courage!"

The guard cupped one huge hand over Iki's mouth, and with the other forced him along the hallway, out into the night and into the waiting van.

Lights burned bright in the Khabarovsk office of the Soviet Ministry of Internal Affairs. Once again Iki sat in the interrogation room, facing Captain Sarnov and his interpreter.

"A long time since we met," he said in faulty Japanese, and repeated the greeting in Russian. The faint smile on Sarnov's face was unmistakable. But, somehow, false. It made Iki suspect the man who held such power over him. "How have you been?"

"You can see for yourself."

"Blame yourself, for being so stubborn. You know you're guilty of the charges. So why not admit them? Cooperate, and you'll be given white bread and cheese for lunch. And cigarettes from time to time."

"I appreciate your kindness, but I can't accept it," Iki said calmly, although offended by the enticement, so transparent, so meaningless to a man in his position. "Let me tell you why. You have no right to question me about war crimes. Your country, not mine, was the one that abrogated the neutrality agreement. Your country attacked my country. Furthermore, I object to your methods of interrogation. They are cruel, inhumane, contrary to law and justice. Now my turn has come to make demands. From now on, if you insist on questioning me, then by all means start in the morning. And please be finished before the hour when even prisoners are allowed to go to sleep."

"You arrogant bastard!" Sarnov exploded. "Keep this up, and you'll find yourself in Magadan!"

He could not have made a more frightening threat. The mere mention of Magadan, gateway to the penal colonies in the frozen vastness of the Kolyma region, was enough to strike terror into the hearts of the most hardened Russian criminals. Iki, too, reacted as did the others of Russia's victims.

Satisfied to see Iki silenced, Sarnov continued more calmly. "Do you admit to contributing to the planning of the war in the Pacific?"

"Yes."

"Which operations did you help plan?"

"Those against Singapore and Manila."

Sarnov leaned back in his chair, choosing his words deliberately. "Now, for the details. What were the objectives? How many troops were involved in the operations? When did troop movements commence? Where were they sent? I want precise answers to all these questions."

Soon before the beginning of hostilities with the United States, the operations in which Sarnov was interested had been planned with great care by a staff of more than a dozen men. They included Iki, who was then twenty-nine years old. For Sarnov's benefit Iki sorted out information that had been known generally among the higher echelons of the Japanese military.

"According to plans drawn up at Imperial General Headquarters, the Navy's bombing of Pearl Harbor was to be followed by Army maneuvers against Singapore and Manila. The 25th Army, consisting of 150,000 men, was ordered to attack Singapore. The 14th Army, consisting of 100,000 men was ordered to take Manila. When diplomatic relations with the United States deteriorated in early November 1941, troops of those units boarded ships at different ports in Japan, Manchuria, and China. The transports rendezvoused at two points—a short distance from Penghu Island, in the Formosa Strait, and near Hainan Island, off the south China coast. If negotiations led to assurances of peace, the ships were to return to port immediately. In the likelihood of war, they were to sail south in time for the armies to land on the Malay Peninsula within one to two hours following the attack on Pearl Harbor, and, two hours after that, on the coast of Luzon in the Philippines."

"A great deal of time would have been required to plan the secret movement of 250,000 troops. When did you begin?"

Obviously Sarnov was trying to uncover evidence of Japan's intent to start a war of aggression.

"Sometime in June of 1941, when a breakdown in diplomatic relationships between Japan and the United States seemed a distinct possibility."

"You can't expect me to believe that. Japan would have had to start planning much earlier."

"You're asking me about routine military planning," Iki replied. "In Japan, as in the Soviet Union, staff headquarters normally were required to be prepared to carry out any military action required by government decisions. War plans were always in readiness, and, naturally, were revised annually in response to changes in the world political situation."

"All right, then," Sarnov said irritably. "If anti-Soviet war plans were drawn up annually, describe those from 1931, the year of the Manchurian Incident, and continuing through 1945."

"I was assigned to Imperial Headquarters in 1940. Therefore, I had nothing to do with plans concerning the Soviet Union except in the year prior to my transfer to the Kwantung Army. I can tell you about those plans. And only those."

Iki described the defensive operations planned for stations along the Soviet-Manchurian border. Sarnov asked a number of detailed questions, then opened his note pad and wrote busily. When at last he finished his report he turned again to Iki.

"You contributed to Japan's planning of the Greater East Asia War. Your crime amounts to abetting capitalism, as stipulated in Article Fifty-eight, Section Four, of the Criminal Code of the Soviet Union." He pushed the report across the table. "Sign here," he demanded.

"I refuse! Japan is a capitalistic nation. The idea is ridiculous, to apply Soviet domestic laws to indict me, a Japanese, for performing tasks in the line of duty for the defense of Japan. Such an indictment is in violation of international law."

"Losers in war can't refuse," Sarnov said icily. "Not anything. And international law means nothing, so far as you're concerned. The Soviet Union will determine what's right and what's wrong for you."

Silenced by the brutality of such logic, Iki could think of nothing to say. Interpreting Iki's silence as consent, Sarnov moved on to a different topic. "A strategic brigade was organized in Manchuria after your transfer to Kwantung Army Headquarters in February of 1944. Is that right?"

"Yes."

"Are you the one who proposed its formation?"

"I was among the planners."

"Why was the unit organized?"

"To penetrate behind enemy lines, sever communication lines, launch night assaults on headquarters and artillery units, and destroy supply depots and other military installations."

"Where was the brigade headquartered?"

"In Kirin, Manchuria."

"How many men were in the brigade? And give me the names of the brigade commander and the staff officers."

That put Iki instantly on guard. His covert mission as a diplomatic courier, as well as his role in planning the war in Greater East Asia, were charges to which he alone need answer. But his answers to questions about the Strategic Brigade could affect the fate of all the men who had been part of the unit.

"You might as well answer," Sarnov said. "We already know who the brigade commander was, and we have the names of the commanders of the subordinate battalions. We know that the brigade was made up of five thousand men, and that its purpose was espionage. Since you helped organize the brigade, I'm sure you can confirm these facts."

"The brigade was organized for the purposes I've already stated," Iki insisted. "It was not an espionage unit."

"We've learned a lot about that brigade. We know that you personally issued the orders for espionage activities when you were operations officer at Kwantung Army Headquarters. You might as well admit it."

"You ought to know, Captain Sarnov, that a strategic brigade is an orthodox army unit specializing in missions behind enemy lines. The men are in uniform, and their actions are military actions."

"If a unit penetrates behind enemy lines to destroy installations, it's an espionage unit. Where's the difference?"

"Military men recognize a clear-cut difference. According to international law, espionage is defined as destructive activity by civilians or military personnel disguised as civilians. An action carried out by a regular military unit of men in military uniform is, by any definition, a military operation."

Sarnov opened a thick volume. "According to Article Fifty-eight, Section Nine, of the Soviet Union Criminal Code, espionage is defined as 'the use of explosives or incendiary material to destroy or damage national facilities, communication lines, military headquarters, etc.' There is absolutely no mention here of the kind of clothing worn."

"Soviet laws mean nothing in this instance. Under international law, the strategic brigade of the Kwantung Army could never be confused with an espionage unit."

"Enough!" Sarnov snarled. "Who are you to criticize the laws of the Soviet Union!"

"That wasn't my intention." Iki forced himself to speak calmly. "What I'm asking you to understand is that you're applying a section of your domestic criminal code to military actions by a Japanese unit which were wholly unrelated to crimes committed by your own citizens."

Despite Iki's expectations of a logical response to a logical statement, Sarnov flew into a rage.

"You're a hopeless fascist! What you need is time to reconsider. And I have a special place where you'll have no trouble concentrating on your problem!"

He yelled for a guard, and issued orders in rapid Russian. The clock on the wall said five. Having been interrogated through most of the night, Iki rose wearily from his chair. The guard led him down the corridor toward a row of closet-like booths. As the guard unlocked the heavy door to one of the booths, Iki wondered if he would be asked to change clothes. And why.

"Get in!" The guard shoved him through the door. Iki's face hit the far wall. The lock snapped and he found himself shut away in a closet six feet in height and two feet square.

Iki had been worn out physically and mentally when he was thrust into the closet. A half hour later, in spite of the sharp pains in his hips and legs, he fell asleep standing up.

Several hours later, the urge to relieve himself awakened him. Light entered the closet through the small air hole overhead. The boards that confined him had been saturated with the urine, vomit, sweat—the foulness of countless victims before him. He gagged at the stench. He shouted to be let out, but no one answered. His bladder felt ready to burst. He pounded on the door and kicked the walls, trying to attract a guard's attention.

At last he heard footsteps approaching. "Quiet, you in there! What do you want?"

"I have to go to the toilet!"

The door was unlocked. Giddy, his legs burning with pain, he fell to the floor the moment he stepped out the closet.

"Get up!" the guard shouted. But when he noticed Iki's pallor, he helped him stand up, and supported him during the walk to the latrine. Grateful to have the freedom to move and to stretch, even briefly, Iki returned to his closet revived—for a while.

Sarnov renewed the interrogation that same afternoon.

"How was it?" he began when they faced each other across the desk. "Have you reconsidered?"

Iki's very spirit revolted in fury. While he was confined in the booth, he had been afraid that he would be left to die in that vertical coffin. Now Sarnov had as much as told him that his torment was a "legal" means of confinement.

"You monsters! You torture everyone you suspect, to force confessions from them."

"Nonsense!" Sarnov said. Iki could not be sure whether he was serious or sarcastic. "The Soviet Union forbids the torturing of prisoners. We have no implements for torture, and we don't permit violence. You were placed in isolation for my convenience. You're not the only one I'm interrogating, you know. If you stop answering my questions, I have to put you in suspension, so that I may question others. As I've told you more than once, if you don't wish to be held in suspension, all you need to do is cooperate with me."

"You're asking the impossible," Iki protested. "I don't care how many times you ask that question. The answer will be the same: the strategic brigade was an operational unit, and no one knows that better than I."

"You're wasting my time," Sarnov said coldly. "You go back into suspension."

Although he knew that former members of the strategic brigade were being subjected to the same horror, Iki wondered how he could bear again the ordeal of the upright coffin.

"You talk big," Sarnov added contemptuously. "Let's see how long you can stand that shoe box."

Iki was interrogated daily by Sarnov and, each time after brief questioning, was sent back to the box. Forced into that unchanging position, he would go through a predictable cycle of responses: first an increasing agony, then a raging torment that found release in shrieks and sobs, then numbness, followed by a merciful exhaustion that left him senseless. He could look forward to only one thing: release from the closet at nightfall, when they put him in his solitary cell for the night. Before long, however, he developed arthritis in the joints of hands and feet and hips, and once his sleep was broken by those stabbing pains they kept him awake for much of the night.

For seven successive days Sarnov questioned Iki and then held him in the closet. On the eighth day they put him in the closet directly, without interrogation. Sweat oozed from every pore as the very idea of being shut up made him groan with fear and pain. Suddenly he imagined he was surrounded by a blaze of red flames. He saw hundreds of Japanese, their bodies afire, fleeing Soviet troops who were invading the streets of burning Shinkyo. A half-crazed woman, holding a small child in one arm, stretched her other arm out to him. But when he tried to reach out to her, a sheet of fire rose up between them. Her stricken face, scorched by flames, floated toward him—

"Yaponskii! Shut up! You're making too much noise!" The guard's shout brought Iki to his senses. "Come! Time for your little chat with the captain." The guard swung the closet door wide, put his arm around Iki's waist, and helped him totter to the interrogation room.

"Do you know who I am?" Sarnov asked, seeing the blank expression on his victim's face. "I've finished the interrogation report. It'll be interpreted for you, in Japanese. So listen carefully."

The report contained not one of Iki's statements. He listened to Sarnov's string of lies, trying hard to concentrate. Among other things, Sarnov made him say that the Kwantung Army strategic brigade had been an espionage unit.

"Here, sign it." Sarnov, mild as milk, put a pen in Iki's hand. "This interrogation will be finished when you sign."

Iki shook his head. "I can't put my name to these lies . . .

You've asked me a thousand times. And I'm telling you again, for one more than a thousand times, that the strategic brigade was a regulation military unit."

Sarnov's half-smile vanished as he cursed Iki in vulgar Russian, gutteral and precise.

"Mr. Iki," the interpeter said softly. "Please sign it. If you don't, you'll be in trouble. What Maxim Gorky said is true: 'Man cannot tamper with fate; it is fate that tampers with man.' "

But, as he must, Iki did not heed the compassionate interpreter.

"To me it's obvious that you're bound by a pledge of loyalty," Sarnov fumed, tossing papers around on his desk. "Loyalty to whom? To the men of the strategic brigade? . . . To the Kwantung Army? . . . Or to Japan?"

"Yes, loyalty to all three."

"What good do you get from being so loyal? Being so obstinate?" Sarnov asked mildly, dropping the hardness in his manner and expression. "Here, look at this."

Sarnov handed him a letter. It was a standard sheet of lined paper, on which messages could be sent to prisoners of war in Siberia. Iki recognized his wife's calligraphy, but hid any sign of eagerness to read it. This was the first letter from his family that he'd received since his capture. He took it with a pretense of calm, and began to read—very slowly, as if wanting to caress each word with his eyes:

I was relieved when I received your letter, dated December 9, 1948, and learned that you were alive and well. Naoko is making good grades in primary school, and Makoto will be starting school soon. I must also send sad news. Your father, always so concerned about your return, died on February 3, 1946, in Yamagata. The cause was pneumonia. Our children keep your portrait beside their desks. They think of you constantly, and with pride. We are waiting for your return. Please keep safe.

He was not ashamed of his tears, when he finished reading. In the letter he'd sent home in June of the year before, from Khabarovsk, he had asked to be fully informed about his immediate family. This reply from his wife, judging from the postmark, had been held up for more than six months by the Ministry of Internal Affairs. He was saddened to think that his aged father had worried about him, up to the moment of his death. But the news of Naoko and Makoto warmed his heart, and his thoughts darted back three years to the joy of having seen them, even from a distance, in Tokyo. How surprised he'd been to notice how fast they were growing. The sight of their thin arms and legs had touched his heart.

Frequently he dreamed about his children—the same recurring dream in which he saw them on the edge of dying from starvation, —and always he awoke bathed in perspiration.

For a single precious moment, his family had crowded from his mind all thought of the strategic brigade, of the torture closet, of this tormentor who clung to him with the tenacity of a leech.

Sarnov could see that Iki had been moved, and he spoke soothingly as he placed a pen in Iki's hand. "Your family is anxiously waiting for you to return to Japan. Come! Sign this report."

Iki did not answer. He was trying to suppress those memories.

"My children are about that age," Sarnov continued relentlessly, his eyes never leaving Iki's face. "I think that's the age when they need a father the most. Your two children are at the age when they are the most lovable. Does your little boy look like you?"

Iki looked away from that mesmerizing face, tried not to hear the relentless voice.

"One of the men in our Political Department was in Japan recently. He told us that many war widows and wives of missing men are marrying again. I would hate to see you return to Japan only to find out that your children have a new father. I think you ought to go back as soon as you can. I'm just advising you as a father who has children about the same age as yours."

That possibility worried Iki. If he stayed away from Japan for many more years, would he lose his family? He weighed the consequences of signing the report. Even if he should sign it, would the Soviet Union free him and allow him to return to Japan? The Russians could so easily capitalize on a confession from the man who was primarily responsible for the missions of the strategic brigade. In that event, his signature would be like a stamp of approval on an order that might send scores of his countrymen to death—or even worse, to a lifetime of hard labor in one of these internment camps with which he himself was so well acquainted.

"No." Iki quietly laid the pen down before Sarnov. "No," he said again, standing up.

This time Sarnov sighed, as if grieved to the heart by a betrayal he did not deserve. "Some day your children will know the shame of having a fascist for a father. The world is changing, and soon the day will come when Japan will be a communist country."

Iki smiled down at the tempter. He had no reason to doubt that his children regarded his photograph with pride. He recalled the portrait, showing him in the lieutenant colonel's uniform, the staff officer's cordon suspended from the right shoulder, his hands on the hilt of his sword. He found the strength he needed in the knowledge that his children continued to remember him with pride and respect.

"I have no pity for the likes of you," Sarnov growled. "You'd better be prepared for what's ahead.

Sarnov no longer worked on Iki. In his solitary cell, Iki slowly recovered from the horrors of the upright coffin. Even as his body mended, however, the enforced idleness tormented him more than ever before. At first, by day and by night, having nothing else to do, he dwelt in troubled thought. Among the greatest of his worries was the possibility that, of all the 700,000 Japanese imprisoned by the Soviets, he must be the only one who still remained captive in Siberia.

Once upon a time the sun's rays coming through the tiny window near the ceiling of his cell had been a reminder of hope. But now those same rays distressed him, for each renewal of brightness signaled another passing day in a life that no longer held any meaning. After a while, he thought no more about his children, or his wife, or Japan. Now he spent the entire day hunched over, his head buried in his arms, thinking of nothing, nothing at all.

In early September, when the sun began to hover above the horizon throughout the night, Iki was summoned to the Khabarovsk office of the Ministry of Internal Affairs, where he had been interrogated more than four months before. There, on September 9, 1949, he appeared before a Soviet military tribunal.

As usual, on the walls of the courtroom hung portraits of Stalin and Beria, side by side, flanked by a pair of red flags. Seated at the center table were four judges, an interpreter, and a stenographer. It was a closed trial, with neither prosecution nor defense counsel present.

As soon as Iki entered the room, the presiding judge declared the court in session. He established Iki's nationality, name, and rank, then announced, "I shall read the court's verdict, based on the indictment presented by the prosecution:

"First, the defendant, Iki Tadashi, lieutenant colonel of the Japanese Army and officer attached to Imperial General Headquarters, did, in 1943, conceal his identity, did assume the guise of a clerk of the Japanese Foreign Ministry, and did secretly enter Kuibyshev, then the capital of the Union of Soviet Socialist Republics. These acts constitute the crime of anti-Soviet intelligence activity, as specified in Article Fifty-eight, Section Nine, of the Criminal Code of the Union of Soviet Socialist Republics.

"Second, said defendant, in his capacity as operations officer of the Army General Staff, did contribute to the planning of the Greater East Asia War for a period of more than three years, from December 1940 to February 1944. Such action constitutes the crime of abetting capitalism, as specified in Article Fifty-eight, Section Four.

"Third, said defendant, in his capacity as operations officer of Kwantung Army Headquarters, did in 1944 participate in the planning of the formation of the Strategic Brigade, and did issue war orders to said unit. These actions constitute the crime of anti-Soviet intelligence activity, as specified in Article Fifty-eight, Section Nine.

"For the above crimes, I hereby sentence you, war criminal Iki Tadashi, to a cumulative total of twenty-five years at hard labor. Although the death penalty is warranted, the Soviet Union has, for humanitarian reasons, abolished capital punishment, instead of which you are given a twenty-five year sentence."

The interpreter rushed through a brief translation of this verdict, which Iki had understood from the beginning.

"If you have any objections," the presiding judge continued, "you may appeal the verdict. What is your wish?"

The act of appeal itself, Iki well knew, would mean that he acknowledged the legitimacy of this spurious trial. Instead, he chose to protest the legitimacy of the verdict.

"I know of the agreement among the Allied Powers to try war criminals in the country where they are imprisoned, but I do not accept unconditional application of the domestic laws of that country. I am a military officer of a capitalistic nation. The fact that I performed my duties loyally for my country is no reason for me to be charged with 'abetting capitalism,' a criminal act according to your national laws. I insist on a retrial based on international law and on recognition of the fact that so-called 'war crimes' have no precedents in courts of law."

"You are ignorant of the fact that this court conducts its trials of war criminals on the basis of a new international agreement."

"If such an agreement exists, I insist on hearing a reading of the text for that agreement."

"This court does not recognize the need for explanations to criminals," the judge said curtly. "We conclude, then, that you do not wish to appeal the verdict. This court is adjourned."

Iki watched, astonished, as the judges left the courtroom. He had been standing before them for only fifteen minutes, and in that brief time he had been tried, found guilty of several crimes, and sentenced to a term of twenty-five years at hard labor. His thoughts raced twenty-five years ahead—if he were still living, he would be sixty-two! Could he survive twenty-five years more of hard labor in Siberia? If his body lived through them, could his mind, his spirit, survive? If they broke, he would become no more than a hollow shell. In the emptying courtroom only he could hear his agonized plea: "Be merciful. Let me die before a firing squad!"

The prisoner transport train left Khabarovsk and headed north. All but two of the fifteen steel cars were filled with women. In those two cars, each of the barred cages held more than twenty men.

Iki's cage compartment held nine other Japanese, as well as Russians, Mongols, and Armenians. Most of the Russians looked like hardened criminals. They occupied the uppermost of the three tiers of bunks, and whiled away much of their time eyeing the belongings of the men below them.

"You cheap Cantonskii, screw your mother!" They shouted the ultimate Russian profanity at the slightest show of resistance to their unruly demands for this, for that, for anything that caught their fancy. The Japanese, who carried little of value on them, ignored their covetous appraisals and their loud curses.

The ten Japanese had either been associated with intelligence duties or had worked for Department of the Justice in Manchukuo. They had been subjected to the same sort of military "trial" as Iki's, convicted of violating Article Fifty-eight of the Soviet Criminal Code, and like him, had received sentences of twenty to twenty-five years at hard labor. Iki first met these other Japanese in Khabarovsk's Red Prison, to which he was transferred following his conviction in September of the year before. Among the nine was Lieutenant Hori Toshio, whom he had seen first in a corridor of the White Prison.

The train, stopping frequently on sidings, crawled northward, across Siberia's Maritime Provinces. Through the small window beyond the iron grating the prisoners could see the snow-covered taiga. At Komsomol'sk the train turned east, and four days later arrived in Sovetskaya Gavan'.

The sun gave little warmth to the convicts who crept down from the transport train. Both men and women prisoners were marched away from the town along a road leading toward distant hills. From the top of a long, steep incline they saw below them an immense prison camp. The compound was packed with close-set rows of barracks, enormous compared with those in the lager at Khabarovsk. The miniature city for convicts bristled with guard towers. The moment Iki and the other Japanese war criminals passed through the gate of lager number five, they knew they had entered a world in which everyone was merely a convict, where no distinction was made regarding anyone's past, whether political or criminal.

Although Iki was resigned to his sentence, he did not welcome the prospect of living in this teeming population of many types of hardened criminals, of many races, until the day in spring when he would board a ship bound for Magadan. As every convict knew, the Magadan coast could be reached only by ship, and the northern seas would not be free of ice until April, at the earliest.

Having spent his first night in a huge barrack constructed of logs, Iki went out into the compound to breathe the fresh morning air. He noticed a crowd of men beside the barbed-wire fence, their attention fixed on a women's barrack across the street. Beneath the eaves of the barrack women lay in groups of twenty to thirty, their bodies white with frost.

"What's happened to them? . . . Are they dead?" he asked a man standing beside him.

"No. Just sleeping."

"Why are they sleeping outdoors?"

"They couldn't get bunks inside. Women are worse than men. We're overcrowded here, but we wouldn't think of kicking each other out of our barracks."

As they watched, a guard went among the sleeping women, prodding one with the butt of his rifle, another with the toe of his boot. All got the lash of his tongue. "Get up pigs! You can't go on sleeping forever."

"Watch out where you go poking, you horny pimp!" one of the women yelled, offering no respect to authority.

The women pushed themselves up, and hung their damp coats, blankets, even dresses on the barbed wire to dry. Some stood around in their underwear, with compacts in hand, applying make-up, indifferent to the stares and cat-calls of the men across the street.

The convicts were not made to labor for the fatherland while they awaited shipment. Such enforced leisure gave the Japanese the chance to talk among themselves about their futures. The more they speculated, the more deeply were they troubled.

Hori Toshio, the youngest among them, told what he had heard. "Between sixty and seventy thousand prisoners are here in Sovetskaya, and we're all going to be shipped off to Magadan in the spring. I wonder what kind of work we'll be doing when we get there?"

A former Manchukuo government official, Tachibana, who spoke fluent Russian, had a ready answer. "From what the Russians have been telling me, I gather that they've found huge mineral deposits along the upper reaches of the Kolyma River. They've opened a number of gold deposits and uranium mines up there. People say the uranium mines are deadly, that convicts die from radiation in a matter of months." Even in remote Siberia, even prisoners were learning about uranium, this newest plaything of warring nations.

"We've nothing to gain from this sort of talk," Iki scolded, hoping to stop the typical convicts' urge to frighten one another with all kinds of imaginings.

The thousands of men and women consigned to this transit camp had reached such a state of degradation that they tried to find release in punishing one another, in beating or even killing each other—often for no apparent reason. And, amazingly, some of them found time and energy for sex. After nightfall, male convicts bribed or intimidated the guards to allow them to sneak through the barbed-wire fence into the women's barracks. Many women, reckless and despondent over having arrived at this literal end of the earth, offered themselves freely to the men. Pairs could be seen each evening, coupling on the ground along the barbed-wire fence that supposedly separated the two compounds.

The searchlight picked out a woman just as she lifted her skirt and, for advertisement, exposed an expanse of white buttocks. Men yelped and whistled as they rushed toward that attraction. A guard in the tower fired a single warning shot, and men and women scattered in opposite directions. But one woman did not rush. She stayed close to the fence, near the spot where Iki sat, seeking solitude.

"That shot didn't scare you," the woman said flatly from beyond the wires. "Are you a Yaponskii samurai?"

"That's right. But you weren't frightened either. You must be a polit-zek."

"Oh, no—nothing that high-class. I was born in a women's lager. I know this kind of place all too well." In response to Iki's questions, she told him more about herself. "I was brought up in a state orphanage, as one of Uncle Joseph's fatherless children. I made a living as a thief and a prostitute, having no other career. But I got caught once too often. Now they're sending me up for fifteen years."

Beneath the heavy make-up, she looked young. And her figure, beneath the plain frock, was still slim. Iki guessed that she could not have been more than twenty-six or twenty-seven years old.

"What happened to your parents?"

"I'm not sure. I guess Papa was stupid. The Party purged him. They shot him just before I was born. Mama and my sister were put in a lager, but I don't know what happened to them after I was born. I'm just a convict, but at least I'm my own boss. Nobody runs me. —Let me show you something."

She opened her blouse part way and showed him a tatoo on her breast—a crude picture showing a man and a woman copulating.

"Why did you put that on? . . ."

"Oh, I didn't do it—they did. Once a woman's a convict, they do this to her to make sure she doesn't live a decent life again on the outside. —Listen, we have a Japanese woman with us. Wait here, I'll go and get her." She sped away, before Iki could tell her not to bother.

Iki doubted her statement, thinking she had probably mistaken a Korean woman, or a Mongolian, for a Japanese. But soon she returned, drawing another woman by the hand.

"Here she is, Yaponskii!"

A very thin woman, dressed in tattered Western clothes, looked at him dully.

"Are you a Japanese?" he asked softly, speaking in Russian, because he could not be sure what she was.

"Yes. I am Japanese," she replied, with an air of complete disinterest.

Iki was stunned. He had never dreamed that a Japanese woman would be among the thousands of convicts being sent to the Kolyma penal colony.

"Where are you from?" he asked in Japanese. "What is your name?"

"I lived in Feng-t'ien. My husband was a civilian worker—" She stopped, as she realized that she was speaking to another Japanese. Quickly she hid her hands behind her back, but not before Iki noticed dark blotches on her wrists. And around her neck, inside the collar, he saw more bruises. He guessed that she, too, bore an indecent tatoo on another part of her body. Struck dumb with pity, he was unable to find one consoling word to say to this broken woman.

In mid-April the Sea of Okhotsk was free of ice, allowing shipments of convicts to sail for Magadan.

"I wish I was going with you, Colonel Iki." Hori, doubly forlorn, lowered his head; his voice broke. Since their reunion on the train, Hori had regarded Iki as something of a commanding officer and a surrogate father.

"Don't lose your nerve," Iki told him sternly. In his heart he pitied Hori, fated to waste his manhood in a colony of convicts. "Have faith in Japan. They won't forget us at home."

Iki and his four companions were among the seven thousand convicts who marched down the sloping road leading to the harbor. Several ships lay at anchor in the bay. When the prisoners reached the docks and learned that all of them were to be loaded aboard a pair of worn out 4,000-ton freighters, they sent up wails of complaints. But no commissar or guard cared in the least what they thought. Prodded by bayonets and clubs, they climbed up the sides of those two rusty derelicts.

The ship's holds had been partly loaded with lumber, across which rough planks were laid to serve as a mid-deck. Although sea ice in the harbor had thawed, the water itself was at near-freezing temperature. Moisture in the convicts' breath quickly crystalized to form a coat of frost on any metal surface, especially the hull plates and bulkheads.

"We'll have to move fast, or we won't get a place to sit," Tachibana warned, as he, Iki, and their fellow Japanese struggled to stay together in the rush of hundreds of convicts, all fighting for a place on the mid-deck. "Here's an open space. Even if it is next to the urine tubs. Not the best place, but let's grab it while we can."

The five Japanese settled down next to the urinals with sighs of relief. Everyone knew that the voyage would last more than ten days if the sea was stormy, and no one, not even the strongest, wanted to stand up for so long a voyage.

Because the shallow northern end of Tatar Straits was closed to maritime traffic, ships bound for Magadan had to go around the southern tip of Sakhalin Island, in order to enter the Okhotsk Sea. Iki and his companions hoped to gain at least a glimpse of Japan when their ship took them through La Perouse Straits between Sakhalin and Hokkaido. But their hope was only a faint one, because they would be kept in the holds almost all the way, and allowed on the upper deck only once a day to receive the single meal for that day.

Toward dawn, the five Japanese, and a few hundred other convicts, were given their turn to come up from below in order to eat their first meal aboard the freighter. For more than twelve hours they had breathed the fetid air of the convict holds. Fortunately, the ship, which had been pitching and rolling until then, sailed now in calm waters in the lee of Sakhalin. The men stood in line, taking deep breaths of the clean, fresh sea air. "Almost like home," said Kawamoto, who came from Shimoda.

The meal consisted of gruel. By the time the Japanese reached the serving counter the ship's supply of earthenware bowls had been exhausted. "Hold out your caps!" the galley-boys commanded.

Iki hesitated. But he had no choice, And, besides, he'd eaten worse meals, under filthier conditions. He held out his grimy cap and watched the gruel being ladeled into it. For a while, he contemplated the watery meal, then shut his eyes and gulped it down, quickly, before the cap leaked. When he looked up from that repast he saw black clouds in the distance, faintly outlined against the brightening sky.

The freighter was sailing directly toward the light of the rising sun. For several minutes the Japanese searched the horizon to the south. Then they saw it, a great high blue mound more solid than cloud or sea.

"It must be Hokkaido . . ." said someone.

"It's Japan," said Tachibana, with a sob.

For a long time the five Japanese clung to the railing, as tears streamed down their cheeks, gazing toward the beloved, unreachable land. No one spoke any more. Each, in his own thoughts, was saying farewell to his native land, which he had little hope of ever seeing again. In a few days they would arrive in Magadan. And from there they would be sent to the deadly mines of the Kolyma region from which few convicts ever returned alive.

8

AT THE EDGE
OF THE WORLD

Since Iki arrived at Lazo, to serve his sentence of twenty-five years at hard labor, a year and a half had passed. They went so slowly that each exhausting day and each wearying night seemed an interminable continuation of the last.

Lazo, known as the "convicts' graveyard," was located on the upper reaches of Kolyma River, at sixty-five north latitude, 152 degrees east longitude, about two hundred and fifty miles north of Magadan. During the nine months of Kolyma's winter, Lazo virtually became an island, cut off from the rest of the continent by a broad plain of snow and ice. The land was dimly lighted by the sun, which hovered above the perpetual blanket of fog for only a few hours each day. A short summer began abruptly in June, when the mantle of snow melted away, revealing miles of desolate, rocky hills with no visible life except a sparse covering of prickly new grasses.

Lazo was only one of several penal settlements in the barren zone lying just south of the perpetually frozen tundra. The lager consisted of a dozen flimsy barracks erected about two and a half miles away from the mines. Rectangular barracks, rocky outcrops, and enormous heaps of rubble were the only shapes that broke the monotony of the sterile landscape.

The convicts' black uniform that Iki wore was thin and ragged. Bits of the cotton padding stuck out from rips in the cheap cloth. A white patch sewn to the back of his jacket bore his number, written in black ink: ON 5–32037. His skin, dry and sallow, stretched tight over fleshless bones. Much of his hair had fallen out. His mouth hung open, and a number of teeth were missing. Yet he was only thirty-nine years old.

* * *

At six o'clock each morning, the inmates of Lazo awoke to the clangor of a hammer striking a piece of steel rail with deafening regularity. Men groped about in the dim light cast by a single five-watt bulb. The glass in the barred windows was covered with ice, and melting icicles from slits between walls and eaves dripped water into the barracks.

A temperature of forty below zero was typical for a morning in late October. At lagers for war prisoners work would be suspended whenever the outdoor temperature fell below minus twenty; but at Lazo, a slave-labor camp, convicts who worked in the mines were relieved only when the temperature registered below minus sixty degrees or when a heavy blizzard prevented them from marching to the shafts.

As he opened his eyes, Iki cursed the coming of morning. He lay on a bunk made of rough boards nailed to a log frame; he had neither mat nor blanket, those being luxuries possessed by only a few men. The convicts slept in the same clothes they wore at work, using their muddy boots for pillows. Two minutes after the signal, a guard came in, swinging a club, shouting commands, and beating prisoners who had not yet left their bunks.

The men ran to the mess hall for a breakfast of black bread and a weak soup made from fish heads and bits of spoiled cabbage. After that hearty meal they ran back to the barracks and dressed for the day's labor. Iki pulled a coat of reindeer skin over the greatcoat of cloth in which he had slept, and tied both about him with a length of rope. He had seen men made insane by freezing that damaged the brain, and each day he took all possible precautions against such a dreaded effect of exposure. He wore the winter cap pulled down over his brow, and wound many strips of cloth about his head, leaving only the eyes uncovered. Hurriedly he wrapped strips of blanket about his feet, over which he pulled thick felt boots, slipped his hands into heavy mittens, and ran outside for roll call.

The barracks chief called out the given names of Russian prisoners, and each responded with his patronym, year of birth, offense, and serial number. Thus the prisoner called "Alexei" would cry out: "Ivanovich Dobronskii, born 1906, twenty years for violating Article Fifty-eight, Section Nine, ON 5–21195."

Iki, called by his surname, answered: "Tadashi, born 1912,

178

twenty-five years for violating Article Fifty-eight, Section Four, ON 5–32037."

Thereupon, he went to join the work-gang. Each man stood with hands clasped behind his back, until the last one had been identified and accounted for. Outside the main gate the barrack chief turned over the team to rifle-bearing guards, one of whom repeated the same instructions each morning: "All convicts are hereby notified that conversation during marching is forbidden. Hands must always be clasped behind the back. Breaking of ranks is forbidden. Falling out of formation will be considered an attempt to escape. Guards will shoot to kill. Understand?"

"Understood," a few prisoners toward the front muttered, merely to please the guards.

Out of the dusky sky snow as fine as powder fell upon the column of ragged convicts slowly moving forward at the urging of the armed guards. They, in turn, were pulled along by dogs on leashes. These, too, had been trained to kill.

As Iki trudged along, thinking about the dreary months he had spent in Kolyma, he would marvel that he still lived. During the first six months after reaching Lazo he had worked above ground, at such tasks as sifting mineral ores and dumping unwanted rubble. But during the last twelve months he had slaved in deep underground shafts, and seldom saw sunlight. He suffered from perpetual weariness, punctuated by spasms of pain in many inflamed joints. His gums bled, and he felt as if his teeth were floating in his jaws. He recognized these symptoms as the progressive symptoms of scurvy, for which no natural remedy could be found in this frigid zone except during the brief summer, when a few antiscorbutic plants managed to grow.

By the time he'd stumbled the two and a half miles to the mine head, all sensation in his limbs were lost. The convicts were driven through a gate to the toolhouse, where each man was given a hand lamp and either a pick or a shovel before being sent underground. The whole crew of two thousand men, divided into teams of twenty-five, began their twelve-hour shift, to work without food or drink in a round-the-clock operation.

Iki fell in with his usual team. This time they were led to a different shaft by their foreman, a one-eyed criminal convict nicknamed Kolyma Volk, "the Wolf of Kolyma." Everyone feared this tough leader, but they also respected him because he treated them fairly as individuals and, somehow, exacted fair treatment for his team from guards and other foremen. Those other foremen, too, deferred to the Wolf.

Kolyma Volk took his gang down a newly prepared shaft at the end of a long tunnel. Iki made the descent slowly. Most of the other men moved quickly down a series of logs laid horizontally, at short intervals, across the shaft to serve as steps of a sort. Iki was much too crippled to keep up with the others. He took one step at a time, resting his pick and lamp on the ramp that supported a log as he lowered himself to the next one, seeking his footing by the faint light of the lamp.

While he lowered himself painfully, rung by rung, his teammates descended into the darkness below. Iki knew the danger of being left alone for many a convict had been lost in the labyrinth of tunnels and shafts, never to be seen again until, perhaps, someone stumbled upon his bones. He pointed his lamp down the gaping shaft, but the beam reached little farther than the next rung. He listened for sounds made by others, but heard only his own wheezing. Although he seemed to be suspended in a lightless, soundless void, he felt no fear. Having lived as a slave in Lazo, he no longer valued his life. Because life was no longer precious, he felt no fear about losing it.

"Hey, Yaponskii! You still up there?" Kolyma Volk's shout echoed along the length of the shaft.

"I'm on my way down. Wait for me."

He continued the descent, trying to move more quickly. When at last he reached the end of the shaft, his legs trembled uncontrollably. Kolyma Volk looked at him closely.

"Why so late? Did you fall asleep on your way down?" He hit Iki on the head, sending him sprawling. "You're as bad as a woman. Even worse!"

"My body's worn out," Iki said, lifting himself. "And I can't do a thing about it. But I'm still an officer of the Japanese Army. And I won't tolerate insults or being knocked about."

"Listen, stupid! You weren't with us as we came down. Everyone was worried. Now we'll start late because of you. We're going to have trouble filling our quota today."

The Wolf, in his gruff way, was telling Iki that he'd become a burden to the entire gang.

"I'm sorry," Iki said, understanding the Volk's concern for the group.

"We don't need apologies in this hell hole. Let's go!" The Volk grabbed Iki's pick and hurried ahead.

Members of their team, a mixed lot of Russians, Armenians, Kirghizeans, Poles, Koreans, and Chinese, waited at the entrance to the newly assigned shaft. Regardless of race all had the same sallow complexion with a purplish gray undertone and the same dull expression. Kolyma Volk issued the day's orders.

"Here's what we do. This shaft fans out into five smaller shafts. The ore's already been blasted loose in the five shafts up ahead. I want twenty of you moles to fill up these hand trucks and bring them back here. As you know, each truck holds a ton, and the quota for each of you is five truckloads. The other five will stay here and roll the trucks to the collection point. That's a hundred yards down this main shaft."

He switched on his flashlight to show the men where the narrow steel tracks from the five new shafts met near the point where they stood.

Iki and four other men went into tunnel four. One of the men in Iki's group was a former Hungarian newspaperman, now a politzek. The other three were Russians—a teenager who had been born in a women's lager and had grown up among thieves, a convicted murderer from Irkutsk, and a former Internal Affairs official who had been sent to the lager in Chita on a false charge and convicted there for a murder he committed accidentally when the prisoners rioted.

The men set their hand lamps on ledges at the sides of the shaft, and worked silently, sharing tools to break up larger rocks and to shovel the fragments into trucks. Every shovelful thrown into a truck sent up swirls of fine dust. The raw ore was much harder than coal. The convicts did not know what kind of ore they were mining. They were not inquisitive to begin with, and even innocent questions about the nature of the ore they were mining could draw the guards' attention. And that could lead to further criminal charges and extended sentences. When Iki worked at the surface, he had seen how this ore was refined into glossy, black grains about the size of sesame seeds. Bagsful of these grains were carried away in airplanes. He suspected that the mines of Lazo yielded uranium. Because of this suspicion he imagined that the shafts in which he worked emitted a dull glow, a glimmer of purest evil.

Lifting each shovelful of loose rock required all the strength Iki could summon. He had to pause to catch his breath between efforts. In two and a half hours each of the other men had filled his truck, but, despite all his effort, Iki's truck was only two-thirds full. His pace fell steadily. When he became too weak to manage the shovel, he picked up large chunks with his hands.

Then, having filled his truck, he could not move it. An unwritten rule among the convicts forbade their seeking help from others. He could hear his joints creak as he applied every bit of strength in his body to start the truck rolling on its tracks. But the heavy thing would not move.

Noticing his difficulty, the Hungarian came over. "Go, goddamn Mustachio!" Cursing Stalin, in that safely indirect fashion, he gave the truck a push that started it rolling.

"Thanks," Iki whipered. He managed to keep the load going along to the relay point. There a huge fellow, with a grunt and a shove, sent it flying along the tracks sloping down toward the collection point. Iki wondered how much longer he could survive in this underworld, where a man's very existence depended upon brute strength.

He went back to the shafthead, pushing a second truck to be filled. Although he worked steadily, not taking rest periods, he fell farther and farther behind his mates. While lifting a large piece of ore, he clenched his jaws and felt warm blood gushing into his mouth. He spat into his glove and found a yellow rootless tooth in a pool of dark blood. Half the enamel had been eaten away.

"Hey, Yaponskii!" the Russian youth called out to Iki, the only one not resting at that time. "Why work so hard? We have a long life ahead or us."

"What innocence!" said the former Internal Affairs official. "Call this a living? Let me tell you—around the time you were still wetting the bed in a woman's lager, I was risking my life on the front lines, fighting the Germans in a holy war, or whatever they call it, in defense of our fatherland. After that, I was betrayed—"

The youth cut him off sharply. "Crying again! It's always the same goddamn story, and we're all tired of hearing it. So give us another tale. Damn!—I'm hungry. What I wouldn't give for a big hunk of bread."

They heard the clumping of Kolyma Volk's footsteps. All four men grabbed their tools and leaped into action.

"You shitheads loafing again?" the Volk growled. "You don't work, you don't eat. I don't give a damn how hungry you get. If you don't fill your quota, you don't fill your bellies!" He glared at them with his good eye and started off to the next shaft.

When the twelve-hour shift ended, they came out from the mine to see a star-filled sky. That in itself was a rare sight in fog-bound Lazo.

Iki hurried to the toolhouse to meet the only other Japanese in Lazo—Major Terada, with whom he had logged and worked on the Baikal-Amur Railroad at Taishet Camp Eleven. Terada, too, had been sentenced to a term of twenty-five years at hard labor.

He worked in the alternate shift, and waited for Iki at the entrance to the toolhouse. Terada, once strong and husky, was almost as gaunt as Iki. But, as with Iki himself, his dedication to the principles of honor and responsibility had not been dulled by slaving in the mines. Often he said to Iki, "We're the only Japanese in Lazo. We must carry on with honor because we represent Japan." And always Iki would nod in agreement.

Iki flapped his mittened hands as he approached Terada. That was their signal, for otherwise neither would recognize the muffled other. They slept in the same bunk—Iki from dusk to dawn, Terada from dawn to dusk—but could meet only when the two shifts were changing.

"How do you feel today?" Terada asked, as almost invariably he did.

"About as good as I look. How about you?"

"Me?—I'm not as worried as you are about good looks," he said, laughing, perhaps at having found something new to say. He noticed the blood around Iki's mouth. "You've lost another tooth?"

"It just fell out . . ."

"You ought to go to the doctor."

"I will—one of these days. Perhaps."

"Well, time to go." Terada's quick laugh did not quite hide his concern. Iki watched him fall into the line of convicts shuffling toward the mine head. He never failed to bid Terada an unspoken farewell after these brief meetings. Each day's meeting, they knew might be their last.

The sky before dawn was black, and a thin layer of mist hung over the camp. Iki walked unsteadily up the path to the dispensary. He was determined to be examined that morning. He knew that in order to survive, he must obtain a release from working in the mines.

Before he walked fifty feet, the dazzling beam of a searchlight picked him out. At that hour the guards in the towers trained the searchlight upon anything that moved. Iki stopped in his tracks, momentarily blinded, and lowered his cap visor over his face. Waving both hands, he signaled to the guards to shift the beam away from him. The spot moved away, but as soon as he started to walk again it found him and followed him closely over the frozen ground. The guards were indulging themselves in a meaningless diversion. Anyone who tried to escape from Lazo into the icy wilderness asked for certain death from the cold, not from the guards.

Even though the dispensary would not open for another hour, thirteen sick men already stood in line. Regulations decreed that no more than twenty among the four thousand convicts at Lazo could be excused from work on any given day. Iki took his place at the end of the line, even though so many others were ahead of him. He would not be the last one for long, for other prisoners would be joining the line soon. His scurvy had become progressively worse, but he had hesitated to risk visiting the dispensary. In order to get inside that little log cabin, he would have to wait outside in subfreezing temperature. A trip to the dispensary, moreover, meant losing his morning meal. If the doctor, after examining him, denied him either treatment or rest, his weakened body could scarcely hold up through twelve hours of labor in the mines without the support provided by breakfast, however bad that might be.

More than fifty convicts waited in line when the dispensary door opened at seven-thirty. Each man entered when an orderly called his name. Their examinations finished, the men emerged from the exit at the rate of about one per minute. Some appeared to be relieved, a few were elated. The others, stumbling along as if blinded, had been ordered to report for work. Nervously, Iki awaited his turn.

At last the orderly called his name, and he entered the dispensary. The several men ahead of him were already stripped, prepared for the doctor's examination. They resembled mummies, with buttocks so shrunken that the anus was revealed. Iki un-dressed, had his temperature taken by a Korean assistant, stood before the doctor, a bored Russian with a graying beard, a bald head, and a heart long since killed by the job that made him, too, a prisoner of his country.

The doctor pressed a wooden stethoscope against Iki's skinny chest for a few seconds. "Everything normal," he declared, signal-ing the next prisoner to step forward.

"Sir," Iki seized his chance. "My teeth are falling out. And please look at these spots on my arms. I'm sure I have an advanced case of scurvy." He showed the doctor the large purple spots around his elbows. The doctor rattled off an opinion in technical language that Iki could not understand. "—and if you're losing your teeth," he continued, "that's due to aging. Normal." Iki heard that well enough.

"But I'm only thirty-nine!" he cried. "My teeth shouldn't be falling out so soon. Besides, I have trouble walking. And these spots on my arms!" he almost wailed, hating the sounds he made. Just like a quavering old man . . .

"Listen, every lazy complainer in this camp tells me the same story," the doctor growled. "When you workers show up here, I don't believe anyone who doesn't have a temperature of at least a hundred and one. Do your fair share of the work. If you do, you'll get plenty to eat, and you'll stay healthy."

An Armenian waiting behind Iki pushed him aside to take his place before the doctor. Iki dressed quickly. As he emerged from the door leading to the freezing world outside, he felt as if he had been cast out from the ranks of the living.

Roll call was being taken at the gate. Iki joined his gang, and soon was marching with them, just as they had done every day for an eternity. The two and a half miles to the mines stretched on without limit, into infinity. The packed snow in the road was fro-zen, and he slipped often. Yet each time he was about to fall, his neighbors held him up and carried him forward. Even so, gradu-ally he fell behind; by the time they had covered two-thirds of the distance to the mines, he was staggering more than a hundred yards behind his proper place in the column. Strangers from other barracks, into whose files he drifted, helped him to fall back a row at a time, thereby concealing his condition from the guards, marching beside the column.

As his last bit of strength was used up, Iki toppled forward. Even as he fell, he saw the German shepherd dogs lunging toward him. Guards trained their rifles on him.

"Come on, Yaponskii," someone said. "Brace up!" A strong hand lifted him by the collar, dragged him back into the formation. A man at either side carried him along, in a team he did not know. The dogs barked fiercely, their sharp fangs white as snow.

"Turn that man over!" a guard shouted, brandishing his rifle. "Right here! Right now!" Iki's comrades ignored him and marched on without saying a word, without turning a head.

The short rest that Kolyma Volk allowed him to take did not make up for the breakfast he had missed, and Iki fell hopelessly behind. If he did not complete at least half of his assigned quota, he would be denied even the bowl of watery cabbage soup. When he felt faint, he called out his wife's name . . . or Naoko's, or Makoto's . . . each time he swung the pick or lifted the shovel. Only his love for his family, and the hope of seeing them again, kept him going.

Four hours later, he delivered his first truckload to the relay point.

"What went wrong up there, Yaponskii?" Kolyma Volk asked, openly sympathetic for once. "Why couldn't you get the day off?"

"I don't think the doctor understood my sickness."

"That old quack won't do a thing for anyone unless he's paid. I'll talk to the boss tomorrow and get you transferred to the laundry. That'll be a soft job."

The lager's choice assignments put convicts in the mess hall and the laundry. But Iki was repelled by the thought of washing prisoners' filthy clothes.

"I'm grateful to you. But I don't think I want to work in the laundry."

"You trying to tell me the laundry isn't good enough for you?" The Volk was hugely annoyed.

"I'm very grateful. But, being an officer in the Japanese Army . . ."

"So, an officer shouldn't be washing convicts' stinking clothes? Well, I'll be damned! I'm glad to see a man with some pride left in him. Don't worry. I'll think of something else for you. Just hang on for today."

As he walked back into the tunnel, pushing an empty truck, Iki thought of Terada, grown pitifully haggard during these past few months. Knowing that Terada was as ill as himself, Iki could not feel comfortable about accepting an assignment on the surface, leaving the only other Japanese in Lazo to waste away in the underground. The night shift was just as brutal as the day shift. He could see no possibility whatever of both him and Terada being transferred to operations above ground. The kindness of Kolyma Volk could not do him any good, he thought. In this hopeless mood, he resigned himself to working in the mines until he dropped dead. And that was likely to happen very soon.

At the end of this desolating twelve-hour shift, Iki crawled up the shaft to the surface. He met Terada at their usual place. The dry skin of Terada's cheekbones was encrusted with crystals of salty sweat, and his eyes were glazed and sunken.

"You don't look at all well, Terada. You have a fever?"

"Not really. But what about you? Haven't you gone to the dispensary yet?"

"Well, the truth is I did go, but—" Iki quickly described what had happened. "So I didn't get the day off. To make matters worse, I had to work without anything to eat. For once, I thought I'd never get through the day . . ."

Terada was surprised to hear so forthright a statement from Iki. Always before, he'd been the perfect Japanese officer, silent even in the time of suffering.

"So that's what happened," he said softly. "You were so late coming up that I worried. I was afraid you might have had an accident down there. I'm glad I worried for no reason. Well, I'd better go."

"Wait," Iki said, disturbed by Terada's appearance. "You're in worse shape than I am. Why don't you forget about regulations and go back to the barrack and rest?"

"You know the answer. If I don't work today, I still have to work tomorrow. And the day after tomorrow. And the day after that—" Gasping for breath, he turned away and plodded toward the mine head.

Iki lay in his bunk, tossing restlessly, unable to sleep because of pain, worry, hunger, cold, and the insatiable bugs. As soon as a man got into his bunk, bedbugs crawled out from every slit and crack in the boards. More bedbugs dropped from the ceiling, falling like a brown rain. Alexei, the White Russian in the bunk next to his, slept peacefully. Iki sat up and saw several swollen bedbugs the color and the size of red beans lolling sluggishly on the boards beside him. Moving around and past them were several thin lines of tiny brown bugs, not yet fed, all crawling toward him, happy for their next meal. Bedbugs had been a constant source of torment to him since the day he set foot on Russian soil. During the first weeks in the barracks at Lazo, he had stayed awake to kill bedbugs—as many as four or five hundred a night—but he no longer had the will or the strength for that losing battle. The best he could do was to crush those that had crawled under his clothes and attached themselves to his flesh. If ever he undressed, waves of bedbugs would have descended on him, attracted by the odor of his exposed body. However shrunken or anemic a man might be, the bugs swarmed over him, eager to drain his body of every drop of its blood.

When, at last, Iki did fall asleep, a guard soon shook him awake.

"Get up, Yaponskii," the guard whispered.

He opened his eyes and saw the hazy outline of a Russian guard. "Your Yaponskii friend's had an accident. He's at the dispensary and is asking for you. Come!"

"Terada—an accident?" Iki slid out of the bunk he shared with Terada. "Is he badly hurt?"

"I don't know. I came to get you because the assistant at the dispensary asked me to. We're not supposed to do these favors for prisoners, you know."

Outside the barracks the guard told Iki to act as if he were sick and being taken to the dispensary. As they neared the entrance, he faded into the night.

Iki rushed inside just as the Korean assistant came through the door from an adjoining room. Also a convict, the Korean had been a practicing surgeon in Manchukuo.

"Thanks for calling me. How is he?"

"Go in and see him," the Korean said, stripping off his bloodied rubber gloves.

"He keeps asking for you. The old quack isn't here tonight, so I was able to bribe the guard to go for you."

He said nothing about the accident, and merely nodded toward the examining room. Iki thanked him again and slipped into the room. Terada lay on a narrow bed, his right hand swathed in bandages.

"Terada, are you all right?"

Terada turned his head, searching for Iki. "I'm glad you came," he whispered.

"It's only your right hand." Iki sighed with relief. "What happened?"

Terada smiled wanly. "It wasn't an accident . . . I chopped off my fingers—"

"What?" Iki gasped. "Why?"

"The work is so hard—it became such torture—that the only thing I could think of was to get out of the shafts. I kept telling myself I had to get out, I had to get out—And the next thing I knew . . ."

Having made this confession, Terada began to sob violently. Iki stood by helplessly, weeping in sympathy for his friend.

Later, after regaining his composure, Terada told Iki what he'd done, and why.

"All along I've pretended because I didn't want you to worry about me. But the truth is, I've been running a high fever for several months. And tonight I knew I couldn't survive another shift in the mine. If I did, I knew I'd collapse during the march back and be shot. So I gave up a few hours of sleep today and stood in line with the rest at the dispensary. One of the men out there was caught with a heated brick tucked in his arm pit, and in punishment all the others of us still in line were chased away. When I left you earlier this evening, I didn't think I'd ever see you again. I didn't think I'd come out of the mine alive. When I knew I might die down there, I became afraid. Suddenly I wanted to live. I didn't want to die wearing this filthy convict's uniform. I didn't want to die in Siberia. If I survived, I might some day get back to my family in Japan. The more I turned these thoughts over in my mind the more obsessed I became with them. How could I get out of the mines? . . . get out of the night shift? . . . stay alive? . . . The only way I could think of was to make myself a cripple, unfit for hard labor.

"After I left you, I went back to the toolhouse, stole an ax, and took it with me down into the mine. At one point, as I walked along the shaft, I felt ashamed of myself—to think I was once an Army officer, my life dedicated to Japan!—and I dropped the ax. But my fever made me giddy. I must have been delirious for a while, because the faces of my wife and children floated up before me in the darkness. When I saw them beckon, 'Come, come,' I fainted. But not for long. I remember walking back up the shaft to get the ax. It was still there, where I'd dropped it. I took my right hand out of the mitten, laid it on a ledge, and swung the ax down —Blood spurted. I look down at my hand with only the thumb left on it. For a moment I was elated . . . I thought now I'll survive! Then the pain started and I fainted."

Terada closed his eyes, and left-over tears stole out from under the lids.

"You can laugh at me," he said after a while. "Remember the first time we logged together, in Taishet? You didn't even have the strength to swing an ax. I wondered then how you'd manage to survive in Siberia. Now I'm the one who turns out to be the weakling."

"I might have done the same," Iki said, "if I'd spent only a week or two in that hellish pit with the fever you've had." In trying to console Terada, he was also speaking the truth. That very morning, the ferocious dogs had strained to get at him when he collapsed. And the guards would have shot him down mercilessly, if his fellow convicts had not saved him. But who could save Terada now, from the penalty the Soviets would exact for his deed?

Outside, beyond the dispensary window, more snow was falling. It fell in sinister silence, smothering everything below, freezing the life out of every living thing it touched.

Three days later, Terada was taken away from Lazo. Alexei reminded everyone that convicts who mutilated themselves were judged guilty of sabotage and therefore were condemned to spend the rest of their lives laboring in a lager farther north in the Kolyma region. Everyone in the camp knew this, but in his delirium Terada had forgotten the fact that no one ever escapes from Soviet justice.

From that day on, Iki was more than ever alone. No one in the camp could speak to him in Japanese, of memories shared and hopes cherished, of Japan, of home.

Several months after Terada's removal, the convict colony at Lazo was still snowbound, although its inmates detected occasional signs of the approaching thaw.

In July the ice and snow were gone, and summer came to Lazo with its usual suddenness. Now the sun, which rose above the horizon for only two to three hours during the days of winter, was visible almost all the time, except near "midnight," when it sank beyond the horizon, only to rise again after an hour or two. Within a few days, the brown, barren land acquired a thin cover of green.

With the help of Kolyma Volk, Iki was reassigned to surface operations, and spent his shift in separating lumps of mineral ore from useless rubble. His last task each day was to search the lager grounds for edible grasses, the only source of vitamins in Lazo. In the coarse, prickly scrub he would look for tender shoots to be boiled and served with the meals. Iki's own signs of scurvy were yielding almost miraculously to the addition of these greens to his diet. "Goddam rabbit food," Alexei called them, along with other Russian prisoners. But Iki and the Korean prisoners did not share their scorn.

One evening, as Iki was preparing to leave his barrack to pick more greens, he saw several convicts running from the mess hall toward the barracks, all shouting crazily. Another brawl, he shrugged. Attracted by the noise, other inmates streamed out of the barracks, eager to enjoy the excitement.

"Mustachio's dead!" Among the cheering men, a few found words to tell the news.

Doubt and astonishment marked the faces of convicts who gathered near the barrack's entrance. Among the men who explained was a polit-zek, formerly a chemist at the University of Moscow. "We saw a photograph of Stalin's funeral on the front page of a newspaper," he told the men around him. "Someone found the paper in a plane that flew into Seymchan Airport. The old bastard died in March. That long ago!"

The prisoners, now gathered in a mob, raised a wild noise of cheers, yells, and whistles. Some wept, some laughed, others embraced their comrades, all rejoiced.

"We're saved!" they shouted. "We're going to be free!" they hoped. "We'll go home!" they prayed.

Iki, caught up in the whirl, enjoyed being part of the exuberant crowd. But one worry nagged him: Beria still controls the Ministry of Internal Affairs. Stalin was ruthless and cruel, but Beria is the most evil of men, a devil. He could not believe that Beria would free the slaves his ministry had imprisoned in so many places throughout the Soviet Union.

"Hey, Iki!" Alexei, his White Russian barrack mate, slapped

him on the back. "You ought to be happy!" Alexei's usually chalk-colored face was flushed with excitement.

"The lager staff has said nothing about Stalin's death," Iki reminded him. "I wonder why?"

"They've kept the news a secret because they're afraid we'll riot when we hear about it. You notice they're not doing a thing to quiet us now. They haven't even called out the guards. They're saying the newspaper account is unreliable. That's a big laugh. It was in *Pravda*."

"But Beria's still alive."

"With Stalin dead, a worm like Beria won't have a chance. Stalin's successors have probably taken care of him already. No mistake about that." He grasped Iki's hand firmly in a gesture of brotherhood and congratulation.

The hope of returning to Japan had been banished from Iki's thoughts when he reached Lazo. But now, as his fellow convicts celebrated the death of a tyrant and summer's sun warmed the land, hope sprang up again in Iki's mind.

"You'll be protesting, to get your trial invalidated, won't you?" he asked Alexei.

"Of course we polit-zeks in this camp will rise up and protest. But first we have to get organized. I guess we'll start on that tonight. I'm excited like everybody else. But I don't know what will come of this for me. If I'm released, I won't have a country to go to. The revolutionary regime in Moscow isn't going to collapse just because Stalin is dead." Alexei shook his head sadly. "Where can I go?"

After that day, production at the Lazo mines fell off markedly, and the lager staff was unable to prevent the slowdown. On the morning of the tenth day, the Lager Commandant ordered all convicts to assemble, in order to hear a formal statement.

"The glorious life of Marshal Stalin came to an end on March 5, 1953," he declared. "Let us all observe one minute of silence in honor of our Great Leader."

The Commandant turned toward a photograph of Stalin draped in black, mounted high on the platform, and bowed his head slightly. The other officers up there with him assumed the same solemn attitude. The convicts massed below them paid little attention to the great leader. They exchanged whispers, speculating on the details of the amnesty, which already they knew had been proclaimed in Moscow. Surely it would grant them reduced sentences, perhaps even immediate release for the luckier ones.

When the ritual silence ended, the commandant cleared his throat to address the convicts. "In memory of the late Field Marshal Stalin, Party Chairman Malenkov, has announced a general amnesty, which I shall describe to you."

To a man, the convicts listened attentively. And what they heard defied belief: the amnesty would apply only to criminals condemned to labor for three years or less, and to polit-zeks who had received a maximum sentence of five years or less. After a moment of stunned silence, the convicts roared in rage. No one at Lazo qualified for amnesty!

Roars of rage were as futile as ever. When the guards restored order and the mob subsided into silence, the commandant made a short announcement about a new law that stipulated separate lager facilities for Soviet citizens and for foreign nationals. The foreigners would be moved out that day, to a camp nearer the coast.

Alexei noticed Iki, just standing at one side of the assembly area.

"Iki! Get moving! You have to get ready."

"What's it all about?" asked Iki, not really trusting anything the commandant had said.

"You're being moved out of Lazo. You'll be on your way home. Looks like Moscow's not entirely blind or heartless after all."

Alexei promised to stay with Iki, to make certain he would understand and do everything necessary to speed his departure. That afternoon the political officer came to their barrack, called out the names of Germans, Hungarians, and Poles, and ordered them to assemble in the area near the main gate. Alexei asked why no Japanese had been called, and received an evasive answer. Soon the first group of foreign convicts departed, speeded on their way by cheers and clapping hands from the many Russians who would remain behind.

The political officer returned and called out the name of a Frenchman. That left only Iki and three Koreans among the many unreprieved Russians. Alexei ran up to the officer.

"Three Koreans and a Japanese officer are still here. Their names are on the register, aren't they?"

"Koreans have been excluded from the amnesty. And no Japanese are here in Lazo. That's all for today."

Iki felt the blood drain away from his face, out of his heart. "I'm a Japanese!" he cried. "I'm interned here as a war criminal!"

"What's your number? . . . And your name?"

"ON 5–32037, Iki Tadashi, Japanese."

The political officer, honestly surprised, looked for Iki's name among all those on his list.

"No," he said. "No Japanese on the roster. This means we have no Japanese here."

"That's ridiculous," said excitable Alexei, as others added their support. "He's a lieutenant colonel of the Japanese Army. Go back to the office and find out! Hurry up before the caravan leaves!"

Still doubtful, the political officer took Iki back with him. As they walked toward the office, two more trucks carrying foreigners left the lager, and Iki's anxiety mounted.

The officer went over the register of foreign nationals, but found no Japanese among them.

"Everyone in the barracks knows I'm a Japanese," Iki protested. "The operations crew knows it, too. Please check the files of prisoners. I'm sure the information will be there."

While Iki stood by, his anxiety bordering on terror, the officer went through the card file. He stopped abruptly and turned upon Iki.

"You're a Korean!" he charged. "You lied in an attempt to get out!" Furious, he lunged at Iki, grabbing him by the collar.

"What are you trying to do to me?" Iki shouted back, pushing him away. "I'm an officer of the Japanese Army! Let me see that card!"

The card, held up for him to see, but not to touch, showed his convict number, name, and sentence. At the very bottom, in the space for nationality, someone had written "Korean."

"You've seen it for yourself. You look like a Korean. You talk like a Korean. Do you still insist you're Japanese?"

"I *am* a Japanese! That card's wrong!"

"You're insulting the staff of this lager. Can you prove you're a Japanese? Can you prove this card's mistaken?"

Iki fell back, appalled—and defeated. A lone Japanese, identifiable only through a number, he was being asked to establish proof of his nationality! The loss of his Japanese identity in a place like Lazo meant the loss of his chance for going home, for surviving. He stood there, dazed and speechless, while the political officer ranted on about lying Koreans, filthy cheating convicts, and the forbearance and magnanimity of the Soviet Union, despite provocations from scum like him.

Iki's many pleas went unanswered. Kolyma Volk, Alexei, even the unhappy Koreans interceded on Iki's behalf, maintaining that he was a Japanese, but to no effect. A careless clerk's slip of the pen had robbed him of his identity.

The few days of summer passed quickly. One morning the convicts awoke to find frost on the ground. September had arrived, and soon the fury of winter would descend upon Lazo.

Among the kinder changes in slave-labor policies since Malenkov's rise to power was a reduction in the number of working hours; instead of two twelve-hour shifts, the convicts worked in three alternating eight-hour shifts. Iki, reassigned to labor underground, forgot the very word for hope. He longed for death to release him. He worked continuously, never pausing, indifferent to hunger or exhaustion. Feelings, memories, sensations receded into nothingness.

"Go easy, Iki—you're killing yourself," the Wolf warned him.

"I'm all right," Iki muttered, turning away.

"Go easy, I said. You're flirting with death, and enjoying it. For you, maybe, that's all right. But you're having a bad effect on the rest of us. I understand how you feel. I felt that way too, long ago. The important thing, for a man, is to stay alive . . ." He stopped when he noticed that Iki wasn't listening. "I came to tell you that we'll be doing some blasting up ahead. It shouldn't be dangerous back here, but you should go down to the relay point to make sure you're safe." He moved on ahead, not sure that Iki had heard him, or would obey.

As soon as Kolyma Volk was out of sight, Iki went back to work. He was swinging his pick, to fill his fourth truck of the day, when he heard the muffled roar. Having been forewarned, he paid no attention to it. A series of dull rumblings and a slight tremor followed the explosion. He stopped, resting his pick. The rumblings didn't sound right. Blasting caused a different set of effects. A strange crackling shot through the tunnel. He wondered if that could be the sound of layers of rock being wrenched apart? The splitting, cracking, jarring scream that alerted miners to a cave-in?

Suddenly the floor under him shook from side to side, slamming him against a wall. An explosive blast, louder than a cannon's roar, rolled through the tunnel. The lamp went out. And out from the darkness came the yells, the screams of terrified men.

In being knocked against the side of the shaft, he broke his left leg. Unable to rise, he crawled forward a few feet. The quakes increased in strength, and the crackling grew louder. Then, in a flash of awareness, the terror he had felt stopped, his mind expanded, and he entered into a beautiful tranquility: when he least expected it, the chance to die had come to him. He wished for the strength to sit cross-legged, with hands joined on his lap. But he could not move his left leg. He touched his left knee, and through the thick trousers felt the warm wetness of blood and a sharp pain. He closed his eyes, accepting the gift of death. Around him the vast earth heaved and trembled. Shouts and shrieks came faintly across an immense distance.

A hoarse cry broke into his peace. "Iki! Where are you? Answer me, Iki!"

He recognized the voice of Kolyma Volk, but neither opened his eyes nor answered. The stony wall beside him cracked open with a deafening roar. He felt the crushing weight, then lost consciousness.

Sounds entered the void in which he felt himself suspended. "You're lucky to be alive, Yaponskii. Your leg hasn't stopped bleeding yet, so lie still." He heard another voice, issuing as a moan from within. Slowly he opened his eyes, and became aware of the cold ground on which he lay. The sky above was an even expanse of darkest gray. As he contemplated the darkness, cursing fate for again having denied him his wish for death, a white glow lit up a segment of the sky and ghostly bands of light, emanating from the Arctic horizon, streamed across the sky, expanding, coalescing, again separating, constantly changing shape and color, shimmering like the folds of a great curtain hanging from the sky. From beyond the pulsating glow came yet another voice—of Colonel Tanikawa, repeating what he had said years earlier: "You must survive and be witness to the plight of Japanese interned in Siberia . . ."

As the first light of dawn crept into the house, Iki rose and quietly slid back the shutters. The pale sky of Osaka in winter was like the midnight sky over Lazo in summer. His wife and children still slept, breathing easily. From the street outside he heard the clatter of milkmen depositing small bottles of milk at the entrances of homes in the neighborhood.

In a few hours he would be walking into the Kinki Trading Company's building, to report for his first day of work.

9

A NEW START

"**P**lease be careful," Yoshiko called out cheerfully, as a good wife should, when Iki left the house on that memorable February morning in 1959.

At breakfast his children had been merry, excited about his going to work for the first time in the two years since he'd returned to Japan. But Iki boarded the train at Suminoe Station with a heavy heart. Could he, at the advanced age of forty-seven, hope to make a success of working for a trading company? At the Army Academy and War College, he and his classmates had been trained to despise money and the means by which it was gained. When they went out to drink together, they had calculated each man's share of the evening's bill in "meters" instead of in yen, just to avoid the taint of that vulgar word. How well would he fit into a trading house, a firm that relied on shrewd calculations to survive and to expand, in a marketplace where competition was at its fiercest? . . . And where acquiring money was one of the most important of a businessman's goals?

Everyone in the office turned to look at Iki when he entered the Personnel Department on the third floor of the Kinki Building. His ill-fitting and old-fashioned suit, the lunch box wrapped in a large green *furoshiki*, the traditional kerchief, the face and wasted body aged beyond his actual years, all drew the interest of young office workers. He asked one of the girls at a desk near the entrance to announce him to the department chief. She asked him to wait, because the chief was busy with a visitor. Most of the men and women seated at a dozen or more desks, aligned in neat rows on the highly polished floor, were in their twenties. The few men who appeared to be holding supervisory positions were slightly older, in their mid-thirties perhaps. Iki felt very uncomfortable in this strange setting, amid people of a younger generation.

The chief of Personnel did not keep him waiting long. A trim, middle-aged man wearing rimless glasses, the chief was rather surprised by Iki's appearance. He had expected a forty-seven-year-old man, of course, but not a candidate with the sunken cheeks and sallow complexion usually found in very old people. Iki's baggy suit and his colorfully wrapped lunch box completed the picture of a repatriated veteran one might have seen ten years earlier.

"Your title is 'Consultant to the President,' " the chief told him. "Have you any special line of work in mind?"

"As you probably know," Iki replied humbly, "the only experience I've ever had has been in the army."

"Yes. The President has told me so. I can understand that you may not want to work directly in buying and selling. How about drawing on your experience in Siberia? Perhaps you can research the potentials of import-export trade with the Soviet Union?"

"I'm really not qualified for that. You see, I was imprisoned during all my years in Siberia. Mostly in labor camps."

The chief suppressed an emerging groan. Never before had he hired a man past middle age, who had no business experience at all, and no special skills. He glanced at the appointment papers, sent down from Daimon's office. "Your base salary is 33,000 yen," he said, hurrying this interview to an end. "Assorted allowances will bring that up to forty-five thousand. Although it isn't much for a man your age, I hope it will be satisfactory."

Because Iki did not keep up with the fluctuating value of the yen, he did not know what his salary represented in the way of purchasing power. Old habits die hard. Nor was he interested in knowing about that as yet. Right now, he was concerned with learning the kind of work he would be considered capable of performing. "To which department will I be assigned?"

"Don't worry about that yet," the chief was saying airily, when the telephone rang. "Yes sir, certainly," he all but bowed. "I've just completed the processing—yes sir!"

"Mr. Iki," he said, much more courteous than he'd been a few minutes earlier. "The President would like to see you, as soon as we're finished here."

Iki took the elevator to the seventh floor, and presented himself to the receptionist. Daimon's own secretary hurried out to greet him, saying, "The President is in conference now, but he would like to have you come in."

Iki found Daimon studying a large graph laid out on the carpeted floor of his office. Standing beside him was Kaneko, chief of the Cotton Yarn Department. Daimon noted Iki's entrance with nothing more than a swift glance. Iki made a slight bow and moved quietly to one side of the room, near the window looking out upon Osaka Castle.

The graph that the two men were studying so intently was busy with zigzagging lines that represented fluctuating market prices of several major commodities since 1950—with blue for rising prices, red for falling ones. Daimon followed the erratic movements of the blue segments. "Are you sure your information's accurate?" he asked Kaneko, a wiry man with dark complexion, wearing a neat pin-stripe suit.

"I'm certain. It came from agents of the Anderson Corporation, a major American exporter of cotton. They're in Japan now to have talks with our government's ministries. They have been given the impression that Japan will lift restrictions on the importation of raw cotton much sooner than we have been expecting. The impression confirms what I've suspected—that our Ministry of International Trade and Industry is eager to find an opportunity to lift trade restrictions."

Kaneko's confidence contrasted markedly with Daimon's restraint. "I'm wondering . . . The graph shows the market just starting to get bullish."

Daimon was weighing two possibilities. On the one hand, the lifting of trade restrictions would result in a sudden increase in raw cotton available to Japanese spinneries, and then the spinneries might flood the market with cotton yarn at low prices. On the other hand, the domestic demand for raw cotton might prove to be insatiable; then the market for cotton yarn would stay firm, despite the lifting of import restrictions.

"What's happening in the producing areas?"

"We just had a radiogram from Mexico City. The price of raw cotton there has fallen below thirty cents."

"So . . ."

Daimon continued to study the zigzag lines. His intense concentration suggested a commander weighing the factors involved in the advance of his army against those concerned in its withdrawal. Iki remembered the tactical map in the Operations room at Imperial General Headquarters. Markers that tacticians used in planning military operations bore the same colors—blue for friendly troops, red for enemy forces. In table-top maneuvers, the red markers would be shifted about to simulate every conceivable tactical threat, and counteroffensives would be devised for each one of them. The decision—whether to advance or to make a tactical withdrawal—would be based on a quick, intuitive assessment of combined tactical and strategic moves, and that decision would be translated promptly into action on the battlefield.

"Keep buying!" Daimon ordered, the commanding general making his decision. "My hunch is that the trend of the market is up."

Daimon had been buying all the cotton yarn offered for sale at the Osaka Exchange since the beginning of the year. Now, in a matter of minutes, he had decided not only to keep his stockpile but actually to increase it. The effect of a wrong decision here could be calamitous. Iki had learned as much when he was initiated into dealings in high finance during his first meeting with Daimon, two months before.

"Kaneko, I hear you've finally quit smoking," said Daimon, drawing on a cigarette as he relaxed.

"I thought I might be more alert if I didn't smoke," Kaneko said, obviously pleased to be receiving the president's attention.

"Once I stopped drinking and smoking," Daimon said. "That was when I held the job you have now. I was misreading the market once in a while—usually when I came to work with a hangover. Being conscientious pays, Kaneko. But don't overdo it. No fun, that way."

Grateful for Daimon's interest in him, Kaneko bowed. He bent to pick up the graph and was turning to go when, for the first time, he noticed Iki standing by the window.

"I want you to meet Iki Tadashi," said Daimon, enjoying Kaneko's surprise. "He's the one I've told you about—the former staff officer at Imperial General Headquarters, who spent eleven years as a prisoner of war in Siberia."

"I appreciate what you've been through," Kaneko said warmly, bowing respectfully. "I was at the southern front. I'm one of the survivors of Leyte."

Iki bowed to Kaneko, as if apologizing for his role in planning the disastrous operation at Leyte. Daimon, impatient, immediately swept Iki into the world of businessmen.

"One thing you should know, Mr. Iki, is that the market is as unpredictable as any living creature—or as any lineup of opposing armies on a battlefield. Cotton yarn is a good example. Kaneko's had several predecessors in his job. Except for me, every chief of the department before him either asked to change jobs or quit the company after suffering a nervous breakdown. Now tell me. What job do you want to start with?"

Daimon's manner, interested but impersonal, was that of the company president addressing an employed consultant, and Iki answered with appropriate respect. "I have two requests to make. First, I would like to familiarize myself with all of the departments of business in this trading company. And, second, I would also like to spend a small part of each day at the Osaka Public Library."

"So? Why go to a library? Our research department has all the material anyone would need to learn about business and trade."

"Please let me explain my rather strange need. I want to read the newspaper files, to find out what happened in Japan during the eleven years I was away."

"Eleven years of catching up?" Daimon was impressed for once. "Certainly. Then go ahead. I'd intended to let you study whatever you want." He turned to Kaneko. "Have someone show Mr. Iki around. And get him a desk in the Textile Division."

"Textile? . . ."

"That's right. Our company got its start in textiles. Anyone who wants to know this company has to know what textiles are all about." With that, Daimon hurried off to the reception room, to meet his next visitor.

As he followed Kaneko down the hall, Iki felt comfortable for the first time. He had taken an immediate liking to this forthright Kaneko. Most people tended to be unfriendly toward former military professionals. Often former enlisted men were the most hostile, because they had been drafted, against their will, into the military forces. Kaneko was one of the few who had ever expressed appreciation for the hardships Iki had endured.

The Textile Division, on the second floor, was as lively as a bazaar. Employees hurried in and out, threading their way among the narrow aisles between ranges of desks. Telephones rang incessantly. Numerous conversations in the office added to the confusion—among Japanese clerks, speaking rapidly in the racy Osaka

202

vernacular, and between Japanese and foreign buyers, among whom blonde Caucasians in sober business suits contrasted with dark-skinned Asians wearing gorgeous tunics or colorful turbans.

Kaneko led Iki to a counter covered with fabric samples. He held up a length of red cloth. "In the textile trade, one must be able to identify the different kinds of fabrics. What would you say this is?"

"Silk, isn't it?" Iki answered, judging by the cloth's sheen and softness.

"It's nylon." He pointed to a grey fabric that looked like material for a man's suit. "What do you think this is?"

"Wool?"

"No, acrylic. The way the world's population is growing these days, cotton, wool, and silk together won't be sufficient to meet the demand for textiles. We're entering the age of synthetics. The future of textile firms will be determined by how well they adjust to the change-over. The trading companies are the businesses that must convince manufacturers and wholesalers to diversify into synthetics. We'll have to develop both domestic and foreign sales channels for the new fabrics at one and the same time. Textiles illustrate how a trading house like ours operates."

Iki had never given thought to textiles, much less discussed the subject with anyone. Further explanations at this time might only confuse him, he admitted ruefully.

"It'll become clear to you in time," Kaneko said, understanding completely. "Now for your desk . . . How would you like to be over there?" He pointed to an open space beside a large pillar at the very center of the office.

Relieved to be home after a tiring day, and not thinking clearly, Iki reached into the mailbox for the key.

"Hi Dad!" Makoto slid the door open.

Seeing his son there shocked Iki into being fully awake. "Well! I'm the one who gets the 'welcome home' for a change."

Yoshiko and Naoko came from the kitchen to greet him. Iki, filling with pleasure, recalled the days he had cleaned the house, gone shopping for fresh food, started the cooking fire, and welcomed his wife and children home.

"You must be tired," Yoshiko said. She took his coat, helped him into a cardigan sweater she had knitted for him. Naoko went back to setting the table for supper. A vase of daffodils stood at the center of the small table. Beside it Yoshiko laid a platter holding a single baked sea bream, expensive fare customarily served only on felicitous occasions.

Conversation that evening was unusually lively. "What kind of work will you be doing?" asked Naoko, full of curiosity.

"That hasn't been decided. After all, I don't know a thing about the company yet."

"But Dad," Makoto said, "you won't quit the company, will you? If you do, Mom will have to go back to work."

"You don't have to worry about that, Makoto." He spoke as if to chide his son, yet was too well aware of the hardships they had endured during his eleven-year absence. But now, with his having accepted Daimon's offer, Yoshiko had quit her job, and Iki could see how delighted Naoko and Makoto were to have their mother at home—for the first time in their memories.

"What's that material called?" Iki asked, leaning forward to peer at Naoko's blouse.

"It's wool, Dad. The blouse is old, but I like the pattern. Mom made it."

"What about your skirt?"

"That's part acrylic."

"A mixture of acrylic and wool?" He looked closely at the material, felt its texture.

"Why are you so interested in her clothes, dear?" Yoshiko asked.

"When Mr. Kaneko showed me around the company today, he took me first to the textile department. There I saw the many different kinds of fabrics Kinki exports. What I thought was silk turned out to be nylon, and what I thought was wool is actually acrylic. Kaneko told me that I must learn to identify all these different fabrics, both old and new."

"You're studying fabrics?—You've never done anything like that before." She turned away from the children, trying to hide the tears of dismay. Such a lowly job, she thought.

"We have nothing to worry about." Iki wanted to regain the good cheer with which they'd begun this festive meal. "I'm fortunate to be joining a company whose boss was kind enough to ask me to come to work. Until now, soldiering is the only thing I've known. Of course I must learn my new profession from the ground up."

The children nodded brightly. "Just like going to school!" laughed Makoto.

"Exactly," said Iki, pleased to see that Yoshiko smiled with them, this time not pretending.

"You've had to work very hard," he said gently to his wife. "I don't know how well we'll manage on my salary, but let's try it for a while."

"Don't worry. We'll manage." She acknowledged, with the slightest of bows, this tender moment between them. "But now that you have a regular job, you'll have to order a new suit made for you. That one is a bit old-fashioned, I think." Her eyes brightened.

"Get one made of nylon!" Naoko cried. "It'll shine!"

"Nonsense! I've never cared about the way I dress. I spent eleven years wearing the same filthy work clothes, day in and day out, and I got used to them. As they got used to me, until they fell apart. Having two suits will be a nuisance." He joined in the laughter that removed any doubts they might have about his willingness to go to work with a lowly trading company.

After dinner Iki sat down at his writing desk—an orange crate, like the children's, covered with sheets of newspaper. He touched his brush to the inkstone and wrote:

Dear Colonel Tanikawa: I trust you are well despite the recent cold weather. After being idle for two years, I have decided at last to embark on what I might call my 'second life.' Kinki Trading Company, here in Osaka, very kindly asked me to accept a position with them, and, having thought the matter over carefully, I have decided to entrust my future to them. All of my former subordinates have found jobs, so I am free now to accept full-time work. I must add that I also feel an obligation to my wife, who worked to support me while I gained back my health.

"My family is delighted, and I wish to share this news with you. I am pained, of course, to think of those few of our comrades who came back from Siberia and are still jobless, some in poor health . . .

He laid down the brush, leaving the letter unfinished, as remembered his reunion with Tanikawa and the other Japanese assembled in Khabarovsk, a few months after his miraculous survival of the disaster in the uranium mines at Lazo.

10

HOMECOMING

On the outskirts of Khabarovsk, a work crew of two hundred and fifty Japanese labored within an enclosed compound. The high wooden fence all around it was intended both to prevent their escape and to hide from Russian view the sight of foreign convict laborers in their midst. Passersby, however, could see a huge construction crane rising almost a hundred feet above the ground.

The Japanese captives had been weakened by more than a decade of forced labor and malnutrition; and the work norms set for them, unchanged in ten years, had become heavy burdens. More than three hundred of the 1,050 Japanese interned in Khabarovsk Camp One were incapacitated by sickness and old age. Yet, as a result of sham physical examinations held the week before, dozens of those ailing men had been reclassified as "physically fit for labor" and reassigned to construction work in near-freezing temperatures.

As always, the men were assigned to teams, each specializing in one kind of task. Iki worked in a team of bricklayers, each man having a quota of seven hundred bricks to set per day. He had been laying bricks for two years, and worked with the dexterity and speed of a professional mason.

Whenever Iki recalled the horrors of his years in the mines of Lazo, he was grateful for the chance to be working with fellow Japanese, and to be speaking the language of home. His injuries in the collapse of the mine shaft had led to his rescue from Lazo. Because of those severe wounds, the inept doctor at Lazo sent him to the hospital in Magadan. There the physician who attended him not only saved his life. That honest man also established his identity as a Japanese, and arranged for him to be reassigned to a camp for Japanese convicts. Not until he arrived at the Khabarovsk lager and once again met comrades from other labor camps—Kamimori, Mizushima, Colonel Tanikawa, and his former orderly Marucho—did he dare to believe that he had survived the icy hell of Lazo.

All the Japanese prisoners had aged prematurely. Although he was only forty-three years old, Iki looked sixty. His haggard face, with its deep wrinkles and startling pallor, marked him as a long-term convict in Siberia. His preference for silence was another characteristic: he worked almost without speech, content with his own private thoughts. His team-mate, Hori Toshio, formerly of the Kwantung Army Tactical Brigade, did not always respect Iki's liking for quiet.

"Colonel Iki," he asked, more than once at the beginning of their partnership, "do you think we'll ever get back to Japan?"

Hori was the youngest of the Japanese who were detained as war criminals in Khabarovsk Camp One. Perhaps because he had spent all the years since youth as a prisoner of the Soviets, his clear eyes and naive conversation suggested the innocence of a man much younger than his thirty-one years. Sometimes, thought Iki, this boy-man resembled a fawn at Nara in search of its mother.

"I'm afraid we'll have to wait until normal diplomatic relations are restored," Iki would reply. He spoke slowly, carefully, trying not to lisp because of the spaces in his mouth left by those teeth lost to scurvy. "But that day will come. You can be sure of it."

"I received a letter from my parents in Fukuoka not long ago. My mother is already sixty years old, and my father is sixty-four. They wrote that they hoped to see me again, while they're still living in this world."

Iki remembered well his first encounter with Hori, as, each escorted by guards, they passed in a corridor in Khabarovsk White Prison, and how Hori had shouted, "Army Second Lieutenant Hori Toshio! Death by firing squad! Tell my father and mother in Fukuoka!"

"Your parents will probably stop aging from the moment they see you." Iki the sober, the serious, surprised himself with this delicate jest.

"Not like Urashima Taro," Marucho cackled. "When you get home, Lieutenant, sir, you'll have to look for a wife right away. With your good looks, you'll be fighting off mobs of eligible girls."

207

Hori blushed, as he usually did when the racier fellows in the barracks talked about women and sex. He was extremely shy in the presence of the strapping—and ribald—Russian women who ran a small store in the lager. Still the dutiful Japanese youth, he treated the older Japanese men with the same respect he had shown his own father.

His quota for the morning nearly filled, Iki turned his attention to Mr. Tachibana. Although the former Manchurian government official was in his sixties and suffering the most serious effects of abnormally high blood pressure, camp officials forced him to work on the construction job. His section of the wall was rising unevenly.

Iki called out to him. "Why don't you rest a bit, Mr. Tachibana? We'll give you a hand in a few moments."

"My goodness, sir," Marucho warned, "that won't do at all. If 'Baboon Face' sees it, we'll all be in trouble."

"I know the wall isn't perfectly straight," Tachibana said, "but I'm doing the best I can."

Not long afterward, Lieutenant Tupchin, the building supervisor—"Baboon Face" to Marucho and most of the other convicts—came to check on their progress. "You stupid bastard!" he raged at Tachibana, waving a thick staff at the poor man. "You call that a wall?"

Tachibana, saying not a word, hung his head.

"Do it over!" Tupchin yelled, kicking down the section Tachibana had raised that morning.

"Lieutenant Tupchin," said Iki, controlling his anger, "what you've done will only delay the project. It won't help your record."

"There won't be any delay, because all of you Japs are going to work overtime—to make up for this. Now get moving, and get it done!" Pushing bricks aside with his cudgel, he stalked away to inspect the work of the next team.

"You go to hell, Baboon Face," Marucho muttered under his breath. "To all the hells, each one worse than the last." Hori went over to Tachibana's side, helping to clear away the heap of bricks.

The temperature meanwhile was falling rapidly, and the morning's light rain turned to sleet. Tachibana rubbed his hands to warm them, and started all over again, laying the first course of bricks.

The Japanese in Khabarovsk Camp One worked together harmoniously, the hardier ones looking after the old and the weak, each man concerned with the good health and eventual return to Japan of the entire group. The ugly, frenzied days of the Siberian Democratic Movement, and of turncoats like Yasuda, were events in the distant past.

While Iki and several others rebuilt the section that Tupchin had kicked down, Tachibana took charge of a group of elderly Japanese gathering firewood for the preparation of lunch. They lit a fire, spent a few moments warming their hands, and started water heating in a metal drum.

"Loafing again!" Tupchin came back, roaring at Tachibana. "Put out that damned fire and get back to work!"

"Please Lieutenant—be reasonable," Marucho said. "You can't have an old man with high blood pressure working so hard in this cold."

"You trying to tell me what I should do?" Tupchin snarled. "What's your name, you?—I'm going to report you to the commandant, and see that you get ten more years."

"I'm sorry!" Marucho yelped as if speared, backing away, with hands raised to ward off further attention. His timidity only increased Tupchin's bullying.

"You lazy old bastards don't do any work! You just sit around on your asses! And you dare to waste the resources of the Fatherland, just to make a fire to warm your damned butts!" This time he kicked over the metal drum, and scattered the glowing embers with his cudgel.

And then Hori challenged him. "These men are too weak to be working out of doors. They deserve a little time to warm themselves, and you know it. We may be convict laborers in your eyes, but to us we're prisoners of war. We're not going to let you ignore international law."

"Don't fool yourself," Tupchin said scornfully. "International law has nothing to do with war criminals, and that's what you are. I'm going to work every one of you damned criminals till you're all dead!" He spat on Hori and walked away.

"Damn you!" Hori yelled. Tupchin turned, lifting his stick to threaten. But Hori was almost on him, with a carpenter's hatchet already swung. Tupchin screamed as Hori struck, and fell slowly forward, blood spurting from a gash in the side of his neck. He lay sprawled on the ground. Hori stood over him in a daze, wet with

Tupchin's blood. Then, realizing what he had done, he began to run, still holding the hatchet in his hand.

"Stop, Hori!" Iki shouted, chasing after him.

"Please! Let me go!" Hori cried, over his shoulder.

"Stop!" Iki repeated. "Don't be foolish!"

"Please! Show me a warrior's pity!"

Iki almost stopped. To all military men of Japan, since the earliest days of the samurai, the asking for a warrior's pity was a plea for a merciful, honorable death. It could not be denied. The greater mercy allowed Hori to die by his own hand. The shame of his being shot to death by guards could not be permitted.

Although many others who did not hear his plea tried to stop him, he outdistanced them all. Before anyone knew what he planned to do, Hori leaped upon the spidery frame that supported the great crane. He climbed all the way to its top, to the operator's cab.

"Please listen to me," he called down, in a voice clear and unafraid. "I did what I had to do. Now I have no choice but to die. And I want to die with pride in myself. I ask all of you to live proudly as Japanese and to return with pride to Japan. I know that what I did was right, and I'm only sorry that my action may cause the rest of you to suffer. Please forgive me."

He drew a flimsy sweat towel from his waistband, slashed open his wrist with the hatchet that had struck Tupchin, and dyed the towel's center with the blood that gushed forth. This banner he tied to the beam of the crane, securing it at two corners so that the flag of the red sun could be seen by everyone below.

Noticing several men climbing up the crane's ladder to catch him, he slammed shut the steel panel that sealed the opening to the top deck and the cab.

"Please listen to my song," he called out, serene now, no longer running from anyone or anything. "It will be my farewell to you."

Standing at attention, he sang the song that every Japanese had learned during the years of the war:

> If I should go to war at sea,
> Let my body soak in the brine.
> If war should take me to the mountains,
> From my body let wild grasses grow.
> I will not look back . . .

The song floated down, clear and sad, upon the hundreds of hushed people watching and waiting below. Many could not bear to look. Many wept. All knew how this saddest story must end. Knowing that Hori planned to leap to death the moment he finished his song, Iki, Kamimori, and Mizushima struggled to lift the heavy steel panel. But Hori had locked it from above and they could not push it open.

"Stop, Hori!" Iki shouted around the edge of the deck. "Think of your parents at home!"

Hori hesitated, but only for a moment. The song would soon end. Every Japanese prisoner on the construction site stood in the space around the foot of the crane. Silent, shaken by emotion, thinking only of the brave and lonely man standing at the very tip of that crane, they waited.

> *. . . I will not look back*
> *If only I may die*
> *In my sovereign's cause . . .*

His voice sank lower and lower as he neared the end of the song. At the last it faded off into a sigh of regret, of longing, of farewell. Low sobs from the men on the ground rose up, in sorrow, in compassion, in farewell.

The death-song ended. From below the Japanese watched in silence as calmly Hori stepped to the edge of the platform and leaped, his arms outspread like wings that had lost their feathers. In the next instant his body lay broken on the ground.

The horrified men of the camp were still debating what to do when Iki, Kamimori, and Mizushima dashed out from the foot of the crane tower. "Quick! Pick him up!" Iki shouted. "The guards—"

But he was too late. A detachment of guards came running in, training their rifles on the Japanese prisoners.

"I want the man who murdered a Soviet officer!" snarled the officer commanding the detail.

"He's dead," Iki snapped back. "As you can see— He was one of us. And we'll bury him." Hearing this, the two hundred and fifty Japanese formed a wall, many ranks deep, shielding Hori's body from the Russians with their own flesh and bones.

"No! I want that body now!"

Frustrated in their attempt to save Hori, horrified and saddened by his senseless death, the Japanese bristled at the Russian's demand.

"And it wasn't murder," persisted Iki. "The fault lay with your Lieutenant Tupchin. Many men are working here who shouldn't be working at all. Tupchin wanted a promotion. He not only forced sick men to work—"

"Enough!" the enraged officer yelled, shaking a fist at Iki. "That's for our investigators to determine. My orders are to bring in the murderer. Hand over the body! —Or else . . ."

Before those cocked rifles and gigantic guards, the Japanese had no choice. Iki was about to give a signal to disperse.

Guards were lifting Tupchin's blood-soaked body to place it on a stretcher, when he groaned.

"He isn't dead!" Kamimori cried. "Then it wasn't murder!"

"Shut up! Hand over that body, or we'll shoot!"

"Go ahead!" Kamimori shouted, taking a resolute step forward. "Go ahead and shoot! Kill a Japanese prisoner of war, and see if you yourself don't end up in a lager! All of you!"

As the Russian hesitated, the Japanese surged forward.

"Hori died for a cause!" "Let's finish what he started!" "We're human beings!" "We demand to be treated like human beings!" "We don't work till our demands are met!"

The Russians retreated before those two hundred and fifty advancing rebels. As they fled, pursued by scores of jubilant Japanese, a few of Hori's barrack mates laid his body on a plank and marched away from the construction site, ignoring the guards as they went. Even the guards recognized that their postures, with legs wide apart and rifles at the ready, were nothing more than gestures of futility.

The sun was setting beyond the hills of Khabarovsk. Seven Japanese, dressed in the black uniform of convicts, were silhouetted against the glowing sky as they accompanied Hori's coffin up the slope to the graveyard for Japanese prisoners. They walked silently, with heads lowered, knowing once again the sadness of burying another of their comrades in foreign soil. Behind them, stiff and surly, marched two Russian guards.

The cortege paused at the side of a large field in which hundreds of wooden grave markers rose above a thick mat of dead leaves and drying weeds. Most of the names and serial numbers painted on the narrow tablets had been worn away by the winds and rains and bleaching suns of too many seasons. So many years had passed that already the oldest graves had sunk, looking like shallow trenches filled with rubbish, rather than like the mounded tombs made for men of Japan.

"Keep moving," a guard told them.

Kamimori, Iki, Mizushima, and Marucho carried the coffin, a plain box made of rough boards. Two of Hori's barrack mates followed, carrying picks and shovels. Several paces behind them came Mr. Tachibana, walking unsteadily and breathing hard.

The Japanese found an unused place big enough to accept Hori in his coffin. The ground was not yet frozen, but it did not yield easily to picks and shovels. The men's jackets were soon stained with sweat, but they worked without resting until they had finished digging and lowered the coffin into the pit.

"We won't forget you, Hori," Kamimori said, aloud, for the spirits of living and dead to hear. "And we won't forget what you tried to do . . ."

Iki could not find release in words. He could think only of the briefness of Hori's life and of the meanness of his death. If only Hori had died in battle, in the flower of his youth! But his karma had called for him to labor in prisons and lagers for ten long useless years before it sent death to claim him. He had tasted nothing of the joys and beauties of life. He left no wife to mourn him. He left no sons to carry on his name. He was a model of youthful innocence all his life, and even in his dying, when he gave his life in defending the rights of his countrymen. The cause was noble, surely, Iki agreed. But the manner of his death . . . —That could never be ennobled . . .

They covered the coffin with softened earth, and carefully shaped a mound over it to mark the place as a grave. They stuck a few twigs of pine into the dirt at the foot of the wooden name tablet driven into the mound, and brought their hands together to pray for the repose of Hori Toshio's spirit.

Darkness was closing in over the hills from the east, and a cold wind moaned through the bare branches of trees on the slopes below the cemetery. In the western sky, ink-black billows of clouds were set off by fine borders of gold, and a slender band of deepest crimson stretched along the far horizon. "If war should take me to the mountains, From my body let wild grasses grow . . ." Hori's death-song haunted Iki's memory, even as that band of crimson put its mark upon his sight. Iki could not speak his grief, but he could feel it, deep within.

The horizon floated before his eyes, brimming with tears, as he bade farewell to Hori the innocent, the victim, the sacrifice.

The death of Hori had an electrifying effect on the Japanese prisoners in Khabarovsk Camp One. Because of him they decided that they would not report for work the next morning. The camp commandant retaliated immediately by threatening to cut their food rations by thirty percent. In doing so, he chose the most effective weapon he could direct against the undernourished prisoners. Alarmed by the threat, barracks leaders and team captains gathered in the mess hall late that night to discuss a course of action.

Kamimori spoke to the men who came to express their support. "We've learned that Lieutenant Colonel Dolgy will be coming here tomorrow morning. Dolgy's in charge of convict administration at the Khabarovsk headquarters of the Ministry of Internal Affairs. He'll be coming with the intention of breaking our strike. When we meet with him, we should make him understand that our talk is to be a formal negotiation between our group and the Soviets. We've never tried anything like this before. What do you think of the idea?"

Dolgy, wiliest of the Internal Affairs officials, had taken only two days to crush the strike that Korean prisoners had attempted in their lager three months before. Iki, like so many others in his camp, felt the thrill of anticipation. At last the longed-for confrontation was near! And, judging by his reputation, Dolgy would be a formidable opponent.

"Kamimori is right," Iki said. "But we don't stand a chance unless we're united. We'll need someone to speak for us. And we'll have to be ready to grab the initiative when we meet with them."

"If all of us try to speak out individually, we'll be cut down as a group," the leader of barrack three said. "We're expecting a long and hard fight. We'll have to be organized for it. Why don't we elect our leader now?"

All agreed on the need for a spokesman. Because the leader in such a confrontation was likely to be severely punished, the group decided to choose him from among those former officers who were below the age of forty-five. Although several men were nominated, ultimately the choice narrowed down to Iki and Kamimori.

"Instead of our voting for one of you," Mizushima suggested, "why don't the two of you talk things over and decide between yourselves? How you decide makes no difference, as far as I'm concerned. I have full confidence in you both."

Iki did not want the discussion to go any further. "I'll serve as spokesman," he said. "After all, I was Hori's team captain, and we were close to each other. This is my responsibility."

Kamimori objected. He rose to explain his reasons to the group, most of whom were confused by this unexpected development. "I'm asking you to let me serve as your spokesman. I understand how Iki feels. And I know he's a good man. But I've represented the Japanese in this lager in many ways, for a longer term than Iki has been here. Besides, my parents are dead, and I'm certain my wife and children died during the evacuation of Manchuria. I'm all alone, and I have nothing to lose."

Kamimori, brief and frank as usual, clearly revealed his courage as well as his consideration for Iki. In the U.S.S.R. a workstrike was considered to be a form of sabotage, an act of sedition, and a spokesman for strikers had to be prepared to accept death.

"But Kamimori—" Iki began.

Kamimori cut him off. "I'll be the spokesman, but I want you to be my alternate, and to advise me. And if anything happens to me, I want you to replace me." His whole body seemed to bounce with determination. "And, of course, I expect all you barracks leaders and team captains to support me."

Lieutenant Colonel Dolgy came to the lager the next morning and quickly assembled all barracks leaders of the Japanese in the administration office. Beside him sat the lager's commandant and its political officer. The portraits on the wall behind them no longer honored Stalin and Beria. Now photographs of Premier Bulganin and Party First Secretary Khrushchev looked down upon the disposition of Soviet justice.

"I don't know what you're demanding," Dolgy began, with obvious contempt for the Japanese representatives standing before him, "but you're convicts. And all convicts must work. That is the law. Your refusal to work is a violation of the law of the Soviet Union. Therefore, you must report for work immediately. If you have demands to make, then present them in a formal manner. They will be considered, while you are working. Not until then."

As soon as Dolgy's statement was interpreted, by Abe, former chief of the Manchurian government's Russian section, Kamimori stepped forward to speak.

"We know very well that our refusal to work does not constitute a formal action. But we want you to know that what happened yesterday at the construction site was not a simple case of ordinary violence. Hori's assault upon a Russian supervisor was not an accident. It was inevitable. In a sense, it was something Lieutenant Tupchin invited and deserved. If Hori hadn't done it, I or someone else among us would eventually have been driven beyond despair to do the same thing. Conditions here are intolerable. Tupchin was only one symptom. We must insist on changes."

Dolgy's predictable response came immediately. "You men are convicts. We are the police. And the judges. An assault with a deadly weapon is a capital offense. And let me add that what you convicts are doing—presenting grievances and demands—is also a criminal act. Remember that."

Iki asked to speak. "Colonel Dolgy, you are the chief administrator for all convicts in this area. We are disappointed to learn that you, of all people, refuse to make a genuine attempt to discover what is going on in this camp. We ask now that you listen to us and learn why we Japanese have finally been driven to take extreme action—only now, after ten years of imprisonment, and of good behavior. We want you to find out how this lager has been administered. And we urge you to try to understand our demands."

Dolgy's frowns did not stop Iki from continuing. "What triggered yesterday's tragedy was the action taken by Lieutenant Tupchin, supervisor of site three. A week ago, your medical officer declared more than eighty of our men unfit for outdoor labor. Lieutenant Tupchin forced sixty-five of those men to rejoin the outdoor labor teams. This same kind of brutality has happened before. We've brought it to the attention of the lager commandant a number of times, but he's refused to listen. Already this year five of our countrymen have died because they were forced to work when they were sick. And not only the sick are in danger. All of us are on the verge of serious illness. And all of us are very close to death.

216

"We have three minimal demands. They must be met if you want to keep us alive and working. First, men with a fever of more than one hundred degrees or a blood-pressure count of over one hundred and fifty, and men suffering from rheumatism or severe intestinal troubles, must be exempted from outdoor labor. Second, prisoners between the ages of fifty-one and fifty-five should be exempted from outdoor labor, and those over fifty-five should be released from all labor. Third, the physician's determination of a man's ability to work must be final. We further insist on the repatriation to Japan of the seriously ill and the elderly. As I have said, we submit these minimal demands so that we may stay alive. Just stay alive. We have resolved that none of us will work until these demands are met."

Dolgy and the other Russians scowled throughout the interpretation. As soon as Abe finished, Dolgy pounded the table with his heavy fist.

"Who are you to make demands? This is mutiny! Mutiny against the Soviet Union!" The Japanese showed their dismay, with exclamations and head-shaking. Seizing the advantage, Dolgy continued angrily. "You men couldn't have plotted this mutiny all by yourselves. Someone must be working behind the scenes. An agitator. An enemy of the state. Whoever he is, he's done his best to agitate and disturb you. Don't let him get the best of you. My advice is for all of you to stop this foolishness and return to work. You do so, and I'll forget what's happened and none of you will be punished for these recent acts of sabotage."

"You are mistaken," Kamimori said. "No one is behind the scenes, trying to influence us. The truth is, we heard you would be coming here to talk to us. Knowing you are chief of the Department of Convict Administration, we obtained the agreement of all Japanese interned here about presenting you with our demands. Our action is not a 'mutiny.' It is an honest attempt to—"

"What's your name?" Dolgy shot back.

"Kamimori Takeshi. Our men chose me to be their spokesman."

"Who's that next to you?"

"I am Iki Tadashi, alternate spokesman."

"So you two agitators organized this mutiny!" Dolgy's voice was thick with hatred. "Call out every prisoner!" he ordered the commandant. "Take roll call!"

"What's the reason for the roll call?" Kamimori demanded.

Both he and Iki were alarmed by the possibility that, in a show of force, the Russians would turn their rifles upon the Japanese. If that confrontation started a riot, or a massacre, hundreds of Japanese might be slaughtered.

"The usual reason—preparation for work," Dolgy said.

"We don't work until our demands are met. Colonel Dolgy, we ask you, once again. Your duty requires you to look into the reasons why we refuse to work. Do you know, for instance, how we suffer because this lager is self-supporting?"

This question annoyed Dolgy. Income from the labor performed by Japanese convicts paid not only for their sustenance but also for maintenance of the lager's facilities and staff. The few Korean and Chinese prisoners in the camp contributed their proportionate share. Two hundred and eighty Russian administrators and guards were the principal beneficiaries of that servitude. Prisoners were treated relatively well at lagers where per capita productivity was high. Khabarovsk Camp One, however, knew only a vicious cycle: prisoners were disabled because of inadequate food and medical care; the drop in their productivity resulted in diminished revenues; then the sick and disabled were forced to return to work to increase revenues so that the lager's administration would not be deprived of its comforts . . .

"Colonel Dolgy," Kamimori continued, "are you aware of the essential difference between this lager and those in which Russians work? Revenues of Russian lagers have remained constant during the past ten years because the capacity of their labor force has remained constant. Russian prisoners come and go regularly, for one reason or another. But no new Japanese prisoners have joined us since we first arrived here. Ten years ago our average age was 32.6 years. Today it's 42.6 years. Men in their forties cannot produce the same revenue through sheer physical labor as can men ten years younger."

"Sir, may I present some figures?" Captain Matsubara of barrack six, a former finance officer, stood up. To everyone's surprise, Dolgy allowed him to speak. "This lager's administration deducts 465 rubles daily from the total wages earned through our labor, leaving us with less than seventy rubles to be spent upon our support. We asked for an accounting of the manner in which that deduction was spent, and were given the following facts and figures. Food was the largest item—260 rubles per day are spent on feeding the staff here. We're being charged a considerable sum for clothing although what we wear is mostly old uniforms discarded by the guards, and dyed black for our use. We've always cleaned our own latrines, but we're charged a 'cleaning fee.' I don't know what the fee for 'cultural items' means, for we've never received as much as one book to read. The deduction of thirty rubles for 'tax' is ridiculous.—Where else in the world do convicts pay taxes? Sir, you have here a case of flagrant embezzlement."

Because these damning figures had been provided by someone in the lager's administration, Dolgy could not challenge Matsubara's statement. But his furious expression promised an inquisition among the lager's staff, in a hunt to find the man who gave that confidential information to a lot of convicts.

"As matters stand," Iki seized the moment to make a bold statement, "a major change is needed in Soviet policies governing Japanese prisoners of war. We ask that you consult Moscow for appropriate instructions."

"Ahh. Now I see what you men are after," Dolgy growled. "You're doing your little bit here to expedite the resumption of diplomatic relations between the U.S.S.R. and Japan. You're hoping to expedite your own return to Japan."

"Again you are mistaken," Iki retorted. "As we said at the start, we're trying to gain humane treatment for those among us who are sick. The rest of us are *not* seeking repatriation through these efforts. Of course, we hope to be sent home, some day. But for now, and here, all we want is a chance for all of us to stay alive until diplomatic relations are restored and we are allowed to return to Japan."

The Japanese prisoners did not want to be used as pawns in the territorial dispute that was developing—their repatriation in exchange for recognition of illegitimate Soviet claims upon lands seized from Japan. They had agreed not to demand prompt repatriation, if doing so would jeopardize Japan's rightful claims to those lands.

Dolgy, aware of these implications, chose not to answer. "I've nothing more to discuss," he said, rising from his chair. Without waiting for the commandant, he strode out of the room, while the guards hurried to catch up with him.

The Japanese prisoners were still on strike when the new year arrived. In the first few days after Hori's death they managed to put aside a secret stock of food, with which to supplement their reduced rations. The lager's staff knew about it—and how pitifully inadequate it was. On the day their "secret" supply was exhausted, the commandant announced the penalty he imposed because they would not work: their daily rations would be reduced to four hundred grams of black bread, fifty-five grams of miscellaneous grains, and five hundred grams of pickled vegetables; no longer would they have access to Soviet radio and newspapers; and they would not be allowed to assemble as a group. Upon hearing this decree, the barracks leaders met immediately in the mess hall. Colonel Tanikawa, who had been confined in the dispensary because of his high blood pressure, joined them there.

"I know what the Russians have in mind," Kamimori said. "We've been on strike for almost four months. But, as you know, we no longer have the solidarity we had at the beginning. They know this. And they know that now our extra food is gone. They're convinced that now we'll break under this latest attack."

"One thing bothers me," Mizushima said. "Was the decision to punish us made by the Khabarovsk staff or by Moscow?"

"I doubt if the staff here has even notified Moscow of our work stoppage," said Major Oba of barrack three. "You remember Colonel Dolgy accused us of agitating to expedite the resumption of diplomatic relations? If Dolgy has reported this strike at all, he's probably reported it as an act of sabotage intended to pressure Moscow for our early repatriation. Although we've bribed a couple of guards to smuggle out our letters to the Soviet Supreme Council and the Red Cross in Moscow, I'm sure they've been intercepted. If they hadn't been, investigators should have been sent out from Moscow long ago. —What do you think, Iki?"

"I'm sure these punitive measures were thought up by the local staff. I doubt if anyone outside Khabarovsk knows why we went on strike. Or even that we are on strike. We shouldn't acknowledge this latest announcement. If we do, we're acknowledging its legitimacy. That'll work against us."

"What can we do, then?" Kamimori asked.

"The important thing is to continue our negotiations with the lager staff, to prolong this situation until Soviet-Japanese relations are restored."

"Three months already," a discouraged barracks leader groaned. "How much longer will we have to keep this up?"

"My guess is until February or March," Iki replied. "We haven't worked on the cement factory and the apartment buildings since October. The staff at Khabarovsk will have to provide Moscow with good reasons for such a significant delay in construction. They'll have to submit a report no later than March or April. And no reasons they can provide will be good enough to satisfy Moscow. When Moscow learns what's happened, some improvements in conditions here will have to be made. But we can't expect important changes until Japan and the Soviet Union resume diplomatic relations."

"And we won't be going home next week, or next month, or next summer," warned Kamimori.

"That means we'll have to take decisive action before we lose the rest of our solidarity," Iki continued. "We've got to get people from the central office of the Ministry of Internal Affairs to come out to Khabarovsk. And we can get them here only by causing trouble that's sure to attract attention in Moscow."

"The idea is fine," Kamimori said. "But how can we do that without using force?" For a long minute no one had an answer to this.

"I can tell you . . ." All attention turned to Colonel Tanikawa. "We can declare a fast unto death," he said quietly, as if he was talking about the weather. "All 1,050 of us are listed in the war prisoners' registry. A fast by 1,050 men is bound to attract international attention. It will become a humanitarian issue that Moscow cannot ignore."

"But we'll be dead by then," Matsubara complained. "We struck to be able to survive and return to Japan. Not to die here, of starvation."

"The 'declaration' is only a means to gain attention," Tanikawa explained. "We start immediately to hoard food—enough to keep us alive while we're on our hunger-strike."

Kamimori thought of a practical concern: "However little we eat at one end, the undigested part of the food's got to come out of the other end. We'll be producing evidence that will betray us."

Tanikawa smiled, like a wise old village elder. "We're in the depths of winter now. The stuff will freeze quickly, as we latrine cleaners know very well. We'll stuff our deposits in those jute bags from the cement factory. The bags and their contents will keep for a while up above, in the attics."

Kamimori agreed that fasting would be a completely passive

and thoroughly effective means of resistance. Whereupon the rest of the barracks leaders voted to recommend the hunger strike to their men. On that same day, the Japanese began to prepare for their campaign. Using gift packages received from Japan, they bribed the supervisor of food supplies, and soon were able to transfer a considerable quantity of food from the warehouse to their barracks. In addition, each man set aside a portion of his daily ration of black bread, to be dried into pieces that would not spoil.

The three hundred sick and elderly Japanese, who would not be asked to fast, were consolidated in two barracks in order to be separated from the strikers. Barracks leaders met each night to compose statements of grievances, which they sent to the authorities in Moscow. Sympathetic underlings in the lager's administrative offices arranged to send these communications through underground channels.

Late one night Iki, with the assistance of Abe, was preparing yet another petition. It was dated January 15, 1956, and addressed to President Voroshilov of the Soviet Supreme Council.

> Dear President Voroshilov, we send you our respectful greetings.
> We 1,050 Japanese of Khabarovsk Camp One commenced a work strike on October 26th last year, hoping that our desperate action would attract the notice of the government of the Soviet Union. We have sent you several letters, explaining why we had no other recourse, but we have received no reply from the central government. We had hoped that your efforts would bring about a fair resolution. However, on January 5th the lager administration announced punitive measures to be taken against us. We have reached the difficult decision to risk death by fasting as the ultimate means of urging you to intervene personally and resolve this conflict in a just and equitable manner . . .

A knock on the barrack door interrupted them.

"Please let us in," a low voice asked. "We represent the Chinese and Koreans in barrack seven."

Iki opened the door cautiously, for the sixty or so Chinese and Korean prisoners in the lager had been openly hostile to the Japanese. Two men slipped in out of the freezing night. By their features Iki recognized one as being a Chinese, the other as a Korean.

"We'd like to join you in your struggle," the Korean said.

Iki and Abe were astonished. How could they respond to so

unexpected a wish? And how could they trust these two men—or all the others in barrack seven whom they claimed to represent?

The Chinese, seeing Iki's reaction, hurried to explain. "We want to apologize for having looked down on you Japanese for so long. We held you in contempt because we saw you bowing to every demand the Russians made. You were always submissive, you never complained. We were distressed by your meekness, because once we considered you the eldest and strongest of our Asian brothers. For too many years we have kept apart. Please forgive us. —When you declared a work strike a few months ago, then a hunger strike this week, our own pride as Asians was strengthened. Now we want to join you in your efforts. Please accept us . . ."

Iki and Abe could not doubt his sincerity. Clasping hands, they recognized the bond that made all Asians brothers.

"We're grateful," Iki said, with unconcealed emotion. "I don't know how to thank you for offering us your support despite your old grievances against us. But, for your sake, I must explain what we hope to do. The people of our country will understand what we are trying to gain, and they will sympathize with us. But if you join with us and defy the Soviet Union, the people in your own countries may condemn you for treason. All of you will surely be placed under suspicion, if not in actual trouble, upon your eventual return to China and Korea. Your countries today are not the ones you remember from before the war. Japan, too, has changed, I know, but not as much as China and Korea. We are more than grateful for your generous intentions, but we've already caused you enough difficulty. We wouldn't think of causing even more troubles for you by encouraging you to join us. —I hope you'll understand our reasoning."

The Korean shook his head sadly. "I fear that you're right. The Communists in China, in North Korea, have changed the thinking in our countries. We're disappointed, but we understand. Thank you for your wisdom, and consideration. Nevertheless, we'll set aside part of our rations for you, and we'll supply you with whatever information we can get from the lager staff. That's the least we can do. We'll be witnesses to what you Japanese do, and we'll talk about it when we return to our own homelands. Your stand here will inspire pride in all Asian peoples. We know you will put up a good fight. We wish you a successful finish."

The two visitors shook hands with the Japanese, and left as quietly as they'd arrived.

Their preparations completed, the Japanese delivered their written declaration to the lager commandant on the nineteenth of January, and prepared to go on their hunger strike for an indefinite period. In all barracks doors were reinforced with strong bolts "borrowed" from the Russians and barricaded with tables and chairs.

The commandant, with a contingent of guards, came that same afternoon into the barracks compound. "My friends!" he said through a big megaphone, "I ask you to call off the hunger strike immediately. You are being very foolish. I am prepared to resume our talks and listen to your grievances when you open the barracks doors."

The Japanese did not answer.

The commandant and the political officer came again the next day, and the day after that, each time repeating their fine words.

A week went by.

Members of the commandant's staff approached the Japanese repeatedly with promises, none of which related directly to their demands. The men in the barracks put themselves on a daily ration of four pieces of hard black bread and water. Despite the weakness brought on by the first stages of hunger, their morale remained high. Their spirits soared when Chinese supporters informed them of a rumored visit by a representative of Moscow. In their elation, some of them went on a total fast, taking only water.

Just before dawn on the tenth day of the hunger strike, one of the men on night watch awakened Iki.

"Colonel Iki. I hear a strange rumbling outside the lager."

Iki hurried up into the attic, past the sacks of frozen excrement, to look out through a peephole. In the pale light reflected from the snow, he made out a column of soldiers approaching the lager, preceded by two small tanks and several fire trucks.

"Wake up!" he yelled to his mates below. "Danger! —They're bringing in troops! Secure the door and windows!"

The men, only half-dressed, strengthened the barricade of tables and chairs with everything else they could move, including their blankets, pillows, and mattresses. The tanks and fire trucks pulled up at the main gate of the lager. A truck equipped with an amplifier drove into the camp itself, and through a loudspeaker someone read out a statement in interpreters' stilted Japanese.

"This message is for you misguided Japanese! We are acting under orders of Lieutenant General Mikhailov, Vice Minister of Internal Affairs. Now you are surrounded by two thousand armed soldiers. Whatever your reasons for this strike may be, you have disregarded the fact that you are convicted war criminals. You have chosen to ignore the laws of the Soviet Union. What you are doing is a grave mistake. Stop this senseless resistance immediately! You have ten minutes to come out of the barracks and line up in formation!"

Looking out through their windows, the Japanese saw soldiers running forward in the glare of searchlight beams, surrounding each of the barracks. They heard the grinding of heavy machinery as the tanks moved into the compound. The Japanese did not answer.

Again the rasping voice came over the loudspeaker: "This is your last warning. Our orders are issued by the highest levels of the government of the Soviet Union. You still have time. Four minutes!—Come out and fall into formation. If you do as we tell you, no one will be hurt. I repeat, this is your last warning!"

No one stirred.

Without another minute's delay, a tank rammed the nuzzle of its long gun against the door of Iki's barrack. A single thrust by the tank broke the door open and pushed down the barricade. Soviet soldiers burst in. The Japanese fought back with sticks ripped from broken chairs, with boards torn from their bunks. But they were far outnumbered by soldiers wielding clubs and rifle butts. Amid yells and shouts and oaths, they were beaten, kicked, and dragged across the floor toward the splintered door.

Again the loudspeaker blared: "We're turning on the hoses! Stop resisting! Come outside or you freeze to death!"

Searchlights were trained on every barrack door. The fire trucks directed streams of water against the barracks walls. With the temperature outside at minus twenty degrees, everyone knew that a jet of water shot at a man would soon kill him. Troops hauled out the Japanese one by one, and pushed them into trucks. The streams of water played nearby, but touched no one.

This eruption of planned violence lasted no more than ten minutes. The silence in the camp was broken only by the heavy rumbling of tanks, withdrawing into the darkness, followed by the fire trucks. When the trucks and the troops departed, the lager was cleared of all militant Japanese. The only Japanese who remained were the three hundred sick ones lying in the dispensary or in the barracks reserved for the weak and the elderly.

Kamimori, Iki, and all barracks leaders and team captains, quickly sorted out from their followers, were herded into lager headquarters. These forty-two Japanese were charged with instigating the hunger strike. The commandant, strutting back and forth before the group, assured them that they would face Lieutenant General Mikhailov, who had organized the night assault. Mikhailov's ruthlessness as a strike-breaker was known in harrowing detail to prisoners in Siberian lagers. In June the year before, he had sent a battalion of tanks against the rebellious prisoners of Karaganda, a lager in Central Asia. When a group of female convicts stripped themselves naked and stood before the tanks with linked arms, he simply ordered the tanks to run over them.

"Kamimori, this way! To the commandant's office," a guard shouted.

Kamimori did not return. The forty-one other Japanese waited, standing, for they were not allowed to sit. More than two hours later a portly man, accompanied by several subordinates, strode in.

"I am Lieutenant General Mikhailov, Vice Minister of Internal Affairs," he told them what they'd already guessed. "I've just finished listening to your spokesman. Now I want to hear from you. I want only one of you to speak on behalf of everyone here."

Iki took a step forward. "Sir, why are you keeping our spokesman isolated from us? And why are you questioning us separately? We want to know what your intentions are." Iki's primary concern was for Kamimori.

"You want to know, eh?" Mikhailov snorted. "Very well. I shall tell you. —I believe that a difference of intentions exists, between you men here and the fellow back there who led you into this useless strike. I wish to learn if the opinions of the damned fool who instigated this strike reflects the thoughts of the rest of you Japanese."

"No one man 'instigated the strike,' as you put it," Iki said. "This entire hunger strike was neither instigated nor planned by any one individual. All of us so-called 'healthy Japanese' planned it together. It was our expression of the outrage felt by all the Japanese who have been interned here for so many years. Colonel Kamimori, the man you talked to earlier, is the one we chose to be our spokesman. You said you wished to listen to only one of us. Please let me speak."

"You may." Mikhailov waved a permissive hand. "And what do you want to say?"

"We've sent many petitions to the Central Government in Moscow, as well as to the Soviet Red Cross. We asked them to hear our pleas. They did not answer. No one came to hear our pleas. Yet you resorted to force of arms, giving us no opportunity whatever to meet and talk with you. Tell us why."

Mikhailov signaled to a subordinate. He brought forth a muddied, torn sign that read "Russians Do Not Enter." Mikhailov held it up for forty-one Japanese to see.

"This sign tells the whole story," he said sternly. "You Japanese have established a settlement, a foreign concession, within Soviet territory. That's one of my reasons."

"That's absurd! How could we establish a 'settlement'! You would understand the ideas behind that sign if you had read our declaration. That sign is directed only at members of this lager's administrative staff. The ones who mistreat us."

"Nevertheless, you have insulted the Soviet Union with your actions. For instance, you declared a fast. Yet you kept on eating Russian food you hid away."

"We've received no food from the lager since the day we declared our intention to fast," Iki said, undaunted. "Technically we've been fasting. But that point is not important. The real issue is the purpose of our hunger strike—which is to improve working and living conditions here, that will enable us to survive so that someday we may return to Japan alive. We're entitled to use any peaceful means to support ourselves physically—and to call attention to our distress."

"You are entitled to nothing. You have no rights—"

Iki refused to stop. "We decided on a hunger-strike as a final, desperate means of attracting the notice of the central government. Local authorities would not even acknowledge our pleas. So we knew we must get an important, responsible representative of the central government to conduct a fair and impartial investiga-

227

tion of our grievances. We are disappointed that you ignored us, and chose to listen only to local authorities. And we regret that you brought in soldiers against us. —Have you, sir, or anyone else of Internal Affairs in Moscow, actually taken the time to read any of the petitions we've sent?"

"Indeed I have. Too much time, for too little reason. And I noticed that all of your petitions were written in the form of diplomatic communications. Who wrote them?"

"We simply wrote what was on our minds," Iki answered, easing past the dangers implied in the question. "We were concerned with writing truths. Any of us could have written those petitions."

Mikhailov studied him coldly. "Truths?" he sneered. "Do you have other requests, Mr. Ambassador?"

"Yes, sir. But I would like to ask how many Japanese were injured today. We are worried—"

"None."

"We hope you will extend good care to the sick and elderly Japanese, who did not participate in the hunger-strike."

"You needn't worry about them."

"We would like you to become acquainted with the actual conditions here. We hope you will study what we have written and grant us our requests."

"I shall read what you have submitted and approve whatever requests I can," Mikhailov said.

The Japanese felt encouraged by the magisterial nod with which Lieutenant General Mikhailov discharged them into the care of their jailers.

Later that same day, on Mikhailov's orders, Iki was confined in a solitary cell in Khabarovsk's White Prison. He had been sentenced to another year's imprisonment "for inciting to rebellion and contributing to disorder in the lager." Kamimori, all barracks leaders and team captains, and even those who had served as interpreters and translators, were imprisoned on the same charge, for the same period.

On the morning of December 18, 1956, ten trucks carrying the last of the Japanese prisoners in Siberia prepared to leave Khabarovsk Camp One.

The newest lager commandant, the newest political officer, and all other administrators and guards gathered in the compound to watch the departure. No longer required to be punishers and jailers, they smiled and waved and exchanged words of farewell with the men who had been their charges. The Japanese, wearing newly issued caps, quilted jackets with high collars, and woolen trousers tucked into heavy boots, smiled, too, despite their mixed feelings. But, being polite, all responded with many a loud "Sayonara!" as well as the several Russian terms that say "Farewell."

The long-suspended negotiations over repatriation between Japan and the Soviet Union had been resumed soon after the hunger-strike at Khabarovsk Camp One began on January 25. Following the Soviet-Japanese accord of October 10th, 1956, all Japanese prisoners of war who could be located were assembled in Khabarovsk from all Russian areas—even from Moscow, the Baikal-Amur region, and Kolyma. About half the Japanese at Khabarovsk Camp One had already left for Japan by the time Iki, Kamimori, and the others were released from the Khabarovsk White Prison and returned to the lager. For them, too, *damoi* was becoming a reality at last.

Each Japanese departing that day had lived through eleven years and four months of imprisonment. Among them was Major Terada Teruo, who had been sent from Lazo to a lager in the arctic tundra, but had miraculously survived, despite his mutilated right hand.

"Dosvidaniya, Yaponskii!" called the women who worked in the lager store.

"Spasibo! Dosvidaniya!" the Japanese shouted back. Some of those women had been very friendly indeed to the younger men from Japan.

The convoy of trucks left the lager, turned on to the highway, and soon rumbled along the main boulevard of Khabarovsk. Its streets were lined with modern apartment houses and tall office buildings. Khabarovsk bore little resemblance to the ramshackle city the Japanese had first seen more than a decade before. The Higher Party School, the municipal hospital, the city plaza, and many of the roads had been built by Japanese war prisoners. Japanese sweat and blood had gone into the laying of every brick and cobblestone, and many lives had been sacrificed to raise those buildings and pave those roads. Hundreds of thousands of Japanese slaves had labored for eleven years to create this new Khabarovsk.

"It should be called 'Japanograd,' " said Kamimori, always a man in search of truth.

The trucks delivered the Japanese to Khabarovsk Station. Iki, as a senior officer, immediately began supervising the boarding of the railway cars.

"Iki!" A deep voice called out to him, across the years, as well as across the space of only a few feet . . . Hoping he'd heard aright, Iki turned and found Chief-of-Staff Hata and his second-in-command, General Takemura, framed in windows of the first-class car, near the front of the train. Never had Iki expected to see them again. He had been told that the Russians heaped their vilest abuses and cruelest treatment on General Hata, because they considered him the Japanese Army's foremost expert on Soviet Russia. Hata showed no sign of his former self-confidence. And General Takemura, shrunken with age, leaned weakly against the window frame.

Released from the spell of surprise, Iki dashed over to stand below them. "You're well!" he cried out as he searched their faces. Unable to say more, he bowed, in respect, to each in turn.

"You had quite a time there, in Khabarovsk," Hata said. "I was in Moscow when I heard about the uprising. You can't imagine how the news gladdened me."

"Yet, to make that happen, a promising young life was sacrificed. —But we'll talk more when we're aboard the ship . . ." The train began to move. Iki bowed again, ran back to his assigned car, and jumped aboard to cheers from his barrack mates.

The train pulled into the port of Nakhodka the next morning. Long before they reached it, air scented with salt and seaweed filled the cars, and the lungs of the exiles. Soon they saw the icy sea spread out before them and, looming high above a pier, the ship they had seen so often in their dreams: the *Koan-maru*, its decks and sides coated with sheets of gleaming ice. Their hearts quickened when they caught sight of the crimson disc, centered upon a field of dazzling white, flying at her stern.

"Banzai!" In their hundreds they shouted from the train. And then, after the noise, the cheering, the jubilation, came the tears of thanksgiving, the sobs of emotion no longer hidden and controlled. Once again they were men with a homeland. "Damoi! Damoi!" they said, as they wept.

The men who were going home waited on the dock, beside the

ship, listening eagerly for their names to be called. Invalids propped themselves up on their litters. Many of the sick ones, who had been unable to stand without the support of others, found strength the instant their names were called, and hobbled up the gangway unaided, as if afraid that a moment's delay would rob them of their chance to escape from the prisons of the dead to the world of the living.

Early the next morning the *Koan-maru* glided slowly across the bay of Nakhodka and sailed out upon the open sea. As the great gray frozen mass of Siberia receded behind them, the prisoners who were going home heard the murmurings from the ice-filled sea, slipping past the bow of the *Koan-maru*. To many of the Japanese these murmurs sounded like the whisperings of comrades fallen on the barren plains of Siberia, their dreams of return unfulfilled, calling out, across the distances, "Remember me! Remember us . . ."

As the ship left Russian waters, her siren gave the signal. Every Japanese aboard her who could stand stood at attention for a moment, raising a silent prayer for those who had not lived to go home. As they prayed, memories of the sufferings they themselves had endured flashed through their minds. Some day, Iki vowed, he would go back to Siberia, with the power and the means to bring home the remains of his comrades for burial in Japan. Until that day, he knew, the spirits of the men who died wretchedly in Siberia would find no repose. And, he thought, hurting with the remembrance, the spirit crying out most plaintively for rest would be that of Hori Toshio.

The color of the sea changed imperceptibly. Soon it rolled blue beneath them. The wind lost its wintry bite. The men knew they were in Japanese waters.

A SECOND LIFE

On the way to report for his first day of work, Iki left the bus at Korai Bridge, happy to escape from the crush of morning commuters. Although this was only February, Japan's sun shed warmth and light upon the favored land below. Despite the two years that had passed since his return to family and home, his memories of Siberia were still intense. He never ceased to be grateful for the comforts that Japan offered both body and spirit, and to marvel at the contrasts that surrounded him as he moved through Osaka's busy streets, among gaily dressed young women and young men soberly attired in Western business suits.

The clock at the entrance to the Kinki Trading Company's building showed eight-thirty, still half an hour before the start of a regular workday. Thinking he was early enough, Iki did not hurry up the staircase leading to the Textile Division. He was not prepared for what he faced there. The second floor seemed almost as crowded with people as was the street outside. Most of the division's employees were already busy at their desks. An office boy, flitting among the desks, was distributing cablegrams that had come in during the night. Many men were shuffling through their messages, or discussing them over the telephone. In all that roomful of activity only the girls were missing: as in all Japanese companies, where women were excluded from positions of responsibility, the lovely file clerks, expecting to work only until they marry, arrived just before nine o'clock.

The department heads sat at impressive desks arranged in a row along a wall of glass at the far end of the room. Kaneko, chief of the Cotton Yarn Department, in shirt sleeves, busily scanned a trade daily newspaper. Two desks away from Kaneko, the chief of the Foreign Trade Department reprimanded Yamamoto, head of the export section, to which Iki had been assigned.

"Look at the chief chewing out Yamamoto," he heard one of the young men say. Unshaven, with hair mussed and shirt rumpled, he obviously had spent the night in the office.

"He must have found an error in our calculations," his companion said, with a look of disgust. "And we worked three nights in a row! I was sure everything balanced out the fourth time around . . ."

"Just once I'd like to finish up without getting the stick. Those damned quarterly reports will kill us yet. —I had to sleep on the couch up here last night, and I think I've caught a cold."

"You were lucky to get as much sleep as you did. I've got a splitting headache. Even worse! This is my extra-duty day. I was wiping the desks and emptying wastebaskets while you snored away on the couch. Can't wait for the new recruits to take over the morning clean-up."

A thick account book landed with a thud on the desk beside the two young men. "When will you squirts learn to use the abacus? You make a fuss about studying English. You dabble a bit in French. But can you add or subtract right? Or multiply? Learn to use the abacus first!" Yamamoto, sputtering, returned to his desk and spun the telephone dial.

"Hello! Osaka Textiles? Extension 276!" with the receiver wedged between his chin and shoulder, Yamamoto flipped through a stack of cablegrams.

"Hello, Mr. Kinugasa? This is Yamamoto of Kinki Trading. How're things this morning?" He began cheerfully enough, soon switched to a note of alarm. "What's that? Reps from seven firms sitting outside your office? I hope you're joking! Listen, a cable just came in from the Congo. It's a big order. What? No, no, not that big. I need 200,000 yards of bold cotton print in any of the basic colors. I've got to have it right away. You open your doors at nine, don't you? That gives me fifteen minutes. Please put us at the head of the waiting list. I'll send someone right over. I'll have him take along the other orders, too—from Hong Kong and South America. Thanks for the favor."

"Ishihara!" he barked before he hung up. A young clerk with a crew cut shot up from his chair. "Take this purchase order over to

Mr. Kinugasa of Osaka Textiles. Representatives from seven other firms are already there. Be sure you get in to see him first. They open at nine."

"It's 8:45 now," Ishihara said, grabbing his jacket. "Can I get there in time?"

"If you run. And if anyone complains about your cutting in, just say you were there first, but had to go to the toilet. The freighter for Africa leaves in ten days. We've got to get our yardage on that ship!"

Ishihara ran for the stairs.

By 8:50 all employees had reported in, and the office was humming. Some younger men rushed out, carrying briefcases stuffed with fabric samples. Many were on the phones, either jabbering excitedly in the Osaka vernacular, or speaking slowly and deliberately in one foreign language or another. Telephones rang constantly.

Iki sat quietly at the center of this madness, isolated in a small pocket of watchful inaction. At nine o'clock he wrapped a notebook in a green and white *furoshiki*, and started off for the prefectural library. He stopped at Kaneko's desk.

"I was so busy, I'd forgotten about you. I'm sorry," Kaneko apologized. "I've been preparing for the bidding on 20-count cotton yarn, which begins at nine-thirty."

"Don't mention it. I can see how busy everyone is. So I'll be leaving for the library."

"The library? Oh yes, of course. To catch up on your newspaper reading. Frankly I don't see how anyone can sit down and read eleven years' accumulation of newspapers. And with two editions daily . . ."

"I feel somewhat presumptuous, taking this privilege, beginning with my first day on the job. I'll be away from my desk till noon. I hope you won't find this arrangement inconvenient." He bowed to Kaneko and, unnoticed by anyone else, left the Textile Division.

Iki walked a short distance along the bank of the Dojima River and crossed a bridge to reach the Osaka Prefectural Library on Nakanoshima, the island in midstream. He went directly to the reading room for the newspaper collection at the far end of the ground floor. Only one other reader had arrived before him.

Iki settled down at the table near shelves filled with numerous bound volumes of newspapers reproduced in reduced print. Rather than rely on books written by historians, social scientists, and political commentators, he wanted to read the news as it had been reported from day to day during his eleven years' absence from Japan. He intended to make his own analyses and arrive at his own conclusions. To read everything included in those newspapers was an obvious impossibility, so he would concentrate on the problems and issues that interested him most. While in Siberia he had read, on rare occasions, Soviet and East German newspapers, invariably outdated; the news articles were slanted, of course, but they had helped to give him some idea of major trends in international affairs. He decided, therefore, to focus his attention on changes that had occurred in Japan.

He considered a great many topics, and ultimately settled upon five that he should explore. These he listed on the first page of his notebook:

1. Changes in the Japanese national character since our defeat in World War II.
2. The substance of the new Constitution.
3. The content of the new system of compulsory education for Japan's children.
4. The changing allocations of appropriations in the national budget.
5. The fate of former professional military men.

He selected the July–December 1945 volume of the *Mainichi Shimbun*. Apparently it had not been opened in years, if at all; beneath a powdering of dust, the binding looked almost new. He searched in the volume until he came to a front page showing a photograph of the surrender ceremony on the maindeck of the U.S.S. *Missouri*, anchored in Tokyo Bay. The accompanying article described the ratification, on September 2, 1945, of the instrument of surrender. It concluded: "The ceremony was attended by a delegation of the Allied Powers, consisting of Supreme Commander MacArthur and representatives of China, Great Britain, the Soviet Union, Australia, Canada, France, the Netherlands, and New Zealand. Representing the Empire of Japan were Foreign Minister Shigemitsu, spokesman for the Government, and

Chief-of-Staff Umezu, spokesman for the Supreme War Council. An atmosphere of austere dignity prevailed at the signing."

Iki studied the photograph, which showed Foreign Minister Shigemitsu signing the instrument of surrender. Standing at attention directly behind him was General Umezu, solemn and dignified in his uniform, wearing the proper cordon, but without his sword. Tears at the sight of his respected chief made Iki put down the volume for a while.

September 2, 1945 marked the beginning of Japan's occupation by the Allied Powers. On September 3rd, the newspaper accounts reported, the Prime Minister, Prince Higashikuni, addressed the National Diet. The Prince summarized the process that brought about the end of the war. He described the Government's policies, designed to meet the needs in these trying times, and stated that the people of Japan should reflect on defeat with a sense of repentance.

In a lower corner of that same front page he saw a small advertisement: "Wanted immediately! 'Special' hostesses! Top salary plus lodging, meals, and clothing. Salary advances possible. Contact Association for Specialized Entertaiment, Ginza, Tokyo." To Iki this as was an unpleasant reminder of the depths to which his demoralized countrymen had sunk. He quickly turned the page, trying to get away from that reminder. He read a press release, dated September 9, of General MacArthur's announcement of policies governing the occupation of Japan:

> 1. The Supreme Commander for the Allied Powers shall issue necessary directives to the Japanese Government, and the United States Occupation Army shall function essentially as an instrument to ensure the implementation of such directives by the Japanese Government.
> 2. Japanese economic arrangements and operations shall be supervised and guided to conform to the general purposes of the occupation.
> 3. Among the major purposes of the occupation are the elimination of militarism and militaristic nationalism and the encouragement of principles of freedom. Freedom of speech, the press, religion, and assembly shall, therefore, be unrestricted except as required to maintain the safety of the Occupation Army . . .

Featured in the September 9th issue was an article carrying General MacArthur's statement, "As a result of defeat in war

Japan has been reduced to a fourth-rate power." News releases over a span of ten days gave Iki a clear picture of his country and his people assailed by troubles and humiliations following their defeat in war.

Just before noon, glancing over his notes, Iki realized how little he had read. And he had just begun! Comforting himself with the thought that, although he may have read little, he had learned a great deal, he left the library.

Back at his uncluttered desk, Iki was eating lunch when the telephone on the next desk rang. All the other employees had gone out to eat, and he alone represented the Textile Division. He reached for the phone, then hesitated; would he know how to respond to business inquiries? He was relieved when the noisy machine stopped ringing, and took another mouthful of cold rice. Naturally, the phone rang again, seeming to be more insistent than ever. Resolutely he picked up the receiver. It shouted immediately: "Let me talk to Sato!"

Iki did not know anyone named Sato. In fact he knew almost no one at all in the Textile Division. But to this command he felt he could give an honest response.

"He's not here at the moment. I'll find out who he is, and—"

"What's the matter with you? He's one of your employees. Listen, get me someone who knows what's going on over there. Any of the girls will do."

"I'm sorry. This is lunchtime and no one else is here. I'll have someone return your call later, if you'll give me your—"

"Cut the nonsense, will you? This is urgent! Take this message, then have someone call me back with an answer. Ready? The request I made the other day regarding—"

"Wait!" Iki begged. "I still haven't—"

"What? Don't you understand plain Japanese? Write this down!" He rattled off several sentences. "Make sure you deliver the message. Tell him Tanaka of Maruei Textiles called. —Who are you?"

"My name is Iki. Now, regarding the specific . . ."

Before he could say more, Tanaka hung up, leaving Iki thoroughly confused, and uncomfortable. He had jotted down a few phrases—"request of the previous day," "February 10," "clearing the shelves," "warehouse ledger," "payment by promissory note"— but the sense of the message completely eluded him. Even though

Tanaka's message seemed to be both urgent and important, he regretted having picked up the phone.

He was putting away the empty lunchbox when Ishihara returned from his hurried mission to Osaka Textiles. Iki repeated what had been conveyed to him over the phone.

"I don't understand any of it," Ishihara complained. "Can't you put these pieces of information together any better than that?"

"As I've told you, none of it was entirely clear to me. He mentioned 'taking something off the shelves on the tenth of February.' He seemed concerned about a 'promissory note,' and asked that Mr. Sato return his call as soon as possible." He hoped that Ishihara would be able to reconstruct the message, but the young man remained mystified.

"Sato is away now. In any case, that's a peculiar message. You're not trying to fool me, are you?"

"No, no! —I am telling you the truth. I'm the foolish one, for not fully understanding what Mr. Tanaka said. But he definitely did call."

"Well, let's try again. Tanaka told you he was 'taking something off the shelves' . . . Say! Are you sure he didn't say 'clearing the shelves'?"

"Yes! That's the word he used."

"Ahhh!" Ishihara fretted. "You don't seem to know the first thing about business, Mr. Iki. Please don't answer the phone any more. That way you'll make less trouble for us." He rushed off, toward a middle-aged businessman entering the office. He greeted the newcomer somewhat abruptly, and led him off to a corner for further talk.

The general commotion grew as the afternoon's market quotations were posted on the big price chart near the center of the room. Unable to share in the reasons for the excitement, Iki decided that his time would be best spent in learning more business terms. And so he listened in on conversations taking place around him. But much of what he heard sounded more like communications in code than talk in good honest Japanese. Even so, he continued to be the silent observer. He guessed that large quantities of unseen merchandise were being bought and sold for large sums of money. And he admired the men and their mysterious system that made such operations possible.

About an hour later Ishihara passed Iki's desk, on the way to his own. Iki dared to stop him, with upraised hand and a smile meant to be apologetic. "Did that person phone again?" Never, in all his career as an Army man, had he been so concerned to gain the good opinion of a lackey.

"Yes, he did. And the first thing he said was 'Who in hell was the idiot that answered the phone?' He jumped all over me, he was so mad."

"Is that so? Then I'm relieved." Noticing the quizzical expression on Ishihara's face, he added, ". . . That the Maruei business was taken care of, I mean."

"I hope you don't mind my asking this," Ishihara said, still wearing the same expression, "but what did you do before you were in the Army?"

"I was an Army man from the start. I've had no experience in any other line of work."

"What school did you attend?"

"The Army War College."

"Really? Never heard of it. What did you major in?"

Now came Iki's turn to be surprised. Just as he had no understanding of the workings of the Textile Division, this young man of the postwar generation had not the slightest conception of an Army officer's career.

"How did a former Army man like you ever get into a rough business like textiles? I can't understand it. To begin with, you don't know the language of business. Isn't that so? Have you found out what 'clearing the shelves' means?"

"No, not yet."

"You probably think that people actually take merchandise off the shelves. Right? But that's wrong. 'Clearing the shelves' means taking inventory. It's done twice a year, usually in March and September."

Ishihara looked upon Iki with undisguised condescension. "You should have gone to work for the Defense Agency. To expect a man your age to start from scratch in a trading company is most unreasonable. I'd say it's unfortunate . . . for everybody."

He sped off along the aisle, the very picture of a young man bound to succeed.

Iki, thus set in his place, felt not so much hurt by Ishihara's patronizing talk as sobered by the realization that, at the age of forty-six, he had committed himself to working in a world too full of men like Ishihara, and Yamamoto, and Tanaka—and, yes, like Daimon Ishizo, too. The next thought was even more distressing: his very livelihood, and the security of his family, from now on depended upon the speed and the success with which he made a place for himself in this world of businessmen.

"Dad, shall we go to the bathhouse?" Naoko asked as soon as they finished washing the supper dishes.

"Fine," Iki said. "Are you coming with us, Makoto?"

"I went with Hayato and his father before supper." Makoto scarcely looked up from the magazine he'd borrowed from his friend.

Iki had not yet succeeded in establishing an easy relationship with his son. He recalled how Makoto had drawn away from him, saying "He's not my father," when his family greeted him at the port of Maizuru two years before. When Iki stepped off the repatriation ship, he bore no resemblance to the handsome lieutenant colonel in the photograph whom his son had regarded fondly for eleven years. The image Makoto had been idolizing vanished in that instant, and with it went his love for his father. Iki hoped that time would heal the wound, but Makoto seldom allowed him to express affection in the way that Naoko did.

The wind along the river bank was cold. Naoko, wearing a long scarf around her neck, leaned against her father's side as they walked.

"After you've worked a while and saved some money," she said, "please build us a room for a bath. Will you? —That's the first thing I want. Then we won't have to walk to the public bath anymore."

"A bath? Of course."

"When do you think you can?" she asked, hugging his arm.

He had no notion of the cost involved, nor how long a time he would need to save enough money to add a Japanese-style bath to their house.

"I'm not sure, but I'll talk over the idea with your mother, and have the bath built as soon as I can."

"Oh, perfect! Mother will be so happy! She's had such a tough time. Before Mother got that job with the city, she worked for anyone who would hire her. She took in sewing and worked late every night. I'm glad you'll be able to do things to make her happy."

240

Yoshiko never talked about the hardships during the war years and their aftermath. Iki was grateful that Naoko spoke freely, reminding him of Yoshiko's troubles.

As usual, they took thirty minutes to bathe and dress, then met in front of the bathhouse for the walk home. When they returned, the kettle of water on the brazier was boiling. Yoshiko made tea.

"How did everything go today, dear?" she asked after Naoko went off to study her lessons.

Iki recalled his helplessness in trying to understand Tanaka of Maruei Textiles, shouting over the telephone, and the disagreeable remarks made by the young clerk, Ishihara, but decided not to talk about them. "Everything was new to me, so it was quite a challenging day. —Say, this tea is delicious. What kind is it?"

His attempt to change the subject did not escape Yoshiko's notice. "I asked about your day because you've been rather glum ever since you came home. Sometimes, you know, you seem to avoid telling me things that are important."

Iki suspected that she was referring to the night the war ended, when he had asked an aide to telephone her, to say that he would be gone "for a short while." That's what he had told the aide to say, even though he knew he would be flying the next day to Manchuria, where he hoped to meet a soldier's honorable death.

"You're the same way, I find," he said, quietly. "You've told me almost nothing about your troubles while I was away. Tonight Naoko mentioned something about them, when she asked me to add an *o-furo* to this house—to make life easier for you now. To make you happy . . ."

When the war ended in August of 1945, Yoshiko took the two children from Tokyo to the home of Iki's parents in Yamagata. However, both his parents died within six months, and Iki's older brother inherited the property. Realizing that their presence was a bother to the brother-in-law's family, she moved to her own parents' home in Osaka. Because her father and brothers had been professional soldiers, they could not find suitable employment. Soon penniless, they sold the family's large house in the city and moved to a village in the countryside. Fortunately, about that time Yoshiko was among the lucky few chosen by lottery to be eligible for a small house in a municipal housing development built on the bank of the Yamato River. But the income from sewing kimonos was so inadequate that, in order to support her children, she worked from time to time as a clerk at a shop near the Suminoe railway station. Eventually, through the intercession of Kawamata Isao, she obtained a job in one of the departments of Osaka's municipal government. Kawamata, a classmate of Iki's at both the Army Academy and the War College, had gone to work with the Defense Agency after he returned from the southern front.

"You were born into an Army family, married an Army man, and knew practically nothing of life outside the military. That must have made matters doubly hard for you." Iki, who daily must adjust to unfamiliar situations and even, at times, to abrasive personalities, could appreciate the trials that had fallen upon his gentle wife.

"I didn't mind . . . because I believed you would return to us some day . . ." She turned away to hide her tears.

"I'm terrible," she forced a giggle. "Lately, I've turned into a crybaby. I've lost the strength that kept me going . . . I never cried while you were away, except when I was angry about being treated unfairly." Lifting the fingers of her left hand to her lips, she laughed. "I'm even becoming forgetful too!" She rose, moved quickly to the dresser, and drew a letter from the top drawer. "This came today—from General Akitsu's daughter."

The sender was Akitsu Chisato of 1–46 Sakuragi-cho, Sakyo-ku, Kyoto. As he opened the envelope, Iki remembered the general's widow, pale with grief, her jet black hair and black kimono glittering with rain drops that had fallen upon her when she came to visit him in Tokyo.

I hope you will forgive me for writing you even before I have had the pleasure of meeting you. I am the daughter of the late Akitsu Noritake. First, I should like to tell you how very happy I am to know that you have returned safely after many long years spent in Siberia. My mother often talked of you and General Takemura. She told me that you were both familiar with the circumstances of my father's death. My mother, I am sad to inform you, died last year.

When I visited General Takemura in Tokyo several days ago, he told me he would visit Kyoto this coming Sunday. He has business to attend to, but he plans to visit me. He said he hasn't seen you in some time, and would be delighted if you could possibly find the time to join us. Such a reunion will surely gladden the spirit of my late father.

I know that you spent many years in cruel detention, and I trust that you have taken good care of yourself.

Most sincerely,
Akitsu Chisato

Again the next day, Iki spent the morning at the library, returning to the Kinki Trading building at one o'clock in the afternoon.

"I see you're just getting in," someone called as he entered the lobby. Ishihara, his youthful directness emphasized by a fresh crew cut, did not slow down for the antiquated veteran.

"Where have you been?" Iki asked, noticing his bulging briefcase.

"We had a little difficulty at customs in Kobe. Our shipping section wasn't able to get it straightened out. So I ran over there and gave them the usual bowing-apologizing routine, to get the merchandise through customs. Because we're merchants, all government offices give us a hard time. They have a long memory—merchants, they never forget, once ranked below samurai, farmers, and craftsmen.

"You're a lucky one," Ishihara rattled on, as they climbed the stairs. "In a class by yourself, spending your mornings in the library—just reading. When I first started working here, they put me on morning clean-up duty for the entire first year. I had to report in by seven. During my second year, I was nothing more than an errand boy, going off on a bicycle to deliver goods, collect accounts, and whatever else they wanted. I was embarrassed whenever I ran into college classmates who had taken better jobs in other companies."

Though Ishihara spoke disparagingly of himself, his cheerful tone conveyed complete satisfaction with himself, never peevishness nor self-pity.

"Please tell me," Iki said, as they approached their desks, "What can a beginner like myself read, to gain a better understanding of the overall structure and workings of our company?"

Ishihara opened a drawer, as neatly arranged as he was. "Here's a booklet for new employees. Haven't they given you one of these? Better yet, take a look at this. It's our annual financial report." He handed Iki the booklet, and a glossy printed report, and hurried off to tell the section chief how he handled the pompous customs official at Kobe Port.

Iki settled down for a careful reading of the annual report. It began with an enumeration of the activities of the company:

1. Importing and selling foreign commodities
2. Wholesaling
3. Importing, exporting, and retailing of scales and measures, sanitary facilities, and hygienic equipment
4. Selling and repairing of automobiles
5. Serving as agent for liability insurance
6. Serving as agent for and manager of real estate and rental properties

The list continued on and on. The more Iki read, the more confused he became. As he studied statements from department heads, he was astonished by the unusual kinds of merchandise the company handled. Many were the expected items of trade—cotton, wool, silk, synthetic fibers, secondary textile products, rice, sugar, and livestock products. Also included, however, were helicopters, other kinds of aircraft, and the latest in communications systems. How, he wondered, would one go about buying and selling such a bewildering assortment of merchandise?

The list of foreign branches was fascinating. Kinki Trading Company had set up fifty-one branches, established in most of the major cities of the United States, South America, Europe, Africa, the Near and Middle East, Australia, and South and Southeast Asia. These branches were staffed by two hundred and sixty employees sent out from Japan. Iki was familiar with geography, but his view of the world had been restricted to the land masses over which armies might be deployed. Now he saw the world as Kinki Trading's vast arena for business operations, with headquarters in fifty-one major cities. He felt a welcome thrill as he thought, "They might have a place for me here after all."

But the pleasure faded the instant he turned to the financial charts—a riot of figures in yen, dollars, pounds, marks, and francs. He would need help to understand any of it. He called Ishihara, calculating at his desk, using a slide rule, not an abacus. "Can you explain these entries to me?"

"That'll be hard to do." Ishihara lit a cigarette as he crossed to Iki's desk. "Because I'll bet you don't know the difference between 'liquid assets' and 'fixed assets.' I don't really know where to begin."

"Why not pick out a section that will give me a general idea of the company's operations, and describe it to me in simple terms?"

"O.K., O.K.," he agreed, using that American expression which, in Iki's opinion, was among the baneful consequences of the Occupation. "Let's take a look at the profit-and-loss statements."

Iki inspected the charts. "Gross sales over the past six months amounted to 212,719,731 yen. Let's see what the total payment was."

"Wait a minute! This is going to take more time than I thought. —The unit there is a thousand yen."

"What? That would make it 212 billion yen!" Iki exclaimed. He was not yet used to the current value of the yen, and actually had been stunned by the prodigious size of the national budget for the coming year—1.5 trillion yen! He made a quick comparison of the two figures and was astounded once again: a single corporation, in only half a year, had grossed one-seventh as much money as was to be appropriated in the government's annual budget!

"Do all of the so-called major corporations have sales equivalent in value to such a sizeable fraction of our national budget?"

"Only the trading companies," Ishihara answered. "But don't be misled by those big figures. Of course, if we could keep all that money we'd be richer than the Bank of Japan. But look at this figure. This is the most telling part of the whole report—it shows a net profit of 828,653,000 yen. As the line at the bottom tells you, that's a mere 0.35 percent of our total sales."

"A net profit of a mere one-third of one percent? I don't understand it."

"Well, a number of factors have to be considered." Ishihara glanced at his wrist watch. "Listen, I gotta run. I don't have time now to be your private tutor. You just look it over. Take your time. Perhaps, after a while, you'll catch on." And off he trotted, to some other more agreeable expenditure of his energy.

Iki remembered, from a course in economics, that a 3.5 percent net profit was not unusual before the war. In Kinki's annual report the decimal point had not been misplaced. But why would a business firm, with a worldwide network of offices and hundreds of employees, be operated for the sake of a mere 0.35 percent profit?

A pert young assistant secretary, slim in a Western-style dress, appeared beside him. "Mr. Ichimaru wishes to see you," she chirped.

Ichimaru, the managing director for textile operations, had just returned from a month's trip in Europe and Africa. His desk, somewhat larger than the others, occupied the center of executive's row.

"The President told me about you," said Ichimaru, following an exchange of greetings. "You've probably been inconvenienced by being thrown together with us in textiles. I hope you won't mind my saying that it's been an inconvenience to us, too. But that's what Mr. Daimon decided, and you or I can do nothing about it. I hear you spend the mornings reading newspapers at the public library. Do you have any idea what the population of the Sudan is?"

"I'm sorry, I don't," Iki answered, taken aback by both the question and the flightiness of this man's chatter.

"I've just made a trip through Europe and Africa. What surprised me is the fantastic rate at which the population of Africa is growing. Take Ghana for instance. When I visited there three years ago, the population was approximately three and a half million. Now it's approximately 4,300,000—an increase of 800,000. Our ambassador in Ghana tried to tell me that the country cannot even take a genuine census. Therefore, no reliable population count is available. After I talked with the ambassador, I had lunch with the assistant manager of the main Paris branch of AFC, a French corporation that's cornered trade in most of West Africa. He remarked on the population growth-rate in the whole continent, and suggested that the Sudan held great potential as a market for Kinki Trading. From that lunch I went straight to the airport, because I wanted to see the Sudan with my own eyes. In villages less than an hour's flight away from the capital city of Sudan, I saw people who wore no clothes—stark naked! I was told that between three and four million people are living in such outlying areas. If we could get all of them to wear just one item of clothing each—like shorts for the men, brief sarongs for the women—do you realize how much yardage that would add up to? A chill ran through me when I thought of the sales potential." Ichimaru talked with all the exuberance of the born trader.

"Do you have any idea, Mr. Iki, why the Sudanese population is growing at such a booming rate?"

"No, I don't."

"They have no electricity in their homes. At night their only diversion is making babies. An improvement in sanitation has occurred since they achieved independence. Nowadays, more of their babies survive. That population increase works to our advantage!" He leaned back, shaking with laughter.

"If you have any special particular requests," Ichimaru coasted into seriousness for the occasion, "you'll have to tell me now. I'm leaving for Tokyo in the morning."

"The truth is," Iki said after a moment's consideration, "I don't yet understand the essential methods of functioning in a trading firm such as ours. I've learned some business terms, and I'm reading the annual report, but I'm still in the dark. I thought I should study every phase of our operations at first hand, starting with textiles. I'd like to see how imported cotton is spun into thread, woven into fabric, and then distributed to wholesalers or diverted to export. I'd like to be led along the route taken by the commodities we handle. I would be grateful if you could make arrangements to permit the study plan I have in mind."

"I don't know if anyone can learn the functions of a trading company that way. But I don't suppose it will do you any harm. I'll have someone guide you. I must say, Iki, you seem to have little confidence in yourself. No matter. I can remember a time when I felt that way, too. My ambition, way back then, was to be a diplomat, and so I majored in French. But I flunked the foreign service exam. I had planned my career so carefully, only to have my plans blow up. But, then, we're adaptable creatures. Once I learned what trading is like, it got to be so much fun that I . . ." Ichimaru's phone rang, and immediately he was chatting away, forgetting Iki and everything else in the office.

Back at his desk, Iki thought about Ichimaru's complete turnabout, in plans, in living, in ambitions. He tried to imagine himself undergoing such a transformation. The change from career soldier to dedicated businessman would require more than the mastering of a new jargon. It demanded a much more fundamental alteration. Did it, indeed, involve a change of character? A virtual conversion, of both body and spirit?

Snow fell upon Kyoto on Saturday night. Next morning the city lay white under a brilliant clear sky.

Iki got off the streetcar at Sakuragi-cho and, following instructions, walked northward along a road that took him through a quiet residential area. The houses and their surroundings had changed little since the prewar years; all he could see of the neighborhood still kept the subdued dignity of the city of tradition, of history. A five-minute walk brought him to a small river, its banks lined with cherry trees, leafless still. He crossed a stone bridge and entered a narrow side street, at the end of which stood a small house surrounded by a wattle fence. The name plate on the pillar of the gate read "Akitsu." He pressed the bell and waited until the sliding door was opened from within.

"I am Iki," he said to the gray-haired servant. "I am sorry to be late."

She bowed respectfully. "We have been waiting for you. I'm sure you had to walk much farther than you expected."

The pair of shoes arranged in the entryway told him that General Takemura was already there. Iki had not seen Takemura since they parted at the dock in Maizuru, himself bound for Osaka, Takemura for Tokyo. After that neither had had the time or the money to travel so long a distance in order to visit the other.

"I'm so glad you were able to come." The attractive young woman, dressed in a crimson kimono, her dark, shining hair drawn tightly into an incongruous ponytail, greeted him from the entryway.

"I am General Akitsu's daughter, Chisato. I wish to apologize for this imposition."

Iki noticed that her skin, white as porcelain, and the oval face resembled her mother's. But the fine nose and large, dark eyes were unmistakably inherited from her father. "I am the one who should apologize," he said, bowing low. "I didn't know you were living this close to Osaka. Had I known, I would have come much sooner to offer my respects at your father's altar."

"Our family is indebted to you for your past kindnesses to my father. I am ashamed of the delay in sending you my greetings since your return to Japan. Mr. Takemura has been waiting anxiously. Please come in."

As Iki slipped out of his shoes, Chisato opened the sliding door to the eight-mat guest parlor facing upon the inner garden.

"Iki! How good to see you!" Takemura called out, leaning forward over a low table. "It's been a long time. I'm glad to see you looking so healthy. But, first of all, the altar . . ."

Iki went directly to the small Buddhist altar and knelt before it to light a stick of incense. A wisp of scented smoke drifted over the small memorial tablet for General Akitsu. With hands placed together, palm to palm, in the attitude of prayer, Iki felt again the long-forgotten emotions as he thought of the late general.

When Iki finished paying his respects to the general, Chisato thanked him gently. "I know my father's spirit has been gladdened." Quietly she excused herself, and slipped out of the room, leaving the two comrades alone for a few minutes.

"Here we are, in General Akitsu's house, meeting for the first time since we returned," Iki said, sitting on a cushion across the table from Takemura. "I feel as if he has helped to bring us together."

"I'm sure he did. I've long been troubled by a sense of unfulfilled obligation to him. Our having met before his altar will ease my conscience, I think." Iki could see that Takemura, now sixty-two years old, would never recover from the effects of those long years spent in Siberia. He was wondering how to break their silence when Chisato returned, bringing the sweet cakes they would taste before she served the tea.

"I want to thank you, Miss Chisato, for inviting Mr. Iki," Takemura said sincerely. "If you hadn't done so, many more years might have passed without our seeing each other."

"I'm the one who should thank you, for remembering my father," Chisato replied, brightening for the first time since they had arrived. "How fortunate for me that I thought to go to your research center when I was in Tokyo."

"You're at a research center?" Iki asked Takemura.

"Yes. This one is the Center for Sino-Soviet Research. I've been working there for the past year and a half. I'm not versatile. My old line, intelligence work, is all I'm good at."

The research center had been established before the war by a select group of Imperial Army specialists on China and the Soviet Union. Takemura, who had been staff officer for Intelligence, and the one responsible for Soviet affairs, had chosen a logical second career.

As he described the nature of his research, Chisato whisked the light-green powder in hot water she poured into a small glazed bowl, until the surface was covered with froth. She placed the bowl before Takemura, who took it in both hands, turned it around in the correct fashion, and sipped the tea. As Chisato prepared a separate serving for Iki, Takemura looked on quietly.

"What are you doing these days?" Takemura asked, when they had finished their tea. "I've heard you're spending all your time finding jobs for men who came back with us on the *Koan-maru.* But you? Are you still without a job?"

"Fortunately, all my men have found work. And I got myself a job about two weeks ago. I'm working for Kinki Trading Company." Iki confessed this more cheerfully than he would have done seven days earlier.

"I'm relieved. To tell the truth, I was worried about you. I'm sure you had good reason for waiting as long as you did. But the time has come, I suppose, to start providing a few luxuries for your family." Although Takemura laughed when he said this, he was expressing a genuine concern for Iki's wife, whom he had met only once, before the war.

"Chisato-san," he said, while she removed the tea bowls, "Iki and I seem to be doing all the talking—I'm afraid we're boring you."

"Not at all. I've enjoyed listening to your conversation. If my father were alive, he would be talking with his friends just the way you two are talking to each other." She smiled, but it was a sad smile.

"Where is the rest of your family?" Iki asked, struck by the quietness of the house.

"No one else is here. I've been living by myself since my mother died. I do have an elder brother, but he has joined a Buddist order, and I never see him."

"I was quite surprised when you first called on me in Tokyo," Takemura said, changing the course of the conversation. "I knew you were General Akitsu's daughter the moment I saw you. I remember that day well, because it was also my first day at the center following several months of recuperation. I took to my bed the day I returned from Siberia. And when I got up, there you were, asking me to tell you about your father's last days."

"My mother often told me what she had heard from you," said Chisato, looking sadly at the altar. "Although I was only a school girl when my father committed suicide, I felt I would never be satisfied until I heard the account of my father's death directly from you or Mr. Iki." She told them how she had searched the published lists of names of soldiers returning from Siberia, looking for those of Takemura and Iki, and how, after ten years, had found them in the very last list of repatriates. She traced Takemura to his address in Tokyo, but decided to wait a few months before visiting him, realizing that he would be busy getting settled. Iki was touched by proof of such devotion to her father's memory.

"Then you, too, spent ten years . . ." He stopped, not wanting to mention the very idea of suffering for anyone.

At that moment, they heard voices at the entryway. Soon the maid slid the door open. "It's that gentleman from Nishijin. What shall I tell him?" No sooner had she said this than a tall, imposing man, wearing the traditional Japanese attire for gentlemen, stepped into the room. His head, pink and shining and balding but for a few strands of white hair, gave him the look of a genial spendthrift.

"You should have given me warning," Chisato said, in some irritation. Nevertheless, she remembered her other guests. "This is my uncle, Akitsu Noritsugu. Uncle, I'd like you to meet Mr. Takemura and Mr. Iki."

"Of course!" he exclaimed. "I owe you many thanks for your kindness to my brother Noritake. Forgive me for intruding this way." He straightened the folds of his kimono and, settling on the mat, made a deep bow. Takemura and Iki glanced at each other, both thinking how thoroughly unlike General Akitsu this man was. He seemed to read their thoughts.

"I'm quite different from my brother Noritake," he laughed, as he moved closer to the table. "I'm a weaver in Nishijin, the cloth making center of Kyoto. We Akitsus have been in the weaving business for three generations, and ours is a proud name in Nishijin. My brother Noritake, being the oldest son, was supposed to carry on the family business. But he wanted to make his career in the Army. So they made me head of the household."

"I never knew that," said Takemura. "Everything about the general suggested that he came from a military family."

"From boyhood my brother said he didn't want to spend his life weaving material for kimonos and obis for women. He refused to take any interest in the family business. —Like father, like daughter, I'd say. This one here is a bit self-centered, too. She's twenty-seven, but she won't get married. I wouldn't mind that so much, if

251

she'd use her time to help me run the family business. But she doesn't. She spends her time working with mud. I just don't understand her." He looked at Chisato, shook his head, and sighed.

"How insensitive of you to say that, Uncle," Chisato protested, not at all happy with his teasing. "Ceramics is an art."

"Ceramics?" Iki interjected, not thinking fast enough. Then, realizing his mistake, he tried to cover it up with a forced smile—and a worse blunder. "Isn't that an unusual profession for a woman?"

"Ah, you think so, too?" said Uncle Noritsugu, delighted with Iki's prejudice. "If she'd take an interest in the tea ceremony, or in traditional painting, she could become a teacher. That's an appropriate career for a woman. But beating and mauling lumps of clay all day long! Just look at her hands!"

"Do you see anything wrong with them?" she retorted, thrusting out her hands."

"You've cleaned them, I see. Usually anyone would notice all that clay, under her fingernails and caked onto her fingers. A stranger would think she was a female ditch digger. I've taken on the job of being her father, but . . ." He shook his head. "I wish you gentlemen would talk some sense into her."

"Uncle, I'll be angry if you say anything more about me before my guests. Please!"

Akitsu shrugged. "I give up, for now—out of consideration for your guests." He turned to them, as good natured as the God of Happiness. "You've come to visit us out of respect for the memory of my brother, so I cannot properly invite you to join me in a little fun. But you've traveled a long distance to come to Kyoto. Why don't you let me show you a few sights about the town. After that we'll go to a geisha house in the Gion Quarter."

"I'm very grateful," Takemura said, "but I have an appointment to see someone this evening."

"If you're free this afternoon, let me at least take you sightseeing."

"In that case," Takemura looked at Iki, "perhaps we can go to Sanzen-in, the monastery in Ohara. I was there in winter twenty years ago, and still remember the snow-covered garden. How would you like to do that?"

"You're true esthetes," Akitsu said with animation, seeing that

Iki agreed. "Only men of taste can appreciate the beauty of San-zen-in in winter, and I'm delighted. Let's go. My car is out in front. On our way back, we can stop at a place where both scenery and saké are good."

The car climbed the winding road along the Takano River and entered the hamlet of Ohara, deep in snow. Rivulets, famed for the purity of their water, coursed beneath a stretch of silver-tipped maples. The landscape, which had blazed with color in autumn, was one of muted beauty now, with the quiet restraint of a *sumie*, a painting done in black ink upon white silk. Near the foot of Mount Hiei, Akitsu stopped the car at the entrance to a path that led to Sanzen-in.

"We'll have to walk the rest of the way," he said, drawing the collar of his heavy cape tightly around his neck. "Stay warm. I don't want you to catch cold."

He led the way and Chisato followed him, the lower half of her face muffled in a pink knit shawl. After Siberia the cold was not at all bothersome to Iki or Takemura, and they were amused by the precautions the Akitsus took.

The approach to Sanzen-in was a long, gradual slope paved with blocks of stone. The monastery itself was enclosed by a stone wall surmounting a low escarpment rising beside the path. The massive gate seemed more appropriate to a fortress than to a monastery. The forbidding aspect of the whole place, Iki thought, would strike the fancy of a man like Takemura.

Akitsu stopped just outside the gate and, stepping easily into the role of a tour guide, even to imitating the stilted language of the souvenir booklet written for pilgrims and tourists, related the history of Sanzen-in in a performance which Chisato affected not to hear at all: "Since the era of the Fujiwara regents in the tenth century, these grounds have been favored by men and women who wish to seclude themselves in order to pray for rebirth in the Pure Land. The grounds are holy to those who devote themselves to invoking the name of Amida Buddha, Lord of the Western Paradise. Among the many famous temples of the Tendai sect in this vicinity are the Shorin-in, Raigo-in, and Jakko-in. These several temples have been subsumed under a monastic entity, called Gyoza, for which Sanzen-in is the administrative center."

They passed through the small door beside the great gate and stood before the main cloister, which seemed deserted. Their many calls for recognition were answered at last, when a young monk appeared and offered to guide them through the ground.

"I come here all the time and know the place well," Akitsu told him. "We'll look around by ourselves. Here, take this—it's an offering in place of admission fees." He handed the surprised monk an envelope thick with paper money, and, without waiting for permission, started to walk along the hallway. The wooden floor glistened, a mirror reflecting the image of Akitsu, floating ahead. The corridor took them through many turns and eventually to the central hall, which opened on a spacious garden. The sight of it took Iki's breath away. The covering of snow had transformed a thick carpet of dark green moss into a sheet of white velvet. The huge maple tress, now leafless and sheathed in ice, glittered at countless points, each like a translucent blue flower. At the center of this magical garden stood the Hall of Paradise, which sheltered the famed Mural of Three Thousand Buddhas.

"It's just as I remember it," Takemura said contentedly. "I'm reminded of the poem: "From year to year, season to season, man is never the same." I've recalled that poem often, but never has its meaning struck so deeply as it does now."

Iki was surprised to hear the taciturn Takemura express such private thoughts. He thought of the many experiences he and Takemura had shared, some good, far too many bad, and, whatever they might have been, surely far more than would fill the lifetimes of ordinary men. He had never visited Sanzen-in before. If he were to return for a second visit after a lapse of twenty years, as Takemura was doing today, would he be a successful member of the world of business? The very question disquieted him. The very uncertainty of the future shattered the serenity he should have felt in this lovely place.

"Mr. Takemura, do you remember the statue of Amida in the Hall of Paradise?" Akitsu asked.

"I do indeed. That beautiful image personifies compassion. When I saw it, twenty years ago, I was able to understand why people of the Fujiwara era believed so readily in Amida's saving grace. May we see the statue today?"

"The hall is kept open the year-around. Let's go over there."

They slipped their feet into *geta*. The men stepped at once upon the snow-covered path leading across the garden. But Chisato stood still, gazing up at Mount Hiei, rising beyond the majestic trees.

"Is something wrong?" Iki asked, breaking the spell the mountain seemed to have cast upon her.

She shook her head sadly. "I'm sorry. My brother Seiki is in one of those cloisters up there on Mount Hiei. I was thinking about him. He performs ascetic practices regularly, and today would be no exception."

"What did your brother do before he entered the monastery?"

"He was in the Army, too, of course. He went back to university after he returned from the Philippines. But he quit school and studied to be a priest. We were quite surprised. He hasn't been down to see us even once since he entered the monastery ten years ago."

Iki could sympathize with General Akitsu's son. He, like Iki himself, a castoff from the military, had found a new way of life. Although I hope it brings him peace, it's not a way I would have chosen, thought Iki.

"Uncle, being the way he is, was very displeased and called him a weakling. At the time, I thought he was anything but a weakling. But I no longer know." She looked intently at Iki. "When I think of what you and Mr. Takemura went through, I become even more confused about what makes a person weak or strong."

The skies above Kyoto were still clear and the next morning. Chisato, dressed comfortably in slacks and a dark brown sweater, sat before the mirror, brushing her long hair. She took but a few moments to tie it into a ponytail and to add a touch of lipstick to an already glowing face.

Kino, the old servant, had gone out, and the house was quiet. Sometimes Chisato felt lonely in such silence, but today she was happy to be spared Kino's chatter. She lingered over her recollections of yesterday's outing, particularly those concerning her father's friends contemplating the beauty of Sanzen-in's snow-covered garden. She thought of the incense burner that General Akitsu had left as a keepsake, and felt a longing to use it.

The incense burner, placed in the *tokonoma* of the guest parlor, was a beautiful piece of Korean celadon porcelain that seemed to have captured the blue luster glowing in the depths of a moonlit pool. General Akitsu had bought it in Manchuria when he was assigned to the Kwantung Third Army Headquarters. He had wanted to buy a Sung vase, but, that being beyond his means, had settled on the incense burner instead. He kept it on display in the *tokonoma*, to admire during the moments of respite from official duties. When they were children, Chisato and her brother Seiki had been warned never to touch the treasured piece. When Chisato's father was appointed director of the Continental Railroad command in 1944, he recognized that Japan was in danger of losing the war, and ordered his wife and daughter to return to Tokyo immediately. He entrusted the cherished ceramic piece to his wife, instructing her not to part with it during the trip home. On the evening before their departure for Japan, he had burned in it his last piece of fragrant sandalwood incense. Chisato recalled this scene with painful awareness of the sadness of beauty.

Not long after her father's suicide, Chisato was taken to Kyoto by her mother. The general's brother, Noritsugu, who had inherited the family home, found them another house to live in. The first thing Chisato did when they moved into the new home was to place the celadon incense burner in the *tokonoma* of the guest parlor, where she could see it daily. The more she saw it the more she became fascinated by its beauty in form and color. Through it she developed a genuine appreciation for ceramics. When she enrolled as a literature major at Kyoto Women's University, she also began an apprenticeship at a potter's studio, despite strong objections from both mother and uncle.

While Chisato remembered so many melancholy events in her short life, the stick of incense she had lighted in tribute to her father vanished in scented smoke.

The clock was striking nine when she locked the house and went to work.

Kano Raizan's studio was situated half way up Gojo Slope, a twenty-minute streetcar ride from Sakuragi-cho, where Chisato lived. Typical of residential dwellings wedged in among shops in the older sections of Kyoto, the narrow frontage of Kano's home was unassuming, but within the gate was a spacious front garden that led to the studio at the rear of the lot. Chisato gently opened the sliding door to the studio. Measuring somewhat less than twenty feet on a side, it consisted of two halves, one with a concrete floor, the other with a raised wooden floor. The master was turning one of the three potter's wheels set up on the wooden floor. Kano produced remarkable works of art. But he had not acquired the fame that would gain him entry into the National Academy of Arts, mostly because of his unwillingness to conform to the patterns of behavior Japanese expected of celebrated artists. He was dedicated to his art, and indifferent to the renown and wealth his genius could bring him. This quality in Kano—what others saw as eccentricity—inspired respect, indeed reverence, in Chisato. Although she had been his disciple for five years, each time she entered his studio she felt the peculiar tenseness of a novice arriving for her first lesson.

Sakuma, Kano's assistant for twenty years, was an unassuming man of unyielding character, very much like the master whom he had served since first he came under his tutelage at the age of thirteen.

Chisato sat down beside a wheel and began to smooth the foot of a tea bowl she had thrown two days earlier.

"That one's no good," the white-haired Kano said gruffly. The remark stung Chisato, for she had shaped the bowl to her satisfaction.

"But, Master . . ."

Kano did not let her finish. "Do it over," he snapped. "This time don't let any preconceived notion direct you. Keep in mind only the idea of 'nothingness.' "

Chisato set the unfinished tea bowl on a stand beside the window and studied it from several angles. It had exactly the shape she wanted. "I don't understand," she said. "It seems to have just the right shape."

"Unlike a vase, a tea bowl requires very little technique to make. Most potters think all they have to do is shape it well. But just look at the tea bowls that are made every day. By almost any dabbler with a lump of clay. They're perfect expressions of inelegant minds. Those potters are ignorant of the spirit of nothingness. A state of nothingness is the essence of the art of tea. When you work on a tea bowl, your mind must merge with the clay that you are shaping. Remember only that while you work."

Even after five years, Chisato was still mystified by this kind of instruction.

"Look at your bowl," Kano said. "You haven't allowed the clay to stretch of itself. You've forced it to take a preconceived form."

257

Abruptly he turned back to his own wheel, resuming his work with Sakuma's assistance.

For a while Chisato was lost in thought, considering her teacher's words. Soon she was kneading a fresh piece of clay, occasionally dipping her fingers in warm water to keep them from becoming numb. The studio was very cold. Only the space near the wheels was heated in order to maintain a temperature that would prevent unfinished pottery from freezing and cracking.

During her first three years as an apprentice, Chisato had done little besides knead clay and clean the studio. Kano had often told her that no one could master the art of ceramics without first perfecting the ability to knead clay. In her fourth year he permitted her to practice on Sakuma's wheel. She had known considerable discouragement. Kano's taunting observation, "It was a mistake to accept a woman as a student," had so disheartened her that, soon afterward, he had grudgingly admitted that she was beginning to show some promise. Now she had her own wheel in his studio. Unknown to her, he was subjecting her to the same kind of testing that every novice-applicant must pass before he is admitted to a profession in traditional craftsmanship.

A final kneading required about two hundred tugging twists and fierce poundings that strained not only the arms but also the torso and legs as well. When at last Chisato placed the kneaded shapeless clay on the wheel, her face was flushed, her whole body perspiring. She flicked on the electrical switch to set the wheel spinning, and soon the lump of clay, guided only by her fingers, assumed the shape of a bowl. It rose with an ease that she knew came from the clay, not from her thought.

"Do you see the difference?" Kano had been observing her. "This one shows the level of awareness that's needed to make a good piece." He permitted himself a rare smile. "—A piece good enough to exhibit."

"Exhibit? . . . My piece?"

"That's right. After today you're no longer a frivolous young lady shopping around for a hobby. You'll have more than enough time to make something suitable for the new ceramicists' show in autumn."

Chisato, elated by Kano's acceptance, thought less about the possibility of exhibiting a piece of her own creation than about the surprise that Uncle Noritsugu must admit, when he heard about her success. "A female ditch digger, indeed!" she muttered, beating another lump of clay in readiness for throwing another work of art.

Bidding on 20-count cotton yarn had begun at nine thirty sharp at Osaka's Cotton Exchange. Nearly sixty agents representing some forty brokerage houses were crowded in front of a platform from which the auctioneer observed their upraised hands.

"Daimatsu buying twenty bales! Hiyoshi buying one hundred! Naniwa buying forty!"

Responding to the brokers' signals the auctioneer called out bid after bid with a speed that amazed Iki. He slapped the table top regularly with a baton, producing a resounding crack to accent the rhythm of his chant.

"I don't understand what's going on," Iki remarked to Ishihara, who had been assigned as his guide.

"I explained it on our way here, but I'll go over it again. All cotton yarn exchanged in Osaka is bought and sold right here, in this room, through brokerage houses licensed by the Ministry of International Trade and Industry. At Kinki Trading, the chief of our Cotton Yarn Department, Mr. Kaneko, handles both buying and selling. While the bidding is going on, he's at his desk with two telephones, one at each ear. He has direct lines to our brokers here. You notice that all these brokers are wearing headphones. Brokers give running reports on the fluctuations in price. Ours will buy or sell according to Mr. Kaneko's instructions. All the brokers you see here are making transactions for small merchants, as well as for large corporations, like Goto and Marufuji. Each time one of those fellows signals with his hand, he's making a bid."

"Which ones work for Kinki?"

"There's one. See that nervous little man with the white face and the sharp eyes? He's with Daimatsu Brokerage. But we use other brokerage firms, too. Hiyoshi and Naniwa are working for us."

"Why don't we rely on just one?"

"If we did, our competitors would be able to trace our every move. Even when he's out to buy big, Mr. Kaneko won't buy it all through Daimatsu. He'll apportion percentages of shares to several brokers. He might even have them bidding against one another, depending on the way the price is fluctuating. He puts it all together—in his head, back there at Kinki—just before the auctioneer brings down the baton."

Iki understood the process, recognizing its similarity to demonstration tactics in the planning of military operations.

During a lull before the start of bidding on 30-count yarn, most of the brokerage agents relaxed in the lounge. The Daimatsu agent, the one Ishihara had described as white-faced and sharp-eyed, approached them. "Hello there!" he called out, recognizing Ishihara. "The market's going to be bullish now that we have Eisenhower's statement this morning on U.S. foreign aid."

"Does that mean an end to the dip caused by last week's news about bumper crops in the U.S.?" Ishihara asked.

"More or less," Daimatsu's agent said, hurrying away as the bell rang to announce bidding on 30-count yarn.

"I'm surprised to hear that," Iki said to Ishihara. "I can understand how production would affect prices. But is the cotton market actually influenced by what the American president says?"

"Of course. The cotton market is affected just as stocks and bonds are—by worldwide weather conditions, politics, war, changes in prime interest rates, even by a rumor that the president of a major trading house may be dying of cancer."

The crack of the auctioneer's baton signaled the start of bidding. All conversation stopped at once, as the brokers turned toward the platform.

The auctioneer's chant rose in pitch as the bidding progressed. "Daimatsu selling twenty! Maruyama buying forty! Oshima buying one hundred!" He scanned the forest of upraised hands. A palm turned toward the auctioneer signified selling. The back of a hand signaled buying. Raised fingers indicated the number of bales. A quick wave of the hand indicated two digits; two waves, three digits.

Daimatsu's agent swung his upraised arm, and the auctioneer brought down his clapper. Transactions involving 30-count yarn, at the current month's unit price of 185 yen, were ended.

The next session was devoted to bidding on futures for March, followed by bids for each of the succeeding months through August.

"More than twenty-two hundred bales of 30-count yarn were bought or sold in yesterday's four bidding sessions," Ishihara said. "Judging by that, I'd say five hundred bales changed in the first session this morning—about seventy-four million yen worth."

One bidding sequence required only ten minutes. Having witnessed successive rounds of bidding for cotton yarn all the way up to six months in the future, Iki couldn't help shaking his head over what seemed to be a quick series of dangerous speculations.

Iki and Ishihara left the cotton exchange and strolled through "wholesalers' row" in the commercial district of Semba. Bolts of cloth were stacked to the eaves in front of shops lining the street. Passing bicycles and three-wheeled motorcycles, loaded down with merchandise, left little space for pedestrians. Iki stopped in front of one of the shops, wanting a closer look at goods on display. Immediately a young clerk rushed up to him.

"Mister, I'll give you a good buy! Look at this—top quality, tight weave, high-grade Australian wool."

Swiftly he unrolled a few yards of a bolt of stuff for men's suits, and started flicking the big black beads on a wholesaler's oversized abacus.

"How's this price?" He allowed Iki only the briefest view of the abacus, which he quickly put away, as if to prevent spying passersby from seeing the low price he was quoting.

Iki was puzzled, for, having been trained in the use of the modern slide-rule, he had no facility with the abacus.

The clerk plucked at Iki's shabby suit. "I believe you've come a long way to do your buying." Again he clicked the big beads. "I'll come down. How's this? I can't go any lower."

"Enough of that," Ishihara said sharply, stepping up and flicking a few of the beads in his turn.

"That's murder," the clerk wailed. Recognizing that Ishihara must be a sharp buyer, he exchanged glances with the head clerk seated inside the shop, and made another calculation on the abacus.

"You win," he said to Ishihara. "I'll compromise. Is it a deal?"

"One eighty-five a yard? No thanks. Next time, maybe." Ishihara sauntered away, and meek Iki followed after him.

"Should you have teased him like that? When you had no intention of buying anything?" Iki was embarrassed, but Ishihara laughed.

"Mr. Iki, you shouldn't let yourself be hoodwinked by the small operators in this neighborhood. Not if you want to be a successful trader."

"Here's something I've been wanting to ask you," Iki said after they had walked a while. "Yesterday you showed me factories spe-

cializing in spinning, weaving, and dyeing. Now that I understand something about how cloth is made, I'd like to know how
the price of cloth is determined."

"A lot of factors are involved—the effect of the international
market on raw cotton in the producing area, for instance. But if I
explained everything, I'd only get you all mixed up. Let me
describe it as simply as I can. First, our company sells raw cotton
to the spinnery, which turns it into thread. We buy the thread
from the spinnery, and sell it to the weaver. We buy the cloth the
weaver makes, sell it to the dyer, then buy back the dyed cloth. At
each stage we make a five percent profit."

"That means our company buys and sells the same merchandise
over and over, making a profit on each transaction. Sounds ruthless."

"Listen," Ishihara said impatiently. "Business is not that simple.
A trading company has to take a percentage on every transaction.
Remember—we're feeding money into every one of those companies. Take the dyeing factory we went to yesterday. They subcon-
tract jobs to dyers, resin makers, fuel suppliers, even a shop that
makes the cores for the bolts: Kinki Trading provides loans to all of
them, in a process of give and take that everyone understands.
This afternoon we'll be going to Kobe to see how ships are loaded.
In order to export its products on these ships, our company has to
draw a letter of credit on a bank. Each time we do that, we pay a
fee. As matters turn out, we're feeding the banks too. So far you've
seen only the surface."

Ishihara, now in his fourth year with Kinki Trading, was frank
in expressing enthusiasm for his work as well as unabashed pride
in appreciating his own capacities as an expert on everything.

"What kind of mystery man are you, Mr. Iki?" He asked one
day, very good naturedly. "You come to us, in the middle of your
life, after a career in the Army, of all places. You're hired as a consultant to the President. And then you spend your time reading
newspapers in the public library, and being taken on guided tours.
I'm baffled."

"I'm nothing special," Iki replied. "Mr. Ichimaru asked me if I
had any requests to make. I said I'd like to be taken on these tours
so that I can find out what a trading company is all about."

"You seem to be in a class by yourself. Nobody else I know ever
had these advantages. Me, for example. When I first started at
Kinki, I worked like a slave. You're lucky."

That afternoon, about half past one, Iki and Ishihara drove into Pier Two in Kobe. Iki had spent several days with Ishihara, observing spinning, weaving, and dyeing plants, then primary and secondary wholesale outlets. After seeing the loading of goods to be exported, he would have completed the schedule of study he had drawn up for himself.

As they walked along the row of warehouses, the sea beyond came into view. Several large merchant vessels, anchored far out in the channel, gave the roadstead a tranquility that was new to Iki, who still associated harbors and ports with warships and naval power. He slackened his pace to breathe in the salt-scented breeze and enjoy the calming effect of the wide stretch of blue.

"Get the hell out of the way!"

Just in time, Iki leaped out of the path of a stevedore's truck.

"Dock workers are a rough lot," Ishihara warned and laughed at the same time.

As they walked toward Yamaichi Wharf, Ishihara explained the operations at the pier. "All exports we handle are delivered to this one wharf. From this point on, the *otsunaka* alone is responsible for getting the goods aboard ship."

"*Ostunaka?* . . ."

"They're agents in charge of loading. An *otsunaka* receives a load of cargo delivered by manufacturers who export through a trading company. He oversees the weighing-in of that load, takes the shipping order to the freight office to get guaranteed space, then obtains customs clearance. He also contracts for the necessary lighters and stevedores to deliver it to the specified ship."

"What's left for Kinki's shipping clerk to do?"

"His job is to prepare the necessary papers—letters of credit, export application, inventory, shipping order, and export permit. On the day of sailing, he's right here to take care of any last-minute emergency."

"He's busy enough, then, I imagine."

"See that freighter out there taking on cargo from a lighter?" Ishihara pointed.

"She's the *Azuma-maru*, an 8,000-ton freighter that's scheduled to set sail at five o'clock for Port Said. She'll be carrying 1,500 tons of rayon and cotton for Kinki Trading."

Loading operations that afternoon were confused and hectic because trucks carrying six hundred crates of rayon from a manufacturer in Toyama had been blocked by deep snow on Suzuka Pass, and arrived at the pier less than an hour before the scheduled sailing. Iki had an unexpected opportunity to observe the *otsunaka* display his skill and tenacity in a conference with the *Azuma-maru*'s officers over keeping the holds open until the delayed cargo could be delivered shipside by three lighters.

By then the time was close to four-thirty. A crane hoisted the crates up from the lighters and into the ship's holds, to be stacked by stevedores. As soon as the sweating stevedores emerged from the holds, the great hatches were closed with deafening thuds and bangings, their echoes blending with the reverberations of the gong that signaled the ship's readiness for the sea.

The stevedores slid down rope ladders to the lighters, which quickly headed back to shore. Iki followed the *otsunaka*, Ishihara, and the Kinki shipping clerk down the swaying rope ladder to the launch that had brought them out from the pier. As the launch moved away, a great blare from her klaxon announced the ship's departure.

The four men stood for a while at the pier's edge, watching the *Azuma-maru* moved sturdily out of the bay toward the sea beyond. She would sail on to Hong Kong and Singapore, then across the Indian Ocean and through the Suez Canal, reaching her destination, Port Said, in a month's time.

Ishihara was unusually wordless as he watched the *Azuma-maru* gliding away. "Mr. Iki," he said, as they started to walk back to their car, "our country's so poor because we lost the war. The only way Japan can rise again is by earning foreign currency. Lots of it. And we businessmen are the ones who can do that!"

After that, Iki found new reason to like Ishihara. "We work in different ways for the same goal," he said.

On the next evening Iki stayed on late at the office, while Kaneko helped him to learn how to identify the different kinds of fabrics. Kaneko provided explanations as Iki examined samples through a magnifying glass.

"Look closely at the weave. See how fine it is? The total thread count, the total of both warp and woof, determines the grade of a fabric. The one you're looking at has 130 strands running vertically and 70 horizontally—a total of two hundred to a square inch. That particular fabric is called 'class-200 poplin.' "

Kaneko pulled out a single thread from a length of 40-count cotton yarn, and waited for Iki to examine it. "Fabrics are typed and graded according to the number of strands woven into a square inch. A specialist in textiles can determine the thread count by feeling a fabric with his fingers. He can do this not only for cottons, but for woolens and synthetics as well."

"How long does he need before developing this skill?" Iki asked.

"Three to four years, I'd say. Such a skill one acquires the hard way—after making many expensive mistakes."

When Kaneko returned to his desk Iki sat slumped in his chair, contemplating the awful prospect of spending at least three years in learning how to identify fabrics. Fortunately for his humor, Ishihara came to invite him to the section meeting, being held that evening. "You might pick up some useful information," said this breezy young man.

Iki joined the dozen members of the Textile Export Section, packed into the customers' lounge. He felt conspicuous among men twenty years his junior.

"First, we'll take up the problem of claims," Section Chief Yamamoto began. "Nairobi Corporation of Kenya is demanding a penalty payment because the nylon yardage we sent them isn't color fast. It's a batch we exported last year. Look at these samples they've returned. The orange has turned brown. You've been in touch with the manufacturers, haven't you, Sato? What did they say?"

Iki remembered that name well. He doubted that he would ever forget his embarrassing attempt to take a telephone message meant for Sato.

"I went right away to Osaka Rayon and raised a fuss because they gave us defective material to export. Their man admitted that they've had smiliar complaints from other exporting firms. Tests of their nylon showed that the fabric is likely to fade badly under strong sunlight. Pink, green, and yellow are the worst offenders. They promised they'd do their best to improve quality in the future."

"That's beside the point," Yamamoto said irritably. "Nairobi Corporation is demanding a penalty payment on sixty thousand yards of defective fabric. What did we sell it for?"

"Forty cents a yard."

"They're asking for eighty percent of the half price."

"A forty percent refund?" Sato squirmed. "At that rate we won't even recover the shipping cost. We've got to negotiate with Nairobi Corporation and—"

"Stupid!" Yamamoto snapped. "You're not thinking. Natural and chemical fibers are on the decline. Synthetics will take over. What's important now is to cultivate markets for the future. So we pay the full amount of the claim. In no other way can we keep Nairobi's trust. Our action will pay off eventually, when the market for synthetics turns into a buyers' market. Try to get Osaka Rayon and other manufacturers to understand this."

Iki approved of Yamamoto's farsightedness. Through his conversations with Ishihara, he had learned that many small Japanese exporters were flooding the African market with rayon, acetate, and other synthetic fiber products without giving any regard to fair prices or to the quality of merchandise. They had undercut one another almost viciously in order to make sales, and evaded all responsibility when buyers approached them with complaints and claims. Importers abroad were becoming aware of the tactics used by those unscrupulous exporters.

"Let's move on to market conditions in the Middle East," Yamamoto said. "Hyodo, what's the trend in the market over there?"

Hyodo had accompanied Managing Director Ichimaru to Europe, then gone alone to the Middle East. He had returned to Osaka only the day before. His lean, sunburned face was heavily lined, giving him the appearance of a man older than his actual thirty-five years.

"Nothing much will happen in Arabia this year," he said bluntly.

"What's that? Everybody in Japan knows that the Middle Eastern countries are getting ready to buy. And buy plenty. If you didn't notice that, you must have been wearing blinders."

Hyodo was unaffected by Yamamoto's sarcasm. "That's what I was told before I went over there. But that advisory was based on reports of last year from the merchants of Aden and Beirut. Those merchants enjoyed a surge in business just before the start of the season for the pilgrimages to Mecca. They're expecting more of the same this year. The trouble is, they're speculators. Or, better, gamblers, who don't have any hard facts to deal from. Therefore, I didn't think I should rely solely on their opinions. Before I talked with them, I went to the bazaars of Aden, Medinah, and Jidda, and checked the amounts and kinds of merchandise in stock. I even got into Mecca. Sales were down even though that was the height of the pilgrimage season. This year I believe that buyers in the Middle East will take no more than a poor half of the two to three million yards the Aden speculators are predicting."

The assistant section chief entered the discussion. "Marufuji, Goto, all the major trading companies, even our own manufacturers, are talking about the large number of orders received from Aden. Some exporters have already drawn up contracts. No one else in Japan has the same information you have. I find that strange."

"The difference," Hyodo replied calmly, "is that none of our competitors' employees have ventured beyond Aden. Marufuji, Goto, and the rest put complete trust in what the Aden speculators are saying. I don't. You just wait and see. We're going to see a lot of trading companies and manufacturers who won't be able to collect on merchandise they've exported. Their customers won't pay up until they sell the merchandise. If they're pressed for payment, they'll simply say that they can't, and they won't. And that, they'll claim, will be in accord with Allah's will."

"When I was stationed in Algeria," another said, "I was burned unexpectedly by an Arab merchant. I told him I'd be willing to wait, if he would pay interest on the principal. I was stunned when he told me that interest payments are not permitted by the Koran. Algeria was an impossible place to do business in."

Yamamoto frowned. "Are you sure about this, Hyodo?"

"I'm positive. Don't look to Arabia for business. They won't come through. The main reason is that few pilgrims are going to Mecca this year. Shop owners everywhere are complaining about the lack of business. To find this out, I disguised myself as a Muslim from Indonesia and joined the pilgrims. I learned that a spreading sickness had wiped out a large number of sheep in Arabia. To make matters worse, the harvests were abnormally low. Most Arabs are simply broke—I could tell that as I traveled along the pilgrimage road. The hotels, which should have been filled to capacity, were almost empty. Instead, pilgrims were camping out in the fields to save money. None of the bazaars was busy."

"You're amazing, Mr. Hyodo!" Ishihara burst out. "How fortunate you weren't caught impersonating a Muslim. Weren't you in danger?"

The young listeners were entranced by the story of his adventure.

"Nothing to it," Hyodo laughed. "I was born with a dark skin, and all I needed was a few days in the sun at Aden to turn browner. When I dressed as a Moslem, all that showed were my eyes and mustache. The customs gave me some trouble, I admit. But I memorized the first few verses of the Koran and repeated them whenever someone looked at me as if I didn't belong. That was enough to get me by. Even my peculiar pronunciation raised no problems, once they knew I came from far-off Indonesia."

As casually as Hyodo talked about his adventure, everyone knew that he had risked his life by pretending to be a Muslim pilgrim.

Yamamoto, meanwhile, had been considering Hyodo's assessment.

"Okay, Hyodo! All trading companies here are buying synthetics in anticipation of exporting to Arabia. First thing tomorrow we'll start selling."

Yamamoto had made the decision for Kinki Trading Company. As Iki knew, each section of the Textile Department was managed independently. Although a section chief ranked below an executive, he had complete responsibility and authority to manage his section as he saw fit.

"Any good ideas for developing new markets?" Yamamoto asked. "We'll keep our hold for a while on markets we've developed in Africa, the Near and Middle East, and Southeast Asia. But the new synthetics will change the competitive situation. Unless we can find new markets and develop them, we'll be losers in the coming export war."

"How about the U.S.?" Hyodo suggested.

"We can't touch the U.S.," Yamamoto answered. "You're talking about the home of synthetics. We wouldn't get to first base with our inferior imitation of their nylon. Besides, even to think of getting our products over the American tariff wall is ridiculous."

"I'm not so sure," Hyodo said. "I'm merely suggesting that we think about it. The American industrial structure will have to change as technological advances are made. The time will come when their labor-intensive industries such as textiles will go into decline. Eventually the U.S. will have to be supplied from abroad. That's when Japan can become an advanced depot in the line of supply."

Iki perked up his ears at Hyodo's use of military terms to describe a business operation. He had already been impressed with the breadth of Hyodo's vision, and by the man's obvious efficiency.

After the meeting, Iki was straightening out papers when Hyodo appeared. "I'd like to introduce myself. I'm Hyodo Shinichiro, also an alumnus of the Army Academy. Class of forty-four."

Iki and Hyodo exchanged views over cups of saké in a basement bar on the underground level of Osaka Station.

"I was astonished when they told me that a former staff officer of Imperial General Headquarters had joined the company," Hyodo said.

The proprietress brought a second bottle of warmed saké and filled their cups. "Sugi-san of Goto Corporation was just here," she said. "He came down from Tokyo on business. He stayed a while, hoping you might drop in on your way home."

"I wish I'd known that," Hyodo replied. "I suppose he spent his time running down Osaka businessmen. It's a habit."

"You're right, he did. And yet you two are close friends, aren't you?" Laughing over her shoulder, she went off to greet other customers.

"I went back to school after the war," Hyodo explained. "Sugi and I were classmates at the University of Tokyo. Now, whenever we're together, he insists on criticizing private trading companies like ours. So we argue constantly. He's with a former *zaibatsu* firm. Lately he's been telling me that the sleeping lions have awakened—the old *zaibatsu* trading companies have regrouped to form giant combines. Frankly, I'd already begun to feel the threat."

"Why didn't you go to work for a firm with *zaibatsu* connections?"

"I'm sure for the same reason you haven't. Beginning with my days at the Junior Academy, I was trained to sacrifice my life for Japan. I grew to hate the money-grabbing *zaibatsu*. I never learned to trust them."

When their conversation turned to the ruinous effects of the postwar era, Hyodo said, "Men of my age group had the most to lose. Our country renounced war, and instantly we were deprived of a purpose in life—not to mention the very means for making our living. Several of my friends were so filled with despair that they killed themselves. A few others gave up trying to adjust to a non-military life and simply disappeared. An Academy graduate who was in Luzon came home and became a Buddhist monk . . ."

"Are you, by chance, referring to Akitsu Seiki?"

"Do you know him? Yes, he's the one. He sent a mutual friend a letter that said, 'For personal reasons I am entering Mount Hiei Monastery. I shall always be grateful for your friendship.' Years have passed, but he's never come down from Mount Hiei."

"I know only his name. His father, General Akitsu, and I were together in Siberia. But tell me—what about you? How did a *zaibatsu*-hater like you come around to joining Kinki Trading?"

"I thought differently about the defeat. Japan reached the depths of despair and poverty, no doubt of that, but she survived. Through those years of adjustment, I felt that I had to do something to help our country . . . the old Academy precept, you know. But what could I do? After considerable casting about, I concluded that Japan's future rested on economic development, especially through foreign trade. That's the reason I went to work for Kinki Trading. They offered me a job, and a chance at a future —for both me and Japan."

Impressed by Hyodo's logical analysis, Iki listened carefully to a history so different from his own.

"But I was disillusioned the day I started," Hyodo said darkly.

"Why? Kinki was the company of your choice, wasn't it?"

"Well . . . I had a purpose, a dream, when I started to work. But right from the beginning I saw that the executives were running the company as if the war had never happened. They were merchants still, conducting business on a day-to-day basis with an eye to earning profits—money-grabbers all, just like those *zaibatsu* executives. I doubt that any of them conceived of the company operating in the broader context of our national economy. Once, when I was reading Bergson during a lunch break, the department chief noticed what I was reading. I'll never forget his comment, delivered with a snarl. 'Instead of wasting your time reading philosophy, do something useful—like practicing on the abacus.' That mentality, I'm sorry to say, still prevails at the executive level of our company."

Hyodo was bitterly critical of firms that relied on the collective strength of a conglomerate to compensate for the lack of foresight and initiative among the individuals who ran the conglomerate's units. "I'm much encouraged to know that a man of your caliber has joined us."

"Wait a minute," Iki said. "I've just joined the company. And all I've learned during these past few weeks is that I'm not cut out to be a businessman. To tell you the truth, I've been miserable."

"You can't be serious. You took part in planning military operations for all of East Asia. You can see how Kinki fits into the world beyond the walls of its building. You know all about logistics. The truth, I'll bet, is that you're tied down by the limited scope of our company operations—which means, of course, the unimaginative policies of our executives."

Iki enjoyed the mild intoxication as he strolled homeward in the dark, between rows of identical houses, all ranged side by side. A radio gabbled merrily in every house. Some houses had small additions, rooms for the family bath, with roofs of galvanized iron pushing out to neighboring eaves. The joyful splashing of water and occasional peals of laughter within reminded him that he'd promised Naoko to add a bath to their house.

When he reached home and slid open the front door, Marucho sprang up to greet him. "Good evening, sir. You are late tonight." Pretending to be the colonel's orderly once again, Marucho took Iki's overcoat and hung it carefully on a hanger. Naoko took his scarf.

"Dad, I had Mr. Marucho cut my hair," she said.

"It looks fine! Marucho-san is an expert. Did you have your hair cut too, Makoto?"

Makoto nodded, and turned back to the radio.

"You're in a happy mood," Marucho said. "Did you stop for a drink on the way?"

"I really enjoyed the day . . . the first time since I joined the company. Let's have a drink together. Yoshiko, please heat up a bottle for us."

"No thanks, not tonight." Marucho shook his head determinedly. "I don't want my wife to get upset. Besides, I can't wait to see my baby. He'll be asleep of course. By the way, Colonel, I was surprised to hear that you've gone to work for the shrewdest money-making firm in Osaka—"

"—So you were worried, and came to see how I was getting along?"

271

"Oh no, sir! A simple barber like me wouldn't have anything to say about your work. Tonight—"

"Tonight," Yoshiko finally had a chance to say something, "Mr. Marucho brought us news about the marriage he's trying to arrange for Mr. Kamimori."

"Kamimori? Good," Iki said. "He's been on my mind for some time."

Kamimori Takashi had lost his wife and children in the turmoil following the Russian invasion of Manchuria. His parents, too were dead, and he lived alone in Tokyo, kept busy with his work at the Defense Agency. In the exchange of letters, Iki had been urging him to remarry. Earlier he had arranged a formal meeting between Kamimori and a widowed classmate of Yoshiko's, but that *miai* did not lead to marriage. So Iki decided to ask for help from Marucho, who had a wide circle of customers and friends and who knew Kamimori well enough to find a suitable match for him.

"Colonel Tanikawa is looking around in Tokyo," Marucho said. "But I hope to be the one who'll find the future Mrs. Kamimori. I owe it to him. We'd all have ended up in the convicts' graveyard in Khabarovsk if Mr. Kamimori hadn't risked his life to lead us when we staged the hunger strike."

"Have you had any luck?" Iki asked.

"I found a good one." Marucho beamed. "Not many people were interested in him because of the tendency to associate returnees from Siberia with communists—or worse! Someone had the nerve to tell me that any man who'd spent eleven years in Siberia must be all worn out. Finished. But now I've finally found someone who'd give her right arm to be Mrs. Kamimori."

"How did that happen? And what kind of a person is she?"

"Just two days ago I was cutting the hair of the neighborhood pharmacist and talking about our experiences in Siberia. Just as I finished describing the Khabarovsk Incident, and Mr. Kamimori's role in it, this guy jumped out of the chair and begged me to ask Mr. Kamimori to consider marrying his younger sister. When I hesitated, he said, 'What're you waiting for? Do it now! Write! I'll run home and get her photograph and a copy of our family history.' I've never seen such an excited man!"

Yoshiko placed a photograph on the tea table. It was a snapshot of a well-dressed woman in her late thirties, a bit plump, with well-rounded features, and a nice smile that did not quite hide the air of sadness.

"She was in Manchuria when the war ended," Yoshiko explained. "Her husband, called into service in the last stage of the war, was killed in combat. They had two children, but the older one died during the evacuation. She and her son, now fourteen years old, are living in Semba with her brother's family."

"What do you think?" Marucho asked. "I went down to the pharmacy during my lunch hour and had a chat with her. She's a quiet woman, doesn't say much. I gathered that she was given very rough treatment by those Russian soldiers during the evacuation of Manchuria. She said she'd be agreeable to marrying as long as her husband is a man who knew hardship in Siberia. His job is not important to her. She has only one condition—that he be willing to adopt her son."

Iki, Yoshiko, and Marucho looked thoughtfully at the snapshot. They knew that two lives—perhaps three—hung in the balance. The raping of Japanese women in Manchuria by the invading Russians had been reported in Japan. Such unfortunate women were condemned forever. And everyone in Japan knew about young women who had been mere children when the war ended, but who were shunned as prospective brides simply because they had lived in Manchuria during that dreadful time of Russian presence.

"People who saw what happened to our Japanese in Manchuria would sympathize with those unfortunate women," Iki said soberly, expressing their common thought. "But I'm afraid most Japanese would not be so understanding . . ."

"Mr. Kamimori would surely be understanding," Yoshiko said. "He would have great compassion for a woman who was subjected to the kind of cruelty his wife and children may have suffered before they died."

Iki thought of the day, more than two years before, when the *Koan-maru*, the repatriation ship they had boarded at Nakhodka in Siberia, arrived in Maizuru in Japan. One of the returning men had searched frantically for his wife. Eventually he located his children on the wharf. He asked them where their mother was, but they wouldn't tell him. He coaxed them for an answer, until finally one of them said, "She went away." "Why?" he asked. "To get married." They clung to their father and sobbed. Another of Iki's men wept without shame when he was told that his wife, believing herself a widow, had married his younger brother. At least one-fourth of the Japanese men who had spent those eleven years imprisoned in Siberia returned to Japan to find their homes broken or their families lost. And Kamimori, robbed of his entire family, was trying to take up living again.

"Let us do what we can to help Kamimori," he said, deciding for them all. "Invite him here to a *miai*."

12

THUNDER IN SPRING

The spacious entryway to Kanaharu, a grand teahouse in the Shimmachi quarter of Osaka, was the scene of a lively farewell. Daimon Ichizo, the host, flanked by several geisha, was bidding goodnight to departing guests.

After their last exchange of bows and expressions of appreciation, he returned to the party room while Satoi, manager of Kinki Trading Company's office in Tokyo, went off to the kitchen to make an urgent telephone call. Geisha immediately flocked around Daimon. Dressed in gay kimonos, their faces powdered a chalky white in the traditional style of their profession, these accomplished women knew exactly the kinds and amounts of attention their guests required.

"You'll have another, won't you, Daimon-san?" urged one of the older women.

Parties with bankers were always tense occasions, and Daimon, freed now of their company, relaxed in the soothing attention of these professional companions.

"I'll have more." He invited two of the geisha to take turns filling his saké cup, which he drained in quick succession. The more he drank, the livelier he became.

"Daimon-san, now is the time for the special." A voluptuous geisha, wearing a wig fashioned into an elaborate towering affair, handed him an oversized cup.

"Why now, Someha?" he asked.

"It's the best way to unwind after entertaining stuffy bankers. I'll join you."

Someha filled Daimon's cup to the brim. Her own cup being filled, she drank the saké in one breath.

Soon Satoi joined them. He looked none the worse for having caroused the whole evening. He was perfectly groomed, with modish suit and matched tie in faultless arrangement, as he sat across the table from Daimon.

"I'm sorry I had to leave you," he said. "I placed a call to Tokyo. About the matter I wished to discuss with you—"

The senior geisha picked up the cue at once. "You girls. Run along now, and help entertain the guests in the other rooms." Then with graceful efficiency she arranged the bottles and cups on the table and moved elegantly out of the room, leaving Daimon and Satoi to themselves.

"You mean the Defense Agency officer we've been trying to recruit?" Daimon asked. "Chief of the Air Division research section, wasn't he?" His change from merriment to seriousness was abrupt. When highly placed officials of national agencies approached retirement age, customarily they left the government service to join private business firms as executives or consultants. Those who had held key positions in important agencies were in great demand; their information, experience, and personal connections became invaluable assets in the business world.

"That's right," Satoi replied. "But I'm afraid he's decided to join Mitsuba Corporation. That call I just made went through to the head of the Air Defense Department of the Agency, and he confirmed it."

"Damn! Done in by Mitsuba again!"

After a long pause, in a calmer vein, he asked "What do you think the total budget will be for the second defense build-up period?"

"No less than one trillion yen. The early warning system and our next mainstay jet fighter are the biggest items in the budget. Everyone is going after the jet-fighter contract. Marufuji and Tokyo Trading, in particular, have hired teams of aircraft specialists. They will use any means to get that contract. We'll have to strengthen our Aircraft Department too. What we need right now is a key man close to the top who can deliver."

Satoi relished the challenge of competition generated by the Defense Agency's plan for the next five years. Revenue from the sale of sophisticated modern weapons was incalculably greater than that from any other single transaction. The firm winning the purchasing contract for the next line of jet fighters would automatically be assured of further contracts for maintenance equipment and spare parts. Aircraft departments of the major trading houses exploited every source of information and used every means of influence to obtain details of the Agency's plans for the next defense build-up period. Needless to say, a company with advance information about the preferred type of aircraft or weapons system would have an exceptional advantage in the subsequent bidding.

"Winning the contract for new weaponry is our top priority," Daimon said. "You're in charge of this assignment, and I'm giving you a free hand. Although you say you need a better man to head our Aircraft Department, I see no sense in replacing the current chief unless you can bring in someone who has contacts with the top levels in the Defense Agency.

The chief of Kinki's Aircraft Department, a machine technician by training, knew little about aviation, and relied entirely on a former Navy rear admiral who had been hired as consultant. The admiral had recruited five Defense Agency officers for Kinki, none above field-grade rank. Clearly, Kinki was disadvantaged in the scramble.

"That's why I want Iki," Satoi said forcefully. "Keeping him in the Textile Division is ridiculous! He's being wasted there."

Satoi, managing director in charge of the whole of Kinki Trading's non-textile operations, was contemptuous of the Textile Division, regarding it as an outdated mercantile wing of the corporation. But he was careful not to offend Daimon with stronger expressions of scorn.

"The difficulty, Satoi, is that I didn't hire Iki for such a purpose. I hired him to help us plan the systems organization we need if we're to meet the reviving *zaibatsu* head on. In fact, I was very careful to avoid saying that I hoped we might profit by his reputation and contacts."

"That isn't at all like you. I don't understand your unwillingness to use one of our own people for the good of the company. You've given me a top-priority assignment. Then why not let me use the one man who might be able to deliver?"

"I repeat, I didn't hire Iki because of the connections he has. Tens of millions of yen in taxes went into training him as a staff officer. I'm after his organizational ability and knowledge of strategy—all proved more than once, incidentally. An order for new

277

weaponry is important to us, of course. It'll generate billions in revenue. But soon we're going to face a trade war with the *zaibatsu* conglomerates. We have to win that war if we want to survive. That's when I intend to use Iki."

"In that case," said Satoi, unwilling to yield, "let me have him temporarily, as a consultant to the Aircraft Department. Only until we can find out which jet fighter the Defense Agency intends to buy."

"If Iki becomes associated in any capacity with a business venture involving the Defense Agency, his reputation is going to be tarnished. If we involve him in a deal like that, and our scheme fails, he'll end up being useless to the company. And that'll be a tremendous waste."

"I can understand that. But we can keep him behind the scenes, completely hidden, and have him advise our Aircraft Department. Almost everyone at the Agency knows Iki. Lieutenant General Kawamata, chief of the Air Defense Department, was his classmate at the Army Academy. The chief of the Air Division, Mr. Harada, is a few years Iki's senior, but I'm sure they know each other. During the war, Harada was a brilliant staff officer, the Navy's pride. Iki was considered his counterpart in the Army."

Satoi elaborated on Iki's many acquaintances in the Agency. "You've got to let me borrow him," he insisted. "All he has to do is help us gain access to the top echelon of the Agency. I won't ask anything more of him. While Iki is with me in Tokyo, we can reorganize the Aircraft Department. That will enable us to compete on an equal footing with Marufuji and Tokyo Trading, maybe even hold our own against Mitsuba. You won't have to worry. I'll do my best to protect Iki's anonymity."

"Alright, then. I'll let you look him over," Daimon yielded to Satoi. "I can see no harm in that. But don't expect things to work out as you hope. —He'll be coming here around eight thirty. I wanted you two to meet, whatever happens, and asked him to join us here."

A few minutes later, a maid brought Iki into the room. In his worn, baggy suit, fifteen years out of date, and carrying books wrapped in the usual green and white *furoshiki*, he appeared thoroughly out of place in that elegant setting.

"Come in, Iki," Daimon greeted him cheerfully. "I asked you to come here because I wanted you to meet the head of our Tokyo office. I hope you didn't have to kill time waiting for our appointment.

"Not at all," Iki replied pleasantly. "I spent the evening reading at the library."

Satoi studied Iki closely while Daimon made the introductions and explained Satoi's role as his deputy in charge of the non-textile division.

"I occasionally go to the Defense Agency on business," Satoi said affably. "Many of the officers seem to know you. Just the other day General Kawamata Isao told me that you and he were classmates. He wants you to join him for dinner if ever you go to Tokyo. He asked me to tell you this, without fail."

"Thanks," Iki said, happy to hear about an old friend. "Kawamata helped my wife gain a job while I was in Siberia. And in the months when food was scarce, he had his relatives in Shiga deliver rice to my family regularly. I can never thank him enough for his kindness."

"General Kawamata is considered to be one of the best men in the Defense Agency," Satoi said. "He'd hoped you would join the Agency. He was so disappointed when you joined our firm that he does his best to embarrass me whenever I see him. He refers to Kinki Trading as 'kidnappers.' " He laughed genially.

"By the way," he went on very casually, "have you seen Mr. Harada of the Air Division lately?"

"I've seen Mr. Harada only once—when I called on him to let him know I was back in Japan. But he's been very kind. He never fails to send a few words of encouragement in his New Year greetings."

Satoi cast a quick glance at Daimon, indicating that Iki had passed his test with highest marks. Daimon knew exactly how to take over. "Say, you two are starting to talk business." He clapped loudly, summoning the geishas. "Forget all that shop talk. This is Iki's first time with me at a teahouse. We're here to relax."

Someha and a half dozen others came into the room to serve them. The geisha who sat down next to Iki stared at him incredulously, but quickly remembered her manners. "I'm very glad you were able to come tonight," she said coyly, as she filled his cup.

While Iki quietly sipped the saké, Someha came to his side. "I want you to drink from my cup," she said. The other geishas followed Someha's example, each in turn offering him her saké cup.

Noticing that Iki was somewhat disconcerted by all this attention, Daimon called out to Someha. "The time has come for you to perform. Show Mr. Iki how well you dance."

As Someha performed the slow and graceful dance called "The White-Heron Lady" to the accompaniment of a samisen and several voices, Daimon whispered to Iki. "You've accepted a difficult challenge, embarking on a new career at your age. Tonight I want you to relax and enjoy yourself."

Iki knew that teahouse parties, at which a few men monopolized the attentions of several geishas, were prohibitively expensive. Although his eyes continued to follow Someha's sensuous motions, he turned over and over in his mind a very disquieting question: why had Daimon invited him to this lavish and intimate party?

About an hour later, after Iki and Satoi left the teahouse, Daimon and Someha remained alone in the room, facing each other across the low table.

"Such a long time it's been!" Someha hissed, her almond eyes flashing angrily.

"I've been busy. Remember?—I was in Australia for two weeks."

"That's your usual excuse for making yourself scarce. Are you sure you weren't in Tokyo, fooling around with another woman?"

"I wish I had been. Unfortunately, a president of a corporation doesn't get around as much as the proprietors of shops in Semba seem to do. Besides, you're all I can handle."

"You'd better be telling the truth," Someha said, managing a satisfied pout. "If I catch you fooling around, you'll never hear the end of it."

Although Someha was an independent geisha, free of the encumbrances of a contract with the teahouse's management, Daimon had been providing her with a generous living allowance.

"The bath is ready," a maid announced, bringing a cotton *yukata* for each of them.

In the *o-furo* at the far end of the hallway, Someha took off the ornate kimono and her underrobes. Then she helped Daimon to remove all his clothing, down to the skin. She followed him into the heated tub. As they enjoyed a luxurious soaking, Daimon ran his hand over her smooth, firm hips. "Your skin is so white and smooth, like silk. Yet it clings to the palm of my hand . . ."

When they moved to the washing area, Someha slowly soaped and rinsed Daimon's shoulders and back. She bade him turn around, and with soap and towel washed the rest of him. In the steam-filled room, Daimon lay back languidly, his eyes closed, yielding himself completely to her soothing attentions. The few evenings he spent with Someha each month were his only times of respite from a perpetual rush of fifteen-minute appointments, telephone conversations, staff meetings, and conferences, dinners, and a dizzying round of travels.

After bathing, Daimon went to a quiet room that opened upon a dimly lit inner garden. A tall bottle of beer and two glasses were in place on the red lacquered table beside the quilted silk bedding.

"I hope the bath water was hot enough for you," said Someha, who had left the bath first to prepare herself for bed.

Daimon's eyes caressed her as she poured the beer. Someha had removed her wig and sponged off the chalky, white liquid make-up. There was a soft glow to her now lightly powdered face. Her smooth white nape, fully revealed by the upswept hairdo, aroused Daimon. He wondered again, as often before, how the voluptuousness of an older, experienced woman could be embodied in this twenty-seven-year-old Someha.

"How can the body of a woman your age have such fullness," he murmured, drawing her close.

"This is how I'm supposed to be. My mother was a geisha and I was brought up to be a geisha. Besides, I enjoy what I do. When you're not here, I spend the evening going from one room to another, helping to entertain all our customers. The madam tells me not to work so hard. I get tipped, of course, but I work every night—more for the fun than the money."

Someha had first caught Daimon's eye at a party at Kanaharu about five years before. Not only was she beautiful and vivacious. She had been expertly trained in dance and the other arts, in notable contrast to so many other geishas who had been hastily pushed into the profession after the war.

Because Daimon was nicknamed "the God of Business," in compliment to his quick rise at Kinki Trading, on nights when he was scheduled to come to Kanaharu Someha did not wear kimono made of double-weave silk, which had a tendency to snag. In this way, she observed the time-honored taboo associating the idea of "snag" with acts that might offend Japanese deities. On those nights, too, she also avoided kimono with diagonal stripes because such a pattern, according to Shinto belief, was ill-omened. One night, when Daimon came to the Kanaharu unannounced, she begged to be excused, saying, "I'm sorry . . . I can't join you tonight because I'm wearing double-weave." Daimon understood the implication in her remark and, at that instant, attracted as he already was by her beauty and artistry, he fell deeply in love with her. Soon afterward he persuaded her to accept him as her exclusive patron, in exchange for a monthly allowance of one hundred thousand yen. Although he might have arranged for her to leave the profession to become his concubine, he knew that he could not support her in an appropriate style unless he diverted company funds to that purpose. He also knew that he would quickly tire of making regular visits to a mistress. Someha, exciting to watch when she was gaily dressed and flitting from one man to another at geisha parties, would probably bore him to death in a small, tidy house hidden away in a quieter part of the city.

"Daimon-san, do you know why our governor is known as Mr. Tea Can?"

"No, I haven't the faintest idea."

Someha could scarcely stop giggling. "The Governor is well known as a man of integrity, with high morals and all that. But he's crazy about . . . well, you know what I mean. Whenever he's invited to a party here, he excuses himself—'to take a short nap,' as he says. He runs off to a back room, to meet a teen-aged geisha he's very fond of. He doesn't dare spend too much time with her, because he's so concerned about his reputation. To save time, he asked the management to place an empty tea can near the pillow, so the girl can park her wig on the thing while they're doing it."

Daimon burst out laughing. "I knew the governor was nick-named Tea Can, but I never knew why." He continued to chuckle, as he imagined the strait-laced governor in a frantic and indecorous state of passion.

"I'm curious about Mr. Iki," Someha said, thinking that Daimon's laughter over the Governor's little secret had lasted long enough. "Is he a former Army man?"

"You have a quick eye," said Daimon.

"Don't be silly! I can't stand soldiers."

"Why not? You couldn't have been more than twelve when the war ended."

"Mama told me all about them. She said they were overbearing. And worse. She didn't mind their taking advantage of war industries to pay for their partying and other goings on, but she couldn't stand the obscene ways they behaved in bed."

"I'm sure a lot of them were that way. But Iki's exceptional, I think. In fact, he's so decent that most other businessmen would consider him a simple fellow, if not a bore. For business purposes he's got to be able to let his hair down once in a while, maybe have an affair or two. Why don't you teach him how?"

"The idea's revolting!" Someha exclaimed. "I noticed how uncomfortable he looked when the girls went close to him. Shrinking away. Drinking almost nothing. I don't want anything to do with a fairy."

"You're so naïve," Daimon said, putting down his glass. "But that's what I like about you. And you're so strong-willed . . . except when you're in bed . . ."He stood up. He had not bothered to tie the sash, and the *yukata* fell away from his body. Someha shed her underrobe and slipped under the covers.

Iki sat in his usual chair in the public library, reading in yet another bound volume of the *Mainichi Shimbun*, impatient with his slow progress. Because of the reduced print, his eyes would begin to throb much too soon, forcing him to stop to rest them. In one morning he could scan no more than two weeks of the *Mainichi's* morning and evening editions.

Almost the whole of the morning edition of May 4, 1947 was devoted to the new constitution, which had become effective the day before. The bannerline read "Embarking on the Great Road of Democracy—the Emperor Becomes a 'Symbol' ":

Yesterday, May 3rd, Japan took to the great road of democracy. A ceremony to commemorate the birth of a democratic Japan was held in His Imperial Majesty's presence at 9:30 a.m., in the outer palace grounds. In his formal address, Prime Minister Yoshida emphasized the need for unremitting effort in order to attain the lofty ideals set forth in the new Constitution. Noteworthy among those who attended the ceremony were Socialist Party leader Katayama, also

Nozaka Sanzo, representing the Communist Party, whose members were conspicuous by their absence at last year's ceremony to commemorate the promulgation of the Constitution.

Iki had studied carefully the new constitution during his recuperation, paying special attention to Article One, which defined the Emperor's status and the people's rights, and to Article Nine, which renounced war and abandoned the rights of armament and belligerency.

Article Nine remained a puzzle to Iki. He did not object to Japan's renouncing war. Eleven years of internment in Siberia had taught him that no country should wage war unless it had unmistakable assurance of winning it. Most nations had inclined toward pacifism since World War II. In Europe, both France and Italy, for example, had renounced war as an instrument of aggression. No country, however, had abandoned its military establishment. Even Switzerland, a perpetually neutral nation, maintained that every citizen was obliged to bear arms.

A warless world was ideal, but it was a dream. The ultimate determinant of conflict between nations was brute strength. Iki fumed at the docility of his own people, who had bowed to the Occupation Force's insistence that they renounce the right to defend their own nation.

Iki stopped again to rest his eyes. Looking out on the Dojima River, he saw a raft of logs being pulled slowly upstream by a small tugboat. The willows and plane trees lining the river's banks had begun to sprout new leaves.

An idyllic spring, he thought, letting his mind wander. He recalled the previous evening, wondering again why Daimon had invited him to a teahouse. Curious, too, that Satoi, manager of the Tokyo office, should be the only other guest, and that Satoi, whom he had not known before, should bring him news of friends from Academy and War College days, most of them now members of the Defense Agency. Iki remembered becoming very cautious after that, expecting Satoi to ask for his help in dealing with his friends in the Agency. But Satoi had been very relaxed, simply passing on friendly gossip, then had happily shifted his attention to the geishas and their suggestive party games, all done to Daimon's delight and Iki's dismay.

Iki, who had far less acquaintance with geishas than most men his age, was not indifferent to the perfume of the women or to their light sensuous touches, fleet as butterflies, upon his hands, arms, thighs. But he could not bring himself to indulge in the vulgar playfulness that Daimon and Satoi enjoyed. Although Daimon had tried to detain him, he left with Satoi, in the company car that had been waiting for him all evening. "I have to make the 10:40 to Tokyo," Satoi said. "Ride with me to Osaka Station, then tell the chauffeur to drive you home." Satoi was running when Iki lost sight of him among the crowd pushing into the station.

He returned to reading the *Mainichi*'s articles on the new constitution. As with many Japanese, he too was perplexed by the contradiction in outlawing potentials for war and simultaneously maintaining the Self-Defense Force.

The Self-Defense Force, created seven years after implementation of the new constitution, was a byproduct of the war in Korea. The antiwar clause had been reinterpreted, both in Tokyo and in Washington, to enable Japan to employ arms to defend herself from external aggression and to maintain sufficient arms for this purpose. Regardless of their quantity or effectiveness, however, those arms constituted potentials for waging war. Former military professionals believed that the constitution should have been amended before Japan's Self-Defense Force was created. West Germany, Iki recalled, had been denied armaments under the Allied occupation. When she decided to become a member nation of NATO, in order to protect herself from the Communist bloc, she promptly legitimatized the possession of weapons and immediately rearmed. The Germans, unlike the Japanese, had responded readily to a logical need; doubtless their precarious geo-political situation had impressed upon them a greater sense of urgency than the Japanese felt. But why, Iki wondered, did his fellow Japanese refuse to acknowledge the very evident fact that the Self-Defense Force was in truth a military force? Why did they despise the military men who could protect their country? Once he asked these questions at a meeting of the self-governing board of the municipal housing project in which he lived. The reply, full of hate, shocked him. "Are you still deluded by dreams of grandeur for Japan? Are you trying to prepare us for another war?"

At noon Iki closed the volume. He sat for a while, thinking about the word "armament," the mere mention of which aroused emotional reactions, at times violent ones, in so many people. He pitied his friends in the Self-Defense Force, dedicated to expanding the nation's military power to protect the very people who looked upon them with suspicion and hatred. He thought of Kawamata Isao, his closest friend among the several whom Satoi had named.

Kawamata, now chief of the Agency Air Defense Department, had been Iki's classmate through the Academy and the War College. Unlike Iki, he had chosen a military career because his family could not afford to send him to Tokyo Imperial University. He had declined a friend's offer to pay for his university education, for he did not wish to be bound by personal indebtedness. When Iki and Kawamata worked together in Operations at Imperial General Headquarters, Kawamata had been especially clever at devising unorthodox tactics to catch the enemy off-guard. When, in 1941, he devised and advocated a strategy to draw the U.S. and the Soviet Union into a mutual war, his colleagues considered him a dangerously imaginative staff officer and arranged to transfer him to the Southern Area General Headquarters.

Recently Iki had heard rumors linking Kawamata with irregularities in the selection and purchase of certain kinds of weapons. His discovery of Kawamata's acquaintance with Satoi disturbed him even more.

Daimon looked out at Osaka Castle, its roof tiles glowing silvery gray under the bright spring sun. He showed no signs of fatigue despite the partying of the night before. Whenever he slept with Someha, the next morning he felt cleansed and vital.

That morning Daimon had attended a meeting of executives, followed by a meeting of directors; after lunch he had met with two groups of important visitors. Now he strengthened his reserve of energy by looking out at the castle. He was thinking about the best way in which he might introduce Satoi's request into a conversation with Iki.

He had never actually told Iki that he would not take advantage of his position in the Army for purposes of Kinki's business, but they had understood, at least tacitly, that he would not do so. Daimon felt a touch of uncertainty about his future action because Iki was a man of such integrity, as unyielding and inflexible as the great hewn rocks that made up the foundation of Osaka Castle.

Unable to think of a way to persuade Iki to accept an assignment that might be considered unethical, Daimon paced back and forth in his office for a few minutes until the huge map of the world drew his attention. He looked at the line of clocks, each showing the exact hour in a different time zone; he admired the red and blue bulbs that identified locations of Kinki's branch offices and agencies throughout those widespread regions.

Daimon zeroed in on the Western Hemisphere—immense, alien, fascinating. Abruptly he sat down and reached for the inter-office phone. "Send for Iki," he said to his secretary. "Tell him to come right away."

When Iki arrived, Daimon greeted him amiably, as if they'd not parted only hours before. "Say, I kept you out late last night!"

"The pleasure was mine," Iki said, standing at stiff, respectful attention. "Like a damned rock," thought Daimon, thrown off balance by that unyielding inflexibility. He had hoped to draw Iki into an easy conversation, and then shift casually but nonetheless sensibly to a talk about aircraft.

"I wanted to ask you if you served anywhere as a military attaché before the war," he said, plunging toward an answer he already knew.

"When I reached suitable age and rank for foreign assignments, Japan was already at war with China. I was assigned abroad, but only to Manchuria, China, and Southeast Asia."

"That's perfect. Just what I'd hoped— I'm taking you on a trip to America."

"Me? . . . To America?"

"That's right. I want you to see the big American cities."

"I'm grateful for the opportunity, sir, but, as you know, I'm still quite ignorant about trading houses. If you'd send me to the United States after I've become more familiar with company business, I'd learn much more. I might even be useful."

"Don't worry about that. You'll learn more about the state of Japan's foreign trade through a first-hand study of Japan's best customer. Just come along with me, as a member of my staff. The most I'll ask of you along the way will be to carry my briefcase, maybe, from time to time. —Or to remind me not to take off my shoes in those fancy hotels."

"But that would require some ability to speak English," Iki argued.

"You studied German. You can read English. Our branch offices in America are full of men who can speak English. If I can get by in English—and I do, well enough—you won't have any trouble either."

"I've been with the company only two months, and know very little about foreign trade. Why am I—" Iki faltered, hoping for a sign from the President. But Daimon looked away, out at the castle, avoiding Iki's glance.

"You're the type who's never satisfied unless he's given full explanations that are beyond doubting. So I'll give you the best reason of all. I want you to come with me because you'll learn from the experience. And, as a bonus, you can stop off in Hawaii on your way back. —To see Pearl Harbor. How's that for a start?" He knew, seeing brightness flicker in Iki's eyes, that he had hit the mark.

"My secretary has all the necessary forms for you to fill out. The administrative section will make all the arrangements for you. Passport should be no problem. You'll need suitable clothes, and a couple of suitcases. Buy whatever you need and send this office the bills. We'll leave Osaka as soon as our itinerary is arranged and the visas come through. So it's all settled." He reached for a stack of memos, ending the conversation and the discomfort of deception.

The moment Iki left the office, Daimon picked up a special telephone and called Kinki's Tokyo office. Satoi answered at once.

"Thanks for keeping me company until late last night," Daimon said heartily. "Did you get the Air Division research group's itinerary in the United States? That's right—the group being sent over to test jet fighters. They're to recommend the new FX. Harada is leading that delegation. You're sure he'll be in Los Angeles by June? Good! Every trading house will be trying to get ahold of that group. You get a jump on them. As for Iki, I'm taking him along with me. What's that? Yes, yes. I understand how you feel about him. But since last night I've developed some ideas of my own." He hung up before Satoi could say another word.

Iki took the stairway, rather than the elevator, walking down slowly as he puzzled over the order to accompany Daimon to the United States.

"Anything wrong, Mr. Iki?" Hyodo called from above.

Iki waited for him. "I'm glad you've come along. I'd like to discuss something with you."

"What is it?"

"The President's just ordered me to go with him to America."

"That's wonderful! I'm glad he's finally come to his senses. What a waste—keeping you just wandering around Textiles! What can I do to help you get ready for the trip?"

"I wanted to ask you about Mr. Satoi. What kind of man is he? What's his background?"

Iki's question drew a frown from Hyodo. "So you've met him. I'm sure you noticed how well he dresses. He's known as a 'dandy'. But don't let that fool you. He's very slick, very capable—the one who started and built up the Aircraft Department. Our expert on the defense industry. And he's always on the move. Even his private secretary doesn't always know where he is."

That set Iki to wondering all the more. Why would a busy man like Satoi have found the time to spend a good part of an evening with him?

"By the way," Hyodo added, "they've just told me. I've been reassigned to the Steel Department."

"The Steel Department? . . . Then what's to become of your plan to send more synthetics to America?"

"I've passed that one on to Ishihara. There's another guy who's on the way up. He pretends to be flighty, a busybody, but he's one of the sharpest men we have. I plan to keep in close touch with him after I'm transferred to Tokyo."

On Sunday morning, Iki and Yoshiko were busy making their small house presentable for the *miai*, the formal meeting between Kamimori and a prospective bride. Naoko and Makoto were sent off to see a movie. After trimming the plants in her small garden, Yoshiko cut a few geranium blossoms to add color to the one room in their house that visitors might sit in.

"I wonder if Mr. Kamimori has lost his way," she said. The appointed hour of noon had only just passed.

"He's been here before," Iki reminded her. "Don't worry."

Iki had seen Kamimori only twice since their return—the first time a month after they arrived in Japan, when Colonel Tanikawa asked all returnees to gather in Tokyo in order to organize the

Sakufukai, a mutual-assistance society; and a second time when Kamimori came to Osaka on behalf of General Kawamata, in an attempt to recruit Iki for the Defense Agency.

"He's coming!" Yoshiko called from the front door.

Peering over her shoulder, Iki saw Kamimori approaching with his characteristic long, firm strides, as if he marched on a parade ground, leading a battalion in review.

"I took the wrong side street," he grinned, mopping his brow with a handkerchief. "It's easy to get lost here, because all the houses look alike. But Osaka gave me a sunny day for a change, and I enjoyed the walk."

"You haven't had lunch yet, have you?" Yoshiko asked as Kamimori stepped out of his shoes and entered the living room. "We have *sushi* for you. Please have some."

"No, thanks. I had lunch at Namba Station. I'll just have tea."

Later, after the necessary exchange of polite greetings he asked, "How does it feel to be a rookie businessman? You probably can guess how surprised we were in the Agency, to learn that you've gone to work for a trading house. Our friends in the Defense Agency were stunned—especially Kawamata. He told me he couldn't understand why under heaven you would join a trading company, of all things. He's the one who hired me up there, and I know how badly he wanted to get you, too."

"Working at Kinki is like being a first grader in grammar school, but I'm getting along. Tell me about Kawamata. I hear he's a prime candidate to succeed Harada as chief of the Air Division. Kawamata is so easygoing and affable . . . Perhaps you ought to warn him about the need to be discreet."

"The man's no longer clean," Kamimori said, his eyes flashing anger. "His rank is Air Lieutenant General. He's in a key position as chief of the Agency Air Defense Department. Yet he hobnobs with scoundrels from trading firms. He's being corrupted."

"You were classmates, Kamimori. If you don't warn him, who will?"

"We may have been classmates a long time ago, but now we're worlds apart in rank. Furthermore, Kawamata's not the kind to take advice—especially from a mere underling."

"We chose the wrong topic to talk about," Iki said, shaking his head. "This is supposed to be a happy occasion. You're meeting the future Mrs. Kamimori—or so we hope."

"And I hope so too—" Marucho's cheerful call brought Yoshiko forth from the kitchen.

At the entrance she greeted Marucho and a serious, round-faced woman, dressed in a striped kimono. Marucho, without stopping to chat, without even introducing the principal in this *miai*, quickly cleared the table, went into the kitchen, and returned with teacups and sweets, which he arranged neatly on the table.

"Hot tea coming up!" he announced cheerfully.

Kamimori pretended to frown. "Iki, are you still ordering Marucho around?"

"Heavens, no!" Marucho chimed in. "I like doing this. Whenever business is slow, I let my wife take care of the shop. I make tea, do the cooking, change the baby's diapers . . . you might call housekeeping my hobby. Don't complain, Mr. Kamimori. Let me have my fun. Oh, I forgot! I'm the go-between for this *miai*."

"Well! And about time!" Iki said, bowing again to the prospective bride.

Seated among them on a cushion, clothed in dignity now, Marucho was at his serious best as he made the formal introductions: "This is an auspicious day, and we have been favored with good weather. Although I am ill-qualified for this role, I am pleased to introduce the two parties to each other—Miss Oda Kimiyo, sister of the proprietor of Oda Pharmacy in Semba district, and Mr. Kamimori Takashi, who is employed in the war history section of the Defense Agency in Tokyo."

"I'm very pleased to meet you." Oda Kimiyo, bowing slightly, spoke for the first time.

"How do you do?" Kamimori replied with a casualness bordering on indifference.

Iki took up the conversation. "Mr. Marucho told me that you lost your husband and older child in Manchuria. In my opinion, no Japanese who didn't live through those terrible months can fully understand the tragedy suffered by our people there. You were lucky to return home safely with your small child."

"I must have been blessed with good fortune," she said quietly. To that summation neither Yoshiko nor the three men could make any response.

Kamimori's eyes were closed; he may have been thinking about his wife and children, who had not survived the evacuation of Manchuria. "How have you been maintaining yourself since

1947?" he asked, with his usual directness. Her résumé did not include a history of employment.

"My child was only six months old when the war ended. By the time we returned to Japan two years later, I was so thin and weak that no one believed I would live much longer. I went to stay with my late husband's parents in Oita, but I was too weak to be useful on their farm. Also, having been raised in Osaka, I didn't do the farm chores at all well. I decided I had no choice but to bring my child with me back to Osaka. We entrusted ourselves to my brother's care."

"Her late husband's parents were farmers of the worst sort," Marucho explained. "They called Kimiyo-san a 'good-for-nothing,' 'freeloader,' and worse, because she was clumsy with the hoe and hated to carry bucketsful of dung from the privy to the fields. They told her to leave the child with them and get out. She bore all their abuse bravely for three years, but her brother found out about them and wouldn't allow her to live that way. He brought her to his home in Osaka."

"I've been helping out at my brother's pharmacy, but most of my energy has been devoted to raising my son."

"Why didn't you bring your son here today?" asked Kamimori.

"I wanted to, but my brother wouldn't let me. He didn't think the child should be present at a formal *miai*, where his mother's marriage would be discussed."

"I don't own a house, and I have no savings," Kamimori said. "I live in quarters provided by the government. My only income is the salary I'm paid as an Agency officer. I have only one question to ask. If you become my dependent, will you be prepared to endure hardship?"

"Hardship is something I am willing to endure," she replied firmly, as if to convince Kamimori. Iki saw that she was inclined to accept the proposal, if Kamimori offered it.

Following this interchange, the *miai* ended very soon because Kamimori insisted that he must leave immediately to catch his train. He went off in a hurry, having paused to offer only the briefest of customary farewells. Marucho took Oda Kimiyo home.

"I wonder if he didn't like her because she has a son," Yoshiko said with a sigh of concern, for Kamimori had left without giving them any hint about his opinion of Oda Kimiyo.

"I don't think the boy was a consideration," Iki said. "He's just being Kamimori. Straightforward. Tactless. Honest."

"How would General Akitsu's daughter be for him? You've described her as a woman of strong character. Wouldn't Mr. Kamimori prefer someone like her?" Iki said nothing. But to himself, he thought, "Not a good match . . ."

Akitsu Chisato sat in the shop's front room, waiting for Uncle Noritsugu.

The name Akitsu-hiko, displayed on the shop curtains, was one of the prominent names in Nishijin, Kyoto's district of silk weavers. The facade of the store, unchanged since the Akitsu family started the business in the mid-nineteenth century, was done in the traditional lattice style. With thirty looms in this central workshop and an additional fifty scattered through subsidiary shops, Akitsu Noritsugu was regarded as one of the ten leading weavers in all of Nishijin.

Chisato admired several obi of gorgeous silk brocades displayed in the window. As she looked over the spools of threads used in making those brocades—gold, silver, scarlet, spring green, every other imaginable hue—and listened to the incessant clatter of the looms in the backroom, she could not believe that her father had grown up here, in this artisan's household.

"Chisato-san! Why didn't you let us know you were here? Please come inside." Aunt Hisako, small, with a graceful manner and the soft speech for which "the Kyoto woman" is admired, wore a kimono of pongee silk dyed a nightingale green.

She stood up, tossing the long hair off the shoulders of her jacket. "When is Uncle coming home? If he's going to be late, I might as well leave."

"He'll be back soon, I know. Stay and keep me company."

She led Chisato through the inner garden to the family's living quarters at the back of the establishment. She liked Chisato, and showed it in many ways. Her three sons were married. The eldest son and his family lived with them, as was the custom, but she did not get along with her daughter-in-law. She preferred the company of Chisato, whom she treated with a mother's fondness.

Chisato liked the inner garden with its little pond, stone lanterns, and carpet of moss. Today, however, the garden shone in the bright spring sunshine, and its very beauty saddened her. Chisato was going to see her brother today, and the occasion made her nervous.

Seiki had not once left the monastery on Mount Hiei. Naturally

293

Chisato had been very much surprised when she received his letter the day before. "Ten years have passed since I entered this monastery," he wrote. "I have at last completed the thousand-day austerity. Of course I must study much harder in order to attain a more profound understanding of Buddhism. Please forgive my self-indulgence in having forsaken my family and friends while I've been engaged in religious training."

Seiki had refused to interrupt that training to visit his dying mother. At her funeral they had kept the principal mourner's seat vacant, expecting him to be present, but he neither appeared nor sent word. Chisato remembered the bitterness she felt as she listened to the priest intoning the Buddhist sutras. Her mother had been able to accept her husband's suicide. She had thought she could rely on her son, but he, too, had deserted her even to the very end. She lay on her deathbed, waiting for Seiki until she drew her last breath. Chisato had asked herself, "How can a man who has lost sight of his humanity succeed in discovering the path of the Lord Buddha?" Only afterwards did she learn something about the severity of the practices of Buddhist austerity, and understand how they might explain Seiki's apparent hardness of heart.

"Why so serious?" her aunt said as she returned with the tea. "You'll be seeing your brother for the first time in ten years. This is supposed to be a happy occasion."

Just then Akitsu Noritsugu came in. "I'm sorry to be late. Business is booming, but it takes a lot out of me." Despite the necessary complaint, he appeared to be thoroughly satisfied, having spent the morning making the rounds of his shops, exhorting the employees to work longer and harder. Orders were pouring in to accommodate the popular revival of interest in wearing traditional clothing during the post-war chase after Western fashions.

"Uncle, I've been told that visitors are allowed to stay no more than two hours at that monastery," Chisato said. "And I'd better be on my way. What do you want me to tell Seiki?"

"Tell Seiki that I bear him no grudge. Now that he's successfully completed the thousand-day austerity, I want him to come down from Mount Hiei and live in the city. I'll do whatever I can to help him get his own temple. I've already discussed this matter with the bishop of our family's diocese."

Such a change of heart delighted Chisato. Never had she expected her uncle to forgive Seiki's "selfishness." The last blow had come when Seiki did not attend his own mother's funeral. Noritsugu, furious over that lack of respect and filial piety, said that he no longer considered him his nephew.

"And what did the bishop say?"

"The bishop also belongs to the Tendai sect, and has long been worried about Seiki. He was astonished when I told him about Seiki's having completed the whole ritual. He said that ordinarily it requires a full seven years, and very seldom has he heard of anyone who's successfully completed it even then. He thinks that because of this distinction Seiki would qualify to hold the chief ministership at one of Tendai's ranking temples anywhere. I want you to persuade him to leave Mount Hiei so that we can all rest easily."

Beneath the gruffness she could hear that Noritsugu was pleading with her to present his arguments. Chisato prayed that she could plead successfully with Seiki.

"Another thing," Noritsugu added. "Tell Seiki about Mr. Takemura and Mr. Iki, who spent eleven years imprisoned in Siberia, under the most dreadful conditions. Far worse than anything he experienced in Luzon. Tell him how they've adjusted to adverse conditions here in this world, how they work quietly, how they're preserving without complaining. —All without retreating into some kind of inn on a mountain top."

Uncle Noritsugu drove Chisato in his new car to the station next to Sanjo Bridge in central Kyoto. From there the tram for Mount Hiei creaked slowly up the tracks to the top of the pass that led from Kyoto to Shiga prefecture. As the tram began its descent on the farther side, Chisato could see the dark blue waters of Lake Biwa through the soft spring haze. Twenty minutes later she arrived in Sakamoto, at the foot of Mount Hiei's eastern slope. After a brief journey by cablecar, Chisato and a group of monks were deposited near the central hall of the monastery. At this higher altitude the air was still chilly.

One of the monks gave her directions to Homa Hall, which, she had been told, stood near her brother's cloister. Homa Hall was located in a valley a considerable distance from the central hall. As she walked along the narrow path that wound through a forest of tall cypress and cedar trees, she thought of the moment she had looked up toward the western slope of Mount Hiei from the snow-covered garden at Sanzen-in. And she remembered Mr. Iki's sur-

295

prise when she told him about Seiki's choice. She recalled how Iki had moved ahead of her, with slow, deliberate steps and bowed head, deep in thought. What had he been thinking then, she wondered . . . that calm, inscrutable man.

She walked for almost fifteen minutes before the tiled roof of Homa Hall, a cluster of dormitories, refectories, and supporting buildings came into view. She opened a brushwood gate in a fence enclosing a small hermitage. The tiny hut perched on a ridge above a deep and narrow valley.

"Hello," she called.

Hardly a breath of air stirred. She stepped into the entry and peered within, into the dimness. The sliding door was open. A tall white-robed figure, with shaven head, looked serenely out at her.

"I'm glad you came," Seiki said quietly, with a smile. "Come in."

Chisato, startled by his deep voice, did not recognize him.

"I'm sorry about coming to see you so suddenly," she said, hurrying before he changed his mind about receiving her. "When your letter came yesterday, I felt I had to see you. Right away. I phoned the monastery several times—to find out where you were. And when I might see you."

"Sit there," Seiki pointed to the threshold of his hut. She obeyed as if in a trance.

Seiki's hut was divided into a small room for study and sleeping, an even smaller kitchen, and a cabinet for a toilet. A writing table and a wicker trunk were the only pieces of furniture. Stacks of books lined the near walls. A monk's robe was spread out on the window sill to air. Below the window the ridge dropped steeply into the valley, from which wisps of mist were rising.

"You've had some difficulty in forgiving me for leaving home as I did," Seiki said, sympathetically, knowing the answer. "I can imagine the problems you've had since Mother died."

Seiki himself had been troubled, once upon a time, because he was unable to help his sister. Chisato understood what her brother left unsaid. But she also guessed that now, after his years on the mountain, nothing in this world troubled him any more.

"I'm the one who should ask forgiveness . . . for having sent you that hateful letter after Mother died. But I knew nothing at all then about the austerities that kept you here."

She studied the changes in Seiki. In childhood he and she had borne a close resemblance to each other. Both were exceptionally fair-skinned and shared their father's handsome features. But even then Chisato's face had reflected brightness and gaiety, whereas Seiki's held a pensiveness suggesting melancholy. Now, after seven years' pilgrimage along the paths that encircled Mount Hiei, Seiki's skin was darkened, his cheeks hollow. But his deep-set eyes were clearer and more tranquil than she'd ever seen them.

"How is Uncle Noritsugu?" Seiki inquired. "I've been a source of worry to him, I know. I hope he's well. He must be in his sixties by now."

"Uncle is in good health, and quite happy because the family business is thriving. He used to say you could at least have explained your wishes before you left us. Of course, I felt the same."

"That's understandable, but at the time I just couldn't—"

By the time Seiki completed the accelerated program at the Army Academy and arrived in Luzon as a newly commissioned second lieutenant, the Japanese Army in the Philippines was facing annihilation. Seiki did not know this, of course. He was appointed colorbearer for the 120th Regiment, which was under orders to defend the outpost on Lingayen Gulf, if necessary to the last man.

The regiment's officers were reduced in number at an appalling rate, and Seiki, then only twenty-one years old, found himself commanding a company of two hundred soldiers. Half his men were killed in their first encounter with American landing forces at Lingayen. Forty more were killed as they retreated toward the jungles in the mountainous northern section of Luzon. The thought of Japan's losing the war never entered Seiki's mind. He fully anticipated taking part in a counteroffensive to attain a final victory, which would bring solace to the spirits of his men who had died for their country.

Then came the announcement of Japan's surrender. To prevent the enemy from capturing the regimental flag, Seiki burned it the night before they were to surrender and be disarmed. The 120th Regiment's colors had been glorified by numerous victories since the Russo-Japanese war. The strong white fabric, displaying sixteen red rays emanating from the central red sun, hung in tatters; only the thick purple cordon forming the banner's edges remained intact. His men wept as flames consumed the flag. After that day,

Seiki was obsessed with the uselessness of the deaths of 143 brave men in his company. They had died to no purpose. And he was the one who had led them to the portal of death.

Seiki returned to Japan at the end of 1945, his spirit shattered, his mind lost in the general confusion. He enrolled as a student at Kyoto University, with no special goal and not much interest in anything. The shock of his father's suicide renewed his sorrow over the deaths of the men he had commanded. In a flash of inspiration, he decided to leave the university and enter the monastery on Mount Hiei. He had neither the strength nor the kindness to tell his mother, whose will to survive had been sustained by her belief that Seiki was preparing himself for a good future. Without saying a word to anyone, he fled to Mount Hiei, to seek guidance from the great priest Jisho.

Novices in Tendai temples on Mount Hiei are permitted to attempt the thousand-day austerity ordeal only after completing the pilgrimage of the Three Thousand Buddhas and then spending one hundred and eight successive days in meditation. Having passed these tests, Seiki began the austerity program, leaving the valley of Mudoji daily, at two o'clock in the morning, to walk eighteen miles on a prescribed route down the eastern side of Mount Hiei to Sakamoto at its foot, then back up Hiei's slopes to the valley. He undertook this walk, regardless of weather, on one hundred successive days each year for the first three years, then on two hundred successive days during both the fourth and fifth years. After he completed his seven hundredth walk during the course of five consecutive years, he submitted to nine continuous days of abstinence from food, water, sleep, and reclining. In the sixth year, the distance covered during each day's walk was increased to thirty-six miles.

A pilgrim made his walk dressed in a white robe, leggings, straw sandals on bare feet, and a broad-brimmed sedge hat, while carrying a lantern in one hand. The clothes gave little protection against the cold weather that marked Mount Hiei's higher elevations in late March, when ordinarily the program of austerities began. While walking over the frosty path, toes were quickly numbed. The sandal thongs cut deeply into the flesh; and, in only a few days, open inflamed cuts developed on the feet. A greater source of discomfort was the heavy dew that drenched the pilgrim's clothes just before dawn at seasons when rain or snow did not fall. The cruelest torment was lack of sleep. The daily traverse increased to fifty-one miles during the last period of a hundred days, allowing a pilgrim only a few hours for sleep. Exhaustion became a formidable adversary. Whenever Seiki caught himself staggering, he strengthened himself by remembering the disgraceful sight of weak novices sprawled beside the paths in helpless weariness. Then he would fix his thought on the purpose of the thousand-day austerity: the awareness of Buddhahood in everything. Man, birds, beasts, as well as plants, rocks, and bare earth —all were to be seen as manifestations of the One, and therefore as worthy of veneration.

Seiki's determination wavered when word of his mother's illness reached him. But he had begun the trial of austerities knowing full well that the merit gained from years of application would be nullified if ever he left Mount Hiei for any reason, even to be treated for an illness that might be fatal. Only a man whose resolve had been unshakable attained the title of Perfect Devotee. So harsh were these austerities that, rarely had more than one or two monks successfully completed them in any decade. Although Seiki, through struggle and dedication, had become a Perfect Devotee, the demands of the body continued to torment him. Accordingly, he reflected often on the imperfection of his spiritual attainments.

"Uncle Noritsugu asked me to bring you a message," Chisato said hesitantly. "Now that you have completed the thousand-day austerities, he would like you to leave Mount Hiei to take charge of a temple in the city. He says he will do all that he can to help you."

"I'm grateful. I'm sorry to remain a source of concern to Uncle and to you, but, the truth is, I'll be starting upon a twelve-year cycle of secluded study. I want to understand the most profound teachings of Tendai Buddhism and, ultimately, attain to the Way of the Bodhisattvas."

Seiki spoke with the quiet resolve of a man whose life is dedicated to the accomplishment of a sacred mission. Chisato, understanding this at once, nodded in fullest agreement.

"I want to entrust something precious to you," he said. "This is why I sent for you. I have been keeping Father's journal of the war in China, which he wrote while he was with the Kwantung Army

Headquarters. He entrusted it to me in 1944, when he returned on leave from Manchuria. I read it then, and have read it since. I know how important a document this is. Father recorded many details about the battles, as well as accounts of what went on behind the scenes, but much of the information he put into in it could not be made public at the time. I left the manuscript with Mother for safekeeping while I was in the Philippines. It's the only thing from the world below that I brought with me to this retreat, and I've kept it here beside me. Recently, in the refectory, I overheard some monks talking about events down below. They said that the Defense Agency is searching for records of the war period and I decided to donate Father's journal to it. Although this is my only keepsake of him, I think it should be read. By many people. It may be useful to the men who are compiling a history of the war. And it may help to prevent another war."

From the mat beside his desk Seiki brought forth a bundle of papers, neatly tied with pale green silken cord. The sheets were yellowing with age, the edges ragged, beginning to tear. Chisato took them eagerly, recognizing at once her father's bold calligraphy. "How wonderful to see this!" she exclaimed, hugging the bundle to her breast, as her thoughts raced ahead.

"Mr. Takemura and Mr. Iki came to Kyoto in February, because they wanted to pay their respects to Father's altar. —You remember them? Mr. Iki lives now in Osaka. I can take Father's journal to him and ask him to deliver it to the Defense Agency's war history section."

"That seems fated. I'm relieved to know that someone who knew Father well will be responsible for them. And I know Father's spirit will approve of him. He had a high regard for Colonel Iki."

Chisato carefully wrapped the journal in her silk *furoshiki*. Holding this precious remembrance of her father was exciting in itself. But the chance that it gave her to see Iki again almost took her breath away. She scarcely remembered saying goodbye to Seiki, already lost amid the shadows in his hermitage.

Following his routine Iki reported in at the Kinki office soon after one o'clock, having spent the morning reading newspapers at the library. At the head of the stairs Ishihara lay in wait for him.

"A visitor waiting for you . . . terrific!" he burbled, practically leering over the railing.

"A visitor?" Iki showed the range of reactions from surprise to suspicion. With Ishihara he never knew what to expect.

"You're a sly one, Mr. Iki. Keeping this from us— She's a real beauty. One look, and I suggested that she wait for you at the Rose Room Restaurant. You know, in the building across the street. That's the usual place. That's okay, go ahead. I'll give the chief a good alibi for you."

"What are you talking about?"

"Hah! You don't have the nerve to admit it! Does the name Akitsu mean anything to you? Miss Akitsu Chisato from Kyoto?"

"Oh, of course! I'd forgotten all about her. Thanks." By now Iki had been consorting with businessmen long enough to know that her visit would send his stock up among them.

Leaving a delighted and amazed Ishihara behind, Iki hurried across the street and took the elevator to the Rose Room on the fifth floor. The office workers' lunch hour was almost over, and the restaurant was half empty. Searching the room, he noticed a young woman in a dark green suit sitting at a table next to a window lined with blossoming azaleas. He thought she might possibly be Akitsu Chisato, but how could he be sure? The modern girl's suit, the long flowing hair falling against a light green silk scarf, contrasted too strongly with the image Iki retained—of a slim, decorous figure in a red kimono, upswept hair gathered plainly into a girlish pony tail. Fortunately Chisato ended the uncertainty; she rose from her chair and waved to him.

"I'm sorry I came without warning you," she said when Iki reached her side.

"I've kept you waiting," he said, pulling up a chair. "I had no idea you'd be coming to see me."

"I came during the lunch hour because I didn't want to disturb you at work. I took your colleague's suggestion and ate lunch here, hoping I might see you this afternoon to discuss something."

"Something urgent?"

"Not really. I came down to see an exhibit of Chinese ceramics in the gift department at Mitsukoshi's. Because your office is nearby, I brought along my father's journal with me, hoping you might have a chance to look at it."

Iki looked with sadness at the packet she gave into his hands. He listened to Chisato's account of her visit with Seiki, and sympathized with their wish to have their father's journal preserved and used for the benefit of others. Naturally, he promised to deliver the manuscript to the appropriate person in the Defense Agency. "I know just the man," he said, thinking of how soon he must take the journal to Kamimori.

"And how is your brother?" he asked.

"Seiki's just finished a course of training he began seven years ago. He's thin, but at peace, I think. He shows an inner strength that he did not have before. To me that peace is most apparent in his eyes. They're clear, tranquil, looking at the world as if nothing more in this world can trouble him. I hope you won't mind my saying that they're very much like your eyes. Seiki's ten years in the peace of Mount Hiei cannot compare, of course, with the eleven years you spent in Siberia. But I've noticed that the eyes of people who've experienced long periods of suffering show much the same quality of quietness and spiritual strength . . ."

Feeling embarrassed by this kind of talk, Iki swept her into a subject that interested him more—the reasons why Seiki wanted to leave the world. Hyodo Shinichiro had mentioned some of them.

"A colleague in my company told me about your brother burning his regimental flag in Luzon when the war ended."

"Seiki has never mentioned that," said Chisato. "Never once did he talk with me about the war or his part in it."

Akitsu Seiki, Iki reflected, is much like his father. Taciturn, withdrawn, not speaking of matters that his conscience did not approve.

"Let's change the subject," Chisato said brightly, feeling that they had said enough about Seiki, at least for now. "One of my works has been accepted for the Exhibit by New Ceramists."

"That's splendid! I'd like to know what your uncle will say about that. 'Female ditch-digger'—isn't that what he called you?" Iki chuckled.

"I haven't breathed a word about it yet to Uncle. He's still hoping I'll tire of ceramics and settle down. But I have no intention of marrying—not for a while at any rate."

"Why not?"

"Ceramics is too much fun. Once you've had the experience of working with clay, of feeling the smoothness with which it glides under your fingers as it takes shape, you're trapped for life."

Chisato noticed that they were the last two customers in the restaurant. "Oh, my!" she said, gathering up her things. "I hadn't intended to take up so much of your time. I hope you will come by to see me the next time you are in Kyoto."

"That's kind of you."

"Someday I'd like you to tell me much more about my father. Please don't forget!" Then, fearing that perhaps she had been too forward, she turned away from him and hastened to the door, not waiting for him to accompany her.

Safely back in the Textile Division, Iki put General Akitsu's journal in his briefcase, and went to work for Kinki Trading, for a change.

He opened his notebook to review what Ishihara had taught him: names of commodities, firms with which they conducted business, and the different types of bills, notes, and drafts. His complete lack of interest in these details of practical business, he thought, hampered his effort to understand the significance of the names and terms he had written down so hastily as Ishihara rattled them off. Self-doubt made him wonder if he would be of any use to the company during his forthcoming trip to the United States, or even on his return to Osaka.

At 3:15 p.m. bidding at the Osaka Cotton Exchange began. Excitement mounted steadily among the clerks clustered in front of the priceboard beside the desk of the chief of the Cotton Yarn Department. Iki approached Ishihara, who had just completed a series of telephone calls and was lighting a cigarette.

"So much activity!" he said, "I haven't been able to tell whether Kinki is buying or selling."

"You don't mean that!" Ishihara gasped. "You actually don't know! The war over cotton yarn is headed for a showdown. We're doing the buying. The man doing the selling is our own president Daimon's most formidable opponent—Kitoh Kansuke, president of Chukyo Spinnery in Nagoya."

Ishihara summarized recent developments for his pupil's benefit. In December, their agents in Djakarta reported that the Indonesian government had decided to acquire a large amount of cotton yarn from Japan as part payment for war reparations. Kinki Trading quietly began to acquire cotton yarn through its trusted brokerage houses, concentrating on 30-count yarn. When, at the beginning of the year, the spinneries announced a fifteen percent cutback in production for the April–June period, Kinki accelerated its buying in anticipation of a future shortage. Later, having acquired seventy percent of its projected total, it lifted the cover of secrecy from its operations. The unit price of 30-count yarn rose promptly from 170 yen to 230 yen. Kinki continued its buying spree, hoping to send the price even higher. Then, today, just as the trend appeared to be going its way, Kinki was unexpectedly deluged by offers to sell. Kitoh Kansuke, president of Chukyo Spinnery, was challenging Daimon's attempt to control the market.

"I think we've been buying an average of ten thousand bales a month—which means we've accumulated forty thousand bales. At ten thousand yen a bale, that's an inventory worth forty billion. At the bidding this morning, the unit price jumped another fifteen yen to 245. Kaneko, our esteemed chief, can't contain his excitement."

Ishihara himself, although not a member of the Cotton Yarn Department, was just as excited as everyone else.

"If the price has risen that much, wouldn't Kinki be wise to sell?" Iki asked. "The book I borrowed from Mr. Kaneko advises moderation. It's emphasis seems to be on correct timing."

"You can't go by the books in a showdown. This is war! Neither side can back down now. It'll end only when either Chukyo or Kinki buckles under."

Kaneko was issuing orders alternately into two telephone receivers, one held against each ear. The lines were routed through two brokerage houses to their agents at the Cotton Exchange. The two houses were among the forty-three whose agents' bidding determined the prices of transactions at the close of each session. Iki recalled observing, several weeks before, the ten-minute bidding session that resulted in a seventy million-yen transaction. Alertness, decisiveness, and the ability to translate decision into action within seconds: Kaneko's capabilities were precisely those required of good combat commanders.

Bidding on 30-count yarn was mounting, and soon Kaneko was issuing orders over three telephones. "It's starting," Ishihara hissed.

The figures on the priceboard showed an abrupt ten-yen drop to 235 yen. Kaneko grew pale.

"I wonder what's happened?" Ishihara muttered. "Chukyo's flooding the market may have started a collapse."

Kaneko resumed his task, calmly directing the bidding on 40-

count yarn. After a few moments, he placed the receivers in their cradles and stood up.

"Get Daimatsu Brokerage on the phone," he ordered. "I'm going up to the President's office, but I'll be right back." His walk, as he left the room, lacked its usual bounce.

As Daimon spun his chair back and forth, Kaneko described the abrupt drop in price. "Four hundred bales were offered for sale at a unit price of 245 yen when the bidding began on the current month's transactions. This unexpected offer caused the price to drop to 235 yen. I was able to hold the price of May transactions at 240 by buying everything that was put up for sale. The amount of yarn Chukyo is putting up for future sales is incredible. I wondered if Mr. Kitoh has lost his mind. In any case, we can't absorb everything he's dumping on the market. I decided to let the price find its natural level today, then consult you on how we should regroup."

"I know what Kitoh's up to," said Daimon. "He's out to break my plan."

Kitoh Kansuke was a formidable opponent. He was president and sole owner of Chukyo Spinnery, whose annual sales grossed twenty-five billion yen. His net worth was estimated at between fifty and sixty billion. A gambler by nature, as well as an aggressive fighter, he would willingly stake that entire fortune to prove his ability to convert a disadvantage into a win.

Submitting to such a power play aroused equal aggressiveness in Daimon Ichizo. His battle of wits with Kitoh, therefore, tended to escalate to the level of titanic trade wars. Each man won often enough, and lost unhurtfully enough, to make the game perpetually exciting.

"We've bought forty thousand bales so far," Daimon said. "How many bales does Chukyo have left?"

"My guess is between five and ten thousand."

"A billion yen will buy ten thousand bales. That damned Kitoh is probably chuckling, thinking we've been done in by the ten-yen drop in price. We can't let him get the upper hand now. Buy everything he puts on the market."

"I didn't anticipate Mr. Kitoh's hitting us hard, just as we were getting ready to sell big," Kaneko said. "Do you think he's increasing his stock by buying direct from other companies?"

"That's entirely possible. He's a brainy old badger! Check out the spinneries and weavers and brokers. Find out the amounts they have in stock. If they're putting yarn up for sale, find out if they actually have the stuff on hand. If they're short-selling, I want to know about it. I've got two conferences to attend this afternoon, then two receptions in the evening before going home. Get in touch with me the minute you have any useful information."

Late that evening Daimon returned to his estate, spread along the foot of a low hill in Shukugawa. The great house, made with rich display of beautiful—and costly—Japanese cypress, was his proof of achievement. Daimon had built it six years before, when he was appointed Kinki's managing director. He himself selected the pieces of golden *hinoki*, and supervised their transportation on a dozen huge trucks from his native Wakayama Prefecture.

Daimon's wife Fujiko came out to welcome him home. Thin and bony, with a very fair complexion, she was not the sort of woman that Daimon favored in bed. Rimmed spectacles that tapered upward accentuated the sharpness of her face.

"Is Reiko still awake?" As usual Daimon asked first about their daughter.

"At eleven o'clock? I'm not sure," Fujiko replied. She hesitated, but only for an instant. "You're holding up well despite the hours you put in every night of the week. I do hope you won't forget that Reiko is of marriageable age. Her chances will be ruined by gossip linking her father with a young geisha."

"Jealous accusations the moment I get home!" Daimon scoffed. "You should know better at your age. I've been playing around with women all my life, and you know it. They're good for me, and good for my work."

"Don't be silly. I forgot how to be jealous years ago. I'm simply saying that you should behave decently for your daughter's sake. At least for a while. I'm worried about her marriage. You have a nerve—"

"Mother, don't . . ." said Reiko, sliding the door closed behind her. Youngest of the four children, she bore little resemblance to her mother. Her face was smoothly curved, and the big round eyes were those of a mischievous child.

"How unbecoming for a woman in her fifties to show jealousy! Besides, what connection can anyone make between my getting

306

married and Father's having an affair? Actually I rather like having a father whom girls consider attractive."

"My word!" Fujiko exclaimed in dismay. "An unmarried young lady is not supposed to talk like that. Because your father's the way he is, you think you can—"

"The trouble is, Mother, you flare up over every little thing. That's why Dad has to find relaxation away from home. Ichiro says the same thing. So do Noboru and Keiko."

Daimon beamed with delight at being so well supported by their two sons and married daughter.

Ichiro worked for the Nihon Pharmaceutical Company in Tokyo. Noboru had joined Mitsuba Trading Company, and for the time being was assigned to Bangkok. Keiko, married to a Frenchman, lived in Switzerland. Fujiko was not happy about that interracial marriage, which, she said too frequently, was allowed to happen by Daimon's general laxity. Now she worried about finding a suitable bride for Ichiro—and, more important, a very eligible young husband for Reiko—a man whose occupation would enable the couple to live near her home.

"Did anyone call?" asked Daimon, anxious to hear from Kaneko.

"Not tonight," Fujiko replied cooly. "Not yet."

"Another overseas call, Dad? They usually wake me up at two or three in the morning. Your voice is so loud it comes right up through the floor."

"Can't be helped, Reiko. But don't worry. The call I'm expecting tonight is a local one."

"Why do you have to work so hard, Dad? You're always on the run. I could understand why, if you owned the company outright. But the profit goes to the corporation, not to you, if you're only the corporation president. Is all this running around worth it?"

Daimon laughed. Reiko was very much attuned to the modern world, and he enjoyed their occasional conversations.

"I hate to lose money," he replied. "To me, a businessman who loses money has committed a great sin. I want to find out how much money I'm capable of making. And to do that, I'm willing to go anywhere, right out to the edge of the earth."

Much too soon, Reiko retreated to her room upstairs, leaving Daimon and Fujiko to themselves. His egoism fell heavily between them, as it always had.

"You're like some kind of monster," she said, no longer feeling the need to hide her thoughts, "the way you work and play twice as hard as most men. You left us all alone for years when you were in China. And yet you seem to know our children better than I do. You certainly have them on your side."

"Nothing extraordinary about me. I simply concentrate on what's important. And forget the rest. I'm serious about my work. I go to women I like for the relaxation I need. When I have time to spare, I come home and spend it with the children. The idea is so simple you might consider it primitive. You've made the mistake of being too fancy in your expectations, coming down hard on me for every little thing that annoys you. —As for this geisha business. My playing around is nothing new. It's been going on since before we were married. You've known it. Everybody knows it. So why do you keep fussing about it?"

Daimon was the third son of a wealthy land owner in Shingu, Wakayama Prefecture. Too ambitious to spend his life as a provincial gentleman of leisure, he took a job with Kinki Trading Company after graduating from the Osaka Higher School of Commerce in 1926. He was only twenty-seven years old when Kinki appointed him branch manager in Saigon, French Indochina. When he was recalled temporarily to Osaka, he yielded to his father's wishes to attend a *miai*, at which he met Fujiko, a graduate of the Kobe Women's Academy and daughter of an Osaka textile wholesaler. To Daimon her chief recommendation was her ability to speak fluent English, a rare skill among young women in those days. Both sets of parents being favorably disposed, Daimon agreed promptly to the marriage although he didn't care much for the upward slant to the eyes that made her look a bit severe. They were married five days before he returned to Saigon. Fujiko reached Saigon two months later, but Daimon was not at the port to meet her. Although he had received a telegram specifying the ship and the time of arrival, he was in the midst of entertaining French Ministry of Trade officials, whose good will he needed in order to ease restrictions on the importing of cotton yarn into Indochina. He and his guests caroused at a night club until dawn, much to the distress of the newly arrived Fujiko. Fujiko's memory of his callousness did not dim with the years. She continued to bring it up, with more hurt to herself than improvement in him.

The angular face, alas, became even more severe. About the only lesson that Daimon learned from all this is the old one that first impressions are seldom wrong. As Fujiko grew older she did not learn to control either her jealousy or her expectations of him. In consequence, he tried to see her as little as possible.

Daimon was relatively wealthy, for he had a considerable inheritance. He did not have fun surreptitiously by siphoning off company funds, as most salaried corporation presidents did. He maintained a clear-cut line between business and personal entertainment. When he caroused for personal pleasure, he did so extravagantly and openly, paying for everything with his own money.

"I had a bit too much to drink at the banquet," he lied to his wife, "so I'll skip the bath and go right to bed."

Without a word, Fujiko closed the partition that sealed him off in the rear bedroom. Beside the pillow were two telephones. Daimon dimmed the lamp, changed his business clothes for a kimono, and lay down. As he began to doze, the telephone rang.

"Sir, this is Kaneko. I'm sorry to disturb you at this hour, but I have some news. Chukyo Spinnery has added a third shift of workers to increase its production of 30-count yarn. Undoubtedly to put more of it on the market."

"This is the time of year for production cutbacks. How reliable is that information? Get it confirmed by morning!"

Kaneko seemed to be just the same as ever while he sat at his desk, sipping tea and gazing out at a clear summer sky. But he didn't really see the sky, or the sprawl of Osaka beneath it. His mind was working furiously, thinking of tactics to use in countering the changing situation in the continuing war over 30-count yarn.

During April, Kinki had bought up all the yarn offered by small sellers. Kaneko had been alternately selling for spot profit and buying at low prices, but when the spring holiday season ended on May 6th he switched to buying exclusively, driving the price beyond the 270-yen ceiling for only the second time since the end of the war. He had no alternative. He must hold the price at that level through the final session to be held in seven days, on the 28th of May, thus frustrating Kitoh Kansuke's scheme to sell more than

Kinki could absorb. If he did not hold, the consequences for Kinki —and for him—would be disastrous.

Kaneko reached for a vial, and swallowed twice the number of tablets he usually took in order to soothe his rebelling stomach. His decisions were almost never made through leisurely conferences. When bidding took place at the Cotton Exchange, he made split-second decisions during each of the four daily sessions; each decision dictated either the buying or selling of yarn valued at tens, if not hundreds of millions of yen. Naturally, this perpetual anxiety taxed both body and mind. Since being promoted to department chief he had quit smoking and drinking in order to maintain complete clarity of mind; his chronic dyspepsia, however, made him lose weight and color.

At 3:15 p.m. Kaneko issued instructions over two telephones. The bidding on 20-count yarn went as expected; successful bids were made for the purchase of futures through the month of October.

Bidding on 30-count yarn would begin in ten minutes. Kaneko had planned his tactics carefully, with the cooperation of Daimatsu, Naniwa, and three other brokerage houses. Transactions made by the forty-three brokerage houses during the past six days had averaged a thousand bales per bidding session. Kinki would make a surprise bid to buy six hundred bales at the closing moment of the final session of the day. One company buying such a great amount would be interpreted unmistakably as an attack aimed directly at Chukyo Spinnery and its president, Kitoh Kansuke.

Kaneko's two telephones were connected directly with the telephones of Daimatsu and Naniwa agents at the scene of the bidding. "What do you think?" he asked the Daimatsu broker.

"Something about Owari worries me." Owari was the brokerage house that handled the bulk of Chukyo's transactions.

"What worries you?"

"I can't say for sure. This is pure hunch. But something fishy is going on."

The clanging of the three-minute warning bell and a sudden rise in the level of the background din pushed Kaneko to a conclusion. "Let's test Owari's reaction. At the start of the bidding I'll give orders to sell rather than to buy."

He switched to the other phone and spoke to the Naniwa broker: "I want you to know that I'm checking out Owari's moves. You go ahead and keep bidding as we planned." He heard the wooden clapper announcing the start of bidding on the 30-count. He ordered the Daimatsu agent to sell one hundred bales at the opening quotation of 270 yen, and the Naniwa agent to buy 110 bales. Because more bids came in to buy than to sell, the unit price rose gradually to 272 yen.

Kaneko relaxed as the tension created in him by the Daimatsu broker's hunch subsided.

"Hiro selling twenty bales! Maruyama selling sixty! Miyako selling twenty! Owari selling four hundred!" Kaneko paled as he followed the auctioneer's chanting over the phone. As more and more buyers turned to selling, the unit price dropped ten *sen* every few seconds. When all bids were accounted for at the sound of the wooden clapper, the unit price for May purchases had dropped to 265 yen.

In the bidding for June futures only Kinki Trading was buying. Brokers working for Chukyo put up vast quantities for sale. Kaneko issued orders over the phone, buying all that was put up for sale in an attempt to stabilize the price. The usual dull ache in his belly became stabbing cramps.

Kinki Trading had bought most of the available yarn at April's closing session. Kaneko was convinced that much of what he had bought was offered by brokers who were selling short, with expectations of making deliveries in the future. "What if all the yarn we bought today is delivered in fact on May 28th?" Kaneko weighed the alarming prospect.

Watching Kinki Trading buy everything in sight, the spinneries, excluding Chukyo, began to hesitate. Some switched back to buying. As a result, the price for June futures closed at 262 yen. Kaneko breathed a sigh of relief. He had shaken off an attack by Chukyo Spinnery, but only for today. If Chukyo should continue its assault tomorrow, the day after tomorrow, and the day after that, Kinki would need enormous capital just to make the marginal payments on the loans it must incur.

Kaneko needed Daimon's backing at this point, but he had flown off to Kyushu and would be out of reach until that night. So Kaneko phoned Daimatsu Brokerage and asked Managing Director Funakoshi to advise him. In ten minutes Funakoshi was at the door. Seeing Kaneko's signal, he slipped inconspicuously into the visitors' lounge.

"I need a reading," Kaneko explained. "Of the bales to be offered at the final May session, how many do you think will be 'bullets,' delivered in kind on the 28th?"

"What readings do you get from your other brokers?" asked Funakoshi, who was Kaneko's most trusted confidant among the agents he knew.

"Of the ten thousand bales we expect to buy, five thousand will probably be 'bullets,' receivable on the spot. The other five thousand doubtless will be 'blanks,' offered by brokers who don't have the yarn and will be short-selling."

"Production was cut back last month, and so a general shortage of yarn on the market has developed. So you probably have an accurate reading. As many as five thousand bales could be 'blanks' . . ." Funakoshi paused, thinking of a surprising possibility. *If*, indeed, brokers who had committed themselves to selling five thousand bales did not have the yarn in hand, and *if* Kinki Trading insisted on delivery in kind on the 28th, those brokers would have to buy yarn on the spot to honor their pledges. They would have no other alternative than to buy from Kinki at Kinki's price, in order to deliver the yarn to Kinki at the agreed-upon price of 265 yen! That would be a windfall for Kinki.

"But be careful," Funakoshi warned. "I suspect something unnatural about the way Chukyo was selling today. If Chukyo has found a way to stock itself, you'd better raise enough capital to pay for—to be on the safe side, let's say six thousand bales. In the meantime, let me find out the number of 'bullets' Chukyo has acquired."

Funakoshi slipped quietly out to the hallway. Kaneko went back to his desk, to phone spinners and weavers whom he trusted. He intended to explore every source of information to learn Chukyo's motives; he would have to be completely safe, in his fortress of facts, if he wanted to repel Kitoh's assault.

On the morning of May 28th, Kaneko and his ten men were busily comparing notes on their final assessment of the impending battle over 30-count cotton yarn.

Ichimaru, managing director of the Textile Division, came over to observe the proceedings. "You sure of that?" he asked Kaneko, who had summarized his department's assessment. "You say that of the ten thousand bales we'll bid to buy, eight thousand will be available for delivery on the spot, and five of those eight thousand will be put up by Chukyo? I can't believe Kitoh would divert half of Chukyo's monthly production to this bidding war."

"There's a ninety percent chance of his doing it," said Kaneko. "That's the reading given to me by Mr. Funakoshi of Daimatsu Brokerage. I've confirmed it by phoning weavers who buy their yarn from Chukyo. They're all crying because Chukyo hasn't sent them any 30-count yarn for the past two to four weeks."

"Then clearly Kitoh is going all-out to win this one. Still, he amazes me. To think he'd stop supplying his regular customers in an attempt to crush us."

Amid much commotion, Daimon, who seldom visited the second floor, arrived to give encouragement to Kaneko. He laughed when he heard Kaneko's projection. "That shark must be desperate if he's gone so far as to choke off the supply lines to the weavers. Incidentally, while we're at it, we can get rid of all the sucker fish riding on Kitoh's back."

"I'm sure we've got correct readings on the intentions of Marufuji, and Toyo," Kaneko said. "They're joining Chukyo in selling. But assessing the intentions of the other firms is like trying to predict which way the undecided votes will go in an election. I think we'll come out on top, and I'm not too worried. But I'd feel much safer if you would release funds for the contingency purchase of an additional one thousand bales. This money would be in addition to the contingency fund already allotted for buying a thousand bales above our previously projected maximum."

The accounting department had refused Kaneko's request for that extra sum. Daimon studied Kaneko, whom he had never before seen so full of battle-spirit.

"Okay! I'll go over to accounting and take care of it."

"That's all right," he said, when Ichimaru objected to the plan. "Kaneko's built the market up to where it is, and he's kept it there. His assessment can't be wrong. Give it all you have, Kaneko. But don't knock yourself out."

In turning to leave, Daimon happened to see Iki, working at his desk.

"Aren't you going to the library today?" he shouted across half the room.

"No, not this morning!" Iki shouted back, surprised by the loudness of his own voice. He pointed to the figures on the price board, revealing his interest in the proceedings in a way that Daimon applauded with a burst of laughter.

At 9:15 the first of the day's four bidding sessions began. Kaneko, at his desk with the two telephones, wore an expression of unusual confidence. The uproar in his stomach had not yet begun. The bidding was progressing as he had anticipated, but an unusual quietness prevailed—the lull before the decisive battle to be fought in the second session. After that, all accounts for the month of May would be settled through the exchange of delivered goods and payments.

Keeping to his tactical plan for the first session, Kaneko ordered the Daimatsu broker to buy. The broker reported that Chukyo Spinnery made no moves. The quiet seemed ominous. But the gloom was dispelled within minutes as the bidding came to an abrupt end with the unit price standing at 273 yen, precisely as the Kinki staff had forecast. Kaneko could almost taste victory, and he relished the sensation. His men were excited, anticipating a triumph that would surely be theirs in two hours.

As the critical second bidding session approached, Kaneko placed a phone call to Funakoshi, who had been his eyes and ears throughout the five months in which he'd set things up for this day's showdown. "This is Kaneko. Have you noticed anything unusual?"

"The 273-yen price would be attractive to some weavers who are well stocked. A few might decide to sell. Most of us expect the price to go higher. I think we're all right."

"Good!" Kaneko tucked in his shirt, swallowed a couple of stomach easers, and picked up the two receivers connecting him with his brokers. At the Exchange, the clap of the auctioneer's baton aroused noisy response. Scarcity of available yarn apparently had induced many brokers to join Kinki in bids to buy, and the unit price gradually climbed. Speculators who had been offering "blanks" were obliged now to buy "bullets" at a higher price, in order to make good on promised deliveries. Responding to all the excitement, Kaneko could feel his pulse throbbing. He had not been wrong in his prediction. Even as he breathed a sigh of thanksgiving, he heard a change in the pitch of the auctioneer's chanting. "Maruyama selling 400 bales! Miyako selling 734! Tokijin selling 210! Yamanaka selling 178! Kyoei selling 114! Tatsumi selling 42!"

Kaneko could not believe his ears. One after another, most of the forty-three brokerage houses had started to sell! Those that had been buying sensed the disadvantage of their position and rushed to join the sellers' horde. Kinki faced an avalanche of opposition—and of cotton yarn. As he felt the helplessness seeping through his body, Kaneko looked down upon the glare of the sheet of glass covering his desk top.

"Mr. Kaneko!" the young Daimatsu agent shouted into the telephone. But Kaneko, his throat tight and dry, could not answer. His hands shook so that he could scarcely hold the phones. With almost every brokerage house selling, Kinki Trading was standing alone against a united opposition that included every spinnery, weaving company, and trading house in Japan. When Kaneko heard the total amount of 30-count yarn put up for sale that morning—fourteen thousand bales!—he groaned.

"Going at a unit price of 273 yen!" he heard the auctioneer shout. No one spoke. No one bid to buy. But Kinki would have to buy. Should he buy now at 273 yen, or wait until the price dropped lower? Kaneko was unable to judge. He listened vacantly as, second by second, the price fell in ten-*sen* stages. "Going at 270 yen 90 *sen*, 270 yen 80 *sen*, 270 yen 70 *sen* . . ." The voice crackling over the wire was sealing his fate. To him the agony of each second stretched into hours, into centuries . . .

"Going at 251 yen . . ."

Dazed as he was, Kaneko knew that he could hold off disaster no longer. "Buy . . ." he moaned into the telephone, and slumped over his desk.

Ichimaru came up behind him and put his hands on his shoulders. "Kaneko, let your assistant take care of bidding on the 40-count stuff. You go and rest." Gently Ichimaru took the telephones away from Kaneko's unhearing ears, put them back in their cradles. Along with all the others in the big room, Iki watched in silence as Ichimaru led Kaneko away.

Word of Kinki Trading's plight spread almost instantly throughout the business houses of Japan. The bidding on futures in the afternoon session compounded the damage Kinki had suffered during the morning. By the end of the day, everyone knew that Kinki Trading had suffered the greatest setback in its history.

The company dining room in the basement was still packed at 12:30. Iki sat by himself, eating rice curry, listening to the gossip being exchanged among half a dozen younger employees sharing the table.

"They're saying we really got burned by Chukyo Spinnery," a clerk said.

"From what I've heard, we lost about five hundred million," another added, with a knowing look. "That means a single department chalked up a loss equivalent to nearly one fourth of the company's net profit for the first two quarters. That error in judgement will cost Mr. Kaneko his job, I'll bet. And here the poor guy was top candidate for managing director. I guess he's reached the end of the line."

"Mr. Ichimaru will take a beating, too. I wonder how big a pay cut he'll take."

"Getting fired isn't so bad, as long as you can stay alive and healthy. The man who ran the Raw Silk Department six or seven years ago dropped close to three hundred million in one of these trade wars. He not only lost his health. He became so neurotic that he had to quit. From the looks of him, Mr. Kaneko will go the same way."

"Those who get assigned to cotton, wool, and silk were born under an unlucky star, I guess. We all get the same pay, but those guys have to work their tails off. We don't get any glory, but exporting rubber slippers is safer work, and a lot more peaceful." They broke into laughter.

While he listened to their chatter, Iki watched Kaneko, sitting alone at the end of the long table reserved for executives. Kaneko picked at his food, while staring off into space. His assistant had replaced him during the afternoon following the debacle and during the next day. But Kaneko was back at his desk on the second day, with a telephone receiver at each ear, directing transactions at the Cotton Exchange. Now he was burdened with the task of selling the vast quantity of 30-count yarn that Kinki had acquired. Overwork, fatigue, and the shame of failure were marking him more each day.

The noisy young men drifted back to work, still gossiping about something. Grateful for the silence, Iki continued to observe Kaneko. He sipped dejectedly at his soup, then pushed it away. Leaving the rest of the meal untouched, he walked unsteadily out of the dining room. Full of pity for the unhappy man, Iki followed him.

Kaneko avoided the elevator, taking the stairs instead. He climbed them slowly, clinging to the rail, sighing often as if moving pained him. To Iki's surprise, he went past the second floor, all the way to the roof, where younger employees were spending their leisure chatting or playing volleyball. Iki followed quietly, unnoticed by Kaneko.

Kaneko walked around the water tank to the far side of the roof. He stood beside the wall at the edge, looking down into the street below. From his distance, for long moment, Iki watched the defeated man, fearing what he might do.

"Mr. Kaneko . . ." he called softly.

Kaneko turned wearily. "Oh, Mr. Iki—"

"How are you feeling?" Iki said casually, as if they'd met in the men's room.

"Exhausted. That last venture took its toll."

"But I must say you put up a magnificent fight. I know this is trite, but the old military saying, 'Victory and defeat are constants in war,' applies to commercial wars as well."

Kaneko nodded. "Of course. Anyone who competes must learn that early in life. —Some of our younger clerks try to avoid that lesson."

"Cigarette?" Iki offered his pack. He remembered Kaneko telling Daimon that he had quit smoking, in hope of increasing his alertness. Without hesitating Kaneko took a cigarette. Iki lit it for him.

"This is my first cigarette in almost a year," he said, slowly exhaling.

"By the way, Mr. Iki, how many children do you have?"

"Two. A daughter in high school, and a son in middle school."

"I spent the war years overseas, so I didn't start a family until the war was over. I'm already fifty, but the oldest of my three children hasn't finished grade school yet. I was hoping I could at least see him through high school."

"You're not really thinking of—" Iki began. He did not know how to continue, because Kaneko could choose any one of many ways in which to end his troubles.

Kaneko knew what Iki was thinking. "Don't worry. I'm not going to jump. There are more honorable ways of 'ending my sorrows,' as people say." He patted a pocket. "I'll resign from Kinki. That ought to be enough for saving face. A businessman's job, Mr. Iki, is to earn money for his employer. I've lost money for the company—five hundred million! So I must do the right thing."

When Iki returned to his desk, he found a note: "The President wishes to discuss an urgent matter with you. Please report to his secretary right away."

Iki went back upstairs again, this time to the seventh floor. As he walked through the president's lounge he was struck by the cold impersonal setting—symbolic, he thought, of a corporation's lack of concern and compassion for its individual employees.

Having received the secretary's nod of permission, he knocked on Daimon's door and entered the office.

"Where've you been?" Daimon asked crossly. "Our agreement was that you'd spend only mornings at the library."

Never before had Daimon spoken so gruffly to Iki. Iki realized that he too must be edgy. Having overseen a venture that resulted in a crippling loss and, even worse, having been outwitted by Kitoh Kansuke, were reasons enough for any man to snarl at underlings.

"I was away from my desk for a while. Sorry." Iki did not mention his talk with Kaneko.

"We had a hard time getting your visa for entry into the United States."

"Oh, is that so?"

"There you go again, with that 'Oh, is that so?' You've got to wean yourself from that stupid military jargon. Do you have any idea why the Americans took so long to give you a clearance?"

Not comprehending the purpose behind the question, Iki could think of no answer to it.

"I'll tell you the reason. You give every appearance of being a staunch patriot—the Rising Sun type. But something in your background has made the Americans suspect that the Soviets sent you back with strings attached, like so many other puppets they converted to Communism in Siberia. Tell me the truth."

Daimon carefully watched Iki's reaction, wanting to catch even the slightest change in his expression. He saw disbelief, dismay, and disgust. Iki said not a word, unwilling to dignify so ridiculous a question with any answer at all.

"I trust you, of course," said Daimon, softening. "Always have.

But we had a problem. We couldn't get you cleared for a visa through regular channels in Tokyo. Our New York office had the Japanese Consul there get in touch with the Japan Desk in the State Department in Washington. Satoi did quite a bit of running around in Tokyo, too, working through the U.S. Embassy there. Our Tokyo office has just sent word that your visa finally came through."

Iki had expected that his past as an Imperial Army officer and as a prisoner in Siberia—not to mention a prisoner who had been a Soviet witness before the International Tribunal in Tokyo—would have some effect on his obtaining clearance from the American government, but he had not anticipated any exceptional difficulties. The fact that these had come up must reflect, he thought, the harsh realities of the Cold War between the Soviet Union and the United States. Why, he wondered again, was Daimon insisting on taking him along to the United States, in spite of such difficulties?

"You have a special reason for my going to the United States?" he asked, bringing his wonder into the open.

"Of course I do! From now on, no one can be useful to a trading house unless he knows the United States—completely, from first-hand. The war in East Asia ended in disaster because men like you, who'd never been to America, were in charge of planning that mess."

Daimon lit a cigarette, waiting before directing his question to Iki: "You saw what happened to us last week. What do you think our primary concern should be as we reflect on that disaster?"

"I can't have anything to say about the commercial aspects of that operation because I didn't understand them fully. But what I do consider very important is the action the company will take against the man who bore the primary responsibility for the operation. I imagine that a big difference exists between the Army's criteria for reward and punishment and those of private industry."

"You raise an interesting point—and one that gives you credit. But let us not forget this basic fact: whether in the Army or in private business, men are the most essential assets. These assets are fostered through systems of rewards, limited by punishments. The difference between the Army and private business is in the approach to punishment. This difference is related to the price of men."

"The price of men?"

"That's right. Your Army got its men cheap, at the cost of a postcard per man. An Army man who fouled up committed *seppuku* or, at the least, was deprived of rank. Replacements were cheap. In private enterprise, on the other hand, each man represents an investment of capital. The company supports him and, incidentally, his family, and trains him, gives him experience, and uses him again and again. We can't get rid of a worker just because he makes a mistake now and then. What we've invested in him would go down the drain. Besides, firing him for making a mistake would affect the morale of the rest of our employees, and the result would be a general drop in efficiency."

"What about Kaneko then?" asked Iki, bringing his worry out into the open. He said nothing about the biased logic behind Daimon's argument.

"I know Kaneko. Better than you, don't forget. I'll bet he's carrying his written resignation around in his pocket, waiting to present it to me. But I won't accept it. A sheet of paper and a broken man won't make up for anything. Now he's responsible for gaining back for Kinki what he's lost. And more. He's going to go through hell during the next two months, disposing of fourteen thousand bales of cotton yarn despite the falling prices. After that, he's got to come through with a project that'll make money for us. If he does, he'll be a better man for the experience. And he's guaranteed a managing directorship. From this, you can see, *seppuku* is not permissible in private enterprise."

"You relieve me of much worry, sir. —About Kaneko, I mean."

"Oh, is that so?—as you like to say. Remember this, Iki. We men of business may be tough. But we, too, play our games according to rules. And we hide our soft hearts as much as possible. You know why? Because soft hearts, like soft heads, can get us into trouble when we're not in control of them."

Later that afternoon, Ishihara came to him with a list of things he would need for his trip to America. Ishihara himself had never been farther from home than Tokyo, but liked to acquire this sort of information just in case the bosses sent him abroad someday. Today he relayed experience passed on to him by Ichimaru, the practiced traveler.

"Be sure to take all the medicines you might need," he warned. "In America, you can't buy most medications without a doctor's prescription. They don't trust people over there, I guess, as we do here. And be sure to take along an extra pair of reading glasses. If you lose your glasses over there, you'll have to go through long complicated procedures—have your eyes examined, get a prescription for lenses, then go to an optician. That's expensive, too." Ishihara plied Iki with advice, much of it unwanted, then tore himself away, in pursuit of other business.

Iki, settling back to peace and quiet, happened to look across the room—and found a reassuring sight: Kaneko, speaking into one or the other of his two telephones, directing Kinki's bidding in the afternoon sessions. Gaunt, and haggard, perhaps, but in control again. And not smoking.

One afternoon Iki went home early to pack for his departure the next day. He marveled at the piles of things Yoshiko thought he ought to take with him.

Naoko, too, wanted to help. "Dad, I brought home two cardboard cartons. You decide what you're going to take with you. Whatever you'll need goes into this carton. What you won't need goes into the other."

"Good," said Iki, rewarding her with a pat on the shoulder. "Get rid of two shirts, two neckties, and three sets of underwear. Get me the two books on that shelf."

Yoshiko overheard him. "But you'll need all your clothes," she insisted. "For all those conferences."

"Not all that. Remember how lightly I traveled when I was in the Army?" He saw no need for two extra suits, five dress shirts and as many neckties, and all those extra sets of underwear.

"But you're going to America as a businessman. You're accompanying Mr. Daimon, and if you're not properly dressed—"

The front door slid open, a cheerful voice called.

"Grandpa!" cried Naoko, running to the entrance.

Sakano gave them his usual bright greeting as he studied the confusion of suitcases and clothing in the front room.

"I'm sorry the house is in such disarray," Iki said, addressing his former teacher at the War College with affection and respect.

"I stopped in because Yoshiko told me you are going to America."

"Won't you stay for dinner?" Yoshiko asked. "That will be a treat for the children."

"I'd like to, but I have to be off right away. To a meeting at the cultural center."

"Gee, Grandpa," Makoto complained. Grandpa knew the current players of all the professional baseball teams in the country, whereas Dad didn't know the difference between baseball and soccer.

"I'll come again," Sakano said, sending Makoto a conspiratorial wink.

The children volunteered to walk with him to the station, but Sakano put them off. "I have something to discuss with your father. We'll walk together to the station next time I come, while he's away, seeing the big world."

As the two men walked beside the Yamato River, Sakano spoke thoughtfully about Japan's low position in the world. And about some of the unexpected consequences of that fall. "Did you know that Harada Masaru of the Defense Agency has finally made up his mind to run for the Upper House?"

"I'd heard that he might eventually go into politics. But I didn't know he was planning to run in the next election."

Harada, who had devised the tactics for the attack on Pearl Harbor, was a man whose character Iki had long admired. He now commanded the Air Division of the Defense Agency. But, according to some sources, he was being corrupted by powerful business interests.

"We in the Veterans Association have been asked to organize an election committee on behalf of Harada. We are willing to do so, of course. But I am looking beyond next year's elections. I've been hoping that someday you will want to serve the country in politics. As a member of the Lower House, to begin with."

Iki wisely said nothing. He knew that his father-in-law had been disappointed when he refused to accept a position with the Defense Agency.

"Many of us remember your reputation—as the Army's answer to Harada, the pride of the Navy. I am pained when Yoshiko tells me that your main interest these days lies in the nature of the fabrics in your children's clothes. Such a waste of a good mind! Yoshiko has had a difficult time, and I can understand her concern that you make best use of your abilities. I agree with her. Perhaps she'd object to your entering politics. I don't know. We've not talked about that. Nevertheless, I wish you would consider the other avenues that are open to you."

Sakano had made a special trip in order to present Iki with a problem to worry about while he was away from his family.

13

AMERICA

Northwest Orient Airlines Flight 138 was exactly on time. After refueling stops in Anchorage and Seattle, it was scheduled to arrive in New York at 10:55 p.m.

The stewardesses were serving after-dinner beverages. Iki sat wedged between Daimon's first secretary Yanagi Kyoichi and Yosano Saburo, Chief of the Foreign Trade Department. Daimon, of course, rode forward, up in the first-class section.

"You must be worn out," Yanagi said to Iki through a cloud of cigarette smoke.

"I'm not as accustomed to long flights as you are. I really am very tired, but I can't sleep. Must be the excitement of my first trip across the Pacific."

"On most flights, we're able to remove an arm rest and stretch out, and get some sleep. This one is especially crowded because it's the only direct flight from Tokyo to New York. Lots of businessmen rush back and forth to Japan these days."

As soon as the stewardesses took the serving trays away, Yanagi dug into his briefcase for manuscripts of speeches that Daimon planned to deliver at several receptions in the United States. After making minor revisions here and there, he went forward to confer with Daimon.

Iki pushed his seat back into what airlines call "a reclining position." Most of the passengers, having done the same, had drawn blankets over themselves and were dozing. Reading lights were extinguished save for the one above Yosano, who had been scribbling continuously except during the cocktail hour and the meal.

Yosano was the head administrator of Kinki's worldwide network of branch offices and agencies. Whenever Daimon traveled abroad, Yosano was responsible for planning his itinerary. He faithfully provided Daimon with summaries of pertinent items of business, and was always at his side as aide and advisor. Although he had slept but a few hours since the plane left Tokyo, he showed no signs of fatigue as he continued to read and revise drafts.

The ostensible purpose of Daimon's trip was to select a general manager who would administer Kinki's entire American operation from headquarters in New York City. Daimon wanted to expand Kinki's American network of offices and at the same time to simplify their control. To implement this plan, he had summoned managers of all North American branch offices to a general meeting to be held in New York.

Upon returning to his seat Yanagi leaned toward Iki. "The President wants you to join him."

Iki exchanged his slippers for shoes, and went into the forward section, which was less than half filled. Daimon, reclining across two seats, held a large snifter of cognac in one hand.

"Yes, sir?" Iki whispered, trying not to disturb an elderly American couple asleep in the next row.

"I thought you might like to join me for a spot of this excellent brandy." Daimon straightened up to make room for Iki, and signaled to a stewardess to bring another glass of cognac. He looked as fresh as ever.

"What do you think of this DC-7?" he wanted to know. "How does it compare with the war planes you've flown in?"

"It's surprisingly quiet and steady, and—" Iki took a quick sip of the brandy. He was about to mention the differences between the big, comfortable, and fast airliner and the plodding PBY Catalina on which he had been flown to Tokyo, then back to Khabarovsk, after his appearance at the Far East Tribunal. He suppressed the useless information, and changed course. "I can't wait to see New York City."

"That's interesting," Daimon laughed. "As I remember, you weren't at all happy about making this trip. Now you're all excited. That's natural, I guess. —Before the war, I traveled everywhere in China and Southeast Asia. In those years, travel was unqualified hard work. Slow. Hot. Uncomfortable. But the war changed everything. Now we travel in style. Many good things come out of war, don't you think? You, especially, should be in a position to notice them, like flying to New York from Tokyo, in one night. Flying to New York is always different, no matter how many times you do it. I still remember how excited I was the first time I flew there seven years ago."

"What was your main thought on arriving that first time in America?"

"After I saw it I asked myself, 'Why on earth did Japan go to war with such a huge, rich country?' Someone should have figured out our chances first. Even on an abacus! The beads would never have balanced out." He shook his head, took another sip of cognac.

"Remember, I didn't have you come along merely to pick up bits of information on business and trading. I want you to spend your time getting to know the outside world better. Japan is so small a country. And still so separate. I told Yosano to let you do whatever you want in America."

"I'm grateful. I'll take full advantage of this opportunity."

When Iki finished his drink he returned to his seat. Yosano was still working over his papers, while Yanagi copied a fresh version of a manuscript revised extensively with red ink.

Both hurriedly put away their papers when the "Fasten Seatbelt" signs flashed on. Iki could not help but feel his heart beating faster at the thought of what awaited him in this fabled America.

As the plane descended a sea of lights appeared below them. Soon Iki saw parallel lines of blue lights ranging in all directions, and in moments heard and felt the rumbling of the plane touching down on the runway. Idlewild Airport was far larger than any other landing field he had ever seen, and he stared, fascinated, at the rows of giant airliners parked in front of immense hangars.

"We're here, Iki." Yosano was standing in the aisle ready to dash outside. Yanagi had already left his seat, heading up the aisle to join Daimon. Iki, clutching at his flight bag, deferred to all but the last of the passengers out of the plane. Daimon and Yanagi were far ahead, walking briskly toward the terminal.

"The President's always in a rush," Yosano said to Iki. "He yells if we don't keep up with him." The two finally caught up with Daimon in the lounge for arriving passengers. Once they'd passed through customs inspection, they turned their luggage over to porters wearing red caps.

Daimon led the way. Seven men from Kinki's New York branch, standing at attention just within the exit, greeted him. "Thanks

325

for meeting me, Masaoka," Daimon said. "I hear you've been doing a fine job."

Masaoka, the lanky manager of the New York branch, responded to Daimon's good humor. "What I do amounts to really very little, but I do my best," he said, laughing nervously and shrugging simultaneously. "Cars are waiting for you outside. Please follow me." He, too, knew that Daimon did not like to be delayed in anything. Three large black Cadillac sedans stood in a row beside the curb. Masaoka led Daimon and Yosano to the limousine in the lead. Iki and Yanagi rode in the second sedan.

Iki looked eagerly at the sights along the way as the three cars sped toward the city. He marveled at the magnificence of the freeway that stretched ahead of them like a wide river. The headlights of hundreds of oncoming cars streaked toward them like tracer bullets over a battlefield. As their limousine approached a bridge over the East River it ascended a rise and, magically, a forest of sparkling skyscrapers floated up out of the darkness. Among the glittering giants of Manhattan, the Empire State Building towered grandly above all the others.

That night, in one of Manhattan's grandest skyscraper hotels, Iki slept soundly in unaccustomed luxury. Never had he even seen such splendor! And, naturally, the mere sight and feel of all this expensive comfort, pleasing to every sense, made him contrast it with his poor man's house in Osaka—and, even more marvelously, with the bestial ugliness of those prison camps in Siberia. The very memory made him wonder, again, why he had been saved from dying amid those horrors. And why, having been saved, he was being exposed now to these opulent trappings, these enticements to the flesh and killers of the spirit.

The next morning, after a late and remarkably heavy breakfast in the American style, he set out for Kinki's New York branch office. He passed through the hotel's lobby, awed by its rich European decor, walked down a flight of marble stairs, and stepped out of an impressive entrance guarded by a doorman garbed in resplendent uniform. Yanagi saw him there, by the curb.

"Sorry I couldn't join you for breakfast this morning," Yanagi explained. "I had to be with the President, while he conferred with representatives of our customers in New York. I just saw them off." He pointed to the flag of Ethiopia, unfurled above the main entrance. "This is where many famous people stay. Each day the Waldorf-Astoria flies the national flag of the important foreign VIP among its guests. The doorman just told me that the Emperor of Ethiopia checked in yesterday."

"Nice custom," Iki said, seeing for the first time in his life the national colors of Ethiopia.

"Enjoy your visit at the branch office. I have to be with the President. We'll be out most of the day. The President will hold a reception here at six o'clock. Be sure you're back for that. He thinks you should be there."

Safely instructed, Iki walked west from Park Avenue to Fifth Avenue, a wide, busy thoroughfare that lay in the shadow of one tall building after another. Most of the men he saw on the broad sidewalk were dressed in dark, well tailored suits and moved along at a brisk pace. Occasionally the roar of subway trains rising through sidewalk grills surprised him. Not everything about this city was pleasing, however. The street was littered with scraps of paper and cigarette butts. A police patrol car sped by, its siren wailing. Taxis and buses cast their fumes over pedestrians. Outside the serene confines of the rich men's hotel lay a bustling, noisy, impersonal city that must frighten many a newcomer. Osaka, big though it was, could not compare with this.

The Kinki Trading Company's office was in an older, twenty-story building on a corner of Fifth Avenue and 50th Street. Iki entered an elevator crowded with men and women of many races —a representation of the people living in this cosmopolitan city. He found the office on the eighth floor and entered it through massive double doors. The familiar emblem of the company graced the wall opposite the doors. A vase of fresh irises added a Japanese touch to the desk of the receptionist, a petite young blonde. She made him feel uneasy in this alien place.

"I am Tadashi Iki . . . May I see Mr. Kaibe?" he inquired, pronouncing the words very carefully.

"Beg pardon," the blonde smiled brightly up at him. "What's that name again?"

Confused by sounds he could not sort out, Iki looked down at her, helplessly. The receptionist repeated her question slowly, and this time he understood her—and she understood him.

He walked through the inconspicuous door the receptionist waved him toward, and stopped short at the sight of the working office—desks and tables to accommodate about a hundred employees, arranged in departmental groups over a vast floor area. This, he admitted, was just like Osaka. He noticed that Japanese employees, without exception, like those at home, sat hunched over their desks in attitudes of diligence, while Americans appeared cheerful and relaxed and, somehow, inefficient, as they typed or talked over the telephones. He almost recoiled in shock at seeing samples of Japanese bicycles, rubber slippers, and dozens of other items that had been sent to New York. Will Americans buy these things, he wondered.

He went to the Textile Department, that being like a touch of home, and introduced himself to a Japanese man working at a table covered with sample swatches. "I came to see Mr. Kaibe of the Grains Section," he said.

"See that fellow over there, pounding a typewriter? He's Kaibe. The market quotations are just coming in. Maybe you should wait a while. Check in with his secretary."

Iki presented himself to an elderly American woman who was seated near Kaibe, then took a chair a short distance away, from which he observed the man at work.

Kaibe, in his early thirties, coatless, with shirt sleeves rolled up and necktie askew, appeared to be concentrating on at least three tasks simultaneously—peering through his glasses at a narrow lateral overhead screen that, at the moment, flashed a signal reading "SB N 240-1/8," listening to the telephone receiver wedged between his left ear and shoulder, and pounding furiously on a typewriter. Iki guessed that he must be analyzing the international market quotations for wheat, barley, corn, and other grains. And Iki could bet here was another Kaneko in the making, giving body and spirit to the cause of Kinki.

Iki had come to see Kaibe at the suggestion of the New York Branch manager, who had described him as "a promising young executive." Masaoka thought that he would be the best person to acquaint Iki with the operations at the New York office and with the life-style of Japanese businessmen working abroad.

A young American man passed Iki and laid a teletype message on Kaibe's desk. Kaibe glanced at the sheet, looked up to check the symbols flowing across the overhead screen, issued an order to the American in rapid English. Iki had time to decode its meaning: "Send another cable to London, and request a definite answer within two minutes."

When Kaibe finished his analysis for the morning, he stretched, lit a cigarette, and spun his chair around to face Iki. Although at first glance he looked somewhat bored, his words, in mercifully simple Japanese, came cheerfully enough. "You're Mr. Iki," he said, rising politely and bowing, the younger man deferring to the older. "I'm sorry you had to wait."

"I must apologize for disturbing you at such a busy time," Iki said, with an acknowledging bow. "I came to see you at Mr. Masaoka's recommendation."

Iki's stiff manner and very proper vocabulary interested Kaibe, but did not affect his good will. "Oh, yes. Mr. Masaoka . . . But Hyodo Shinichiro is the one who told me you'd be here. He sent me a radiogram from Tokyo several days ago. He and I went to work for Kinki at the same time, and we were together in the Planning Office. He asked me to do whatever I could for you here. He even sent me a description. I must say, Hyodo has an accurate way of describing people." He laughed so agreeably that Iki could not be offended.

In fact, he took an immediate liking to Kaibe. "I met Hyodo only a few weeks ago, the day after he returned from Arabia. But I haven't seen his since he was transferred to Tokyo. How very kind of him to remember me."

Kaibe started to discuss the general routine at this branch office, but Iki interrupted him. "I'm curious about those symbols you were studying—like 'SB N 240' and 'C U 205.' What do they stand for?"

"Oh those . . . They're current market quotations at the Board of Trade in Chicago. The initial letters are abbreviations. 'SB' for soybeans, 'C' for corn, and so forth. The next letter is a code for the month of the year. And the numbers represent the prices in cents for the particular months cited."

"I've seen how textiles are affected by the market. Therefore, I can imagine how sensitive you must be to fluctuations in grain prices."

"I've become used to it. But I've learned that I have to stay in good physical condition to keep up with time differences in trinational trade. This morning, for instance, I had to get up at four o'clock to take an important phone call from London. I've put in a long day already."

"What is 'trinational trade'? I haven't heard that term before."

"It's not 'trinational' in the true sense of the word," Kaibe said, removing the heavy-rimmed glasses to rub his eyes. "It refers to transactions between two foreign counties in which Japan is involved as a third party. Ordinarily we export Japanese products, to the U.S., let's say, and import American goods into Japan. In trinational trade, however, we arrange import-export trade between two non-Japanese countries."

"Sort of like a go-between at home, arranging a marriage?"

"Exactly, and with a good commission besides. —Each day," Kaibe continued, "I sell American wheat and soybeans not only to Japan, but also to Southeast Asia and Europe as well. Prices are set at the Chicago Board of Trade, but London is the headquarters for grain transactions. Before I leave this office at the end of a day, I always call London to instruct our men there to offer grain for sale at prices based on that day's Chicago quotations—for example, "X tons of soybean offered to X nation, to be delivered during X month at X price, send reply tomorrow morning." The replies are on my desk by the time I get here at eight the next morning. The minute the Chicago Board of Trade opens, the day's quotations start to flow across the screen, and I sit here and buy and sell according to what I see. If I notice a drastic shifting of prices, I get in touch with London before I make my decision."

"I'm curious about one thing," Iki said. "I heard you telling your American assistant to send a cable to London and get an answer within two minutes. Why don't you use the radio-telephone if it's so urgent a matter?"

"For one thing, you need time to get a phone call through during working hours. So we have our own direct cable connection between New York and London. That allows almost instantaneous communication. Furthermore, printed figures are much more reliable than those quoted orally."

Kaibe checked his wristwatch. "It's almost noon, Mr. Iki. If you don't mind eating the equivalent of a take-out Japanese box lunch, won't you join me? I'm sorry I can't offer you anything better, but I have to stay at my desk. I'm expecting a call from a freight broker."

"They have *o-bento* in America too? I'd be delighted to join you." Iki was relieved, for he had been very uncomfortable during breakfast in the hotel's ornate dining room—and too full, ever since, of fried bacon and eggs, oily potatoes, things Yoshiko never served at home.

Kaibe took two wrapped sandwiches and two cartons of hot soup from the cart brought by the negro youth who came daily to cater to the office staff.

"This is tuna." Kaibe unwrapped one of the sandwiches for Iki to see. "Japanese don't make tuna sandwiches, unfortunately, but Americans are quite fond of them. That's one reason why Japan can export so much canned tuna to the U.S. I've come to like it. Especially for lunch."

The telephone rang. "Hello, Jack? . . . Yes, I think I will . . ." Kaibe laughed as he talked, discussing a matter in English that was much too rapid for Iki to follow exactly. He seemed to be considering a choice among freighters to ship fifteen thousand tons of soybeans in response to an order from London. The conversation with Jack being completed, he dispatched a cable to London, stating the name of the freighter, the port and date of sailing, and the shipping charge. As soon as he received a confirming reply, he scanned a tape flowing past him to the accompaniment of rapid clicking.

"What's that?" Iki asked.

"Oh, it's printout provided by the news services. Every imaginable kind of news comes in on the teleprinter. It's just said that the fighting between the two Chinas over P'eng-hu Island has stopped. At least for the while. I doubt that there'll be any more news that might have a bearing on the grain market. So let's go. I think it's safe for us to leave."

"You came here at the best time of the year," Kaibe said, rolling down the window of his dusty Ford Comet. "In July and August, New York is as hot and muggy as Tokyo. But in May the whole country outside the city is beautiful."

They were driving along Fifth Avenue. Interesting, even overwhelming, but not beautiful, Iki thought. "You might call Fifth Avenue and Park Avenue the two spines of Manhattan. The Empire State Building, Rockefeller Center, the Metropolitan Museum —all are in this vicinity. The whole area symbolizes American culture and prosperity. I hated this city when I first came here. Having been stationed in London, when I was with the Textile Division, I was accustomed to European manners. In London people apologize if they so much as accidentally brush against someone. I remember my first day in New York. A man bumped into me and

331

walked right on without saying a word. I felt foolish, because I had said 'Pardon me' even though he was at fault. I turned to see what he was like, and was bumped by another man. He didn't say a word either. I was disgusted. But now I like the speedy, on-with-the-business pace of New York. It's exciting."

Iki could observe much of the excitement as they drove south on Fifth Avenue. The buildings stretched skyward, the only direction in which they could expand. Pedestrians and cars alike appeared to vanish into crevices among unbroken blocks of skyscrapers. But the heights of the buildings shrank the farther south they drove, and even the appearance of pedestrians changed. Fewer well-dressed Caucasians were seen. More of the men wore open-collared shirts and casual jackets. Blacks and Puerto Ricans were plentiful. The scene matched Iki's idea of a typical American "downtown."

Kaibe turned toward Broadway and parked the car near that important street. "Most of our customers are in this neighborhood. The textile trade—jobbers and cutters—are concentrated here on Broadway, between 30th and 40th streets. You can always find one or two of our salesmen making the rounds in this vicinity."

The several wholesale shops they passed looked very much the same, each one with bolts of material stacked high in rooms about a thousand square feet in area. In none of the shops did they see more than a half dozen employees. They stopped in front of an unusually small, dismal store on the ground floor of a shabby building. The sign above the shop's door said "Knox Company." Through the dirty window they saw the back of a small thin Japanese bending over the counter. He had unrolled several bolts of fabric samples, which were being inspected by a large man with bushy eyebrows and a large hooked nose.

"That's Itokawa, in charge of Textiles," Kaibe whispered. "He's up against the man we call 'Eagle Nose.' That guy is so crafty that even our shrewdest dealers in Osaka wouldn't stand a chance against him. Let's go in and watch."

The two slipped in quietly, and pretended to be looking at fabrics.

"But Mr. Knox," Itokawa was saying, "none of our competitors can beat our price on this Bemberg Georgette fabric. If you give your order, I'll throw in extras."

"Man, you been telling me the same sorta crap for three weeks.

Listen, there's plenty of this stuff floatin' round. Why should I bother to buy it from a Japanese?"

"All I ask is that you give us a try. You'll like our material. I'm sure of it."

"Okay, then. So I'll like it. What're the extras you been talkin' about?"

"I'll come down from eighty-nine cents to eighty cents a yard. And we'll pay the cost of adding the print."

"Is that all? Listen! The fella from Marufuji Company said they'll give me an exclusive print, and not reproduce it for a year."

"A year? I don't believe it!"

"That's your problem. Furthermore, I want guaranteed delivery. If the order can't be shipped off to me in plenty of time, it has to be air-flown in. If you agree to all that, maybe I'll think it over."

"But . . . but . . ." Itokawa sputtered. "If I say okay to all your conditions, how much will you buy?"

"Three thousand yards."

"Is that all? . . . Only three thousand yards? . . . Okay, okay. It's a deal," he agreed miserably.

"Good," Knox said, breaking into a grin. "Now make way for the next Japanese salesmen."

Itokawa looked back in surprise. "Mr. Kaibe! I'm embarrrassed that you were watching," he burst out in Japanese. "That man really took me!" He threw his samples into a large suitcase and rushed outside, holding the heavy suitcase in one hand, his briefcase in the other. Kaibe and Iki hurried after him.

Outside, safe from "Eagle Nose's" scrutiny, Kaibe introduced Iki to Itokawa. "All our men in the Textile Department go from one wholesaler to the next, as Itokawa's doing, trying to make sales."

"Eagle Nose" had made Itokawa very unhappy. "In Japan my wife tells her friends how lucky she is, having a husband who was chosen for an assignment in New York. If they could only see me, pounding the streets, as a door-to-door salesman! They would laugh—my wife, too! By the way, you're driving aren't you, Mr. Kaibe? I have to make a few more stops, so I'll find a taxi."

The slight body of Itokawa, leaning to one side against the weight of his oversized suitcase, soon vanished in the crowd pushing along the sidewalk.

Later Kaibe drove Iki toward Wall Street. "Our men in Textiles are trying hard, but Itokawa's experience shows how little they can do at present. They can get only small orders, so the gross sales figures for Textiles are always much smaller than those of our other departments. The branch manager is constantly jumping on them. But I agree with what Hyodo says about the future of textiles in the U.S. A labor-intensive industry like textiles won't be able to keep up with changes brought on by technological advances. The American industry hasn't been adapting to these changes. Soon the U.S. will have to import textiles in large quantities. And we in Japan are ready to produce. Our men are manning an outpost, so to speak. They receive no glory for their work, much less thanks, but they're keeping the lines open so that Kinki Trading will have a competitive edge when the real battle over textiles begins." Military terms, Iki noticed, had become a part of the traders' jargon.

Kaibe maneuvered his car expertly through the crowded traffic and entered Wall Street. To Iki this famous place looked like the bottom of a canyon walled in by towering buildings that denied the street its sunlight. Young men in shirt sleeves rushed back and forth along the sidewalks as if they knew where they had to be at precisely what time.

"Branches of foreign companies with offices in New York have had to register as overseas-affiliated firms because of state legislation passed two years ago. That legislation was basically tax-economy measure, intended to make Wall Street banks indispensable to companies like ours. Probably our President, and Mr. Yosano, and our branch manager are sitting in one of those banks right now, trying to raise capital."

Iki felt squeezed in by the walls of steel and concrete that closed in on them from both sides. A break in the wall in the middle of one block admitted a beam of dazzling sunlight. As they drove past Trinity Church, Iki caught a glimpse of a patch of blue that was as bright and clear as the early summer skies in his native Yamagata. The roar of a speeding van drew his attention. As it raced past them, it flaunted a message—"To Hell with Khrushchev"—painted across the rear panel. The slogan made him realize that he was actually living in one of the belligerent countries waging the Cold War. Just when relations between the U.S. and the Soviet Union seemed to be warming, an American U-2 reconnaissance plane had been shot down over Soviet territory. The furor that incident raised in both countries had aroused the old antagonisms again.

The main ballroom of the Waldorf-Astoria Hotel was the scene of a reception presented by Kinki Trading Company. Receiving the guests at the entrance were Daimon and Masaoka, newly appointed general manager for Kinki in America.

The reception was a stag affair, held for the convenience of businessmen in the city, who could come straight from their offices after working hours. Many were Jewish merchants, either textile wholesalers or dealers in general goods. Also present, to Daimon's unconcealed delight, were high-ranking executives of Dupont and Barrington, First National City Bank, Continental Corporation, a giant among grain exporters, Lance Aircraft Corporation, and Beach Corporation, a manufacturer of helicopters.

By seven o'clock more than three hundred men mingled sociably around bars and food tables arranged along the middle of the ballroom. Iki stayed close to Kaibe Kaname, observing the novel experience of an American-style cocktail reception, or "business party" as Japanese called such an affair. Having seen so few Japanese on the streets of the city during the day, he was impressed by the unexpectedly large number who appeared at the reception.

"Are they all Kinki employees from Japan?" he asked Kaibe.

"No. Some are from other Japanese corporations or organizations. But all members of our New York branch, including local hires, are here tonight. The purpose of the reception is to entertain our guests, but it's partly to show our strength, too. Of course, our host's attitude, as you must know by now, is 'the more the merrier,' " Kaibe chuckled.

"Seriously," he continued, "many of the other Japanese you see here are the true resident elite—representatives of Mitsuba, Goto, Marufuji, the Bank of Japan, the Bank of Tokyo, JETRO, the Consulate General, the major steel and electrical companies."

An announcement from the master of ceremonies quieted the conversation. He introduced Daimon, who took his place at the microphone. Flushed more with pleasure than with whiskey, he looked out upon the men who were his guests.

"I am honored because so many of you are present with us this evening," he said in English, finding occasional help in his notes. "I am happy to announce that Kinki Trading Company has

335

unified its American operations, and that we are elevating Mr. Masaoka, currently manager of our New York office, to be general manager of all our branches in the United States. We take this step with the hope that Kinki Trading Company, by expanding the scope of its operations, will be able to contribute significantly to the ever-growing trade between the United States and Japan. We intend to develop our American operation in full compliance with the laws of the United States and in conformity with the interests of the United States. I shall be grateful for your words of counsel and for your assistance as we work together toward a better future. Thank you very much."

When the applause ended, Masaoka stepped up to the microphone. Iki noted that he was perfectly groomed, Westernized from the careful cut of his hair to the pointed tips of his elegant shoes in the latest fashion from France.

"We sincerely thank each of you for having taken the time to be with us this evening," Masaoka said in easy unaccented English. "I haven't yet found words to describe adequately my gratitude for the experiences I have enjoyed in this great country. Since I first arrived in New York City, I've made it a point to study current American management practices and to apply them to the management of our New York office. I realized from the start that I must approach my work as most American citizens do, and I've endeavored to instill this attitude in all of our employees . . ." Beads of perspiration caused by the heat of the spotlights formed on Masaoka's forehead as he spoke.

"Mr. Masaoka is very capable, wouldn't you say?" Kaibe whispered to Iki. "He was formerly branch manager in Sydney. One of the first things Mr. Daimon did after becoming president was to select Mr. Masaoka for the post here in New York. The choice drew considerable criticism, expressed openly by most of the North American branch managers as well as by Kinki's managerial staff in Europe. They spoke of him as 'the Australian country gentleman'—a clear case of resentment and jealousy, I'd say . . . In a month's time, he made himself over into the American-type executive you see up there now. You have to give him a lot of credit."

Masaoka finished his graceful speech, and Iki admired the poise with which he responded to enthusiastic applause. A model in every respect, he concluded.

"What changes will be made in Mr. Masaoka's role, now that

he's to become general manager?" he asked. "As New York branch manager, wasn't he more or less the equivalent of president of Kinki Trading in the United States?"

"His promotion is going to make a big difference. Kinki Trading was locally incorporated, and therefore enjoyed preferential tax treatment in New York. In other respects, it's been treated in the same way as is any other foreign branch office. But it had no autonomy. For instance, we couldn't hire anyone to work here without an okay from the home office in Osaka. The purpose behind the reorganization is to allow a more autonomous operation in the United States. The general manager for America will be given authority to make many decisions independently—for example, on all transactions involving less than a million dollars."

Kaibe took two glasses of Scotch whiskey and soda from a waiter's tray, gave one to Iki, and led him to the buffet. Soon he was deep in conversation with the head of an importing firm specializing in portable radios and television sets made in Japan. He introduced the American to Iki, trying to back away from conversation with anyone who didn't speak Japanese.

"What position do you hold in your company, Mr. Iki?" the American asked affably.

Very uncomfortable in this noisy setting, Iki explained that he served as a consultant to the president. "I entered Kinki Trading Company in February of this year, so I am a very new man," he added.

Noticing Iki's age, the American decided that he must have been plucked out of another firm. "For whom did you work before?"

While Iki searched for unfamiliar English terms, Kaibe came to his rescue. "He was a very capable member of Japan's General Staff during the war."

"In the Army or the Navy?"

"The Army."

"What rank did he hold?"

Kaibe had to turn to Iki for the correct English equivalent. "Lieutenant colonel," Iki said hesitantly.

An executive of Beach Corporation overheard the exchange and moved over to join the group. Noticing Iki's discomfort, Kaibe exchanged a few pleasantries with the man, then led Iki away to a corner.

"You should enjoy talking with them, Mr. Iki. Things are different here. American businessmen respect retired military officers. So—" Kaibe's attention wandered from Iki's past and present. "Please excuse me. I've heard rumors about some Russians coming here to buy American wheat. The man who just passed us is the business manager of Continental Grain. I want to sound him out."

"Here? At a cocktail reception?"

"Of course! All this drinking and cocktail chatter are just excuses. These parties are the best places for people to pick up information. Of all kinds."

Kaibe went after his quarry. Iki, all alone, studied the crowd. The party was in full swing, and the chatter and laughter made conversation very difficult. The slight intoxication caused by mixing whiskey with nervousness was agreeable, but it did not obscure Iki's recognition of his own amazement at being present in such a novel and exotic world—and his perplexity, as he wondered why had he been brought into this alien setting.

The annual meeting of the board of managers for Kinki's North American district was about to begin. Iki had been invited to observe the proceedings, and sat with the recording secretary at a small table that had been set apart from those for the managers, arranged in a U at the middle of the room. From his seat he looked out upon the silvery spire of the Chrysler Building, which rose nearby.

Managers of the six branches and two offices in North America sat with their staff assistants, who were fully prepared with information for answering questions regarding their operations. They were tense because Daimon himself was present, to discuss the changes made necessary by the reorganization that raised Masaoka to be general manager over them.

Daimon at the head table, was flanked by Masaoka and Yosano. Seated at the parallel tables in the U configuration were Kaibe and the three department heads of the New York branch, the district managers of San Francisco, Los Angeles, Chicago, Houston, and Dallas, and the managers of the Portland and Seattle offices.

Masaoka started the proceedings. "This meeting of the Board of North American branch managers is now in session. With the institution of a general managerial system, much more will be expected of all our North American branch offices. Those of us

338

who are working in foreign offices were especially selected from among the three thousand employees of Kinki Trading Company, and we must gear ourselves to live up to the expectations of the home office. This year we have the unusual honor of welcoming our President to our meeting. I ask all of you to be candid in your reports, so that we may discuss them to our mutual benefit for the purpose of strengthening our over-all operation."

Masaoka's remarks were as polished as was his appearance, enhanced this morning by a superbly cut pinstripe suit. He himself presented the first report, on the aggregate results of the previous year in North America: "Gross sales last year totaled one hundred and ninety-five million dollars, representing a seventeen percent annual growth rate. A breakdown by areas shows sales of one hundred and forty million for San Francisco, eight million for Dallas, and seven million for Chicago. The principal commodities again were textiles, steel, machinery, and food items. There have been no significant changes. But we're encouraged by the export last year of automobiles and electrical appliances made in Japan. Even though the number was negligible, it represents a beginning compared to year before last, when sales were practically non-existent. Hereafter, we hope to concentrate only on major commodities with good growth potentials."

Masaoka, thoroughly aware of Daimon's preference for precise information rather than for general descriptions, presented facts and figures he had committed to memory. He was much relieved by Daimon's approving nods, given frequently while he spoke.

"Now we shall hear individual reports on current status as well as future planning. May we begin with Los Angeles?"

The Los Angeles Branch Manger was a small but husky man, wearing an exceptionally colorful necktie. He rattled off a long series of figures in a loud, clear voice. Iki checked his statements against a list of commodities, which had been distributed beforehand. Plywood and steel were the major items exported from Japan to Los Angeles. Textiles, canned tuna, and fresh tangerines were among the lesser items. The major items exported to Japan from Los Angeles were helicopters, scrap iron, and petroleum.

"Compared with New York and Chicago, Los Angeles is still a huge provincial town that's largely untapped," the Los Angeles Branch Manager continued. "It holds great potentials for expansion, both in the amount of trade and in the variety of merchandise we handle. We now enjoy a large balance in favor of exports to Los Angeles, so I plan to work toward increasing imports to Japan from Los Angeles to achieve a closer balance between import and export. But we're handicapped by trade practices there to which we are not accustomed. Also, we on the West Coast tend to incur more bad debts than our offices do elsewhere. The reason for this is interesting. Los Angeles attracts many businessmen who have failed on the East Coast and gone West in hopes of making a quick recovery. We could reduce bad debts and concentrate on trading if you would send us an attorney, preferably someone from our own legal section, to anticipate such defaults or to follow through on them when they occur. In view of Los Angeles' steadily increasing population—by at least ten thousand people a month—I suggest a policy with primary emphasis on growth. The Bank of America and other such institutions are willing to provide financing. Los Angeles, I might add, is quickly becoming the economic center of the entire West Coast."

Daimon was pleased with such an optimistic report and with the manager's dynamic presentation. The fact that the newer Los Angeles branch had quickly overtaken the long established branch in San Francisco added to his satisfaction with the aggressive manager from the southern area.

"Now may we now have the report from San Francisco?" Masaoka said.

The San Francisco Branch Manager could not conceal his resentment at being surpassed by his counterpart in Los Angeles. Nonetheless, assuming a bland expression, he rose to present his report. Iki, after consulting his list, found very little difference between the commodities handled by the Los Angeles and the San Francisco branches.

"The situation at San Francisco is about the same as that just described by the Los Angeles Branch Manager. I also intend to pursue a policy with emphasis on expansion. San Francisco is the most important West Coast metropolis, of course, and is the home of a majority of corporations in the American West. Naturally I'm regularly in touch with executives of these corporations. Because San Francisco is the western gateway to the United States, Japanese visitors seldom fail to make it their first stopping point. An inordinate amount of time and considerable sums of money are diverted to entertaining visiting Japanese executives. Those visitors expect me to give them my personal attention. I would like to request an increase in our budget and the assignment of at least one experienced young executive to help me manage the branch office."

The subtle manner in which he responded to the remarks of the man from Los Angeles, Iki thought, pointed up the relative sophistication of San Francisco and of Kinki's suave manager there.

"When I first arrived in Chicago, I was shocked to find Kinki at the very bottom of the ladder," the Chicago Branch Manager began. At thirty-eight, he was the youngest of the company's executives in North America. "I realized that Kinki could not compete with Japan's so-called Big Three—Mitsui, Mitsubishi, and Sumitomo. They'd tied up most of the available trading rights even before World War II. Until recently, the primary mission of our Chicago branch has been a kind of step-by-step invasion into the established territory of the Big Three. But I've learned that that's very difficult to accomplish, a near impossibility. So I've decided to look for profitable items of trade that the Big Three have not yet taken over. For example, I intend to concentrate on selling sheet iron to auto parts manufacturers in the Detroit area, portable radios and television sets, as well as parts for these, to electrical appliance manufacturers in the Chicago area. I, too, would like to have my staff increased. And I ask permission to lower the commission rates I charge."

Daimon scowled at this third request for an increased budget. "What's the size of Chicago staff?" he demanded.

"We have seven men. Four from the home office, and three local hires."

"Seven should be more than enough for a branch with gross sales of only seven million dollars. We spend a lot of money to send you men abroad. You ought to be thinking of ways to increase efficiency rather than expenses."

"I don't wish to be disagreeable," the young man from Chicago replied, undaunted. "But I'm convinced that an adequate staff is a prerequisite to growth. The best we can do with our seven men is to keep our operations from losing ground. We can't really expand. I want to get Kinki firmly established in Chicago before the Big Three *zaibatsu* corporations take over the area completely."

"All right," Yosano intervened. "Your request is noted. The President and I will discuss this with Personnel when we get back to Osaka, and see what we can do for you."

The men in charge of the offices in Seattle and Portland

described even worse circumstances. Each of them had only one employee, and both offices were swamped daily with unmanageable numbers of radiograms, phone calls, and visitors, mostly from Japan.

The final regional report came from the branch manager at Dallas. He tended to mumble as, haltingly, he described the previous year's operations. After a few minutes Iki realized that he was describing how the Dallas branch had been saddled with a huge uncollectable debt. Much had gone wrong in transactions related to cotton.

"All I hear from you is excuses," Daimon said, with brutal clarity. "You've told me nothing about the causes. Start from the beginning and give me a point-by-point description of the whole process."

Everyone felt sorry for the man, so obviously marked for trouble. After a few awkward moments, he began to trace the course of events that led to the debacle.

His second attempt at an explanation told Iki more about the problem. Of the 2.3 million bales of raw cotton imported annually by Japan, one million came from the United States. Troubled by declining sales and profit in his district, the Dallas Branch Manager had decided to acquire some of his cotton through direct purchasing from growers instead of buying it through shippers. Two years earlier, he had borrowed extensively from banks in Los Angeles, precontracted with one of the large cotton growers in Texas for the purchase of the whole crop, and thereby acquired ten thousand bales. Encouraged by this initial success, in the following year he drew up a precontract for fifty thousand bales at a unit price of $130 and paid eighty percent of the total purchasing price in advance. Then frost destroyed the whole planting before the harvest. The grower rejected the manager's plea for a refund of the advance, or even for a part of it, claiming that an "act of God" is clearly an exclusion. Thus the four million dollars could not be recovered.

"The cause was unpredictable weather conditions," the manager from Dallas said. "In other words, it was an inevitability . . . not the fault of any particular person . . . I took all necessary precautions. I consulted all available data from the United States Weather Bureau as well as from civil meteorological institutes. I was confident that everything would work out, and yet . . ."

"Don't tell me it was inevitable!" Daimon shouted him down. "You don't enter into a contract without considering every possible contingency. That's the 'A' in the ABC of business. You made a mistake in the first place, to take that big a risk after only a year's experiment."

"But I discussed it with the home office. I did not make the decision on my own . . ."

"In business we cannot make allowance for excuses," Daimon snapped. "Tell me, what do you intend to do now?"

"I'm sorry. Cotton is growing well this year, and I think the outlook for profit is good. I've been preparing plans for diversifying along new lines. I'm confident I can erase the debt and get the Dallas branch back into the black."

"New lines?" Daimon snorted. "How can you start up something new when you're carrying interest payments on four million dollars?—You say that cotton is growing well this year. But who knows what'll happen to the weather in Texas between now and harvest time? Remember last year? How can a man with your past record speak confidently about getting back into the black?"

Daimon's retort, everyone realized, labeled the Dallas manager a failure. Iki felt the harsh reality of business—and of businessmen —as if his own back were feeling the lash of Daimon's scorn.

And yet Daimon did not destroy the man from Dallas then and there. That would come later and quietly, in private. Instead, Daimon addressed the whole group, as the confident leader of a thriving company.

"Let me add a final word. Thanks to you men stationed abroad, Kinki Trading has been able to come as far as it has in the fourteen years since the end of the war. Having heard your reports, I realize this all the more, and I want to thank each and every one of you. You've crossed barriers that once seemed insurmountable. But your real work lies in the years ahead. We're far behind the Big Three. The ratio of our relative strengths is ten for Mitsui, ten for Mitsubishi, five for Marufuji, and only three for Kinki Trading. But our opportunity is coming. The United States is heading toward another great economic boom. Already Americans are talking about the "golden sixties." The U.S. government is starting to look favorably on increased trade with Japan. It'll be a rough trade war, with only the fittest surviving through the next ten years. The new general managerial system is intended to strength-

343

en our organization in North America. You men are on your own now. My expectations of you are high. If Kinki Trading Company succeeds in America, that will be an inspiration to our branches in all other countries in the world. Give the Company your best support!"

The next evening Iki was invited to supper at Kaibe Kaname's apartment in the borough of Queens. Kaibe lived with his wife and young son in one of the many big apartment buildings in Jackson Heights.

The dining table was set in a corner of the large living room that opened upon an enclosed balcony five stories above the ground level.

"I'm sorry I've dropped in so unexpectedly." Iki drew upon the usual formulas of apology. "I'm afraid I have put you to a lot of trouble."

Mrs. Kaibe, even on short notice, had prepared several traditional Japanese dishes for the traveler so far from home. After just two days of exposure to American meals, Iki longed for the taste—and restraint—of Japanese foods.

Iki had been asked to join Daimon and the district managers for dinner at a restaurant, but had excused himself in order to visit Kaibe's home. He wanted to see how a Japanese businessman and his family lived in America.

"We didn't have time to prepare adequately," Kaibe apologized in his turn, "but I'm glad to see you enjoying whatever little things my wife has made."

"I was planning to serve an American-style meal," Mrs. Kaibe said. "But my husband told me no. He told me to put together whatever we have, as long as it's Japanese food. I am happy to do so—for many reasons. Thanks to you, my husband is actually having dinner at home tonight, at the regular hour. That seldom happens. I'm sure our boy is delighted."

She indicated their six-year-old son, sitting withdrawn among the potted plants on the balcony. He ignored her.

"Shigeru," Kaibe called to him. "Uncle Iki from Japan is with us. Come in, and ask him to tell you about Japan." Shigeru ignored him, too.

"He's very shy." Kaibe did not disguise his concern.

"Because of the language problem?" Iki asked.

344

"I don't think so. He's in first grade, and already speaks English much more fluently than my wife does."

"Dear, it's not shyness or difficulty with English," Mrs. Kaibe said. "He's lonesome. New York has no schools for Japanese children, Mr. Iki, so we've sent him to a regular public school in the neighborhood. He doesn't enjoy it because a few boys there call him 'Jap,' and pick on him in other ways. He comes home and sees other children playing with their fathers, or doing things with them, like washing the car. He sees them eating supper together and telling each other what they did during the day. But in our family, Papa usually doesn't get home until close to midnight, so our family almost never has a chance to be together. The same sad story is true in the homes of all businessmen from Japan. Shigeru feels left out—in school, in the neighborhood, even at home, because at home he has no one to talk to except me. I don't wonder, then, that he is withdrawn, that he tries to live in his own dream world."

"You shouldn't talk that way in front of him," Kaibe scolded her mildly. "If Shigeru hears you say it too often, his shyness may become full-blown autism."

"He's becoming a clear case of autism," Mrs. Kaibe dared to say. "His homeroom teacher told me so, at the last PTA meeting. You've never been to a PTA meeting because your company keeps you so busy. You don't even know that the census taker who came here the other day couldn't believe that any man would work between sixty and seventy hours a week. He asked me what kind of a job you had, that took so much time."

Iki well understood that Kaibe's wife was using this opportunity to express her frustrations. And he wondered if Kaibe, who worked daily at a murderous pace and bore the additional burdens of trying to please both an unhappy wife and a neurotic child, might not be the first of Kinki's men in New York to suffer a breakdown.

"I'm sorry that you must listen to our bickering," Kaibe said. "My wife feels the strain of the constant struggle to speak English to everyone outside this apartment. And she, too, has no one to turn to for help. I'm afraid her irritability is becoming chronic. —But," he laughed, "you see she is not autistic . . ."

Mrs. Kaibe herself laughed at that. "Oh, my! I've been terribly rude. To think Mr. Hyodo asked us to take especially good care of you! I'm sorry." Looking around for a safer subject, she asked, "How did you like the *miso* soup?"

"I enjoyed it thoroughly. A taste of home! I'd like to have some more."

The buzzer sounded. "We're expecting Mr. Itokawa," Mrs. Kaibe said, hurrying to open the door.

"Ah, the fragrance of *miso!*" Itokawa exclaimed, as he came in. "Do you have some for me?"

"Did your guest get off all right?" Kaibe asked.

"I saw him off, but it was murder." He slumped into a chair, tired and wan.

"Why? What happened?"

Itokawa didn't answer until he'd swallowed some of the excellent soup. "Ah! I feel revived!" Only then did he bow to Iki. "I've really been run over flat today. When I got back to the office, after spending the whole day covering my usual downtown route, Masaoka told me to take care of an executive from a Japanese machinery firm. He was booked for a 7:10 p.m. flight. I told him that it was a dinner flight, but he insisted on eating a Chinese meal first. So I took him to a restaurant in Chinatown, then drove him to the airport—with plenty of time to spare. He isn't used to traveling abroad. His English is poor, so I had to help him get through the boarding procedures. That was when he discovered he'd left his dentures at the restaurant."

"Why in the world would he leave his teeth at a Chinese restaurant?" Kaibe chuckled.

"He went to the washroom to clean the things, and forgot them on the basin. But, he was a Class A guest, so what could I do? Luckily, I had an hour to run about in, before the plane took off. I drove back to Chinatown and out again to the airport at breakneck speed. I found the dentures—who else would want them?—but I almost smashed into another car at the approach to the airport."

"What is a Class A guest?" asked Iki.

"You should know how we handle this steady stream of feather merchants. We've set up four classes, from 'A' to 'D.' We pick up class 'D' visitors at the airport, deliver them to their hotels, and say 'Sayonara.' We take 'C' class visitors out to dinner. Class 'B' visitors get dinner and a night on the town—usually a strip-tease or a blue film. Class 'A' visitors are given the full treatment, twenty-four hour service. Whatever they want . . ." He sighed dramatically, wiping his sweaty face with Mrs. Kaibe's paper napkin.

Kaibe enlarged upon the resident businessman's woes. "I never complain about work at the office, however hard or demanding it may be. But I can't stand entertaining these lousy visitors from Japan. If we do everything we can to please them, they go back home and tell their friends about our extravagant spending here in America. If we economize, in order to forestall such gossip, they're thoroughly displeased. They say that we skimp on the entertaining and keep the money that should have been spent on them. The ones who demand and get the most all too often are the very ones who complain the loudest when they get back to Japan. And usually they're the ones who pester us with requests for hired women."

"If a Japanese visitor brings his wife, too," Mrs. Kaibe added, "I'm assigned to take care of her. I'm expected to have lunch with her, take her shopping, even carry her luggage. At first, I resented being treated as a personal maid, but I'm used to that now."

"I can understand how you feel," Itokawa said. "I consider entertaining as a part of my job, at least for now, and I'm resigned to it . . . I tell myself I'm paying the price for something I did in a previous life. But I resent having to spend my free time as the manager's houseboy. When I was with the branch in San Francisco, that sleazy manager never failed to call me up on Sundays. Usually I'd end up taking his four kids to the zoo. He even made me paint his doghouse. That was too much! I couldn't have been *that* bad in a previous life!"

Iki laughed, but no one else did.

"It's no laughing matter, Mr. Iki," Kaibe said. "You have to please everyone above you, if you want to get ahead. In an organization as large as ours, you don't dare offend an administrative superior who makes personnel decisions. Once he takes a dislike to you, he'll see that everything goes against you—regardless of how well you produce on the job."

Itokawa got up from his chair. "I must go. Already I'm five minutes behind schedule. The man I'm supposed to meet is arriving on the 10:05 flight from Paris."

"Who are you meeting this time?"

"The head of the Chemical Fiber Department at New Japan Spinnery. I'm afraid this means another greasy dinner in China-

347

town. But I'll have to take good care of him anyway. Manufacturers like New Japan Spinnery have been willing to share our current deficits. Without them, we'd never be able to offer the discounts that American textile dealers demand.—Thanks for the soup, Mr. Kaibe," Itokawa called over his shoulder, as he headed for the door.

While Mrs. Kaibe cleared the table, Kaibe and Iki sat talking in the living room.

"So there you are!" Kaibe called out to his son, concentrating upon putting together a model airplane. "Come and join us. Uncle Iki will tell us about the beautiful kites of Japan."

Shigeru looked up for an instant, then turned back to the pieces of balsa wood. He did not react at all to Iki's urging, whether in English or in Japanese. Iki recognized the signs of rebellion lurking behind the indifference. He had seen them in his own son.

Kaibe shook his head. "What to do about our children? That's the most distressing problem for almost all Japanese stationed abroad. I had to leave my family in Japan while I worked in the London Office. I came to New York by myself, and was here for a year before they could join me. But I'm better off than Hyodo, who lived apart from his family for several years when he was working in the Middle East and Southeast Asia. His children were babies when he left them. By the time he was reassigned to Japan, they were going to elementary school. At first, of course, they resented him because he took his wife's attention away from them. Later, when they seemed to be a little friendlier, he was thinking that everything was getting back to normal. But one Sunday he received the shock of his life when he took them out for a drive. A car suddenly shot out in front of theirs, and all the kids shouted, 'Watch out, Mr. Hyodo!' "

Other people may have laughed over the story, but Iki thought it pathetic. He had been kept apart from his family for eleven years. Now, although they had been reunited for almost three years, he had not succeeded in breaking down the barrier that Makoto—and time—had put up between them. He looked at Shigeru, and saw in him a younger Makoto. And a sadder one, precisely because he was so young. How would he be when he reached Makoto's age?

"Mr. Kaibe, do you really think I can make the grade as a businessman?" Iki asked abruptly. "For one thing, I don't think I can possibly bear to live in a foreign country. And apart from my family."

"I doubt if you would be expected to do the kind of work we do. According to Hyodo, you'll be given an assignment only you can perform."

"I can't imagine what that will be. The only knowledge I've picked up is about the Japanese Army and the inside of Siberian prison camps. What can I possibly do in the big world of trading companies?"

"I think you've been brought along on this trip to gather ideas that will help you to decide what kind of work you'll do eventually."

Kaibe's friendliness and sincerity comforted Iki somewhat, but did not resolve his problem. The question that he'd been asking himself ever since he reached New York still baffled him. Why did Daimon bring him to America?

A taxi delivered Iki to his hotel soon after ten o'clock that night. Because he was scheduled to leave for Washington, D.C. the next morning, he wanted to talk with Daimon for a few minutes. But Daimon had not yet returned to his suite. Iki took a shower and went to bed. During the short time he'd been in New York, he had seen something of Kinki Trading Company's local operations, attended a lavish cocktail reception that had unnerved him, observed a meeting of district managers, and visited Kaibe's home. He was worn out by such unrelenting demands upon his mind and body. He switched on the bedside radio for music to soothe him, but found only the blarings of jazz or the thumpings of rock and roll. Impatiently he cut the radio off. When he switched off the lamps in the room, a soft, faint light from outside stole in through the curtains. He went to the window, parted the curtains, and looked out upon the immense city. A half moon cast its cold glow on the groves of darkened skyscrapers. The world outside his room seemed to be enwrapped in the silence of death. The street below was dark and deserted.

Iki lay down again, switched on the bedside lamp, and examined the front page of the *New York Evening Post*. A small headline disturbed him thoroughly: "Japanese Military Mission Visits Pentagon." The brief article stated that a Japanese mission headed by Harada Masaru, Chief of the Air Division, National Defense

Agency, had visited the Pentagon and conferred with the Secretary of Defense about upgrading Japan's defense capabilities.

Iki put down the paper, to rest his eyes, but not his troubled mind. My being in the United States at the same time as the Harada Mission is a surprising coincidence, he thought. He recalled how his father-in-law had praised Harada, who planned to leave the Defense Agency to campaign for a seat in the Upper House of the Diet. He remembered, too, Sakano's question, put to him just before he left Japan: "Why don't you consider serving the country in politics? . . . instead of devoting the rest of your life to a trading company?" The memory of that conversation—and of Sakano's scorn for businessmen—pained him. The possibility of a connection between Harada's mission and his own presence in America bothered him all through the night.

"A letter from Dad!" Naoko chirped happily when she found the airmail envelope with the American stamps in the family's mailbox. The rainy season of early summer had begun on schedule, and one wet gloomy day had followed upon another ever since Iki's departure twelve days before. Naoko danced into the house, waving the letter over her head.

"You're dripping water all over the place," Yoshiko reminded her. "Please take off your raincoat." Only then did she put aside the dress she was making for Naoko. "Where is it from?"

"From Washington! The capital of America! Read it, Mother. Hurry!"

Yoshiko looked for a few moments at her husband's handwriting, opened the letter, and for Naoko's sake read aloud:

I hope you are all well. This is my fourth day in America. As I mentioned briefly on the first postcard, everyone in our New York office has been very kind to me, and I am getting along quite well. Today I came to Washington, D.C. alone. This trip is not related to company business. I came because I've wanted to see Washington ever since I was in the Army. It is not only the capital of the United States. It is the nerve center of world politics.

Washington, as you children know, was a planned city, started during the time of the first American president, George Washington. The streets radiate from the Capitol, at the hub of the city. Buildings here are mostly about ten stories high, quite unlike the very tall New York skyscrapers. Surprisingly, the city has the quiet dignity of an old European city. The White House, which I've seen so often in photographs and newsreels, is much smaller than I expected. In fact, I asked a guard if I had come to the right place."

Naoko burst out laughing.

I was impressed by Arlington Cemetery, with its tens of thousands, perhaps hundreds of thousands of identical white grave markers. An elderly American couple shouted 'Damned Jap!' at me. They probably lost a son in the Pacific War. Anyway, I was shocked by their behavior. I have almost forgotten that terrible war. They made me realize that we Japanese must strive much harder toward reaching mutual understanding.

Tomorrow I return to New York. Later I'll visit Detroit, then fly by way of Chicago to Los Angeles. The rainy season must have begun at home. Please take care."

Hearing the front door being opened, Naoko called, "Makoto! Come quick! A letter from Dad!"

"Only me," answered Yoshiko's father.

"Grandpa! What a pleasant surprise!" both Yoshiko and Naoko cried out.

"I went to the prefectural office, so I thought I'd stop in to see how you are. Have you heard from Tadashi?"

"Oh, he's fine. We were just reading a letter from him. He wrote to us from Washington."

"Washington? What does he say? I'd love to read it," Sakano said, dabbing at his rain-soaked cuffs with a handkerchief.

"Stay with us tonight, Grandpa. I think this rain will last all night."

"Thanks," he nodded, delighted to be asked.

Naoko sat at her desk, doing homework, while Sakano, comfortable on a thick *zabuton*, read Iki's letter. Yoshiko brought a cup of black tea for her father, and some of the sweet cookies that he loved.

"Just this one letter from Washington?" he asked, when he'd finished reading it.

"Yes. Why do you ask?"

"No special reason . . . By the way, Mr. Harada of the Defense Agency has decided definitely to run for the Upper House in the next election. He announced his intention just before he went off

351

for a visit to America. I'll be busy working for him with the election committee of the Veterans' Association."

"I'm surprised to hear that Mr. Harada is entering politics."

"I told Tadashi about it when I saw him last. I've meant to ask you— What do you really think about Tadashi's new career as a merchant? Are you happy about it?"

"Why do you ask?" Her father's seriousness puzzled Yoshiko.

"For a man like Tadashi to spend the rest of his life working for an import-export firm is shameful, I think. I can understand your wish for a quiet, secure life now at last. But if your wish is holding Tadashi back, you really ought to think it over. I think he'd make an excellent candidate. He commands great respect, especially among all those returnees from Siberia whom he helped to get jobs. And their families, and their friends. He's a good man at heart. Now that he's regained his health, and has had his teeth fixed, he looks like a leading man who has aged very well."

"He's never talked about going into politics," Yoshiko said with unusual sharpness. Not that she didn't agree with Sakano about her husband's virtues. She just didn't want him to lose them, in the dirty business of politics.

"Wait a minute." Sakano put up a hand. "I didn't come here to argue or to put pressure on you. I just want to hear how you feel about his future. Tadashi said he was being sent to the United States to broaden his perspective as a businessman. He's so close-mouthed that I can't learn a thing from him. I've been wondering if he wasn't ordered to accompany Mr. Daimon to assist in contracting for the purchase of the new line of jet fighters for our Defense Agency. Did he say anything to you about the reasons for his trip?"

"How can his visit to America be related to jet fighters, I wonder?"

"When the veterans' election committee met day before yesterday, someone mentioned that the Defense Agency's fact-finding mission is now in the United States. Harada is head of that mission, and General Kawamata of the Air Division is with him. The mission will visit Los Angeles to try out planes that have been recommended as replacements for the entire line of current fighters. Test pilots from our Air Self-Defense Force are supposed to meet the mission in Los Angeles. Tadashi's itinerary shows that he'll be in Los Angeles when the mission is there. So, naturally, I wondered."

Yoshiko frowned. She remembered the ugly scrambling among trading companies three years earlier, over a contract for the initial line of jet fighters. Before it was settled, a colonel in the Defense Agency committed suicide. Her voice trembled as she said, "I hope Tadashi doesn't get involved in that sort of thing."

The manager and key staff members of Kinki's Los Angeles branch watched as the Boeing 707 arriving from Chicago touched down easily at 1:40 p.m. A few minutes later, when Daimon entered the passenger lounge, the manager rushed up to him. "Sir, the local Japanese press wants to run an article on your visit. I've given the reporter most of the information. A picture is all they need. I know you must be tired, but I hope you won't mind posing for the photographer."

He signaled to a young Japanese-American, who quickly took half a dozen shots of Daimon, as seen from assorted angles.

"Sir, this way," the manager said. "We have your luggage in the car."

"That was quick," said Daimon, pleased by his man's efficiency.

Soon they were speeding along one of Los Angeles's fantastic freeways. Daimon and Yosano occupied the wide rear seat of a Cadillac sedan. Iki sat in front with the manager, who drove. The multi-colored necktie he wore was even gaudier than the one he'd flourished in New York.

"Sir, did you enjoy Detroit and Chicago?" the manager asked Daimon alone. "We received frequent reports on your many activities there. With so much business to attend to, I wonder that you had time at all to rest."

"I enjoyed Detroit. I was fascinated by the growth of the automobile industry. Annual production of seven to eight million units is astounding—a number that's almost inconceivable to us."

"I certainly agree. As I mentioned the other day in New York, jet aircraft and communication technology, especially the new electronics devices, are experiencing remarkable growth in the Los Angeles area. I'm looking forward to showing you the main plants. All our employees here are excited about your coming, and are looking forward to meeting you."

The manager, small and athletic, with a fine suntan, kept up an easy conversation throughout the drive downtown from the airport. By the time they arrived at the Biltmore Hotel another Kinki man had registered the whole party. The manager himself ushered Daimon to his suite. Daimon enjoyed every moment of this grand entrance. "You men in Los Angeles certainly see to everything," he said, in his most affable manner.

"You are kind to say that." The manager bowed and beamed— almost like an inn-keeper, Iki thought sourly. "I'll be back for you after you've had a chance to shower and rest."

"I'll just take a shower. No need to rest. I'll be ready in thirty minutes, so wait for me in the lobby. I want to go to the office right away."

The Los Angeles office of Kinki Trading Company had a staff of twenty-five—ten men from the home office in Japan and fifteen from Southern California. The manager bowed almost reverently as he opened the door for Daimon, saying, "I'm afraid you'll find it a little cramped."

Daimon was greeted by a huge portrait of himself hung on the wall facing the entrance. A vase full of bright golden chrysanthemums stood beneath and to the right of it. Iki, last in line, almost stopped in shock. Once upon a time, and not that long ago, he thought, only the Emperor would have received such homage . . . golden chrysanthemums!

"I didn't know chrysanthemums were grown in Los Angeles," Daimon said, with undisguised pleasure.

"My wife inquired around and found them. She hoped they would offer a pleasant welcome for you. Of course, they represent the spirit of welcome and respect from our entire staff."

Daimon responded with a restrained nod of approval.

After addressing the staff in the conference room, giving a speech that both praised and exhorted, Daimon left immediately with Yosano and Yanagi to visit his legal consultant, several local banks and branches of Japanese banks, city government offices, and Japanese-American groups. Iki was free to go wherever he liked, under the care of Hanawa Shiro, a young Japanese member of the staff.

Hanawa, dressed in a light blue suit and wearing the most opaque of sunglasses, had the relaxed manner of a Japanese-American overlying the burdens of a melancholy imported straight from Japan. He tried never to look directly at Iki, and spoke so softly that sometimes his words drifted away before Iki could hear them.

He held the car door open for Iki. "Where would you like to go?" he all but whispered.

"I've never been in this city before, so that's hard to say . . . Oh, yes, I'm told that jet aircraft and electronics are thriving industries here. How about showing me one of the plants?"

"You're scheduled to visit an aircraft plant in a few days. With the Big Boss, I think. Besides, it's already past three o'clock. Too late. Why don't we just drive around a bit?"

Iki thought that he would rather talk with this oddly restrained young man than be taken on a routine sightseeing tour, but, being polite, said nothing.

"Well," Hanawa decided, "let's drive out to the coast. I'll take you down Hollywood Boulevard, then along Sunset Boulevard into Beverly Hills, then across to Santa Monica Beach."

Hanawa, who undoubtedly had driven innumerable Japanese visitors around town, seemed utterly bored. In spite of so bad an example, Iki became interested in the tropical effect of the place—palm trees lining the boulevards, the cream-colored stucco houses with red tile roofs, the healthy tanned faces of the people. After driving along a freeway for ten minutes, Hanawa took the car down a wide and busy street.

"Here we are," he said, with little enthusiasm, "Hollywood Boulevard, the street of movie stars. You can see the handprints and footprints of some of them in the sidewalk. Look over there on the right. Recognize that building?"

Seeing Iki's ignorance of such a noted phenomenon, Hanawa instructed: "That's Grauman's Chinese Theater. All the famous stars, the Academy Award winners, have left their handprints there. By the way, Mr. Iki, who's your favorite actress?"

"I'm afraid that I haven't seen many foreign movies. But I used to like Marlene Dietrich," he answered with a shy smile. "I guess my favorite now is Ingrid Bergman."

"Ingrid Bergman's handprint is in the middle of this block," Hanawa said, smiling for the first time, apparently amused by Iki's reluctance to admit his admiration of beautiful actresses. He stopped the car, and Iki forced himself to get out for a look at the famous slab of sidewalk. But handprints in hardened concrete are disenchanting at close range, and, duty done, he returned to the car.

Hanawa picked up speed as he drove along the wide street through the foothills. Residences, mostly of modern design, were only partly visible beyond high fences or through thick foliage. Their elegant, often extravagant, styles were appropriate, he supposed, for their celebrated occupants—all movie stars, popular singers, wealthy doctors, and renowned attorneys, according to Hanawa.

Another twenty minutes' dashing along Sunset Boulevard brought them to the blue waters of the Pacific, looking molten under the afternoon sun. Hanawa circled down to the coast highway.

"Let's stop somewhere along here," Iki ventured to suggest, when they had driven past a strip of drive-in restaurants and aged unkempt houses to a quieter part of Santa Monica Beach. Hanawa pulled off the road, and the two walked out upon the broad stretch of sand. Sitting beside Hanawa, who seemed to be interested only in the horizon, Iki found a few moments of peace as he listened to the low murmur of the incoming waves. How many years had passed since last he had sat beside the sea?

Yet, feeling that he must say something, he turned to his host. "Have you been here long?"

"Fairly long, I suppose . . . Well, actually not so long, I guess. Depending on how you look at it. First I was assigned to the San Francisco branch, but I got in trouble over a woman there, and was sent—you might even say exiled—to El Paso in Texas, on the Mexican border. That happened three years ago." Hanawa talked dispassionately about all this part of his past, as if he were discussing someone else.

"She was a well-educated American girl," Hanawa continued. "After we had lived together for a year—happily, I should add—I asked her to marry me. I was so stunned when she said that she couldn't possibly marry an Oriental that I simply fell apart. Naturally, I left her. Before long, people started saying all sorts of things about me. You know how they are. And, besides, I couldn't do a decent day's work. Eventually the bosses hustled me off to El Paso, to run a one-man operation."

"What kind of operation is that?"

"As low as one can go." Hanawa dropped one hand toward the sand. "It means living in cheap hotels in small ugly towns, and trading with the locals, mostly Mexican and blacks. I spent two years in and around El Paso without once seeing a Japanese face or speaking a Japanese word. I got so homesick that I almost went crazy. I started walking out into the desert to shout aloud the names of every Japanese person, place, or thing I could think of, to sing Japanese songs at the top of my lungs. I was desperate to hear anything that sounded like our beautiful Japanese language. Instead I heard the howling of coyotes and the sighing of the wind. By sheer luck I was reassigned to Los Angeles. Another half year out there and I would have ended up in a madhouse."

Las Vegas emerged, a brilliant ornament, from a desert of dark shadows. As they drove into the sparkling city, they saw gorgeous and gaudy neon signs advertising the famous places, bearing names like "Tropicana,', "Flamingo," "Sands," "Desert Inn."

Daimon's party had flown by jet airliner early that morning from Los Angeles to Dallas, surveyed Texan cotton fields in a chartered Cessna, returned to Los Angeles, then rushed on to Las Vegas, accompanied by the Los Angeles manager. After checking in at the Stardust Hotel, they went down to the lobby to spend their first wholly free evening in America.

The roulette tables, under brilliant chandeliers, were surrounded by a crowd of gamblers, some dressed in tuxedos and formal gowns, other in casual sportswear or business suits.

Daimon placed his bets with keenest attention, as if he were playing the cotton market in Osaka. Yasano and Yanagi, too, at the same table, challenged the spinning wheel.

"Why don't you try it?" Yanagi said to Iki, standing behind him, always the observer. "If the ball falls on your number, you get back thirty-six times your wager."

So Iki sat next to Yanagi when that chair was vacated. Since this was the twenty-sixth day of June, he chose to place a silver dollar each on twenty-six and six. Daimon placed ten dollars each on twenty-nine, ten and twenty-eight. As soon as all bets were laid, the croupier set the roulette wheel to spinning. Bettors held their breath as slowly the wheel came to a stop and the fickle white ball tumbled across several compartments, settling at last in slot twenty-eight.

"Luck is with me tonight," Daimon exclaimed, as the croupier pushed several stacks of chips toward him.

"The numbers he bet on refer to a date," Yanagi confided to Iki. "In 1954—Showa 29 in Japan—he made a killing on the twenty-eighth day of October by selling cotton he had bought at rock bottom prices soon after the end of the Korean War."

Daimon increased his bets for the next few spins of the wheel, while sipping on a scotch and soda a hostess brought him.

"It's time for the dinner show," he announced to his associates. He tipped the dealer generously before rising from the table. Iki had lost six silver dollars. Daimon, needless to say, won much more than he lost.

By some magic known best to the manager from Los Angeles, the maitre d' recognized them as they entered the show room, and escorted the honored visitors from Japan to a reserved table in the front row. The show had already begun. Dancers clad in spangled silver lamé were performing high kicks to the accompaniment of a very loud and brassy orchestra.

"I think you'll like this show," the Los Angeles manager said into Daimon's ear. "They're a famous troupe from Paris."

"They'll do wonders for my eyes," Daimon said, gazing at the line of dancers, all flaunting fans and feathers, and long white legs. "Those girls have beautiful bodies."

By the time they finished their salad and began upon the steak and red wine, the spotlight shone upon a soloist, completely nude but for her G-string ornamented with a jeweled butterfly. Daimon did not watch the dancing; his attention was fixed on that small alluring butterfly.

The moment they finished dinner the Los Angeles manager said, "Sir, I know you're tired, after such a busy day. I think you should get a good night's rest."

"You're right." Daimon rose promptly. "Iki, you should get back to your room, too. You must be tired after the long day we've had."

"I'd like to chat for a while with the Los Angeles—"

"I'll talk to you tomorrow," the manager said, before Iki could finish. "Get a good night's sleep."

Back in his room, Iki took a quick shower in the huge bathroom lined with colored tiles. He inspected with some curiosity the assortment of perfumes and cosmetics arranged on the marble counter before a large mirror, and wondered why they should be there. Comfortable in clean pajamas, he was about to get into bed when a light knock sounded at his door. Thinking that Yanagi wanted to talk to him about tomorrow, he put on his bathrobe and opened the door. Standing before him was a smiling young woman wearing a bright red satin dress and a silver lamé cape.

She ignored Iki, desperately trying to tell her that she must have come to the wrong room, and slipped past him. When she tossed her cape on a chair and winked at him, Iki sagged with embarrassment. "I do not need you," he said, remembering the English words at last. "I do not wish you here."

"But honey," she said, puckering her painted lips into an invitation, "I've been reserved for you for tonight. All night." In an instant she slithered out of her dress and the slip beneath it. Although cosmetics made her face look youthful, her body was not. And now Iki understood why the others had insisted on sending Daimon and himself off to bed. He was not surprised that Daimon, a notorious womanizer, should be provided with a bed mate wherever he went. But why had he been so favored? Naturally, he being a man, his lust was aroused by the sight of this naked woman. But at the same time he resented having been given this hired woman as a reward in advance for some unknown obligation yet to be thrust upon him. The thought of being bought so cheaply offended him. However much he admired Daimon's daring and skill, he realized, he must be wary of him—and not only until this expensive excursion to America was finished, and he could learn why he'd been brought along in the first place.

On the following Monday morning, Iki went with melancholy Hanawa to visit the Lance Aircraft Plant in Palmdale.

Lance, the largest of American aircraft manufacturers, concentrated on production of military rather than civil aircraft. Its main office and parts plant were located in Burbank, about ten miles north of the city of Los Angeles. The assembly plant was built in Palmdale, some thirty miles farther north, near a desert area.

"We'll be taking a look at the Lance F-77 today," said Hanawa as they raced along the freeway. "The F-77 is Kinki's choice for the next FX jet fighter. I imagine you know quite a bit about the preferences of the Defense Agency."

"Not at all. My title is Consultant to the President, but actually

I sit at a desk in the Textile Division. I'm still learning the business. I know that Japanese trading companies work as agents for American firms. But I don't know who represents whom, much less which aircraft each is trying to sell to the Defense Agency. Are there jet fighters other than the F-77 that the Defense Agency might be interested in?"

"I'm surprised that you don't know," Hanawa said with evident disbelief. "You're not just fooling me? There are three others, each backed by a different trading company—the Conway F-106 by Goto, the Norton F-5 by Marufuji, and the Grayson F-11 by Tokyo Trading. All those Japanese firms have sent top-level officials to Los Angeles, so there's a lot of maneuvering going on in the city now."

"I thought that Mr. Daimon came to establish a general managerial system in America. But now I wonder if he's not planned all along to get involved in this business of jet fighters." Iki was still very much puzzled by Daimon's motives because not once had he spoken—at least in Iki's presence—on the subject of aircraft. Nor was he scheduled to tour any of the aircraft manufacturing facilities in the Los Angeles area.

Hanawa honked his horn and accelerated to a speed that frightened Iki as he passed a car. In a while he veered off onto a ramp that made a leisurely curved descent to street level. Soon they pulled up at the entrance to a large building, resembling a hangar.

A tall, lean American in his late thirties came out to meet them. "Hi there, Shiro! How are you?"

"Hello, Buck. I've brought Mr. Iki of Kinki Trading Company to meet you." He turned to Iki. "This is Mr. Buchanan Collins. Usually a member of the Public Relations Staff guides visitors around the plant. Mr. Collins is an engineer. He has very kindly agreed to show us around today."

Collins drove them in a jeep to the parts manufacturing plant at the far side of the huge compound. Judging by the high wire fence around the building and the security guards at the gates, Iki guessed that the building housed more than one secret project.

Within, they saw stacks of sheets of duraluminum, and complicated machines for making parts for electronic equipment. The many workers, dressed casually in short-sleeved shirts and slacks, bent over their tasks. From the farther recesses of the building came the shrill sounds of metal grinding against metal.

Iki stopped beside a conical object shaped like the nose of a bullet. "Is this the head of a fuselage?"

"Yes, it is," Collins said. "This rocket-shaped fuselage is a characteristic of the F-77, which I think is a masterpiece of design for jet fighters. The plane has amazing speed and acceleration, as well as a reserve thrust that gives it a remarkable rate of climb. The fuselage is fifty-eight feet and three inches long. As you see, it is shaped like a long, slender bullet. The stubby wings will remind you of the flippers on a seal. It's a totally new concept in aircraft design, and I'm very proud to be a member of the team that created it."

Collins pointed to a trapezoidal piece of duraluminum sheeting, about seven feet long. "This is an F-77's wing," he said. However high the speed of the F-77 might be, Iki could not believe that a pair of such short wings could lift a fuselage fifty-eight feet long.

Collins took Iki to one of those unbelievable flippers. "The wing is very small and very thin. What would you say the thickness of the leading edge is?"

Iki inspected it, and drew back, impressed by its sharpness. "I can't say," he admitted, shaking his head

"About .5 millimeter?" Hanawa guessed.

"Actually, the leading edge tapers from .25 down to .13 millimeter."

"How can you make such thin wings?" Iki asked. He did not have an expert's knowledge, but he did know that all wings he'd every seen were ribbed frames covered with sheet metal or canvas. The wing of the F-77 appeared to consist of frame and surface covering, but that was an illusion: it was a single piece of metal.

When he commented on this, Collins gave him a grin of approval. "The wing is made from a single sheet of duraluminum by means of electrolytic etching. The process by which that's done is one of our top secrets. The Japanese Defense Agency mission and you two gentlemen from Kinki Trading Company are the only outsiders we've shown the wing to. I trust you'll keep this information confidential. I can explain everything about it a lot better with an F-77 before us. So let me take you out to Palmdale."

Soon they were airborne, in a helicopter on which the Lance Corporation insignia was prominently displayed. "I've been visiting Lance regularly," Hanawa spoke directly into Iki's ear, in order to be heard over the roar of the engine, "and this is the first time I've been allowed even to see the wing of an F-77. This is also my first trip to Palmdale by helicopter. I've always had to drive all the way to Palmdale—two and a half hours through the city, the suburbs, and finally across the desert over dusty roads. I'm lucky to be tagging along with a VIP." Iki, somewhat annoyed at being raised to such importance, had to admit that he enjoyed the comforts of privilege—and the added minor reward of seeing Hanawa looking almost happy, for a change.

In a few minutes they left the city of Burbank behind, as the helicopter flitted over the narrow desert toward a range of barren mountains. The land below was sere and brown, its monotony relieved only occasionally by white patches of rock salt and clusters of pale green cactus. Only few dozen miles inland from the fertile coast, California's earth turned into a desert—stark mountains, succeeded by a plain that stretched on, seemingly endless, beyond the eastern foothills of the Sierra Nevada mountains. Iki was fascinated by the changing landscape, unfolding below him. Seen from this lower altitude, the immenseness of the American continent was overpowering. And I am seeing only a small part of California, he thought—of this one state, into which all the islands of Japan can be fitted, with room to spare . . .

The helicopter swept over yet another mountain ridge, and hovered above a level plateau. "Those are Lance's assembly plants." Hanawa pointed to three barracks-like structures. "The airstrip, too, belongs to Lance."

Collins brought the helicopter down gently. What appeared to be military barracks were large factories built on a site about two hundred and fifty acres in extent. A newly assembled plane was taxiing along a concrete road toward the runway.

"That's one of our four-engined Jetstars," Collins said as he led them to the nearest building. "It's used widely in both commercial and military aviation. The president of the United States flies in one of those."

As they entered the spacious buildng, Iki stopped in his tracks, staring in amazement at the F-77. It was like some fantastic bird out of science fiction. With a rocket-like fuselage fifty-eight feet long and seven feet in diameter, a bullet nose tapering to a needle-thin pitot tube, and those stubby wings projecting from the rear half of its body, it was nothing like his idea of an airplane.

He had many questions to ask. Wanting to be correct, he phrased them in Japanese, which Hanawa interpreted for Buck Collins.

"What was your purpose in producing a plane of such unconventional design?"

"Everyone who's seen it asks me that, especially pilots. Some even ask if we really expect this funny thing to fly. The answer is easy: we've proved it. This thing flies beautifully! The F-77 is a jet fighter designed to achieve maximum efficiency at Mach 2. To achieve that purpose, we had to design stubby, rectilinear wings. Simplicity of design and light-weight construction were our principal aims."

"At what altitude can this plane fly at Mach 2?"

"At thirty to forty thousand feet."

"How quickly can it reach that altitude?"

"In two and a half minutes. It can accelerate to Mach 2 within four minutes."

This F-77 would be ideal for use in defending Japan, Iki thought. Japan needs jets that can take to the air almost instantly, to intercept unidentified aircraft detected on our radar screens. But how well can a plane with such small wings maneuver?

"A plane's maneuverability increases in direct proportion to the span of its wings," he said, remembering back to the time when he served as an intelligence officer in the Japanese Army. "Japan's Zero Fighters were designed on that principle."

"Things have changed since then, Mr. Iki. Almost everything is different in supersonic flight. Now our primary concern is thrust. The greater the thrust, the greater the mobility. Or maneuverability, as you called it in the old days. In supersonic jet warfare, loops and barrel rolls are not necessary functions anymore. Mobility is the capability of changing directions while in pursuit of an enemy target. Efficiency is measured by the degree of acceleration per second. The amount of reserve thrust is the determining factor."

Despite Collins' patient efforts to explain them, Iki still did not fully comprehend the current concepts of jet warfare.

"Mr. Iki," Hanawa said, putting an end to a series of yawns, "test pilots of Japan's Air Self-Defense Force have been flying the F-77 for three days at Edwards Air Force Base. Why don't we go over there and watch them? Your former classmate, General Kawamata Isao, is there."

"Kawamata?" Iki asked, in disbelief.

Edwards Air Force Base lay thirty miles northeast of Palmdale, near the middle of the wide Mojave Desert. No fences marked its perimeter. Only a gate, astride the road leading to the base, and an MP guarding it, told Iki where he was. At least fifty jets— fighters, reconnaissance planes, and trainers—were parked in neat rows on the huge field. Men in the gray uniforms of test pilots or the blue of Air Force officers strode between the planes and administration buildings. Several jets took off with a thunderous roar, and flew eastward in tight formation.

A young lieutenant serving as public relations officer took over as guide for Iki and Hanawa. "We train quite a few pilots sent to us here by Japan's Self-Defense Force. They're enrolled in our regular academic subjects while they receive training in flying one or more of our aircraft. We also train pilots from West Germany, the Netherlands, Belgium, and Italy. Usually the Japanese boys have a little difficulty with their English at first, but after a while they do exceptionally well. The four test pilots who have come with your Defense Agency mission are all graduates of our flight training school. They're over there now—at the Testing Center."

The lieutenant pointed to a tower some distance away from the main Air Force control tower. Iki watched a Japanese pilot—distinguished by his flight uniform—climbing into a Lance F-77, parked in front of that farther tower. A short man, he was almost hidden in the cockpit of the sleek, silvery fuselage. Iki, a survivor from a different war, rejoiced at the sight of a Japanese aviator sitting at the controls of an American plane as its test pilot, about to take off from an American Air Force base in California.

The lieutenant conducted them to the Testing Center control tower. They took an elevator to the top level, and slipped into the control room. Directly behind the four air traffic controllers stood several American officers and six members of Japan's Defense Agency Air Division. Iki did not see Harada, who was said to be heading the mission, but immediately noticed General Kawamata Isao.

Kawamata looked across at Iki for an instant, then returned his attention to the runway. Everyone in the tower was caught up in the events unfolding below.

"Cleared for take-off!" the tower's chief controller said into the microphone. The F-77's afterburner gave off an explosive burst of green flame. Within moments the aircraft rose with a shriek into the sky. As the plane disappeared into the brilliant blue far beyond the base, the pilot's voice issued from the tower's speakers.

"Altitude five thousand, speed Mach 0.6 . . . ten thousand, Mach 0.7 . . ." In two and a half minutes, the F-77 reached 40,000 feet.

"I'm now at forty thousand and going into acceleration . . . Mach 1.2 . . . 1.4 . . . 1.6 . . . 1.8 . . ."

"Mach 2!" the pilot exclaimed, and the men in the control tower cheered.

"I'm going for altitude," the pilot said hoarsely.

The jet went into a steep climb. Reports of his altimeter readings came in quick succession: "45,000 . . . 50,000 . . . 55,000 . . ." His air speed fell gradually from Mach 2 to Mach 1.4 by the time he reached the upper limits.

"I'm now at 60,000. Returning to base."

Within a few minutes they heard the pilot say, "Low station," referring to the approach altitude of five thousand feet. Soon afterward they saw a small shiny dot appear in the distance. In thirty seconds it achieved its transformation into a body with wings, and a drag-chute opening behind it, at the far end of the landing strip, a mile and a half long.

When the F-77 taxied to a stop, the ground crew swiftly removed the canopy. The pilot pulled off his oxygen mask and climbed out of the plane. A jeep brought him straight to the control tower.

He was a slight and imperturbable man in his mid-thirties. His face still bore the imprint of the oxygen mask's rim. He stood at attention before General Kawamata, saluted, and asked, "Sir, how were the test results?"

"Splendid, Koizumi! Congratulations! Two minutes thirty-two seconds to reach forty thousand feet. And another two minutes thirty-eight seconds to accelerate to Mach 2. We'll discuss the other details at our meeting." His expression revealed the pride in the pilot's achievement that he could not very well put into words.

The pilot saluted and marched out of the control room. His flight suit was wet from the seat down to the thighs. The damp stain showed how terrible is the strain upon a man's body when he flies at twice the speed of sound. Recalling the moments of exhilaration he had experienced during the successful events of his own earthbound military career, Iki regarded the airborne pilot with good-natured envy. A whole new realm of sensations and triumphs to experience!

"Good to see you, Iki." Kawamata, smartly dressed in uniform, with a pair of golden cherry blossoms on each shoulder strap, kept a trim body and an athlete's vigor that gave him the appearance of a man many years younger than Iki. "Fourteen years," he added, touching his hand briefly to Iki's shoulder. "No, I take that back. Eighteen years since we served together at Imperial Headquarters. I haven't seen you since my reassignment to Southeast Asia during the war."

"Our meeting here is a remarkable coincidence," said Iki, responding happily to this undoubted friendliness.

"You rascal!" Kawamata laughed. "You came all the way from Japan to watch this test flight."

"Quite the contrary. My company's president thought that I should see the United States, to help me be more useful in the import-export business. We went to our branch offices in New York and a few other cities. While visiting the Lance factory in Palmdale, I was told that members of Japan's Air Self-Defense Force were here at Edwards conducting a test flight of the F-77. So I came over here, too."

"Then you didn't know I'd be here?" Kawamata directed a suspicious glance at Hanawa, standing—inscrutable as ever, behind those sunglasses—next to Iki. "We've finished our tests for the day. Why don't you two join me for a drink at the Officers' Club?"

Hanawa answered, almost too quickly. "Thank you, but I have something to talk over with the Public Relations Officer. So you two go ahead. And take your time."

In the bar at the Officers' Club, Iki and Kawamata took a table that looked out toward the barren desert beyond the landing strip, and toasted each other with cold beer.

"I'm grateful for all the help you've given me," Iki said. In person now, as he had done earlier in a letter, he thanked Kawamata for the assistance he had given the Iki family during his internment in Siberia. In concluding, he expressed regret for having declined Kawamata's invitation to accept a position with the Defense Agency.

"Think nothing of it," Kawamata said. "I could understand your feelings. You had the worst experience of us all. But I've been worried about your health."

"I was in very poor condition when I got back, but thanks to two years of idleness my health is getting back to normal. And my family is well. And how are things with you? How is your family?"

"The same. No children. And my wife hasn't changed a bit." Kawamata broke into an impish grin.

Kawamata's wife had been a beautiful and accomplished geisha. The Minister of War at first refused to recognize his request to marry her. They had been living together as man and wife for two years when finally they were permitted to hold the formal nuptial ceremonies. The War Minister gave his consent only after Kawamata's beloved was adopted by a reputable family, thanks to the intercession of his regimental commander. All the gossips, as usual, had predicted ruin for Kawamata, both at home and in the Army. But they had been proved wrong in every respect save one. No sons—or daughters—came to add heaven's blessing to the marriage.

Kawamata had always been a bold and exuberant man, even to the point of committing an occasional indiscretion, Iki recalled. He studied Kawamata, who appeared little changed but for the added dignity that comes with rank and, perhaps, with experience.

"I didn't see Mr. Harada at the control tower," Iki said, following a hunch.

"Oh, he's here at the testing site with us. This afternoon he's been called over to Base Headquarters, to confer with General Burkland."

"Does he still insist on flying?" At one time Harada had been considered the best pilot in the Japanese Navy.

"Yes, he does. We've been here for two weeks now, test-flying these remarkable jets. They are unbelievable! We've taken turns flying them—he and I, among the rest."

Out of interest in the subject, Iki followed through. "I understand that your group from Tokyo came to America to choose the next FX fighter. Can you tell me what kind of plane it must be?" Neither he nor Kawamata stopped to consider that a textile salesman from Osaka had any right to ask this question—or receive an answer to it.

"Our ideal plane has to have a top speed in excess of Mach 1.6 if it's to contend with Soviet jets of the next decade. It must have combat capability in altitudes up to 60,000 feet. It must be able to climb to 40,000 feet within three minutes. Its flight radius must be at least two hundred nautical miles. And it must be able to take off and land on a strip no longer than 2,300 feet."

"Have you found such a plane?"

"The Lance F-77 can reach Mach 2 in a few minutes, but it requires a long runway. The Grayson F-11 can take off from an aircraft carrier deck, but it takes ten minutes to reach Mach 2. As you can see, finding the perfect plane is not easy."

Four Japanese officers entered the room, sat down at the bar, and ordered draughts of cooling beer. Among them was the pilot who had just flown the F-77.

"Koizumi! Come join us," Kawamata called to him. Koizumi, wearing a fresh uniform with lieutenant colonel's insignia, came to their table and bowed politely. Kawamata introduced him, explaining that he and Iki had been classmates in both the Army Academy and the War College. "Tell my old friend how you feel, flying the F-77," he urged.

"Uncomfortable at first, off balance almost, because the cockpit is so far up front, and I'm so low down in it. But the more I flew it, the more I was impressed by it. This plane is really a marvel. I never imagined that any aircraft could reach forty thousand feet in less than three minutes. Our best fighter now, the F-56, takes seventeen minutes to reach that altitude. —Then, of course, we find other marvels. At fifty thousand feet, even in daytime, we can see the stars out there in the sky. Beautiful! I'd never experienced that before. The plane's only shortcoming is the need to roll once before leveling off from a steep climb."

"Being a layman, I'm not fully informed about these matters," Iki said, "but I'm inclined to think that the design doesn't offer much stability. Isn't it dangerous?"

"It is. It makes no allowance at all for recovery if the engine flares out at a low altitude. The F-77 has already been called 'widow-maker' and 'flying coffin.' Actually, those nicknames refer to low-altitude bombers used by the West German Air Force. Even so, the F-77 is an ideal interceptor because it can get into the stratosphere with such fantastic speed."

A Japanese civilian came into the bar to call members of the misson into conference. Koizumi drained off the last of his beer and led the pack out of the bar.

"We have to analyze the data from Koizumi's test flight," Kawamata said, pushing himself up from the table. "Then we'll compare them with information on the same aircraft compiled by similar missions sent here from West Germany, the Netherlands, and Italy."

"Let's get together for a more leisurely talk after we're back in Japan."

"Have you forgotten?" Kawamata said. "We're to meet sooner than that. Right here in America—in Los Angeles. When Mr. Daimon invited me to dinner there, he said you'd be joining us. See you there." He moved away quickly to the door.

Iki felt a flash of anger as he took in the information Kawamata had just given him. The rendezvous in Los Angeles had been planned even before he left Japan. The vague doubts that had been troubling him during these days in America fell away. Now, in their stead, he saw the new scene clearly, himself among the actors in it.

Daimon and Iki were ushered into one of the quieter, Japanese-style rooms of the Mikado Restaurant in Beverly Hills.

Kawamata, who was assigned quarters at Edwards Air Force Base, had arranged to come into Los Angeles to attend a Japanese social function in "Little Tokyo," from which he would slip away to make an inconspicuous visit to the Mikado.

The soft strains of *koto* music drifted into the room, where Daimon and Iki sat sipping tea. A young Japanese-American girl served them. Daimon noticed, with much amusement, how awkwardly she moved in the tight-fitting kimono the management forced her to wear. When he joked to her in Japanese, she didn't understand what he said. Rather than add to her distress, he turned to Iki.

"Your meeting General Kawamata at the air base was a remarkable coincidence. How many years have passed, since you last saw him?"

Iki resented Daimon's pretended innocence, and showed it. "I believe both you and Mr. Satoi know the answer to that question. To be frank, I want to say that, as far as I am concerned, I've not been assigned to Kinki Trading's project to persuade our Defense Agency to buy the American F-77 jet fighter. If you would like me to introduce you to General Kawamata, I'd be happy to do so. But I ask that you not involve me in these evasive games you seem to be playing."

The big smile faded from Daimon's face—for only an instant.

"I've never heard you speak so candidly," he said with a chuckle. "People seldom take me by surprise, but you've certainly done so."

"I should make my thoughts clear," Iki said, slowly, with utmost clarity. "If your intention is to have the three of us dine together just so that I can help sell the F-77 to the Defense Agency, then I must say that I cannot agree to this. As I've said, I'll be happy to help you two get acquainted. But then I must excuse myself from further talk about deals involving the F-77. I'll go back to the hotel while you talk."

Daimon held up his big hands. But they signified only good nature, not surrender. "I understand your feelings. Still, I'm discouraged by your refusal to adapt . . . And by the time and place you've chosen in which to be so stubborn. Listen to me, and try to understand my point of view. We're trying to land a contract to sell between two hundred and fifty and three hundred jet fighters, each of which costs a million dollars. If we succeed in selling the F-77 for Lance, our Machinery Division will finally get off the ground. Success in this venture means our getting up to ten years of business in just supplying parts for those fighter planes. Furthermore, we'll establish ties with American heavy industry and machinery manufacturers. Those are business connections that we haven't been able to make so far. This contract is essential to Kinki's future. Leave everything to me—just this once."

Daimon's zeal and eloquence had no effect at all on Iki. He sat there, hard of face—and of mind.

At that moment the waitress brought in Kawamata Isao. "I'm sorry I've kept you waiting," he said. "The Japanese Consul cornered me at the reception, and I had some difficulty in tearing myself away."

"I'm afraid I've imposed on you," Daimon said, drawing himself erect, as good manners required. "I'm Daimon Ichizo. We should have met much earlier, but I was wary of misunderstandings that might arise if we were ever seen together in Tokyo—or anywhere in Japan for that matter."

"The pleasure is mine. Mr. Satoi has told me much about you, and I've been looking forward to meeting you."

He declined Daimon's urging to take the seat of honor in front of the *tokonoma*. "Let me sit here, beside my old friend Iki. You asked me to join you so that we could get reacquainted. Remember? . . ." His lazy grin and toss of the head sent a subtle message to Daimon . . . and to the sensitive Iki.

"If a Defense Agency officer is seen with a trader, is that a cause for concern?" Iki asked, in a tone clearly lacking in humor.

"I'm afraid the Agency would be embarrassed. And your own company, too, would be embarrassed if word got around that a member of the Agency's mission was invited to join your President for a private dinner. News commentators and journalists in Japan have pinned the label 'war-mongers' on those of us who serve in the Self-Defense Force. 'Death merchants' is their sneer for the trading companies we deal with. And each time we revise our plans to defend Japan from foreign agression, we're accused of 'bleeding the public.' "

The waitress interrupted them, bringing delicacies in the Japanese style and bottles of saké. Daimon filled Kawamata's cup and Iki's, waiting until the waitress went off again before resuming the conversation. He went straight to the point. "Of the four jet fighters, which do you think the Agency is likely to choose?"

Kawamata answered with a frankness that shocked Iki. "The Conway F-106 is by far the best interceptor. It has the best electronic guidance system of any plane in the world. You might say it's the Cadillac of jet fighters. So its price rises accordingly. Estimates range as high as $2,300,000 per plane, which puts it far beyond our reach. The Norton F-5 is attractive, because it's the cheapest among the four. But it's not yet in production. We visited the plant, but were shown only a prototype. Besides, it hasn't been adopted by the American Navy or Air Force, so there's almost no chance of our becoming interested in it."

"That leaves only Lance and Grayson," said Daimon. "I've been told that test flights of the Lance F-77 have given remarkable results. —Isn't that so, Iki?"

Shaking his head in irritation, Iki began to protest. But Kawamata, laughing easily, shrugged away his objections. "As you surely know, Mr. Daimon, the selection of the next mainstay jet fighter for Japan will not necessarily be based on our evaluations. The National Defense Council will make the decision. The name 'National Defense Council' has a nice ring to it, but it's made up

371

entirely of politicians—the Prime Minister, Vice Premier, Finance Minister, Foreign Minister, and director generals of the Economic Planning Agency and Defense Agency. The head of the Ministry of International Trade and Industry is a member *ex-officio.* Those politicians are going to make the decision. As matters now stand, I think they'll choose the Grayson F-11 Hornet."

Koto music from overhead speakers dropped into the silence. "That's news to me," Daimon said at last, giving no other clue to his disappointment. "When did they make that decision?"

"It hasn't been made definitely, as yet. At the Council's last meeting, its members may have reached an understanding that approximates a decision. We were informed of it on the eve of our departure from Tokyo. According to some rumors, not all, Mitsubishi Heavy Industry was ordered to come up with Grayson's production planning. The orders were said to have come from two sources—the chief of MITI's Heavy Industry Bureau and the chief of the Equipments Division of the Defense Agency Secretariat."

"That's strange. From what I've heard, Grayson has made only two F-11's for testing purposes. And furthermore, that plane hasn't been adopted by the U.S. Air Force. Who in Japan is favoring the F-11?"

"The Prime Minister."

That jolted Daimon.

"American aircraft manufacturers are turning to missile development," Kawamata explained. "As a result, a reduction in force of about one hundred thousand aircraft workers has occurred. The Grayson Corporation has been hard hit because it didn't move into missiles. But it can save itself for the while if it sells us the fleet of planes we need for the next defense build-up period. People at Grayson have been sending us brochures and all kinds of supporting data by the ton, through trading companies, ever since we began planning the second build-up period. And they've done a lot of entertaining in Japan. In the best places . . .

"Now that the selection process has reached the stage where politics counts, they're resorting to any means they can use. Their means aren't necessarily legitimate. I'm sure you've heard about Mr. Nozoe, the former admiral who's now one of the Prime Minister's trusted advisors. He was in Hawaii a month ago, as a guest of the American Navy, staying in a guest house on an Air Force base."

Nozoe had been Japan's Ambassador to the United States until the outbreak of the Second World War. Iki had known him well before his assignment to Washington. "How does that tie in with the selection of the next mainstay jet aircraft?" he asked. "Nozoe has many friends in the American Navy. Such an invitation would seem quite natural, and honorable."

"Having been a Navy man, Mr. Nozoe is familiar with the performance of current Grayson carrier-based jets. He's given them a higher evaluation than the Lance jets on several points—such as flight radius, take-off and landing needs, versatility in the air, and safety factors. Now, tell me: what would you make of the news that the Prime Minister's top aide, Mishima, also went to Hawaii while Nozoe was there? Mind you, the Diet was in session at the time. Mishima flew to Hawaii 'for personal reasons,' the announcement said—'to control a flare-up of his asthma.' His wife went with him, in the role of ever-faithful nurse. However healthy Hawaii may be for asthmatics, only fools will believe that he could be cured of his ailment in ten days—which, incidentally, included time for a trip to and from Los Angeles. The whole deal was cooked up by Grayson's agent, Tokyo Trading Company."

"Tokyo Trading has become the kingpin among aircraft importers," Daimon said with a scowl, "because they're totally unscrupulous up there. Their men will go to any lengths to get what they want. They must have arranged with Grayson to fill the coffers of the Prime Minister's party with campaign contributions."

Daimon, dissecting motives and personalities as only he could, tapped the table to emphasize the points he made. "What is the explanation for the National Defense Council's haste? Why did the Prime Minister's party feel the need to decide on the Grayson jet even before you Agency men left Tokyo on this fact-finding mission?"

"Indeed, your question goes right to the heart of the matter. I think the answer is that the Diet is going to be disbanded soon. If that happens, another general election will be called. And that means, of course, the need to pour lots of money into the party's campaign chests."

"In Osaka we've already been asked three times for campaign contributions," Daimon said.

"The Prime Minister's party needs much more money than whatever sums it can squeeze out of you business people. It has to provide financial support for all candidates running on its ticket.

Grayson Corporation appears willing to pay a commission of three hundred thousand dollars for each plan. That's about ten million yen. *For each plane!* I'm sure that Mishima went abroad to collect a part of the advance payment—either in Honolulu or in Los Angeles."

Kawamata's eyes were dark with anger. "I've looked away from most of what is going on. But not any more. Those politicians are selecting the FX on the basis of whether or not their choice will benefit the Prime Minister's party. They're putting the nation's system of defense in jeopardy, simply in order to maintain a majority in the Diet and to keep the position of prime minister within their party. This is no mere corruption. It's treason!"

"Iki," Kawamata resumed in a calmer vein. "They tell me that you want nothing to do with this FX business. How can you remain aloof, knowing about this rotten situation at home?"

"That's an odd question to ask," Iki retorted. "The corruption you've described, and my unwillingness to meddle in this aircraft business are entirely separate issues. If you're concerned about acquiring the best jet fighter for Japan's defense, you don't need any help from me. Get together with your colleagues in the Defense Agency, and determine the right countermoves to win your campaign. —That's elementary strategy, as you must remember."

Kawamata shook his head. "Of course I remember. But that's not to be done as easily as you think. Our biggest problem is inside the Agency itself. The post of director general of the Defense Agency is appointive. It's always gone to a senior member of the Liberal Party, a puppet of the Prime Minister, naturally. The Self-Defense Force is also a problem. It evolved out of the Police Reserve Force, so the key positions are filled by former members of the Police Bureau. No doubt they are good men, morally, but still they have the mentality of policemen. They're incapable of thinking about the problem of national defense with patriotic selfless concern. The worst among them is Chief Secretary Kaizuka, or "Emperor Kaizuka" as everyone calls him, because of the authority he's built into his position. He exercises greater power than the director general. He holds a tight rein on the directors of the Ground, Maritime, and Air divisions of the Defense Agency, because each is obliged to him for his appointment. What Kaizuka has, then, is an effective command staff. I've put it in terms you understand."

Iki caught the sarcasm. And to his discomfort he felt the stirring of interest in this problem.

"You and I know from experience, Iki, that some staff officers will try to outwit their commanders, and direct their units in ways to suit themselves. To do that, they need the backing of someone who outranks the commander. In the Defense Agency, the ambitious ones are forever concerned with second-guessing not only Kaizuka but also his political friends as well. As a result, within the Air Self-Defense Force, men with real ability are being sent off to serve in remote district commands. The central command is being filled with men who'll obey 'Emperor Kaizuka.' Take Harada, for instance. Now that he knows Kaizuka wants the Grayson F-11, everyone's watching to see how long he'll stick to his own opinion."

"That's an insult to Harada!" Iki protested. "He's a man of character."

"True, he is. But rumors say that he'll run for the House of Councillors in the next election. If he intends to do that, he can't cross an important politician like Kaizuka. At least not publicly."

"But now we must talk about you, Iki," said Kawamata, shifting his sights to their primary target. "If you've kept your ideals about working for the good of Japan, then help me get the Lance F-77 selected. The F-77 will certainly receive the mission's endorsement as the best aircraft available that we can afford. Member nations of NATO are in the process of replacing their jet fighters. France, West Germany, Italy, and Canada appear to have decided on the F-77. We can't allow our government to be swayed by money-grabbing politicians to buy a plane that hasn't even been tested. If they win, Japan would become a laughing-stock for the rest of the world."

Such a direct appeal caught Iki as none of Daimon's devious schemings could. The flicker of concern that showed in his face did not escape Daimon's notice.

The Branch Manager, his wife, and five key staff members of Kinki Trading Company's Los Angeles office were gathered near the boarding gate at the air terminal.

"Sir, I had Mr. Yanagi carry on a box of Havana cigars for you. My wife chose the gifts for Mrs. Daimon and your daughter. I hope they will be pleased."

"Thanks," Daimon said. "I'm sure my wife and daughter will be delighted."

Without missing a word in Daimon's formal patter of farewell, the Branch Manager glowed with pride in the sunshine of such approbation. "Please take good care of yourself," he said. "Our San Francisco staff will be at the airport to meet you there. I'll phone them again when your plane is airborne."

"I want to thank you for everything," Daimon said. "And will you make sure that Iki is taken care of?"

Iki was leaving Daimon's party to fly the southern route to Hawaii. From there he would return, alone, to Tokyo.

"Because we don't have an office in Honolulu, I got in touch with a Japanese society over there. Everything is taken care of, both here and there. Mr. Iki will be boarding a Pan American plane, scheduled to leave thirty minutes after you depart."

"Then I have no worries," Daimon said, shaking the manager's hand. To Iki, standing behind the party of well-wishers, he said, "I'm sorry about those few disagreeable moments during dinner last night. But, as you heard, the matter we discussed is of greatest importance to our company. Give it some thought."

From Daimon, seeming to be his usual casual self, this little speech managed to convey both an apology and an order. "You're probably tired," he added. "So relax a bit in Hawaii. Don't be all business—the way you were in Las Vegas. You can't succeed in business unless you're willing to loosen up and have a little fun from time to time." Giving Iki a friendly tap on the shoulder, he strutted off toward the gate, followed by Yosano and Yanagi.

The honors rendered, the well-wishers quickly left the airport to resume the day's duties at Kinki's office, entrusting Iki to the care of Hanawa Shiro.

"I hope we meet again," Hanawa said as he gave Iki his boarding pass at the Pan American gate.

"So do I," said Iki, touched by such a show of sentiment from the phlegmatic Hanawa. "I doubt that I'll have many opportunities to travel abroad, but I'm sure that we'll meet again. Meanwhile, I expect to hear good things about you and your work."

Hanawa took off his sunglasses as he said goodbye, shaking

hands. Then Iki saw why the man wore those impenetrable spectacles. The misery hidden behind them was too deep for anyone else to bear.

The Pan American Clipper touched down at Honolulu International Airport on schedule at 6:30 p.m. Soon after Iki arrived at the Moana Hotel on Waikiki Beach fatigue from the long flight hit him. He declined an invitation to dinner from the president of the local Japanese society, ate a light supper instead, and went to bed.

He was fully awake at five o'clock the next morning. He had slept soundly, and his body felt rested. He drew back the flowery curtains and looked out at the expanse of sea, dark under a graying sky, the crests of low breakers moving in upon the shore. The early hour, the sight of the sea here, in this very place, made him remember why he had wanted to come to Honolulu.

At that very hour, on the eighth of December in 1941, December seventh in Hawaii, the first wave of 183 of Japan's attack planes was airborne, flying on a direct course to the island of Oahu.

He had come to Honolulu because he wanted to see Pearl Harbor. Although a visit to the harbor was included in a schedule of tours drawn up for him, he felt a strong desire to see it now. Dressing quickly, he went down to the hotel's lobby. He found a taxi parked near the entrance, and asked the sleepy driver to take him to a place that commanded a view of the famous harbor.

"You want to see Pearl Harbor at this hour?" the driver asked, trying to put him off. "Still too dark, yet. If you wanna see the *Arizona*, wait a while and then take the Pearl Harbor cruise."

"I'm not interested in that cruise. I just want to see the harbor from above. Now."

"Every Japanese from Japan wants to see Pearl Harbor," the driver grumbled. "But watch youself. Americans still remember December 7th."

Nonetheless, he drove Iki west on a highway that took him past Honolulu's airport and Hickam Air Force Base, then northward, hugging the eastern shore of Pearl Harbor, to the small town of Aiea. By the time the driver took them up the winding road to the top of Aiea Heights, the sun had risen above the mountains of Oahu. Iki left the taxi—and the driver huddled down in it, to wait for him—and followed a hiking trail that led to a low hill. Far below lay the harbor, resembling a crane in flight, narrowing at the ocean end into a channel as slender as the neck of that crane. Six gray ships were moored in the southeast loch. A white, oblong structure, seeming to float on the quiet water, marked the grave of a sunken man-of-war. The bodies of more than eleven hundred men who died with the *Arizona* lay entombed within her broken hull.

The slopes of the Koolau Range behind him, and of the Waianae Mountains in the distance to the right of Pearl Harbor, lay exactly as he had visualized them many years before. The topography of Oahu had been fixed in his memory when he participated in naval operational planning at Imperial General Headquarters.

The attack on Pearl Harbor was a masterstroke, conceived, planned, and accomplished under the direction of Fleet Admiral Yamamoto Isoroku. On November 22, 1941, the Combined Japanese Fleet, commanded by Vice Admiral Nagumo, assembled in the coastal waters of Etorofu in the southern Kuril Islands, having secretly set sail from Japan's Inland Sea under strict radio silence. Then the great fleet sailed eastward, along the northern edge of the Pacific, away from the usual route of merchant vessels and beyond the range of patrol planes from the Hawaiian Command.

The attack on Pearl Harbor began while Japan slept, at 3:25 a.m. An hour later, the Japanese Army made a surprise landing on the Malayan coast, according to a plan drawn up by a team of staff officers that had included Iki himself. The complex plan, which led to the fall of Singapore, had been carried out in close cooperation with the Navy. Convoys carrying 150,000 soldiers of the 25th Army, under the command of Lieutenant General Yamashita Hobun, had rendezvoused in waters far south of Hainan Island, in order to evade detection, then sailed a thousand more miles through dangerous waters to reach the Malay Peninsula.

During the weeks preceding the commencement of hostilities with the Allied nations, Iki had lived at headquarters in Ichigaya, engaged in operational planning that frequently continued far into the night. He returned to his home in Koenji only once, at the end of November, to get some clean clothes. Soon after dusk that evening, utterly weary, he fell into a troubled sleep.

"Is December 8th to be a special day?" Yoshiko asked him the next morning. "You mumbled that date several times in your sleep."

"Clothes rationing will start then," he lied, realizing how completely he was absorbed in the planning that would plunge Japan into war.

Now, on this summer day so many years later, he stood upon a peaceful island looking down upon Pearl Harbor. Those years in which he had lived out his boyhood fantasies about war, Iki thought, had been the most satisfying time in his life. But the exhiliration had been too brief, even the remembrance of satisfactions had all but vanished, pushed out by the horrors that had followed the times of triumph.

The pain of Lieutenant Hori's death lingered in him still. How could he forget, even for a moment, Hori the Innocent, or the cruel needlessness of his dying? Or the poignancy of his death-song?

> *If I should go to war at sea,*
> *Let my body soak in the brine—*
> *If war should take me to the mountains,*
> *From my body let wild grasses grow—*
> *I will not look back . . .*

And now, here, at Pearl Harbor, how could he not remember all those American warriors who had died or suffered during the years of the war that he had helped to start?

The last contingent of Japanese prisoners of war who had survived those brutal labor camps sailed from Nakhodka on a winter morning in 1957. Iki remembered the frozen land falling away into the distance, as the *Koan-maru* sailed beyond the limit of Russian waters. The faint murmurings rising up from the ice-filled sea seemed like the voices of comrades who had fallen on the barren plains of Siberia, their dreams of return unfulfilled, their hopes for life never to be gained. Some day, Iki had vowed then, aboard the *Koan-maru*, he would return to Siberia to bring home the bones of his comrades. Until that time, the spirits of the men who had died there in wretchedness and in despair would not find repose.

That would be his supreme mission—to be undertaken at a time when Japanese citizens would be able to travel again in the Soviet Union. And to be able to complete his mission, he knew, he must gain the power that would draw the support of the nation.

Hyodo Shinichiro, a fellow graduate of the Army Academy, had not hesitated in selecting a new profession. "I felt I must do something to help my country," he had said. "But what could I do? I decided that Japan's future would rest on economic development, especially on foreign trade. That's the reason I went to work for Kinki Trading."

And Ishihara, also, who was much too young to have remembered Japan before the war, when she was recognized as a first class international power, shared Hyodo's awareness of mission, and Daimon's. "Our country's poor because we lost the war," he said to Iki that day the two of them watched a small Japanese freighter sail from Kobe, its holds filled with textiles consigned to Africa. "The only way Japan can rise again is by earning foreign currency. We businessmen are the ones who can do that."

Iki remembered Daimon's homily, delivered the morning they met: "If you think you should make amends for the lost war, then put your training and experience in tactical warfare to good use. Apply it to planning the strategy we need to develop our country's economy." Daimon had intended to sting Iki into action, but Iki had not responded as Daimon had planned.

He thought again about Ichimaru's complete change of plans— from failure to be accepted in the diplomatic corps to becoming an expert in marketing management. He tried to imagine himself passing through such a transformation. That would require more than a mastery of new jargon, of new methods. It demanded a more basic alteration, almost a change of character. A caterpillar does this, when it emerges from its cocoon to become a butterfly. Why cannot I, he asked himself, leave behind this empty useless shell of a man who dwells only in the past?

The blast of a horn shattered the morning's calm. The cab driver was tired of waiting. The sun, risen high above the valleys of the Koolau ridge, was transforming the sea beyond Pearl Harbor's entrance into a shimmering expanse of turquoise in all its hues. Flags on the warships in the harbor fluttered gently.

Iki knew that the time for deciding had come. Even at the age of forty-seven, he had enough years of life in him to complete still other tasks. He felt the stirring of a new response to Daimon's challenge. Although he had been drawn into the world of business, an unwilling recruit, his three weeks' sojourn in the United States had given him an appreciation of the arena in which trading companies operated. To serve his country as a businessman, he realized, was an honorable calling, and a calling he must not refuse. Businessmen, he had seen, commanded power. Yet the ways in which they used that power were too often influenced by politicians. Honesty, integrity, love of one's country, loyalty to one's countrymen—these traits were little esteemed by men whose self-interest could dictate the course of Japan's future. Instead, working with others like Kawamata, he would use that power to help his country rise once again to greatness.

For many years, ever since Japan's defeat in that useless war, he had looked upon the world as a barren place. He had become unproductive, grudging, unyielding. Looking into the past, into old newspaper files where history was dead, he had failed to see the future, where history is still being shaped. Even his visit here this morning, to see Pearl Harbor, was a clinging to the past, instead of a welcoming of the future—as full of promise, as green and lovely and fertile as was this Hawaiian hillside, awakening to a new day. Shaken almost to tears, he looked around him, his mind opened at last. Why else had he been saved from the torments of Siberia? Why was he the fortunate one, to have survived?

In this strange setting, so far from home, yet so much a part of the modern world into which he was entering, he made his decision.

SURVIVORS
OF SIBERIAN PRISONS
WHO WERE INTERVIEWED

Baba Yoshimitsu
Fujimoto Haruo
Hara Shiro
Hasegawa Uichi
Hata Ikue
Imai Ganji
Ishida Saburo
Ishide Tomoji
Kikuchi Hiroshi
Kurosawa Yoshiyuki
Kusachi Teigo

Mori Yoshinobu
Okamura Aiichi
Sakama Fumiko
Sakama Hunichi
Shibuya Kiyoshi
Shimanuki Takeji
Shindo Akira
Suzuki Toshio
Takehara Kiyoshi
Uchiyama Hiroshi
Yakubukuro Munenao

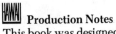 Production Notes

This book was designed by Roger Eggers. Composition and paging were done on the Quadex Composing System and typesetting on the Compugraphic 8400 by the design and production staff of University of Hawaii Press.

The text and display typeface is Compugraphic Caledonia.

Offset presswork and binding were done by Vail-Ballou Press, Inc. Text paper is Writers R Offset, basis 50.